American Environmental History

BLACKWELL READERS IN AMERICAN SOCIAL AND CULTURAL HISTORY

SERIES EDITOR: Jacqueline Jones, Brandeis University

The *Blackwell Readers in American Social and Cultural History* series introduces students to well-defined topics in American history from a sociocultural perspective. Using primary and secondary sources, the volumes present the most important works available on a particular topic in a succinct and accessible format designed to fit easily into courses offered in American history or American studies.

American Environmental History

Edited by

Louis S. Warren

Blackwell
Publishing

BLACKWELL PUBLISHING
350 Main Street, Malden, MA 02148-5020, USA
9600 Garsington Road, Oxford OX4 2DQ, UK
550 Swanston Street, Carlton, Victoria 3053, Australia

First published 2003 by Blackwell Publishing Ltd

5   2007

Library of Congress Cataloging-in-Publication Data

American environmental history / edited by Louis S. Warren.
p.   cm. –(Blackwell readers in American social and cultural history)
Includes bibliographical references and index.
ISBN 0-631-22863-2 (hbk: alk. paper) — ISBN 0-631-22864-0 (pbk: alk. paper)
1. Human ecology–United States–History.   2. Nature–Effect of Human beings
on–United States   3. United States–Environmental conditions–History.
I. Warren, Louis S.   II. Series.

GF503 .A445 2003
333.7´2´0973—dc21

ISBN-13: 978-0-631-22863-9 (hbk: alk. paper) — ISBN-13: 978-0-631-22864-6 (pbk: alk.
paper)

A catalogue record for this title is available from the British Library.

Set in 10 / 12 pt Plantin
by Kolam Information Services Pvt. Ltd, Pondicherry.
Printed and bound in the United Kingdom
by TJ International, Padstow, Cornwall

The publisher's policy is to use permanent paper from mills that operate a sustainable
forestry policy, and which has been manufactured from pulp processed using
acid-free and elementary chlorine-free practices. Furthermore, the publisher ensures
that the text paper and cover board used have met acceptable environmental
accreditation standards.

For further information on
Blackwell Publishing, visit our website:
www.blackwellpublishing.com

For Spring, Jesse, and Sam

Contents

Series Editor's Preface

The purpose of the Blackwell Readers in American Social and Cultural History is to introduce students to cutting-edge historical scholarship that draws upon a variety of disciplines, and to encourage students to "do" history themselves by examining some of the primary texts upon which that scholarship is based.

Each of us lives life with a wholeness that is at odds with the way scholars often dissect the human experience. Anthropologists, psychologists, literary critics, and political scientists (to name just a few) study only discrete parts of our existence. The result is a rather arbitrary collection of disciplinary boundaries enshrined not only in specialized publications but also in university academic departments and in professional organizations.

As a scholarly enterprise, the study of history necessarily crosses these boundaries of knowledge in order to provide a comprehensive view of the past. Over the last few years, social and cultural historians have reached across the disciplines to understand the history of the British North American colonies and the United States in all its fullness. Unfortunately, much of that scholarship, published in specialized monographs and journals, remains inaccessible to undergraduates. Consequently, instructors often face choices that are not very appealing – to ignore the recent scholarship altogether, assign bulky readers that are too detailed for an undergraduate audience, or cobble together packages of recent articles that lack an overall contextual framework. The individual volumes of this series each focus on a significant topic in American history, and bring new, exciting scholarship to students in a compact, accessible format.

The series is designed to complement textbooks and other general readings assigned in undergraduate courses. Each editor has culled particularly innovative and provocative scholarly essays from widely scattered books and journals, and provided an introduction summarizing the major themes of the essays and documents that follow. The essays reproduced here were chosen because of the authors' innovative (and often interdisciplinary) methodology and their ability to reconceptualize historical issues in fresh and insightful ways. Thus students can appreciate the rich complexity of an historical topic and the way that scholars have explored the topic from different perspectives, and in the process transcend the highly artificial disciplinary boundaries that have served to compartmentalize knowledge about the past in the United States.

Also included in each volume are primary texts, at least some of which have been drawn from the essays themselves. By linking primary and secondary material, the editors are able to introduce students to the historian's craft, allowing them to explore this material in depth, and draw additional insights – or interpretations contrary to those of the scholars under discussion – from it. Additional teaching tools, including study questions and suggestions for further reading, offer depth to the analysis.

Jacqueline Jones
Brandeis University

Acknowledgments

Thanks to Bill Cronon and Mark Fiege for their thoughtful advice, and to my research assistants, Robert Chester and Phil Garone, for their help.

The editor and publisher are grateful to the following for permission to reproduce material:

Rachel Carson, "Elixirs of Death," from *Silent Spring*. Copyright © 1962 by Rachel L. Carson, renewed 1990 by Roger Christie. Reprinted by permission of Houghton Mifflin Company and Pollinger Ltd. All rights reserved.

William Cronon, "A World of Fields and Fences," from *Changes in the Land*, pp. 127–48, 199–203 (excerpted). Published by Hill & Wang, 1983.

William Cronon, "The Trouble with Wilderness; or, Getting Back to the Wrong Nature," from *Uncommon Ground*, edited by William Cronon. Copyright © 1995 by William Cronon. Used by permission of W. W. Norton & Company Inc.

Alfred W. Crosby, "Ills," from *Ecological Imperialism: The Biological Expansion of Europe, 900–1900* (1986), pp. 196–216 (excerpted). Reprinted with the permission of Cambridge University Press.

William M. Denevan, "The Pristine Myth: The Landscape of the Americas in 1492," from *Annals of the Association of American Geographers* 82(3) 1992, pp. 369–385 (excerpted). Reproduced by permission of Blackwell Publishing.

Olive K. Dixon, *The Life of "Billy" Dixon: Plainsman, Scout and Pioneer* (1987), pp. 81–3 (excerpted). Reproduced by permission of State House Press.

Paul Ehrlich, *The Population Bomb* (Sierra Club, 1969), pp. 5–8. Reproduced by permission of the Sierra Club.

John C. Ewers, "Horse Breeding," from *The Horse in Blackfoot Indian Culture: With Comparative Material from Other Western Tribes* (1955, reprinted 1969), pp. 53–5 (excerpted). Reproduced by permission of Smithsonian Institution Press.

J. Brooks Flippen, *Nixon and the Environment*, pp. 1–16, 46–49, 83–87, 98, 233–6, 243–4, 250, 254–5 (excerpted). Published by University of New Mexico Press, 2000.

Dan Flores, *The Natural West: Environmental History in the Great Plains and Rocky Mountains*. Copyright © 2001 by the University of Oklahoma Press. Reprinted by permission.

Lois Gibbs, "Foreword," from *Toxic Struggles: The Theory and Practice of Environmental Justice*, edited by Richard Hofrichter, pp. 1–3 (excerpted). Published by New Society Publishers, 1993. Reprinted by permission of Lois Gibbs.

Robert Gottlieb, "Reconstructing Environmentalism: Complex Movements, Diverse Roots," from *Environmental History Review* 17(4) Winter, 1993, pp. 1–19 (excerpted).

Public Law 159, July 14, 1955, from *Environmental Statutes 2001 Edition*, pp. 322–323 (excerpted). Reproduced by permission of Government Institutes, Rockville, Maryland, USA.

William Hornaday, *Our Vanishing Wildlife: Its Extermination and Preservation*, pp. 110–113 (excerpted). Published by New York Zoological Society, 1913.

Benjamin Heber Johnson, "Conservation, Subsistence, and Class at the Birth of Superior National Forest," from *Environmental History* 4(1) January 1999, pp. 80–99 (excerpted).

Jacques Le Moyne de Morgues, "Method of tilling the Ground and sowing Seed," from *The Work of Jacques Le Moyne de Morgues*, Vol. II (1977), p. 119. Text extracts from *The Work of Jacques Le Moyne de Morgues*, Vol. I (1977). Copyright © The British Museum. Reproduced by permission of the Trustees of the British Museum and British Museum Publications Ltd.

Jacques Le Moyne de Morgues, "The Offering of a Stag to the Sun," from *The Work of Jacques Le Moyne de Morgues*, Vol. II (1977), p. 133. Text extracts from *The Work of Jacques Le Moyne de Morgues*, Vol. I (1977). Copyright © The British Museum. Reproduced by permission of the Trustees of the British Museum and British Museum Publications Ltd.

Peter Matthiessen, "Procession of Game," from *Wildlife in America* p. 166. Published by Viking, 1959.

Richard K. Nelson, "The Watchful World," from *Make Prayers to the Raven: A Koyukon View of the Northern Forest* (1983), pp. 14–32 (excerpted). Reproduced by permission of University of Chicago Press and the author.

Frederick Law Olmsted, "The Rice District," from *The Cotton Kingdom: A Selection*, pp. 72–3. Published by Bobbs–Merrill, 1981.

"National Environmental Policy Act," from *Public Law* 91–190, Jan. 1, 1970, 83 Stat, pp. 852–4. Reproduced by permission of Sweet & Maxwell Ltd.

"National Park Service Act," from *Sixty-Fourth Congress*, Sess. I, Ch. 408, 1916, pp. 535–6 (excerpted). Reproduced by permission of Sweet & Maxwell Ltd.

Gifford Pinchot, *The Fight for Conservation*, pp. 42–52 (excerpted). Published by Doubleday, Page and Co., 1910. Reproduced by permission of Random House, Inc.

Carl Pope, "The Politics of Plunder," from *Sierra* Nov/Dec 1988. Reproduced by permission of *Sierra*, the magazine of the Sierra Club.

Charles E. Rosenberg, "Introduction" and "The Epidemic," from *The Cholera Years: The United States in 1832, 1849 and 1866* (1962, revised edition 1987), pp. 1–7, 13–39 (excerpted). Reproduced by permission of the University of Chicago Press and the author.

The Saturday Evening Post, "Fallout: The Silent Killer" from *Saturday Evening Post* Aug. 29, 1959, pp. 26–7, 87, 89, 90 (excerpted). Reprinted with permission of The Saturday Evening Post © 1959 (Renewed).

Junipero Serra, *The Writings of Junipero Serra*, edited by Antonine Tibesar, vol. 4 (1966), pp. 398–401 (excerpted). Reproduced by permission of the Academy of American Franciscan History.

The Sierra Club, "The Letter That Shook a Movement," from *Sierra* May/June 1993, p. 54. Reproduced by permission of *Sierra*, the magazine of the Sierra Club.

S. Fred Singer, "The Economic Costs of Environmental Overregulation," from *Human Events* Aug. 7, 1993. Reproduced by permission of Human Events.

Mart A. Stewart, "Rice, Water and Power: Landscapes of Domination and Resistance in the Lowcountry, 1790–1880," from *Environmental History Review* Vol. 15, Fall 1991, pp. 47–64 (excerpted).

Ellen Stroud, "Troubled Waters in Ecotopia: Environmental Racism in Portland, Oregon," in *Radical History Review*, Vol 74, pp. 65–95. Copyright © 1999, MARHO, The Radical Historian's Organization, Inc. All rights reserved. Reproduced with permission from Duke University Press.

Alan Taylor, "'Wasty Ways': Stories of American Settlement," from *Environmental History* 3(3) July 1998, pp. 291–309 (excerpted).

Ben Wattenberg, "The Population Explosion is Over," from *NYT Magazine*, Nov. 23, 1997, pp. 60–3 (excerpted). Copyright © 1997 by the New York Times Co. Reprinted by permission.

Mark Douglas Whitaker, "Jobs vs. Environment Myth," from *Institute for Southern Studies News Release*, Thursday, November 16, 2000.

"Wilderness Act," from *Public Law* 88–577, Sept 3, 1964, 78 Stat, pp. 890–1 (excerpted). Reproduced by permission of Sweet & Maxwell Ltd.

Gilbert L. Wilson, *Buffalo Bird Woman's Garden: Agriculture of the Hidatsa Indians* (1917). Published by Minnesota Historical Society Press, 1987, pp. 9–15, 30–31. Used with permission.

Introduction: What is Environmental History?

What is environmental history? At its most fundamental level, environmental historians explore the changing relations between people and nature. Such a broad definition can be more of a hindrance than a help, however. So let's be more specific. Environmental historians study how people have lived in the natural systems of the planet, and how they have perceived nature and reshaped it to suit their own idea of good living. More than this, the field of environmental history encompasses the investigation of how nature, once changed, requires people to reshape their cultures, economies, and politics to meet new realities. As we'll see in the pages that follow, such processes are not without social friction and unrest. People in history have battled mightily, and often, over what constitutes the best way of living in nature.

As a field of study, environmental history has been around for more than a generation. To many, it is most familiar as the history of the environmental movement. Obviously, the kinds of relations and processes I am discussing here go far beyond that, but, to be sure, the field includes the history of environmental reform and politics as a central concern.

The articles and documents in this volume illuminate how people have lived in the natural systems of the American landscape since before the time of Columbus to the present day. Read with enthusiasm and care, they will provide some startling and illuminating new perspectives on American history. The early centuries of American history were a period of enormous transformations. We shall see how American Indians lived on the earth and worked both to change it and to maintain its abundance. The coming of European colonists brought new organisms to the Americas, with consequences both disastrous and liberating for Indians. We shall read how colonists introduced the natural products of America's ecosystems to the enormous demands of the market system, and how early American settlers sought to transform forests to farm fields to escape their poverty.

Environmental history is not just about the countryside. It encompasses also the tangled relations between people and nature at the heart of the city. Thus, we shall explore how concentrating people in nineteenth-century cities with close trade links to Eurasia brought new and dangerous disease and fire environments to the American people, and how Americans ameliorated those conditions, sometimes with controversial measures that linked city to countryside in new ways.

The nineteenth century was a period of rapid industrialization and urbanization. Together, these two trends underwrote huge changes in America's natural systems, many of them destructive, with the result that a new political movement arose at the turn of the last century, through which many Americans sought to better manage the ways in which nature was used. The history of conservation provides a window on dramatic environmental *and* social change. It was inspired partly by the fear that a dissipated nature would harm centers of culture, the cities. Conservationist solutions entailed radical approaches to allocating nature's bounty, new ways of determining who was entitled to water game, lumber, and water, and to how much.

Environmental history offers not just new ways of thinking about history, but new ways of thinking about nature, too. Perceptions of nature have changed over time. In exploring how, historians question many of the most pervasive and popular understandings of nature around us. Thus, we shall see how Americans went from abhorring the wilderness to loving it as America's distinctive landscape, a kind of natural badge of American identity. And we shall ask whether the new valuing of wilderness did not come with a host of other problems, some of which may have created new obstacles to environmental protection.

Calamitous events are often the birth pangs of new thinking, and World War II and the Cold War together brought a revolution, or perhaps several revolutions, in environmental thought. The modern environmental movement, with its beginnings in various strands of conservation in the early twentieth century, reached maturation after 1945 in the public anxieties over insidious new environmental hazards such as radiation, pesticides, and air pollution. Amidst these concerns, environmentalism rose to such heights that politicians from across the political spectrum competed with one another for environmentalist support, with the result that the 1960s and 1970s saw a blizzard of environmental legislation with bipartisan authorship.

Almost as soon as it had begun, the environmental movement attracted critics. Among the most persuasive of these came from the political left, alleging that the movement was overwhelmingly concerned with securing quality of life for America's most powerful people, middle- and upper-class whites, while ignoring living and working conditions of the poor and peoples of color. Continuing attempts to address the problems of environmental racism have done much to transform the environmental movement in recent years. Environmental concern and racial prejudice arguably have reinforced one another at times, a tendency which helps explain historical genesis of the movement for environmental justice.

A very different critique of the environmental movement hailed from the political right. The successes of the environmental movement were followed, in the 1980s, by a backlash which has become an enduring political sub-movement. By the end of the twentieth century, environmentalism was under frequent attack from conservatives, who saw it as an obstacle to efficient government and traditional economic opportunity and entrepreneurialism.

For all the vehemence of conservative critics, Americans in general retain a pervasive belief in the need to protect clean air, clean water, and environmental systems. It may be that these beliefs are now a central feature of American culture – yet another example of how our ideas about nature and our responsibilities to it continue to evolve. This volume ends with some documents of ongoing environmental concerns and developments: some worrisome, some hopeful. At the beginning of the twenty-first century, as concerns about global warming and other ominous threats trouble many, the discipline of environmental history provides key insights into environmental relations and problems of the past. It can teach us not only how we might better understand our current predicaments. But more than that, in instructing us about how people once saw nature, it offers powerful insights into how they saw themselves and one another. In illuminating how Americans have perceived changed, and been changed by nature, environmental history teaches us much about how they have understood and shaped their politics, culture, and society.

I

The Natures of Indian America before Columbus

Given that so many people believe that America before Columbus was a version of the Garden of Eden, the history since then is usually understood as a fairly straightforward story, which goes like this: when Indians dominated America, the place was beautiful and natural. When Europeans arrived, they trashed the place.

The truth is far more complicated and interesting, however. William Denevan explores pre-contact Indian America with an eye to seeing how Indians shaped and changed the natural worlds around them. To be sure, most Indians did not impose as great a strain on natural environments as subsequent non-Indian settlers or modern industrial capitalism eventually would. But nonetheless, they did alter the earth around them in important ways. This is a key insight of environmental history: all peoples change nature to achieve their notion of the good life. To suggest that any people does not do this – that some people are *part* of nature without being willing or able to change it – is to remove them from history and to dehumanize them.

As you read Denevan's article, ask yourself how Indian changes to the natural environment before 1500 were different from the kinds of alterations, modifications, and wholesale changes in nature that your society makes today. Is there any way in which they were similar? How does it change your perception of American history to consider that Indians did not live in a Garden of Eden?

The Pristine Myth: The Landscape of the Americas in 1492

William M. Denevan

This is the forest primeval...

Evangeline: A Tale of Acadie
(Longfellow, 1847)

What was the New World like at the time of Columbus?...

Scholarship has shown that Indian populations in the Americas were substantial [in 1492], that the forests had indeed been altered, that landscape change was commonplace. This message, however, seems not to have reached the public through texts, essays, or talks by both academics and popularizers who have a responsibility to know better....

The evidence is convincing. By 1492 Indian activity throughout the Americas had modified forest extent and composition, created and expanded grasslands, and rearranged microrelief via countless artificial earthworks. Agricultural fields were common, as were houses and towns and roads and trails. All of these had local impacts on soil, microclimate, hydrology, and wildlife. This is a large topic, for which this essay offers but an introduction to the issues, misconceptions, and residual problems. The evidence, pieced together from vague ethnohistorical accounts, field surveys, and archaeology, supports the hypothesis that the Indian landscape of 1492 had largely vanished by the mid-eighteenth century, not through a European superimposition, but because of the demise of the native population. The landscape of 1750 was more "pristine" (less humanized) than that of 1492.

Indian Numbers

The size of the native population at contact is critical to our argument. The prevailing position, a recent one, is that the Americas were well-populated rather than relatively empty lands in 1492. In the words of the sixteenth-century Spanish priest, Bartolomé de las Casas, who knew the Indies well:

All that has been discovered up to the year forty-nine [1549] is full of people, like a hive of bees, so that it seems as though God had placed all, or the greater part of the entire human race in these countries. (Las Casas, in MacNutt 1909, 314)

Las Casas believed that more than 40 million Indians had died by the year 1560. Did he exaggerate? In the 1930s and 1940s, Alfred Kroeber, Angel Rosenblat, and Julian Steward believed that he had. The best counts then available indicated a population of between 8–15 million Indians in the Americas. Subsequently, Carl Sauer, Woodrow Borah, Sherburne F. Cook, Henry Dobyns, George Lovell, N. David Cook, myself, and others have argued for larger estimates. Many scholars now believe that there were between 40–100 million Indians in the hemisphere (Denevan 1992). This conclusion is primarily based on evidence of rapid early declines from epidemic disease prior to the first population counts (Lovell 1992).

I have recently suggested a New World total of 53.9 million (Denevan 1992, xxvii). This divides into 3.8 million for North America, 17.2 million for Mexico, 5.6 million for Central America, 3.0 million for the Caribbean, 15.7 million for the Andes, and 8.6 million for lowland South America. These figures are based on my judgment as to the most reasonable recent tribal and regional estimates. Accepting a margin of error of about 20 percent, the New World population would lie between 43–65 million. Future regional revisions are likely to maintain the hemispheric total within this range. . . . In any event, a population between 40–80 million is sufficient to dispel any notion of "empty lands." Moreover, the native impact on the landscape of 1492 reflected not only the population then but the cumulative effects of a growing population over the previous 15,000 years or more.

European entry into the New World abruptly reversed this trend. The decline of native American populations was rapid and severe, probably the greatest demographic disaster ever (Lovell 1992). Old World diseases were the primary killer. In many regions, particularly the tropical lowlands, populations fell by 90 percent or more in the first century after contact. Indian populations (estimated) declined in Hispaniola from 1 million in 1492 to a few hundred 50 years later, or by more than 99 percent; in Peru from 9 million in 1520 to 670,000 in 1620 (92 percent); in the Basin of Mexico from 1.6 million in 1519 to 180,000 in 1607 (89 percent); and in North America from 3.8 million in 1492 to 1 million in 1800 (74 percent). An overall drop from 53.9 million in 1492 to 5.6 million in 1650 amounts to an 89 percent reduction (Denevan 1992, xvii–xxix). The human landscape was affected accordingly, although there is not always a direct relationship between population density and human impact (Whitmore et al. 1990, 37).

The replacement of Indians by Europeans and Africans was initially a slow process. By 1638 there were only about 30,000 English in North America (Sale 1990, 386), and by 1750 there were only 1.3 million Europeans and slaves (Meinig 1986, 247). For Latin America in 1750, Sánchez-Albornoz (1974, 7) gives a total (including Indians) of 12 million. For the hemisphere in 1750, the *Atlas of World Population History* reports 16 million (McEvedy and Jones 1978, 270). Thus the overall hemispheric population in 1750 was about 30 percent of what it may have been in 1492. The 1750 population, however, was very unevenly distributed, mainly located in certain coastal and highland areas with little Europeanization elsewhere. In North America in 1750, there were only small pockets of settlement beyond the coastal belt, stretching from New England to northern Florida (see maps in Meinig 1986, 209, 245). Elsewhere, combined Indian and European populations were sparse, and environmental impact was relatively minor.

Indigenous imprints on landscapes at the time of initial European contact varied regionally in form and intensity. Following are examples for vegetation and wildlife, agriculture, and the built landscape.

Vegetation

The Eastern forests

The forests of New England, the Midwest, and the Southeast had been disturbed to varying degrees by Indian activity prior to European occupation. Agricultural clearing and burning had converted much of the forest into successional (fallow) growth and into semi-permanent grassy openings (meadows, barrens, plains, glades, savannas, prairies), often of considerable size. Much of the mature forest was characterized by an open, herbaceous understory, reflecting frequent ground fires. "The de Soto expedition, consisting of many people, a large horse herd, and many swine, passed through ten states without difficulty of movement" (Sauer 1971, 283). The situation has been described in detail by Michael Williams in his recent history of American forests: "Much of the 'natural' forest remained, but the forest was not the vast, silent, unbroken, impenetrable and dense tangle of trees beloved by many writers in their romantic accounts of the forest wilderness" (1989, 33). "The result was a forest of large, widely spaced trees, few shrubs, and much grass and herbage . . . Selective Indian burning thus promoted the mosaic quality of New England ecosystems, creating forests in many different states of ecological succession" (Cronon 1983, 49–51).

The extent, frequency, and impact of Indian burning is not without controversy. Raup (1937) argued that climatic change rather than Indian burning could account for certain vegetation changes. Emily Russell (1983, 86), assessing pre-1700 information for the Northeast, concluded that: "There is no strong evidence that Indians purposely burned large areas," but Indians did "increase the frequency of fires above the low numbers caused by lightning," creating an open forest. But then Russell adds: "In most areas climate and soil probably played the major role in determining the precolonial forests." She regards Indian fires as mainly accidental and "merely" augmental to natural fires, and she discounts the reliability of many early accounts of burning.

Forman and Russell (1983, 5) expand the argument to North America in general: "regular and widespread Indian burning (Day 1953) [is] an unlikely hypothesis that regretfully has been accepted in the popular literature and consciousness." This conclusion, I believe, is unwarranted given reports of the extent of prehistoric human burning in North America and Australia (Lewis 1982), and Europe (Patterson and Sassaman 1988, 130), and by my own and other observations on current Indian and peasant burning in Central America and South America; when unrestrained, people burn frequently and for many reasons. For the Northeast, Patterson and Sassaman (1988, 129) found that sedimentary charcoal accumulations were greatest where Indian populations were greatest.

Elsewhere in North America, the Southeast is much more fire prone than is the Northeast, with human ignitions being especially important in winter (Taylor 1981). The Berkeley geographer and Indianist Erhard Rostlund (1957, 1960) argued that Indian clearing and burning created many grasslands within mostly open forest in the so-called "prairie belt" of Alabama. As improbable as it may seem, Lewis (1982) found Indian burning in the subarctic, and Dobyns (1981) in the Sonoran desert. The characteristics and impacts of fires set by Indians varied regionally and locally with demography, resource management techniques, and environment, but such fires clearly had different vegetation impacts than did natural fires owing to differences in frequency, regularity, and seasonality.

Forest composition

In North America, burning not only maintained open forest and small meadows but also encouraged fire-tolerant and sun-loving species. "Fire created conditions favorable to strawberries, blackberries, raspberries, and other gatherable foods" (Cronon 1983, 51). Other useful plants were saved, protected, planted, and transplanted, such as American chestnut, Canada plum, Kentucky coffee tree, groundnut, and leek (Day 1953, 339–40). Gilmore (1931) described the dispersal of several native plants by Indians. Mixed stands were converted to single species dominants, including various pines and oaks, sequoia, Douglas fir, spruce, and aspen (M. Williams 1989, 47–48). The longleaf, slash pine, and scrub oak forests of the Southeast are almost certainly an anthropogenic subclimax created originally by Indian burning, replaced in early Colonial times by mixed hardwoods, and maintained in part by fires set by subsequent farmers and woodlot owners (Garren 1943). Lightning fires can account for some fire-climax vegetation, but Indian burning would have extended and maintained such vegetation (Silver 1990, 17–19, 59–64).

Even in the humid tropics, where natural fires are rare, human fires can dramatically influence forest composition. A good example is the pine forests of Nicaragua (Denevan 1961). Open pine stands occur both in the northern highlands (below 5,000 feet) and in the eastern (Miskito) lowlands, where warm temperatures and heavy rainfall generally favor mixed tropical montane forest or rain forest. The extensive pine forests of Guatemala and Mexico primarily grow in cooler and drier, higher elevations, where they are in large part natural and prehuman (Watts and Bradbury 1982, 59). Pine forests were definitely present in Nicaragua when Europeans arrived. They were found in areas where Indian settlement was substantial, but not in the eastern mountains where Indian densities were sparse. The eastern boundary of the highland pines seems to have moved with an eastern settlement frontier that has fluctuated back and forth since prehistory. The pines occur today where there has been clearing followed by regular burning and the same is likely in the past. The Nicaraguan pines are fire tolerant once mature, and large numbers of seedlings survive to maturity if they can escape fire during their first three to seven years (Denevan 1961, 280). Where settlement has been abandoned and fire ceases, mixed hardwoods gradually replace pines. This succession is likely similar where pines occur elsewhere at low elevations in tropical Central America, the Caribbean, and Mexico.

Midwest prairies and tropical savannas

Sauer (1950, 1958, 1975) argued early and often that the great grasslands and savannas of the New World were of anthropogenic rather than climatic origin, that rainfall was generally sufficient to support trees. Even nonagricultural Indians expanded what may have been pockets of natural, edaphic grasslands at the expense of forest. A fire burning to the edge of a grass/forest boundary will penetrate the drier forest margin and push back the edge, even if the forest itself is not consumed (Mueller-Dombois 1981, 164). Grassland can therefore advance significantly in the wake of hundreds of years of annual fires. Lightning-set fires can have a similar impact, but more slowly if less frequent than human fires, as in the wet tropics.

. . . Most ecologists now believe that the eastern prairies "would have mostly disappeared if it had not been for the nearly annual burning of these grasslands by the North American Indians," during the last 5,000 years. A case in point is the nineteenth-century invasion of many grasslands by forests after fire had been suppressed in Wisconsin, Illinois, Kansas, Nebraska, and elsewhere (M. Williams 1989, 46).

The large savannas of South America are also controversial as to origin. Much, if not most of the open vegetation of the Orinoco Llanos, the Llanos de Mojos of Bolivia, the Pantanal of Mato Grosso, the Bolívar savannas of Colombia, the Guayas savannas of coastal Ecuador, the *campo cerrado* of central Brazil, and the coastal savannas north of the Amazon, is of natural origin. The vast *campos cerrados* occupy extremely senile, often toxic oxisols. The seasonally inundated savannas of Bolivia, Brazil, Guayas, and the Orinoco owe their existence to the intolerance of woody species to the extreme alternation of lengthy flooding or water-logging and severe desiccation during a long dry season. These savannas, however, were and are burned by Indians and ranchers, and such fires have expanded the savannas into the forests to an unknown extent. It is now very difficult to determine where a natural forest/savanna boundary once was located (Hills and Randall 1968; Medina 1980).

Other small savannas have been cut out of the rainforest by Indian farmers and then maintained by burning. An example is the Gran Pajonal in the Andean foothills in east-central Peru, where dozens of small grasslands (*pajonales*) have been created by Campa Indians – a process clearly documented by air photos (Scott 1978). *Pajonales* were in existence when the region was first penetrated by Franciscan missionary explorers in 1733.

The impact of human activity is nicely illustrated by vegetational changes in the basins of the San Jorge, Cauca, and Sinú rivers of northern Colombia. The southern sector, which was mainly savanna when first observed in the sixteenth century, had reverted to rainforest by about 1750 following Indian decline, and had been reconverted to savanna for pasture by 1950 (Gordon 1957, map p. 69). Sauer (1966, 285–88; 1975, 8) and Bennett (1968, 53–55) cite early descriptions of numerous savannas in Panama in the sixteenth century. Balboa's first view of the Pacific was from a "treeless ridge," now probably forested. Indian settlement and agricultural fields were common at the time, and with their decline the rainforest returned.

Anthropogenic tropical rain forest

The tropical rain forest has long had a reputation for being pristine, whether in 1492 or 1992. There is, however, increasing evidence that the forests of Amazonia and elsewhere are largely anthropogenic in form and composition. Sauer (1958, 105) said as much at the Ninth Pacific Science Congress in 1957 when he challenged the statement of tropical botanist Paul Richards that, until recently, the tropical forests have been largely uninhabited, and that prehistoric people had "no more influence on the vegetation than any of the other animal inhabitants." Sauer countered that Indian burning, swiddens, and manipulation of composition had extensively modified the tropical forest.

"Indeed, in much of Amazonia, it is difficult to find soils that are not studded with charcoal" (Uhl et al. 1990, 30). . . .

The Amazon forest is a mosaic of different ages, structure, and composition resulting from local habitat conditions and disturbance dynamics (Haffer 1991). Natural disturbances (tree falls, landslides, river activity) have been considerably augmented by human activity, particularly by shifting cultivation. Even a small number of swidden farmers can have a widespread impact in a relatively short period of time. . . .

Indian modification of tropical forests is not limited to clearing and burning. Large expanses of Latin American forests are humanized forests in which the kinds, numbers, and distributions of useful species are managed by human populations. . . .

. . . There are no virgin tropical forests today, nor were there in 1492.

Wildlife

The indigenous impact on wildlife is equivocal. The thesis that "over-kill" hunting caused the extinction of some large mammals in North America during the late Pleistocene, as well as subsequent local and regional depletions (Martin 1978, 167–72), remains controversial. By the time of the arrival of Cortéz in 1519, the dense populations of Central Mexico apparently had greatly reduced the number of large game, given reports that "they eat any living thing" (Cook and Borah 1971–79, (3) 135, 140). In Amazonia, local game depletion apparently increases with village size and duration (Good 1987). Hunting procedures in many regions seem, however, to have allowed for recovery because of the "resting" of hunting zones intentionally or as a result of shifting of village sites.

On the other hand, forest disturbance increased herbaceous forage and edge effect, and hence the numbers of some animals (Thompson and Smith 1970, 261–64). "Indians created ideal habitats for a host of wildlife species ... exactly those species whose abundance so impressed English colonists: elk, deer, beaver, hare, porcupine, turkey, quail, cuffed grouse, and so on" (Cronon 1983, 51). White-tailed deer, peccary, birds, and other game increases in swiddens and fallows in Yucatán and Panama (Greenberg 1991; Gordon 1982, 96–112; Bennett 1968). Rostlund (1960, 407) believed that the creation of grassy openings east of the Mississippi extended the range of the bison, whose numbers increased with Indian depopulation and reduced hunting pressure between 1540–1700, and subsequently declined under White pressure.

Agriculture

Fields and associated features

To observers in the sixteenth century, the most visible manifestation of the Native American landscape must have been the cultivated fields, which were concentrated around villages and houses. Most fields are ephemeral, their presence quickly erased when farmers migrate or die, but there are many eye-witness accounts of the great extent of Indian fields. On Hispaniola, Las Casas and Oviedo reported individual fields with thousands of *montones* (Sturtevant 1961, 73). These were manioc and sweet potato mounds 3–4 m in circumference, of which apparently none have survived. In the Llanos de Mojos in Bolivia, the first explorers mentioned *percheles*, or corn cribs on pilings, numbering up to 700 in a single field, each holding 30–45 bushels of food (Denevan 1966, 98). In northern Florida in 1539, Hernando de Soto's army passed through numerous fields of maize, beans, and squash, their main source of provisions; in one sector, "great fields ... were spread out as far as the eye could see across two leagues of the plain" (Garcilaso de la Vega 1980, (2) 182; also see Dobyns 1983, 135–46).

It is difficult to obtain a reliable overview from such descriptions. Aside from possible exaggeration, Europeans tended not to write about field size, production, or technology. More useful are various forms of relict fields and field features that persist for centuries and can still be recognized, measured, and excavated today. These extant features, including terraces, irrigation works, raised fields, sunken fields, drainage ditches, dams, reservoirs, diversion walls, and field borders number in the millions and are distributed throughout the Americas (Denevan 1980; see also Doolittle 1992 and Whitmore and Turner, 1992). For example, about 500,000 ha of abandoned raised fields survive in the San Jorge Basin of northern Colombia (Plazas and Falchetti 1987, 485), and at least 600,000 ha of terracing, mostly of prehistoric origin, occur in the Peruvian Andes (Denevan 1988, 20). There are 19,000 ha of visible raised fields in just the sustaining area of Tiwanaku at Lake Titicaca (Kolata 1991, 109) and there were about 12,000 ha of *chinampas* (raised fields) around the Aztec capital of Tenochtitlán (Sanders et al. 1979, 390). Complex canal systems on the north coast of Peru and in the Salt River Valley in Arizona irrigated more land in prehistory than is cultivated today. About 175 sites of Indian garden beds, up to several hundred acres each, have been reported in Wisconsin (Gartner 1992). These various remnant fields probably represent less than 25 percent of what once existed, most being buried under sediment or destroyed by erosion, urbanization, plowing, and bulldozing. On the other hand, an inadequate effort has been made to search for ancient fields.

Erosion

The size of native populations, associated deforestation, and prolonged intensive agriculture led to severe land degradation in some regions. Such a landscape was that of Central Mexico, where by 1519 food production pressures may have brought the Aztec civilization to the verge of collapse even without Spanish intervention (Cook and Borah 1971–79 (3), 129–76). There is good evidence that severe soil erosion was already widespread, rather than just the result of subsequent European plowing, livestock, and deforestation. Cook examined the association between erosional severity (gullies, barrancas, sand and silt deposits, and sheet erosion) and pre-Spanish population density or proximity to prehistoric Indian towns. He concluded that "an important cycle of erosion and deposition therefore accompanied intensive land use by huge primitive populations in central Mexico, and had gone far toward the devastation of the country before the white man arrived" (Cook 1949, 86).

Barbara Williams (1972, 618) describes widespread *tepetate*, an indurated substrate formation exposed by sheet erosion resulting from prehistoric agriculture, as "one of the dominant surface materials in the Valley of Mexico." On the other hand, anthropologist Melville (1990, 27) argues that soil erosion in the Valle de Mezquital, just north of the Valley of Mexico, was the result of overgrazing by Spanish livestock starting before 1600: "there is an almost total lack of evidence of environmental degradation before the last three decades of the sixteenth century." The Butzers, however, in an examination of Spanish land grants, grazing patterns, and soil and vegetation ecology, found that there was only light intrusion of Spanish livestock (sheep and cattle were moved frequently) into the southeastern Bajío near Mezquital until after 1590 and that any degradation in 1590 was "as much a matter of long-term Indian land use as it was of Spanish intrusion" (Butzer and Butzer 1993). The relative roles of Indian and early Spanish impacts in Mexico still need resolution; both were clearly significant but varied in time and place. Under the Spaniards, however, even with a greatly reduced population, the landscape in Mexico generally did not recover due to accelerating impacts from introduced sheep and cattle.

The Built Landscape

Settlement

The Spaniards and other Europeans were impressed by large flourishing Indian cities such as Tenochtitlán, Quito, and Cuzco, and they took note of the extensive ruins of older, abandoned cities such as Cahokia, Teotihuacán, Tikal, Chan Chan, and Tiwanaku (Hardoy 1968). Most of these cities contained more than 50,000 people. Less notable, or possible more taken for granted, was rural settlement – small villages of a few thousand or a few hundred people, hamlets of a few families, and dispersed farmsteads. The numbers and locations of much of this settlement will never be known. With the rapid decline of native populations, the abandonment of houses and entire villages and the decay of perishable materials quickly obscured sites, especially in the tropical lowlands.

We do have some early listings of villages, especially for Mexico and Peru. Elsewhere, archaeology is telling us more than ethnohistory. After initially focusing on large temple and administrative centers, archaeologists are now examining rural sustaining areas, with remarkable results. See, for example, Sanders et al. (1979) on the Basin of Mexico, Culbert and Rice (1990) on the Maya lowlands, and Fowler (1989) on Cahokia in Illinois. Evidence of human occupation for the artistic Santarém Culture phase (Tapajós chiefdom) on the lower Amazon extends over thousands of square kilometers, with large nucleated settlements (Roosevelt 1991, 101–02).

Much of the rural precontact settlement was semi-dispersed (*rancherías*), particularly in densely populated regions of Mexico and the Andes, probably reflecting poor food transport efficiency. Houses were both single-family and communal (pueblos, Huron long houses, Amazon malocas). Construction was of stone, earth, adobe, daub and wattle, grass, hides, brush, and bark. Much of the dispersed settlement not destroyed by depopulation was concentrated by the Spaniards into compact grid/plaza style new towns (*congregaciones, reducciones*) for administrative purposes.

Mounds

James Parsons (1985, 161) has suggested that: "An apparent mania for earth moving, landscape engineering on a grand scale runs as a thread through much of New World prehistory." Large quantities of both earth and stone were transferred to create various raised and sunken features, such as agricultural landforms, settlement and ritual mounds, and causeways.

Mounds of different shapes and sizes were constructed throughout the Americas for temples, burials, settlement, and as effigies. The stone pyramids of Mexico and the Andes are well known, but equal monuments of earth were built in the Amazon, the Midwest U.S., and elsewhere. The Mississippian period complex of 104 mounds at Cahokia near East St. Louis supported 30,000 people; the largest, Monk's Mound, is currently 30.5 m high and covers 6.9 ha. (Fowler 1989, 90, 192). Cahokia was the largest settlement north of the Río Grande until surpassed by New York City in 1775. An early survey estimated "at least 20,000 conical, linear, and effigy mounds" in Wisconsin (Stout 1911, 24). Overall, there must have been several hundred thousand artificial mounds in the Midwest and South. De Soto described such features still in use in 1539 (Silverberg 1968, 7). Thousands of settlement and other mounds dot the savanna landscape of Mojos in Bolivia (Denevan 1966). At the mouth of the Amazon on Marajó Island, one complex of forty habitation mounds contained more than 10,000 people; one of these mounds is 20 m high while another is 90 ha in area (Roosevelt 1991, 31, 38).

Not all of the various earthworks scattered over the Americas were in use in 1492. Many had been long abandoned, but they constituted a conspicuous element of the landscape of 1492 and some are still prominent. Doubtless, many remain to be discovered, and others remain unrecognized as human or prehistoric features.

Roads, causeways, and trails

Large numbers of people and settlements necessitated extensive systems of overland travel routes to facilitate administration, trade, warfare, and social interaction (Hyslop 1984; Trombold 1991). Only hints of their former prominence survive. Many were simple traces across deserts or narrow paths cut into forests. A suggestion as to the importance of Amazon forest trails is the existence of more than 500 km of trail maintained by a single Kayapó village today (Posey 1985, 149). Some prehistoric footpaths were so intensively used for so long that they were incised into the ground and are still detectable, as has recently been described in Costa Rica (Sheets and Sever 1991).

Improved roads, at times stone-lined and drained, were constructed over great distances in the realms of the high civilizations. The Inca road network is estimated to have measured about 40,000 km, extending from southern Colombia to central Chile (Hyslop 1984, 224). Prehistoric causeways (raised roads) were built in the tropical lowlands (Denevan 1991); one Maya causeway is 100 km long, and there are more than 1,600 km of causeways in the Llanos de Mojos. Humboldt reported large prehistoric causeways in the Orinoco Llanos. Ferdinand Columbus described roads on Puerto Rico in 1493. Gaspar de Carvajal, traveling down the Amazon with Orellana in 1541, reported "highways" penetrating the forest from river bank villages. Joseph de Acosta (1880, (1) 171) in 1590 said that between Peru and Brazil, there were "waies as much beaten as those betwixt Salamanca and Valladolid." Prehistoric roads in Chaco Canyon, New Mexico are described in Trombold (1991). Some routes were so well established and located that they have remained roads to this day.

Recovery

A strong case can be made for significant environmental recovery and reduction of cultural features by the late eighteenth century as a result of Indian population decline. Henry Thoreau (1949, 132–37) believed, based on his reading of William Wood, that the New England forests of 1633 were more open, more park-like, with more berries and more wildlife, than Thoreau observed in 1855. Cronon (1983, 108), Pyne (1982, 51), Silver (1990, 104), Martin (1978, 181–82), and [M.] Williams (1989, 49) all maintain that the eastern forests recovered and filled in as a result of Indian depopulation, field abandonment, and reduction in burning. While probably correct, these writers give few specific examples, so further research is needed. The sixteenth-century fields and savannas of Colombia and Central America also had reverted to forest within 150 years after abandonment (Parsons 1975, 30–31; Bennett 1968, 54). On his fourth voyage in 1502–03, Columbus sailed along the north coast of Panama (Veragua). His son Ferdinand described lands which were well-peopled, full of houses, with many fields, and open with few trees. In contrast, in 1681 Lionel Wafer found most of the Caribbean coast of Panama forest covered and unpopulated. On the Pacific side in the eighteenth century, savannas were seldom mentioned; the main economic activity was the logging of tropical cedar, a tree that grows on the sites of abandoned fields and other disturbances (Sauer 1966, 132–33, 287–88). An earlier oscillation from forest destruction to recovery in the Yucatán is instructive. Whitmore et al. (1990, 35) estimate that the Maya had modified 75 percent of the environment by A.D. 800, and that following the Mayan collapse, forest recovery in the central lowlands was nearly complete when the Spaniards arrived.

The pace of forest regeneration, however, varied across the New World. Much of the southeastern U.S. remained treeless in the 1750s according to Rostlund (1957, 408, 409). He notes that the tangled brush that ensnarled the "Wilderness Campaign of 1864 in Virginia occupied the same land as did Captain John Smith's 'open groves with much good ground between without any shrubs'" in 1624; vegetation had only partially recovered over 240 years. The Kentucky barrens in contrast were largely reforested by the early nineteenth century (Sauer 1963, 30). The Alabama Black Belt vegetation was described by William Bartram in the 1770s as a mixture of forest and grassy plains, but by the nineteenth century, there was only 10 percent prairie and even less in some counties (Rostlund 1957, 393, 401–03). Sections of coastal forests never recovered, given colonist pressures, but Sale's (1990, 291) claim that "the English were well along in the process of eliminating the ancient Eastern woodlands from Maine to the Mississippi" in the first one hundred years, is an exaggeration.

Wildlife also partially recovered in eastern North America with reduced hunting pressure from Indians; however, this is also a story yet to be worked out. The white-tailed deer apparently declined in numbers, probably reflecting reforestation plus competition from livestock. Commercial hunting was a factor on the coast with 80,000 deer skins being shipped out yearly from Charleston by 1730 (Silver 1990, 92). Massachusetts enacted a closed season on deer as early as 1694, and in 1718 there was a three-year moratorium on deer hunting (Cronon 1983, 100). Sale (1990, 290) believes that beaver were depleted in the Northeast by 1640. Other fur bearers, game birds, elk, buffalo, and carnivores were also targeted by white hunters, but much game probably was in the process of recovery in many eastern areas until a general reversal after 1700–50.

As agricultural fields changed to scrub and forest, earthworks were grown over. All the raised fields in Yucatán and South America were abandoned. A large portion of the agricultural terraces in the Americas were abandoned in the early colonial period (Donkin 1979, 35–38). In the Colca Valley of Peru, measurement on air photos indicates

61 percent terrace abandonment (Denevan 1988, 28). Societies vanished or declined everywhere and whole villages with them. The degree to which settlement features were swallowed up by vegetation, sediment, and erosion is indicated by the difficulty of finding them today. Machu Picchu, a late prehistoric site, was not rediscovered until 1911.

The renewal of human impact also varied regionally, coming with the Revolutionary War in North America, with the rubber boom in Amazonia, and with the expansion of coffee in southern Brazil (1840–1930). The swamp lands of Gulf Coast Mexico and the Guayas Basin of Ecuador remained hostile environments to Europeans until well into the nineteenth century or later (Siemens 1990; Mathewson 1987). On the other hand, Highland Mexico-Guatemala and the Andes, with greater Indian survival and with the establishment of haciendas and intensive mining, show less evidence of environmental recovery. Similarly, Indian fields in the Caribbean were rapidly replaced by European livestock and sugar plantation systems, inhibiting any sufficient recovery. The same is true of the sugar zone of coastal Brazil.

Conclusions

By 1492, Indian activity had modified vegetation and wildlife, caused erosion, and created earthworks, roads, and settlements throughout the Americas. This may be obvious, but the human imprint was much more ubiquitous and enduring than is usually realized. The historical evidence is ample, as are data from surviving earthworks and archaeology. And much can be inferred from present human impacts. The weight of evidence suggests that Indian populations were large, not only in Mexico and the Andes, but also in seemingly unattractive habitats such as the rain forests of Amazonia, the swamps of Mojos, and the deserts of Arizona.

Clearly, the most humanized landscapes of the Americas existed in those highland regions where people were the most numerous. Here were the large states, characterized by urban centers, road systems, intensive agriculture, a dispersed but relatively dense rural settlement pattern of hamlets and farmsteads, and widespread vegetation and soil modification and wildlife depletion. There were other, smaller regions that shared some of these characteristics, such as the Pueblo lands in the southwestern U.S., the Sabana de Bogotá in highland Colombia, and the central Amazon floodplain, where built landscapes were locally dramatic and are still observable. Finally, there were the immense grasslands, deserts, mountains, and forests elsewhere, with populations that were sparse or moderate, with landscape impacts that mostly were ephemeral

Map 1.1. Selected features of the prehistoric cultural landscape. Some cities and agricultural works had been abandoned by 1492. The approximate limit of agriculture and the distribution of terraces is based on Donkin (1979, 23); other features were mapped by the author.

or not obvious but nevertheless significant, particularly for vegetation and wildlife, as in Amazonia and the northeastern U.S. In addition, landscapes from the more distant past survived to 1492 and even to 1992, such as those of the irrigation states of north coast Peru, the Classic Maya, the Mississippian mound builders, and the Tiwanaku Empire of Lake Titicaca.

This essay has ranged over the hemisphere, an enormous area, making generalizations about and providing examples of Indian landscape transformation as of 1492. Examples of some of the surviving cultural features are shown in Map 1.1. Ideally, a series of hemispheric maps should be provided to portray the spatial patterns of the different types of impacts and cultural features, but such maps are not feasible nor would they be accurate given present knowledge. There are a few relevant regional maps, however, that can be referred to. For example, see Butzer (1990, 33, 45) for Indian settlement structures/mounds and subsistence patterns in the U.S.; Donkin (1979, 23) for agricultural terracing; Doolittle (1990, 109) for canal irrigation in Mexico; Parsons and Denevan (1967) for raised fields in South America; Trombold (1991) for various road networks; Hyslop (1984, 4) for the Inca roads; Hardoy (1968, 49) for the most intense urbanization in Latin America; and Gordon (1957, 69) for anthropogenic savannas in northern Colombia.

The pristine myth cannot be laid at the feet of Columbus. While he spoke of "Paradise," his was clearly a humanized paradise. He described Hispaniola and Tortuga as densely populated and "completely cultivated like the countryside around Cordoba" (Colón 1976, 165). He also noted that "the islands are not so thickly wooded as to be impassable," suggesting openings from clearing and burning (Columbus 1961, 5).

The roots of the pristine myth lie in part with early observers unaware of human impacts that may be obvious to scholars today, particularly for vegetation and wildlife. But even many earthworks such as raised fields have only recently been discovered (Denevan 1966; 1980). Equally important, most of our eyewitness descriptions of wilderness and empty lands come from a later time, particularly 1750–1850 when interior lands began to be explored and occupied by Europeans. By 1650, Indian populations in the hemisphere had been reduced by about 90 percent, while by 1750 European numbers were not yet substantial and settlements had only begun to expand. As a result, fields had been abandoned, while settlements vanished, forests recovered, and savannas retreated. The landscape did appear to be a sparsely populated wilderness. This is the image conveyed by Parkman in the nineteenth century, Bakeless in 1950, and Shetler as recently as 1991. There was some European impact, of course, but it was localized. After 1750 and especially after 1850, populations greatly expanded, resources were more intensively exploited, and European modification of the environment accelerated, continuing to the present.

It is possible to conclude not only that "the virgin forest was not encountered in the sixteenth and seventeenth centuries; [but that] it was invented in the late eighteenth and early nineteenth centuries" (Pyne 1982, 46). However, "paradoxical as it may seem, there was undoubtedly much more 'forest primeval' in 1850 than in 1650" (Rostlund 1957, 409). Thus the "invention" of an earlier wilderness is in part understandable and is not simply a deliberate creation which ennobled the American enterprise, as suggested by Bowden (1992, 20–23). In any event, while pre-European landscape alteration has been demonstrated previously, including by several geographers, the case has mainly been made for vegetation and mainly for eastern North America. As shown here, the argument is also applicable to most of the rest of the New World, including the humid tropics, and involves much more than vegetation.

The human impact on environment is not simply a process of increasing change or degradation in response to linear population growth and economic expansion. It is instead interrupted by periods of reversal and ecological rehabilitation as cultures collapse, populations decline, wars occur, and habitats are abandoned. Impacts may be constructive, benign, or degenerative (all subjective concepts), but change is continual at variable rates and in different directions. Even mild impacts and slow changes are cumulative, and the long-term effects can be dramatic. Is it possible that the thousands of years of human activity before Columbus created more change in the visible landscape than has occurred subsequently with European settlement and resource exploitation? The answer is probably yes for most regions for the next 250 years or so, and for some regions right up to the present time. American flora, fauna, and landscape were slowly Europeanized after 1492, but before that they had already been Indianized. "It is upon this imprint that the more familiar Euro-American landscape was grafted, rather than created anew" (Butzer 1990, 28). What does all this mean for protectionist tendencies today? Much of what is protected or proposed to be protected from human disturbance had native people present, and environmental modification occurred accordingly and in part is still detectable.

The pristine image of 1492 seems to be a myth, then, an image more applicable to 1750, following Indian decline, although recovery had only been partial by that date. There is some substance to this argument, and it should hold up under the scrutiny of further investigation of the considerable evidence available, both written and in the ground.

Acknowledgments

The field and library research that provided the background for this essay was undertaken over many years in Latin America, Berkeley, and Madison. Mentors who have been particularly influential are Carl O. Sauer, Erhard Rostlund, James J. Parsons, and Woodrow Borah, all investigators of topics discussed here.

References

Acosta, Joseph [José] de. 1880 (1590). *The natural and moral history of the Indies.* Trans. E. Olmston, Hakluyt Society, vols. 60, 61. London.

Bennett, C. F. 1968. *Human influences on the zoo-geography of Panama.* Ibero-Americana 51. Berkeley: University of California Press.

Bowden, M. J. 1992. The invention of American tradition. *Journal of Historical Geography* 18:3–26.

Butzer, K. W. 1990. The Indian legacy in the American landscape. In *The making of the American landscape,* ed. M. P. Conzen, pp. 27–50. Boston: Unwin Hyman.

——, **and Butzer, E. K.** 1993. The sixteenth-century environment of the central Mexican Bajío: Archival reconstruction from Spanish land grants. In *Culture, form, and place,* ed. K. Mathewson, pp. 89–124. Baton Rouge, LA: Dept. of Geology, Louisiana State University.

Colón, C. 1976. *Diario del descubrimiento,* vol. 1, ed. M. Alvar. Madrid: Editorial La Muralla.

Columbus, C. 1961. *Four voyages to the New World: Letters and selected documents,* ed. R. H. Major. New York: Corinth Books.

Cook, S. F. 1949. *Soil erosion and population in Central Mexico.* Ibero-Americana 34. Berkeley: University of California Press.

——, **and Borah, W.** 1971–79. *Essays in population history.* 3 vols. Berkeley: University of California Press.

Cronon, W. 1983. *Changes in the land: Indians, colonists, and the ecology of New England.* New York: Hill and Wang.

Culbert, T. P., and Rice, D. S., eds. 1990. *Pre-columbian population history in the Maya lowlands.* Albuquerque: University of New Mexico Press.

Day, G. M. 1953. The Indian as an ecological factor in the northeastern forest. *Ecology* 34:329–46.

Denevan, W. M. 1961. The upland pine forests of Nicaragua. *University of California Publications in Geography* 12:251–320.

——. 1966. *The aboriginal cultural geography of the Llanos de Mojos of Bolivia.* Ibero-Americana 48. Berkeley: University of California Press.

——. 1988. Measurement of abandoned terracing from air photos: Colca Valley, Peru. *Yearbook, Conference of Latin Americanist Geographers* 14:20–30.

——. 1991. Prehistoric roads and causeways of lowland tropical America. In *Ancient road networks and settlement hierarchies in the New World,* ed. C. D. Trombold, pp. 230–42. Cambridge: Cambridge University Press.

——, **ed.** 1992 [1976]. *The native population of the Americas in 1492,* 2nd ed. Madison: University of Wisconsin Press.

Dobyns, H. F. 1981. *From fire to flood: Historic human destruction of Sonoran Desert riverine oases.* Socorro, NM: Ballena Press.

——. 1983. *Their number become thinned: Native American population dynamics in eastern North America.* Knoxville: University of Tennessee Press.

Donkin, R. A. 1979. *Agricultural terracing in the aboriginal New World.* Viking Fund Publications in Anthropology 56. Tucson: University of Arizona Press.

Doolittle, W. E. 1990. *Canal irrigation in prehistorical Mexico: The sequence of technological changes.* Austin: University of Texas Press.

———. 1992. Agriculture in North America on the eve of contact: a reassessment. *Annals of the Association of American Geographers* 82(3): 386–401.

Forman, R. T. T., and Russell, E. W. B. 1983. Evaluation of historical data in ecology. *Bulletin of the Ecological Society of America* 64:5–7.

Fowler, M. 1989. *The Cahokia atlas: A historical atlas of Cahokia archaeology.* Studies in Illinois Archaeology 6. Springfield: Illinois Historic Preservation Agency.

Garcilaso de la Vega, The Inca. 1980 [1605]. *The Florida of the Inca: A history of the Adelantade* Hernando de Soto. 2 vols. Trans. and ed. J. G. Varner and J. J. Varner. Austin: University of Texas Press.

Garren, K. H. 1943. Effects of fire on vegetation of the southeastern United States. *The Botanical Review* 9:617–54.

Gartner, W. G. 1992. The Hulbert Creek ridged fields: Pre-Columbian agriculture near the Dells of Wisconsin. Master's thesis, Department of Geography, University of Wisconsin, Madison.

Gilmore, M. R. 1931. Dispersal by Indians a factor in the extension of discontinuous distribution of certain species of native plants. *Papers of the Michigan Academy of Science, Arts and Letters* 13:89–94.

Good, K. R. 1987. Limiting factors in Amazonian ecology. In *Food and evolution: Toward a theory of human food habitats,* ed. M. Harris and E. B. Ross, pp. 407–21. Philadelphia: Temple University Press.

Gordon, B. L. 1957. *Human geography and ecology in the Sinú country of Colombia.* Ibero-Americana 39, Berkeley: University of California Press.

———. 1982. *A Panama forest and shore: Natural history and Amerindian culture in Bocas del Toro.* Pacific Grove: Boxwood Press.

Greenberg, L. S. C. 1991. Garden-hunting among the Yucatec Maya. *Etnoecológica* 1:30–36.

Haffer, J. 1991. Mosaic distribution patterns of neotropical forest birds and underlying cyclic disturbance processes. In *The mosaic-cycle concept of ecosystems,* ed. H. Remmert, pp. 83–105. Ecological Studies, vol. 85. Berlin: Springer-Verlag.

Hardoy, J. 1968. *Urban planning in pre-Columbian America.* New York: George Braziler.

Hills, T. L., and Randall, R. E., eds. 1968. *The ecology of the forest/savanna boundary.* Savanna Research Series 13. Montreal: McGill University.

Hyslop, J. 1984. *The Inka road system.* New York: Academic Press.

Kolata, A. L. 1991. The technology and organization of agricultural production in the Tiwanaku state. *Latin American Antiquity* 2:99–125.

Lewis, H. T. 1982. Fire technology and resource management in aboriginal North America and Australia. In *Resource managers: North American and Australian hunter-gatherers,* ed. N. M. Williams and E. S. Hunn, pp. 45–67. AAAS Selected Symposia 67. Boulder, CO: Westview Press.

Lovell, W. George. 1992. "Heavy shadows and black night": disease and depopulation in Colonial Spanish America. *Annals of the Association of American Geographers* 82(3): 426–43.

McEvedy, C., and Jones, R. 1978. *Atlas of world population history.* New York: Penguin Books.

McNutt, F. A., trans. 1909. *Bartholomew de las Cases: His life, his apostolate, and his writings.* New York: Putnam's.

Martin, C. 1978. *Keepers of the game: Indian-animal relationships and the fur trade.* Berkeley: University of California Press.

Mathewson, K. 1987. Landscape change and cultural persistence in the Guayas wetlands, Ecuador. Ph.D. dissertation, Department of Geography, University of Wisconsin, Madison.

Medina, E. 1980. Ecology of tropical American savannas: An ecophysiological approach. In *Human ecology in savanna environments,* ed. D. R. Harris, pp. 297–319. London: Academic Press.

Meinig, D. W. 1986. *The shaping of America. A geographical perspective on 500 years of history,* vol. 1, *Atlantic America, 1492–1800.* New Haven: Yale University Press.

Melville, E. G. K. 1990. Environmental and social change in the Valle del Mezquital, Mexico, 1521–1600. *Comparative Studies in Society and History* 32:24–53.

Mueller-Dombois, D. 1981. Fire in tropical ecosystems. In *Fire regimes and ecosystem properties: Proceedings of the Conference,* Honolulu, 1978, pp. 137–76. General Technical Report WO-26. Washington: U.S. Forest Service.

Parsons, J. J. 1975. The changing nature of New World tropical forests since European colonization. In *The use of ecological guidelines for development in the American humid tropics,* pp. 28–38. International Union for Conservation of Nature and Natural Resources Publications, n.s., 31. Morges.

——. 1985. Raised field farmers as pre-Columbian landscape engineers: Looking north from the San Jorge (Colombia). In *Prehistoric intensive agriculture in the tropics,* ed. I. S. Farrington, pp. 149–65. International Series 232. Oxford: British Archaeological Reports.

——, **and Denevan, W. M.** 1967. Pre-Columbian ridged fields. *Scientific American* 217(1):92–100.

Patterson, W. A., III, and Sassaman, K. E. 1988. Indian fires in the prehistory of New England. In *Holocene human ecology in northeastern North America,* ed. G. P. Nicholas, pp. 107–35. New York: Plenum.

Plazas, C., and Falchetti, A. M. 1987. Poblamiento y adecuación hidráulica en el bajo Río San Jorge, Costa Atlantica, Colombia. In *Prehistoric agricultural fields in the Andean region,* ed. W. M. Denevan, K. Mathewson, and G. Knapp, pp. 483–503. International Series 359. Oxford: British Archaeological Reports.

Posey, D. A. 1985. Indigenous management of tropical forest ecosystems: The case of the Kayapó Indians of the Brazilian Amazon. *Agroforestry Systems* 3:139–58.

Pyne, S. J. 1982. *Fire in America: A cultural history of wildland and rural fire.* Princeton, NJ: Princeton University Press.

Raup, H. M. 1937. Recent changes in climate and vegetation in southern New England and adjacent New York. *Journal of the Arnold Arboretum* 18:79–117.

Roosevelt, A. C. 1991. *Moundbuilders of the Amazon: Geophysical archaeology on Marajo Island, Brazil.* San Diego: Academic Press.

Rostlund, E. 1957. The myth of a natural prairie belt in Alabama: An interpretation of historical records. *Annals of the Association of American Geographers* 47:392–411.

——. 1960. The geographic range of the historic bison in the southeast. *Annals of the Association of American Geographers* 50:395–407.

Russell, E. W. B. 1983. Indian-set fires in the forests of the northeastern United States. *Ecology* 64:78–88.

Sale, K. 1990. *The conquest of paradise: Christopher Columbus and the Columbian legacy.* New York: Alfred A. Knopf.

Sánchez-Albornoz, N. 1974. *The population of Latin America: A history.* Berkeley: University of California Press.

Sanders, W. T.; Parsons, J. R.; and Santley, R. S. 1979. *The Basin of Mexico: Ecological processes in the evolution of a civilization.* New York: Academic Press.

Sauer, C. O. 1950. Grassland climax, fire, and man. *Journal of Range Management* 3:16–21.

——. 1958. Man in the ecology of tropical America. *Proceedings of the Ninth Pacific Science Congress, 1957* 20:104–10.

——. 1963 [1927]. The barrens of Kentucky. In *Land and life: A selection from the writings of Carl Ortwin Sauer,* ed. J. Leighly, pp. 23–31. Berkeley: University of California Press.

——. 1966. *The early Spanish Main.* Berkeley: University of California Press.

——. 1971. *Sixteenth-century North America: The land and the people as seen by the Europeans.* Berkeley: University of California Press.

——. 1975. Man's dominance by use of fire. *Geoscience and Man* 10:1–13.

Scott, G. A. J. 1978. *Grassland development in the Gran Pajonal of eastern Peru.* Hawaii Monographs in Geography 1. Honolulu: University of Hawaii.

Sheets, P., and Sever, T. L. 1991. Prehistoric footpaths in Costa Rica: Transportation and communication in a tropical rainforest. In *Ancient road networks and settlement hierarchies in the New World,* ed. C. D. Trombold, pp. 53–65. Cambridge: Cambridge University Press.

Siemens, A. H. 1990. *Between the summit and the sea: Central Veracruz in the nineteenth century.* Vancouver: University of British Columbia Press.

Silver, T. 1990. *A new face on the countryside: Indians, colonists, and slaves in South Atlantic forests, 1500–1800.* Cambridge: Cambridge University Press.

Silverberg, R. 1968. *Mound builders of ancient America: The archaeology of a myth.* Greenwich, CT: New York Graphic Society.

Stout, A. B. 1911. Prehistoric earthworks in Wisconsin. *Ohio Archaeological and Historical Publications* 20:1–31.

Sturtevant, W. C. 1961. Taino agriculture. In *The evolution of horticultural systems in native South America, causes and consequences: A symposium,* ed. J. Wilbert, pp. 69–82. Caracas Sociedad de Ciencias Naturales La Salle.

Taylor, D. L. 1981. Fire history and fire records for Everglades National Park. Everglades National Park Report T-619. Washington: National Park Service, U.S. Department of the Interior.

Thompson, D. Q., and Smith, R. H. 1970. The forest primeval in the Northeast – a great myth? *Proceedings, Tall Timbers Fire Ecology Conference* 10:255–65.

Thoreau, H. D. 1949. *The journal of Henry D. Thoreau*, vol. 7, *September 1, 1854– October 30, 1855*, ed. B. Torrey and F. H. Allen. Boston: Houghton Mifflin.

Trombold, C. D., ed. 1991. *Ancient road networks and settlement hierarchies in the New World*. Cambridge: Cambridge University Press.

Uhl, C.; Nepstad, D.; Buschbacher, R.; Clark, K.; Kauffman, B.; and Subler, S. 1990. Studies of ecosystem response to natural and anthropogenic disturbances provide guidelines for designing sustainable land-use systems in Amazonia. In *Alternatives to deforestation: Steps toward sustainable use of the Amazon rain forest*, ed. A. B. Anderson, pp. 24–42. New York: Columbia University Press.

Watts, W. A., and Bradbury, J. P. 1982. Paleoecological studies at Lake Patzcuaro on the west-central Mexican plateau and at Chalco in the Basin of Mexico. *Quaternary Research* 17:56–70.

Whitmore, T. M., and Turner, B. L. II. 1992. Landscapes of cultivation in Mesoamerica on the eve of the conquest. *Annals of the Association of American Geographers* 82(3): 402–25.

Whitmore, T. M.; Turner, B. L. II; Johnson, D. L.; Kates, R. W.; and Gottschang, T. R. 1990. Long-term population change. In *The earth as transformed by human action*, ed. B. L. Turner II, et al., pp. 25–39. Cambridge: Cambridge University Press.

Williams, B. J. 1972. Tepetate in the Valley of Mexico. *Annals of the Association of American Geographers* 62:618–26.

——. 1989. Contact period rural overpopulation in the Basin of Mexico: Carry-ing-capacity models tested with documentary data. *American Antiquity* 54:715–32.

Williams, M. 1989. *Americans and their forests: A historical geography*. Cambridge: Cambridge University Press.

Documents

Richard Nelson, "The Watchful World"

Reprinted from *Make Prayers to the Raven: A Koyukon View of the Northern Forest* (Chicago and London: University of Chicago Press, 1983)

Because most pre-Columbian Indians did not have a written language, there are few primary sources that describe their understandings of the natural world. For this reason, we're going to turn first to an anthropologist's account of Indians and their views on nature. Technically, what we are looking at here is a secondary source, which describes how American Indian hunters, the Koyukon people of Alaska, understood the natural world.

There are at least two limitations to the usefulness of this document. First, it is by a white anthropologist, Richard Nelson, so we must remind ourselves that we are actually receiving this account of the Koyukon world view second hand. Nelson often quotes Koyukon people's descriptions of their beliefs from interviews he had with them (these appear in italics). But he also quotes his own thoughts as recorded in his journal during his research (these appear in roman, and end with "Huslia Journal," and the date of the entry). Be careful not to confuse the two.

Second, Nelson was describing Koyukon beliefs of the 1970s. To assume that Indian beliefs of the distant past were similar to the 1970s Koyukon views is risky. Indian peoples were and are culturally diverse. Just because a community of people in Alaska thought in particular ways in the 1970s does not mean that their ancestors of centuries back, much less Indians living thousands of miles away at the same time, thought similarly. (Would your modern-day beliefs about religion and nature be a good indicator of the convictions of your ancestors in, say, 1490?) Nevertheless, other evidence suggests that historical Indian beliefs had many parallels to Koyukon religion. Richard Nelson provides us with a coherent interpretation of Indian natural understandings, and for this reason his account remains one of the most useful introductions to the subject.

Nelson describes a perception of nature that was alive and well at the time he lived amongst the Koyukon. The way of life and world view he describes are in fact still vigorous, especially in the remote reaches of Alaska, the Canadian north, and even in places in the continental United States. In this sense, the cultural world he sketches for us here is part of modern America – thinking about it as just "history" would mean missing one of the most important insights which environmental history has to offer: that not all people think about nature in the same way. Nelson is attempting to present us with a view of nature through Koyukon eyes. Whatever else we say about his interpretation, there is no doubt that Koyukon people see the natural world as a universe of spirits, most of them having great and potentially dangerous powers. Environmental history often leads us, in surprising ways, to the connections between peoples and their creators.

What in the Koyukon view of nature strikes you as different from your own understandings of nature? Is the Koyukon world generally more "natural" than your world? And is "nature" one thing among the Koyukon? Or is it a whole world of separate entities, spirits, presences, and forces? Do different parts of Koyukon nature have different meanings?

* * *

There's always things in the air that watch us.

A Way of Seeing

... Traditional Koyukon people live in a world that watches, in a forest of eyes. A person moving through nature – however wild, remote, even desolate the place may be – is never truly alone. The surroundings are aware, sensate, personified. They feel. They can be offended. And they must, at every moment, be treated with proper respect. All things in nature have a special kind of life, something unknown to contemporary Euro-Americans, something powerful. . . .

Over a span of millennia, the Koyukon people and their ancestors have sustained themselves directly from their surroundings. The intimacy of their relationship to nature is far beyond our experience – the physical dependence and the intense emotional interplay with a world that cannot be directly altered to serve the needs of humanity. This close daily interaction and dependence upon an omnipotent natural universe has profound importance to the Koyukon people and provides a theme upon which their cultural lives converge.

Koyukon perceptions of nature are aligned on two interconnected levels. The first of these is empirical knowledge. The practical challenges of survival by hunting, fishing, and gathering require a deep objective understanding of the environment and the methods for utilizing its resources. In short, the Koyukon people are sophisticated natural historians, especially well versed in animal behavior and ecology.

But their perception of the natural environment extends beyond what Westerners define as the empirical level, into the realm of the spiritual. The Koyukon inherit an elaborate system of supernatural concepts for explaining and manipulating the environment. From this perspective the natural and supernatural worlds are inseparable, and environmental events are often caused or influenced by spiritual forces. Detailed explanations are provided for the origin of natural entities and for the causation of natural events (which seldom, if ever, take place purely by chance). Furthermore, behavior toward nature is governed by an array of supernaturally based rules that ensure the well-being of both humans and the environment.

It is important to understand that Koyukon beliefs about nature are as logical and consistent as they are powerful, but that they differ substantially from those prevailing in modern Western societies. Our own tradition envisions the universe as a system whose functioning can be explained through rationalistic and scientific means. The natural and supernatural worlds are clearly separated. Environmental events are caused by ongoing evolutionary and ecological processes, or else they happen purely by chance. Finally, modern Western cultures regulate human behavior toward nature and its resources primarily on the basis of practical rather than religious considerations.

For the traditional Koyukon Athapaskans, ideology is a fundamental element of subsistence, as important as the more tangible practicalities of harvesting and utilizing natural resources. Most interactions with natural entities are governed in some way by a moral code that maintains a proper spiritual balance between the human and nonhuman worlds. This is not an esoteric abstraction, but a matter of direct, daily concern to the Koyukon people. Failure to behave according to the dictates of this code can have an immediate impact on the violator's health or success. And so, when Koyukon people carry out their subsistence activities they make many decisions on the basis of supernatural concerns. The world is ever aware.

From the Distant Time

As the Koyukon reckon it, all things human and natural go back to a time called *Kk'adonts'idnee*, which is so remote that no one can explain or understand how long ago it really was. But however ancient this time may be, its events are recounted accurately and in great detail through a prodigious number of stories. *Kk'adonts'idnee* (literally, "in Distant Time it is said") is the Koyukon word for these stories, but following from its conversational use I will translate it simply as Distant Time.

The stories constitute an oral history of the Koyukon people and their environment, beginning in an age before the present order of existence was established. During this age "the animals were human" – that is, they had human form, they lived in a human society, and they spoke human (Koyukon) language. At some point in the Distant Time certain humans died and were transformed into animal or plant beings, the species that inhabit Koyukon country today. These dreamlike metamorphoses left a residue of human qualities and personality traits in the north-woods creatures.

Taken together, the Distant Time stories describe a primordial world and its transfiguration into modern form. Some are so long that a single narration may require many evenings, even several weeks of evenings, for a complete telling. Stories of this kind – widely known as legends, myths, or folklore – are found throughout North America and elsewhere. It is common practice, however, to vastly underrate their significance in the lives of people like the Koyukon. They are not regarded as simple entertainment (though they are appreciated as such), and they are certainly not considered fictional. Stories of the Distant Time are, first of all, an accounting of origins. They are a Koyukon version of Genesis, or perhaps of Darwin. Woven into the plots of many stories are innumerable subplots or asides, which often describe the origins of natural entities.

The scope of Distant Time stories ranges from the minute to the cosmological. They explain the beginnings of entities that inhabit the sky – the sun, moon, and aurora. They account for certain weather phenomena, such as thunderstorms, which are the transformed embodiment of a formerly human spirit. For this reason thunderstorms have consciousness and can be turned away by people who know how to influence them. Features of the earth, such as prominent hills or mountains, are also given some accounting in these stories. For example, a hill near Huslia is called "Giant's Firemakers" (*Yiłkuh tł' aala'*), because it was formed when a giant man lost his flints there.

A central figure in this ancient world was the Raven (it is unclear, perhaps irrelevant, whether there was one Raven or many), who was its creator and who engineered many of its metamorphoses. Raven, the contradiction – omnipotent clown, benevolent mischief-maker, buffoon, and deity. It was he, transformed into a spruce needle, who was swallowed by a woman so she would give birth to him as a boy. When the boy was old enough to play, he took from beneath a blanket in her house the missing sun and rolled it to the door. Once outside, he became Raven again and flew up to return the sun to the sky, making the earth light again.

And it was he who manipulated the natural design to suit his whim or fancy. When he first created the earth, for example, the rivers ran both ways, upstream on one side and downstream on the other. But this made life too easy for humans, he decided, because their boats could drift along in either direction without paddling. So Raven altered his creation and made the rivers flow only one way, which is how they remain today.

There are hundreds of stories explaining the behavior and appearance of living things. Most of these are about animals and a few are about plants. No species is too insignificant to be mentioned, but importance in the Koyukon economy does not assure a prominent place in the stories. Many of the stories about animal origins are like this one:

> *When the burbot* [ling cod] *was human, he decided to leave the land and become a water animal. So he started down the bank, taking a piece of bear fat with him. But the other animal people wanted him to stay and tried to hold him back, stretching him all out of shape in the process. This is why the burbot has such a long, stretched-out body, and why its liver is rich and oily like the bear fat its ancestor carried to the water long ago.*

At the end of Distant Time there was a great catastrophe. The entire earth was covered by a flood, and under the Raven's supervision a pair of each species went aboard a raft. These plants and animals survived, but when the flood ended they could no longer behave like people. All the Distant Time humans had been killed, and so Raven recreated people in their present form. My Koyukon teachers were well aware of the biblical parallel in this story, and they took it as added evidence of the story's accuracy. None suggested that it might be a reinterpretation of Christian teaching.

Distant Time stories were usually told by older people who had memorized the lengthy epics and could best interpret them. But children were also taught stories, simpler ones that they were encouraged to tell, especially as they began to catch game. Doing this after setting out their traps or snares would please the animals and make them willing to be caught.

Today's elders can recall the long evenings of their youth, when Distant Time stories made the hours of darkness pass easily. In those days houses were lit by burning bear grease in a shallow bowl with a wick, or by burning long wands of split wood, one after another. Bear grease was scarce, and the hand-held wands were inconvenient, so in midwinter the dwellings were often dark after twilight faded. Faced with long wakeful hours in the blackness, people crawled into their warm beds and listened to the recounting of stories.

The narratives were reserved for late fall and the first half of winter, because they were tabooed after the days began lengthening. Not surprisingly, the teller finished each story by commenting that he or she had shortened the winter: "I thought that winter had just begun, but now I have chewed off part of it." Or, more optimistically, "When I woke up in the morning, my cabin was just dripping with water!" In this case the narrator implies that the spring thaw has suddenly begun.

Distant Time stories also provide the Koyukon with a foundation for understanding the natural world and humanity's proper relationship to it. When people discuss the plants, animals, or physical environment they often refer to the stories. Here they find explanations for the full range of natural phenomena, down to the smallest details. In one story a snowshoe hare was attacked by the hawk owl, which was so small that it only managed to make a little wound in its victim's shoulder. Koyukon people point out a tiny notch in the hare's scapula as evidence that the Distant Time events really took place.

The narratives also provide an extensive code of proper behavior toward the environment and its resources. They contain many episodes showing that certain kinds of actions toward nature can have bad consequences, and these are taken as guidelines to follow today. Stories

therefore serve as a medium for instructing young people in the traditional code and as an infallible standard of conduct for everyone.

*Nobody made it up, these things we're supposed to do. It came from the stories;
it's just like our Bible. My grandfather said he told the stories because they would
bring the people good luck, keep them healthy, and make a good life. When he
came to songs in the stories, he sang them like they were hymns.*

The most important parts of the code are taboos (*huƚaanee*), prohibitions against acting certain ways toward nature. For example, in one
story a salmon-woman was scraping skins at night with her upper jaw,
and while doing this she was killed. This is why it is taboo for women to
scrape hides during the night. Hundreds of such taboos exist, and a
person who violates them (or someone in the immediate family) may
suffer bad luck in subsistence activities, clumsiness, illness, accident, or
early death. In Koyukuk River villages it is a rare day when someone is
not heard saying, *"Hutlanee!"* ("It's taboo!").

Personalities in Nature

Stories of the Distant Time often portray the animal-people as having
distinctive personalities, and this affects the way a species is regarded
today. Often these personalities can be known only through the stories,
because the animals do not visibly express them any longer. People
sometimes have strong positive or negative feelings about particular
species because of the way they are portrayed in the stories.

The sucker fish, for example, was a great thief in the Distant Time and
so it is not well thought of. One man told me he could never bring
himself to eat this fish, knowing what it had been and fearing that it
would make a thief of him:

*Even in springtime, sometimes we run short of food. But if we catch a sucker in
the net, I just can't eat him.*

People will sometimes characterize someone by referring to an animal's personality. In fact, Jetté . . . writes that Yukon River Koyukon may
inquire about a person by asking, "What animal is he?" Someone known
as a thief may be described as "just like a sucker fish." When a person
talks big, promises a lot but accomplishes little, or gets ahead by trickery,
he or she is said to be "just like a raven." Although Raven is the creator,
he is portrayed in the stories as a lazy trickster who usually finds a way to
get ahead by the efforts of others. The Koyukon have a kind of jocular

respect for ravens, mocking their personality but still awed by their spirit power.

When I asked about relatedness among animals, people usually answered with reference to their social behavior and personality. For example, a Distant Time story reveals that bears and porcupines are cousins, and people cite as proof their occasional sharing of a den. When relatedness is not mentioned in a story it may be revealed by a tendency to "get along." Muskrats and beavers often live close together and they eat the same kinds of plants, so they are considered relatives. Wolves may kill a loose dog, which shows that the two are not related.

Animal relationships are also shown by shared characteristics, but usually not those chosen by Western taxonomists. One story of the Distant Time says that all the smaller animals were related as sisters who lived together in an underground house. These included red squirrel, mink, fox, several owl species, short-tailed weasel, ptarmigan, and others. Another related group includes the four water mammals: otter, mink, beaver, and muskrat. Stories also reveal that the raven is mink's uncle. And in obviously paired species, the larger is considered the older brother to the smaller – brown bear to the black bear, for example, and flicker to the woodpecker.

The Koyukon people conceptualize a natural order, but its structure and foundation are quite different from our own. No one described to me a system of phylogeny or biological interrelatedness, but I did not probe this matter exhaustively and may have failed to ask the right questions. Such a system might exist, or perhaps the world's makeup is sufficiently explained in the stories.

The Place of Humans in a Natural Order

When Raven created humans, he first used rock for the raw materials, and people never died. But this was too easy so he recreated them, using dust instead. In this way humans became mortal, as they remain today.

How does humanity fit into the world of nature and the scheme of living things? For the Koyukon, humans and animals are clearly and qualitatively separated. Only the human possesses a soul (*nukk'ubidza*, "eye flutterer"), which people say is different from the animals' spirits. I never understood the differences, except that the human soul seems less vengeful and it alone enjoys immortality in a special place after death. The distinction between animals and people is less sharply drawn than in Western thought – the human organism, after all, was created by an animal's power.

The Koyukon seem to conceptualize humans and animals as very similar beings. This derives not so much from the animal nature of humans as from the human nature of animals. I noted earlier, for example, that today's animals once belonged to an essentially human society, and that transmutations between human and animal form were common. One of my Koyukon teachers said, however, that after the Distant Time people and animals became completely separate and unrelated.

Animals still possess qualities that Westerners consider exclusively human, though – they have a range of emotions, they have distinct personalities, they communicate among themselves, and they understand human behavior and language. They are constantly aware of what people say and do, and their presiding spirits are easily offended by disrespectful behavior. The interaction here is very intense, and the two orders of being coexist far more closely than in our own tradition. But animals do not use human language among themselves. They communicate with sounds which are considered their own form of language.

The closeness of animals to humans is reinforced by the fact that some animals are given funeral rituals following the basic form of those held for people, only on a smaller scale. . . . In these cases, at least, animal spirits are placated much as human souls are after death.

Most interesting of all is animal behavior interpreted to be religious. "Even animals have their taboos," a woman once told me. From her grandfather, she learned that gestating female beavers will not eat bark from the fork of a branch, because it is apparently tabooed for them. The late Chief Henry had told her of seeing a brown bear kill a ground squirrel, then tear out its heart, lungs, and windpipe and leave them on a rock. Again, the organs must have been taboo (*hutłaanee*). . . .

Nature Spirits and their Treatment

From the Distant Time stories, Koyukon people learn rules for proper conduct toward nature. But punishment for offenses against these rules is given by powerful spirits that are part of the living, present-day world. All animals, some plants, and some inanimate things have spirits, vaguely conceptualized essences that protect the welfare of their material counterparts. They are especially watchful for irreverent, insulting, or wasteful behavior toward living things. The spirits are not offended when people kill animals and use them, but they insist that these beings (or their remains) be treated with the deference owed to the sources of human life.

Not all spirits are possessed of equal power. Some animal species have very potent spirits called *biyeega hoolaanh*, which are easily provoked and highly vindictive. These dangerous spirits can bring serious harm to anyone who offends them, taking away luck in hunting or trapping and sometimes causing illness, disability, or even death. Animals possessed of such spirits include the brown bear, black bear, wolverine, lynx, wolf, and otter. The beaver and marmot have similarly powerful spirits but are not so vengeful.

The remaining mammals, birds, fish, and some plants and inanimate things have less powerful spirits. Although these are very real and can inflict punishment (usually bad luck in taking the species), all my instructors agreed that no Koyukon word exists for this kind of spirit. In response to my perplexed questioning, one person explained:

> *The animal and its spirit are one in the same thing. When you name the animal you're also naming its spirit. That's why some animal names are hutłaanee – like the ones women shouldn't say – because calling the animal's name is like calling its spirit. Just like we don't say a person's name after they die ... it would be calling their spirit and could be dangerous for whoever did it.*

While most Koyukon adults seem to concur on the basic premises of their ideology, they vary widely in their opinions about the specifics and apparently do not feel inclined toward a rigid, systematized theology. This often left me confused, no doubt because of my Judeo-Christian background; and if my account of certain concepts is amorphous or inconsistent it properly reflects my learning experience. Koyukon people must find us painfully compulsive and conformist about our systems of belief.

... When an animal is mistreated, I was told, its individual spirit is affronted but all members of its species may become aloof from the offender. In former times, shamans could manipulate spirits for the opposite effect. They made dream visits to "animal houses" that were filled with spirits of a particular animal, then attracted them to certain parts of the country to enrich the harvest there.

Many other supernatural beings inhabit the traditional Koyukon world ... but these seem to have little importance today. Perhaps Christian teachings displaced or undermined these beliefs, unlike those concerned with spirits of natural entities. Devices used to catch and kill animals – such as nets, snares, and deadfalls – also have powerful spirits (*biyeega hoolaanh*) with many associated taboos. Like the spirits of natural entities, these are still considered important today. For example, if a person borrows someone else's snare, he or she may take sick or die from its spirit power. Similarly, stealing a snared animal exposes the thief to grave danger from the spirits of both the snare and its catch.

Proper treatment of natural spirits involves hundreds of rules or taboos (*hutłaanee*), some applying to just one species and others having much more general effects. The rules fall into three main categories – first, treatment of living organisms; second, treatment of organisms (or parts of organisms) that are no longer alive; and third, treatment of nonliving entities or objects. I will briefly summarize these rules. . . .

Treatment of living organisms

Koyukon people follow some general rules in their behavior toward living animals. They avoid pointing at them, for example, because it shows disrespect, "like pointing or staring at a stranger." They also speak carefully about animals, especially avoiding boastful talk about hunting or trapping exploits.

A man who said he would trap many beavers was suddenly unable to catch any; and someone who bragged about bear hunting was later attacked and seriously hurt. In fact, bears are so powerful that every word spoken about them is carefully chosen. Trapped animals are also treated respectfully, and powerful ones like the wolf or wolverine may be addressed in special ways before they are killed. One man said that he always asks trapped animals for luck: "My animal, I hope that more of you will come my way."

Keeping wild animals as pets is also prohibited, except for species whose personality traits are valued in humans. A child who keeps a red fox will become mischievous, but if a boy raises a hawk owl he will acquire its hunting skill and cleanliness. People seldom keep pets, because they are likely to suffer, offending their spirits and causing illness or bad luck for those involved in their captivity. A woman told me of losing her small child about a year after the death of a baby hawk owl her family had kept. The tragic connection was clear.

Taking individual animals away to zoos, even catching and releasing them alive as part of studies, is a spiritual affront that can cause a species to shun the area. For this reason Koyukon people are opposed to wildlife research in their country if it involves live capture of animals.

> We have respect for the animals. We don't keep them in cages or torture them, because we know the background of animals from the Distant Time. We know that the animal has a spirit – it used to be human – and we know all the things it did. It's not just an animal; it's lots more than that.

Following from this, Koyukon people believe that animals must be treated humanely. The spirits are not offended because humans live by hunting, but people must try to kill without causing suffering and to avoid losing wounded animals. A starving moose, mired in deep snow near Huslia, was fed daily until it regained strength and could walk away. Once a man found a black bear with cubs, driven from their den by groundwater, hopelessly starving in the deep snow. He ended their suffering, then dismembered and covered their unusable carcasses, lest he offend their spirits by killing without at least symbolic utilization. "We'll come back for this later," he told his companion, a placating remark that he knew he would not abide by.

Treatment of killed game

The rules for showing respect to killed animals and harvested plants are myriad. I will give some general principles and a few illustrations here . . . .

> Today I was told about a man who had once jokingly stuffed debris into the opened jaws of a dried pike head nailed on a cabin door to ward off bad spirits. His companions were horrified that he would open himself to retaliation from the animal's spirit. "When you do something like that – when you don't show respect for animals – it's just like making fun of the Bible." [Huslia journal, March 1977]

The remains of animals and plants are treated with the deference owed to something sacred. For example, when fur animals (such as mink, beaver, or wolf) are brought inside the house for skinning, their names should not be mentioned, nothing should be burned lest the smell offend their spirits, metallic noises should be avoided, and even if it is unfrozen and skinned the carcass should be kept indoors overnight. One way to prevent difficulties is to plug the nostrils of smell-sensitive animals like mink by smearing lard on them. Cloth may also be wrapped around an animal's head to protect it from offensive noises.

> *I had bad luck with fox this year. Come to think of it, I was using noisy power tools while I had a fox in the house. Guess that's why . . . it's got really sensitive ears. When you get bad luck like this you just have to let it wear off. There's nothing else you can do.*

There are also rules for proper butchering of game – for example, certain cuts that should be made or avoided for a particular species. There are rules for proper care of meat, such as keeping all meat covered when it is outside, protecting it from scavengers or from any insinuation that it is not respected. And a multitude of rules govern who eats an animal or parts of it. Young adults and especially women of childbearing age are subject to a wide array of these....

Finally, there are regulations to ensure that unusable parts of animals are respectfully disposed of. For example, bones of water animals such as beaver, muskrat, and mink should be cast into a lake or river. Bones of large land animals should be put in a dry place away from the village or completely burned in a remote spot. And the remains of small animals ought to be hung in bushes or burned. . . . Adherence has declined today, but many people scrupulously avoid leaving animal remains to rot on the ground (especially where someone might walk over them) or mixing them with household trash.

Punishment for ignoring or violating these regulations depends on the power of the living thing and the gravity of the offense. Spirit vengeance can be as severe as death or decades of bad luck in catching a species. Disregarding the prohibitions against eating certain foods usually causes clumsiness or other physical problems. Only old people who no longer hunt can eat red-necked grebe, for instance, because this bird is awkward on land. A young person who ate it would become slow and clumsy or would have children with these shortcomings. I never understood whether animal spirits cause such "contagious" reactions, but the innumerable food taboos are generally respected as an important way of protecting health and well-being.

Many of the rules apply to everyone, regardless of age or sex. But a large number of special restrictions apply to women between puberty and menopause. Koyukon women are skilled and active providers – they hunt, fish, trap, and gather on their own or along with men. Although they are competent and productive, they are somewhat limited by their possession of special power that can easily alienate or offend natural spirits.

The menses (*hutlaa*) has its own spirit that contains the essence of femininity, and it can bring bad luck with animals, feminize men and alienate animals from them, or even cause sickness or death. To avoid these dangers, Koyukon women were traditionally secluded during menstruation (some pubescent girls are still briefly sequestered at the first menstruation), and they continue to follow a multitude of special taboos regulating their use of animals and their behavior toward them.

Spirits of the physical world

Elements of the earth and sky are imbued with spirits and consciousness, much in the way of living things, and there are codes of proper behavior toward them. Certain landforms have special powers that must be placated or shown deference, for example. Even the weather is aware: if a man brags that storms or cold cannot stop him from doing something, "the weather will take care of him good!" It will humble him with its power, "because it knows."

> *In falltime you'll hear the lakes make loud cracking noises after they freeze. It means they're asking for snow to cover them up, to protect them from the cold. When my father told me this, he said everything has life in it. He always used to tell us that.*

The earth itself is the source of a preeminent spiritual power called *sinh taala'* in Koyukon. This is the foundation of medicine power once used by shamans, and because of it the earth must be shown utmost respect. One person who was cured by medicine power years ago, for example, still abides by the shaman's instructions to avoid digging in the earth. Berry plants have special power because they are nurtured directly from the earth. "People are careful about things that grow close to the ground," I was told, "because the earth is so great."

The Manifestations of Luck

Luck is the powerful force that binds humanity to the nature spirits and their moral imperatives. For the Koyukon people, luck is a nearly tangible essence, an aura or condition that is "with" someone in certain circumstances or for particular purposes. Luck can be held permanently or it can be fleeting and elusive. It is an essential qualification for success – regardless of a person's skill, in the absence of luck there is no destiny except failure.

The source of luck is not clearly explained, but most people are apparently born with a certain measure of it. The difficulty is not so much in getting it as in keeping it. Luck is sustained by strictly following the rules of conduct toward natural things. People who lose their luck have clearly been punished by an offended spirit; people who possess luck are the beneficiaries of some force that creates it. Koyukon people express luck in the hunt by saying *bik'uhnaatltonh* – literally, "he has been taken care of."

> *If a person has good luck, catches game, it is because something created the world, and that is helping him to get what he needs.*

Luck, or the absence of it, is specific to particular animals or even certain activities. A woman who violates tanning taboos may fail in preparing hides. Each person is possessed (or dispossessed) of luck for all the entities he or she interacts with. Thus a man told me that he had always been lucky hunting bears until he inadvertently treated one the wrong way. For many years afterward his luck was gone – he never took a single bear. Finally the effect wore off and since regaining his luck he has killed at least one bear each season.

Luck can be passed along to others, but it is a lot like money. The one who gives it up may be left with nothing. To illustrate, when beaver snaring was made legal years ago, it was very hard for young people to learn how to do it. The older men knew but were reluctant to reveal their ways, because telling someone how to make a trapping set also gives him your luck. Eventually people reach an age of inactivity, when their measure of luck becomes superfluous. Then they can confer their luck on others by simply wishing it so. This is why children often present their first-killed game to elders, and why young hunters give liberal shares of their catch to old men who no longer go out onto the land.

Possessions like sleds, fishnets, rifles, or snowshoes are also infused with luck. A man lamented to me that one of his high-caliber rifles had failed to kill a bear coming out of its den although it was at close range. He had to use another gun to finish the animal. This gun was "out of luck," he explained, and he suspected that a young woman had rendered it useless by stepping over it.

Putting on another person's mittens can either take away his luck or give him yours. Once I was traveling with a man whose hands became painfully cold, so I offered him my extra mittens. He finally took them, explaining that since I was leaving Huslia I could get along without luck in things like trapping. But a short while later he decided to take them off and endure the cold instead.

Luck is a finite entity, specific to each natural thing or even to certain activities. It can be lost, transferred, and recovered. Luck binds people to the code of proper behavior toward the natural world. And so success in living on the land involves far more than a mastery of technical skills. It requires that a sensitive balance be maintained between each person and the conscious forces of the environment. . . .

The Koyukon View of Nature

For traditional Koyukon people, the environment is both a natural and a supernatural realm. All that exists in nature is imbued with awareness and power; all events in nature are potentially manifestations of this power; all actions toward nature are mediated by consideration of its consciousness and sensitivity. The interchange between humans and environment is based on an elaborate code of respect and morality, without which survival would be jeopardized. The Koyukon, while they are bound by the strictures of this system, can also manipulate its powers for their own benefit. Nature is a second society in which people live, a watchful and possessive one whose bounty is wrested as much by placation as by cleverness and craft.

Moving across the sprawl of wildland, through the forest and open muskeg, Koyukon people are ever conscious that they are among spirits. Each animal is far more than what can be seen; it is a personage and a personality, known from its legacy in stories of the Distant Time. It is a figure in the community of beings, once at least partially human, and even now possessed of attributes beyond outsiders' perception.

Not only the animals, but also the plants, the earth and landforms, the air, weather, and sky are spiritually invested. For each, the hunter knows an array of respectful gestures and deferential taboos that demand obedience. Violations against them will offend and alienate their spirits, bringing bad luck or illness, or worse if a powerful and vindictive being is treated irreverently.

Aware of these invisible forces and their manifestations, the Koyukon can protect and enhance their good fortune, can understand signs or warnings given them through natural events, and can sometimes influence the complexion of the environment to suit their desires. Everything in the Koyukon world lies partly in the realm beyond the senses, in the realm we would call supernatural.

From Gilbert Wilson, *Buffalo Bird Woman's Garden*

Reprinted from *Buffalo Bird Woman's Garden: Agriculture of the Hidatsa Indians* (St Paul: Minnesota Historical Society Press, 1987)

While European and Euro-American conquerors preferred to see all Indians as hunters, in fact, many American Indians were also formidable agriculturalists. Indeed, a whole range of wild plants were domesticated by American Indians, and their legacy is with us today. Maize, most beans, squash (including pumpkins), tomatoes, avocadoes, chocolate, and tobacco – to name just a few – developed from centuries of careful effort by Indians, most of them women, to make wild plants more useful to people. Buffalo Bird Woman was of the Hidatsa people, from the upper Missouri River in what is now North Dakota. Her people lived in this region for centuries before their conquest by the United States. Her reminiscence of cultivating the river bottoms in the latter 1800s is more than just one woman's personal story. It is testimony to centuries of planting and cultivating on the American continent. Various Indian peoples farmed and hunted along the Missouri River, in the well-watered eastern part of the continent, from southern Maine to Florida, and in the southwest, along the Rio Grande. To make a living by growing corn amidst the Great Plains, where a dry climate and ferocious winters conspire to frustrate even many modern farmers, was no mean feat. Many people lived by a mix of farming, hunting, gathering, and trade. Most appear to have thought about animals in ways similar to the Koyukon of the late twentieth century. Plants also had spiritual powers. Compare Buffalo Bird Woman's account to the excerpt from *Make Prayers to the Raven*. The garden is a woman's world. What conflicts did Hidatsa farmers have with one another? How did they resolve them? How did access to iron tools change Hidatsa farming?

* * *

Soon after they came to Like-a-fishhook bend, the families of my tribe began to clear fields, for gardens, like those they had at Five Villages. Rich black soil was to be found in the timbered bottom lands of the Missouri. Most of the work of clearing was done by the women.

In old times we Hidatsas never made our gardens on the untimbered, prairie land, because the soil there is too hard and dry. In the bottom lands by the Missouri, the soil is soft and easy to work. . . .

Dispute and its Settlement

About two years after the first ground was broken in our field, a dispute I remember, arose between my mothers and two of their neighbors, Lone Woman and Goes-to-next-timber.

These two women were clearing fields adjoining that of my mothers; . . . the three fields met at a corner. . . . [M]y father, to set up claim to his field, had placed marks, one of them in the corner at which met the fields of Lone Woman and Goes-to-next-timber; but while my mothers were busy clearing and digging up the other end of their field, their two neighbors invaded this marked-off corner; Lone Woman had even dug up a small part before she was discovered.

However, when they were shown the mark my father had placed, the two women yielded and accepted payment for any rights they might have.

It was our Indian rule to keep our fields very sacred. We did not like to quarrel about our garden lands. One's title to a field once set up, no one ever thought of disputing it; for if one were selfish and quarrelsome, and tried to seize land belonging to another, we thought some evil would come upon him, as that some one of his family would die. There is a story of a black bear who got into a pit that was not his own, and had his mind taken away from him for doing so! . . .

Beginning a Field in Later Times

As I grew up, I learned to work in the garden, as every Hidatsa woman was expected to learn; but iron axes and hoes, bought of the traders, were now used by everybody, and the work of clearing and breaking a new field was less difficult than it had been in our grandfathers' times. A family had also greater freedom in choosing where they should have their garden, since with iron axes they could more easily cut down any small trees and bushes that might be on the land. However, to avoid having to cut down big trees, a rather open place was usually chosen.

A family, then, having chosen a place for a field, cleared off the ground as much as they could, cutting down small trees and bushes in such way that the trees fell all in one direction. Some of the timber that was fit might be taken home for firewood; the rest was let lie to dry until spring, when it was fired. The object of felling the trees in one direction was to make them cover the ground as much as possible, since firing them softened the soil and left it loose and mellow for planting. We sought always to burn over all the ground, if we could.

Before firing, the family carefully raked off the dry grass and leaves from the edge of the field, and cut down any brush wood. This was done that the fire might not spread to the surrounding timber, nor out on the prairie. Prairie fires and forest fires are even yet not unknown on our reservation.

Planting season having come, the women of the household planted the field in corn. The hills were in rows, and about four feet or a little less apart. They were rather irregularly placed the first year. It was easy to make a hill in the ashes where a brush heap had been fired, or in soil that was free of roots and stumps; but there were many stumps in the field, left over from the previous summer's clearing. If the planter found a stump stood where a hill should be, she placed the hill on this side [of] the stump or beyond it, no matter how close this brought the hill to the next in the row. Thus, the corn hills did not stand at even distances in the row the first year; but the rows were always kept even and straight.

While the corn was coming up, the women worked at clearing out the roots and smaller stumps between the hills; but a stump of any considerable size was left to rot, especially if it stood midway between two corn hills, where it did not interfere with their cultivation.

Figure 1.1. Drawn from specimen made by Yellow Hair. Length of specimen, following curvature of tines, 36 ½ inches.

My mothers and I used to labor in a similar way to enlarge our fields. With our iron hoes we made hills along the edge of the field and planted corn; then, as we had opportunity, we worked with our hoes between the corn hills to loosen up the soil.

Although our tribe now had iron axes and hoes from the traders, they still used their native made rakes. These were of wood (Figure 1.1), or of the antler of a black-tailed deer (Figure 1.2). It was with such rakes that the edges of a newly opened field were cleaned of leaves for the firing of the brush, in the spring.

Trees in the Garden

Trees were not left standing in the garden, except perhaps one to shade the watchers' stage. If a tree stood in the field, it shaded the corn; and that on the north side of the tree never grew up strong, and the stalks would be yellow.

Cottonwood trees were apt to grow up in the field, unless the young shoots were plucked up as they appeared. . . .

Figure 1.2. Drawn from specimen made by Buffalo Bird Woman. Length of wooden handle, 42 inches; spread of tines of antler, 15 ½ inches.

The Watchers

The season for watching the fields began early in August when green corn began to come in; for this was the time when the ripening ears were apt to be stolen by horses, or birds, or boys. We did not watch the fields in the spring and early summer, to keep the crows from pulling up the newly sprouted grain; such damage we were content to repair by replanting.

Girls began to go on the watchers' stage to watch the corn and sing, when they were about ten or twelve years of age. They continued the custom even after they had grown up and married; and old women, working in the garden and stopping to rest, often went on the stage and sang.

Two girls usually watched and sang together. The village gardens were laid out close to one another; and a girl of one family would be joined by the girl of the family who owned the garden adjoining. Sometimes three, or even four, girls got on the stage and sang together; but never more than four. A drum was not used to accompany the singing.

The watchers sometimes rose and stood upon the stage as they looked to see if any boys or horses were in the field, stealing corn. Older girls and young married women, and even old women, often worked at porcupine embroidery as they watched. Very young girls did not embroider.

Boys of nine to eleven years of age were sometimes rather troublesome thieves. They were fond of stealing green ears to roast by a fire in the woods. Sometimes – not every day, however – we had to guard our corn alertly. A boy caught stealing was merely scolded. "You must not steal here again!" we would say to him. His parents were not asked to pay damage for the theft.

We went to the watchers' stage quite early in the day, before sunrise, or near it, and we came home at sunset.

The watching season continued until the corn was all gathered and harvested. My grandmother, Turtle, was a familiar figure in our family's field, in this season. I can remember her staying out in the field daily, picking out the ripening ears and braiding them in a string.

Images of Florida Indians planting and making an offering of a stag to the sun

Reprinted from Trustees of the British Museum, *The Work of Jacques Le Moyne de Morgues* (London: British Museum Publications, 1977)

The remaining items are engravings based upon paintings made by a French painter, Jacques Le Moyne de Morgues, who lived in Florida in the 1560s, and grew to know the Saturina and Timucua peoples. Look for the ways that different features of Indian economy connect to each other and to the earth. The first image is of Indian men and women planting a field. Although the engraving is not always accurate (since these people did not have plows, the field would have been planted in hillocks, not rows), it remains one of the best pieces of evidence we have about Indians and the earth in the 1500s. How did men assist women in the preparation of these fields? Note the way that men fashioned hoes from fish bone. Who did the fishing? To what degree was fishing a vital part of the economy of these people as a source of food, and as a source of farm implements?

Then note the second image, which depicts a religious offering. Here, the Indians have filled the body of a deer with produce and raised it to the spirits in hopes that the spirits will respond by making "grow again in their kingdom good things similar to those offered." Notice how the hunting of deer (these people were superlative hunters *and* farmers) is vital to the success of the harvest. Without hunting, there would be no offering to the spirits who make the crops grow. Without farming, there would be no gifts to place inside the offering. In this way, Indian hunters and farmers worked within the same villages to connect the nature of the hunt and the nature of the garden, balancing the spirits' gifts, and making balanced offerings to the spirits in return.

Figure 1.3. Method of tilling the ground and sowing seed (no. P119). The Indians cultivate the soil carefully. The men know how to construct hoes out of fish bones for this purpose, to which wooden handles are fitted, and they dig the ground easily enough since it is rather light. Then, when it is thoroughly broken up and levelled, the women sow beans and millet or maize, several of them going ahead and making holes by prodding a stick into the ground, into which are dropped beans and millet grains. The sowing finished, they leave the fields in order to avoid the winter time which is rather cold – inasmuch as the region lies between west and north – and lasts for about three months from December 24 to March 15. Since they go naked they take themselves off to the woods. When winter is over they go back home and wait for the crops to ripen. After gathering the harvest they store the produce for consumption all the year round, not using it for any commercial purpose except perhaps bartering it for some common household article. Courtesy of the British Museum.

Figure 1.4.   The offering of a stag to the sun (no. P133). Every year, a little before their spring (at the end of February, in fact), the chief Outina's subjects take the skin, complete with antlers of the biggest stag they have been able to catch. They stuff it with all kinds of the choicest plants that their land produces, sew it up again, and deck the horns, the throat, and the rest of the body with their more special fruits made up into wreaths or long garlands. Thus decorated, it is carried away to the music of pipes and singing into a very wide and beautiful plain, and there it is placed on a very tall tree trunk, with its head and chest turned towards the sunrise, prayers being repeatedly uttered to the sun that he should cause to grow again in their kingdom good things similar to those offered to him.

The chief with his sorcerer is nearest to the tree and gives the lead in what is said, with the people who are farther away responding. When they have greeted the sun the chief and the rest of the people go away leaving the skin there until the following year. This sort of ceremony is repeated each year. Courtesy of the British Museum.

2

The Other Invaders: Deadly Diseases and Extraordinary Animals

European colonists did not arrive alone in the Americas. They brought a great deal of baggage, some of it unintentionally. Many of the most significant changes in America's natural environments came about through autonomous workings of natural organisms that accompanied colonists and traders. These included disease-causing microbes, or pathogens, domesticated animals such as cows, sheep, and horses, and also weeds, or plants – many of them imported – that grew in conditions of disturbance brought on by plowing, grazing, or other colonial activities.

The impact of these organisms was enormous. Together, they remade much of American nature to better suit the new arrivals from Europe. While all of them had different effects, which varied from one region to the next, it is fair to say that without these small, often microscopic "co-invaders," it is unlikely that Europeans would have conquered those vast sections of the Americas which their descendants now dominate.

In the material presented below, we see how the linking of the Americas to the rest of the world in the early colonial period (and even after) meant that the nature of the New World was suddenly attached to the nature of the Old World, often with astounding consequences. Alfred Crosby explores the impact of microscopic germs, viruses, and plasmodia on American Indians, and particularly the impact of smallpox and its role in the conquest of the Americas and Australia. This piece is taken from one of Crosby's most famous books, but some of his terms need to be explained. Crosby refers to "Pangaea," which is the name scholars give to the world's single great land mass before it broke into continents millions of years ago, long before people existed. In part, Crosby argues that after the world split into separate continents, different disease environments eventually emerged in different places. To cross the ocean becomes, in Crosby's narrative, to cross "the seams of Pangaea."

The people who cross the ocean, sailors, he occasionally refers to by their Portuguese name, *marinheiros*, because many of the earliest European sailors and explorers were Portuguese. And finally, he refers to "Neo-Europes," by which he means those parts of the world outside Europe where the *marinheiros* and other Europeans settled and successfully transformed the natural environment into some approximation of European nature. These include the temperate zones of the Americas, Australia, New Zealand, and parts of southern Africa, among others. In Crosby's analysis, the process of making a strange new environment into a "neo-Europe" was the key to success for any European colonial regime.

In this excerpt, keep a close eye on *how* these diseases come to the Americas, and pay special attention to the way in which long isolation from the disease environments of Eurasia makes American Indians especially vulnerable at the time of contact. Why did Europeans bring diseases to Indians, without Indians having diseases of their own to kill Europeans? Also, you might ask why disease did not play the same role in the Europeans' attempted conquest of Africa, where pathogens worked in the opposite direction, often undermining the power of the colonists. Does the fact that natural organisms often worked to European and Euro-American advantage mean that the conquest was "natural"? Or were settlers who took the land from dying Indians merely exploiting the environmental conditions they had created, intentionally or otherwise?

Indian responses to the conflagration of smallpox and other Eurasian ailments are as much a part of environmental history as the epidemics themselves, but it is important to keep in mind that not all the Eurasian biota that arrived with the Europeans were so bad for Indian peoples. The documents in this chapter offer us a window on Indian perceptions of smallpox, and also suggest how Indians made use of another European organism which flourished in the Americas, the horse.

Virgin Soil Epidemics
Alfred W. Crosby

...We must examine the colonial histories of Old World pathogens, because their success provides the most spectacular example of the power of the biogeographical realities that underlay the success of

European imperialists overseas. It was their germs, not these imperialists themselves, for all their brutality and callousness, that were chiefly responsible for sweeping aside the indigenes and opening the Neo-Europes to demographic takeover. . . .

The isolation of the indigenes of the Americas and Australia from Old World germs prior to the last few hundred years was nearly absolute. Not only did very few people of any origin cross the great oceans, but those who did must have been healthy or they would have died on the way, taking their pathogens with them. The indigenes were not without their own infections, of course. The Amerindians had at least pinta, yaws, venereal syphilis, hepatitis, encephalitis, polio, some varieties of tuberculosis (not those usually associated with pulmonary disease), and intestinal parasites, but they seem to have been without any experience with such Old World maladies as smallpox, measles, diphtheria, trachoma, whooping cough, chicken pox, bubonic plague, malaria, typhoid fever, cholera, yellow fever, dengue fever, scarlet fever, amebic dysentery, influenza, and a number of helminthic infestations. The Australian Aborigines had their own infections – among them trachoma – but otherwise the list of Old World infections with which they were unfamiliar before Cook was probably similar to the list of Amerindian slaughterers. It is worth noting that as late as the 1950s it was difficult to get a staphylococcal culture from Aborigines living in the sterile environs of the central Australian desert.

Indications of the susceptibility of Amerindians and Aborigines to Old World infections appear almost immediately after the intrusion of the whites. In 1492, Columbus kidnapped a number of West Indians to train as interpreters and to show to King Ferdinand and Queen Isabella. Several of them seem to have died on the stormy voyage to Europe, and so Columbus had only seven to display in Spain, along with some gold trinkets, Arawack finery, and a few parrots. When, less than a year later, he returned to American waters, only two of the seven were still alive. In 1495, Columbus, searching for a West Indian commodity that would sell in Europe, sent 550 Amerindian slaves, twelve to thirty-five years of age, more or less, off across the Atlantic. Two hundred died on the difficult voyage; 350 survived to be put to work in Spain. The majority of these soon were also dead "because the land did not suit them."[1]

The British never shipped large numbers of Australian Aborigines to Europe as slaves or servants or in any other category, but in 1792, two Aborigines, Bennilong and Yemmerrawanyea, did sail to England as honored pets. Despite what we can assume was good treatment, they did no better than the first Amerindians in Spain. Bennilong pined and declined and showed indications of a pulmonary infection, but he did survive to return to his home. His companion succumbed to the same infection (perhaps tuberculosis, which was very widespread in Western Europe at the end of the eighteenth century) and was buried beneath a stone inscribed "In memory of Yemmerrawanyea, a native of New South Wales, who died on the 18th of May, 1794, in the 19th year of his age."[2]

We have some idea of the source of the Aborigines' morbidity and mortality: pulmonary infection. But what killed the Arawacks in 1493 and 1495? Maltreatment? Cold? Hunger? Overwork? Yes, and no doubt about it, but could this be the entire answer? Columbus certainly did not want to kill his interpreters, and slavers and slaveholders have no interest whatever in the outright slaughter of their property. All or almost all of these victims seem to have been young adults, usually the most resilient members of our species – except in the case of unfamiliar infections. The hale and hearty immune system of one's prime years of life, when challenged by unprecedented invaders, can overreact and smother normal body functions with inflammation and edema. The most likely candidates for the role of exterminator of the first Amerindians in Europe were those that killed so many other Arawacks in the decades immediately following: Old World pathogens.

. . . Let us restrict ourselves to the peregrinations of one Old World pathogen in the colonies, the most spectacular one, the virus of small-pox. Smallpox, an infection that usually spreads from victim to victim by breath, was one of the most communicable of all diseases and one of the very deadliest.[3] It was an old human infection in the Old World, but it was rarely of crucial importance in Europe until it flared up in the sixteenth century. For the next 250 to 300 years – until the advent of vaccination – it was just that, of crucial importance, reaching its apogee in the 1700s, when it accounted for 10 to 15 percent of all deaths in some of the western European nations early in the century. Characteristically, 80 percent of its victims were under ten years of age, and 70 percent under two years of age. In Europe, it was the worst of the childhood diseases. Most adults, especially in the cities and ports, had had it and were immune. In the colonies, it struck indigenes young and old and was the worst of all diseases.

Smallpox first crossed the seams of Pangaea – specifically to the island of Española – at the end of 1518 or the beginning of 1519, and for the next four centuries it played as essential a role in the advance of white imperialism overseas as gunpowder – perhaps a more important role, because the indigenes did turn the musket and then rifle against the intruders, but smallpox very rarely fought on the side of the indigenes. The intruders were usually immune to it, as they were to other Old World childhood diseases, most of which were new beyond the oceans. The malady quickly exterminated a third or half of the Arawacks on

Española, and almost immediately leaped the straits to Puerto Rico and the other Greater Antilles, accomplishing the same devastation there. It crossed from Cuba to Mexico and joined Cortés's forces in the person of a sick black soldier, one of the few of the invaders not immune to the infection. The disease exterminated a large fraction of the Aztecs and cleared a path for the aliens to the heart of Tenochtitlán and to the founding of New Spain. Racing ahead of the *conquistadores*, it soon appeared in Peru, killing a large proportion of the subjects of the Inca, killing the Inca himself and the successor he had chosen. Civil war and chaos followed, and then Francisco Pizarro arrived. The miraculous triumphs of that *conquistador*, and of Cortés, whom he so successfully emulated, are in large part the triumphs of the virus of smallpox.

This first recorded pandemic in the New World may have reached as far as the American Neo-Europes. The Amerindian population was denser than it was to be again for centuries, and utterly susceptible to smallpox. Canoeists of the Calusa tribe often crossed from Florida to Cuba to trade in the early sixteenth century, and certainly could have carried smallpox home to the continent with them; and peoples in at least sporadic contact with each other ringed the Gulf of Mexico from areas where the disease was rife all the way around to the thickly populated regions of what is now the southeastern part of the United States. The Mississippi, with villages rarely so much as a day's journey apart along its banks, at least as far north as the Ohio, would have given the disease access to the entire interior of the continent. As for the pampa, the pandemic certainly spread through the Incan Empire to present-day Bolivia, and from there settlements with easy access to each other were sprinkled across Paraguay and down along the Río de la Plata and its tributaries to the pampa. Smallpox may have ranged from the Great Lakes to the pampa in the 1520s and 1530s.

Smallpox is a disease with seven-league boots. Its effects are terrifying: the fever and pain; the swift appearance of pustules that sometimes destroy the skin and transform the victim into a gory horror; the astounding death rates, up to one-fourth, one-half, or more with the worst strains. The healthy flee, leaving the ill behind to face certain death, and often taking the disease along with them. The incubation period for smallpox is ten to fourteen days, long enough for the ephemerally healthy carrier to flee for long distances on foot, by canoe, or, later, on horseback to people who know nothing of the threat he represents, and there to infect them and inspire others newly charged with the virus to flee to infect new innocents. To give one example (a precise rather than sensational example), most of the Abipones with whom the missionary Martin Dobrizhoffer was living in mid-eighteenth-century Paraguay fled when smallpox appeared among them, some as far as eighty kilometers. In some instances this quarantine-by-flight worked, but often it simply served to spread the disease.

The first *recorded* epidemic of smallpox in British or French North America erupted among the Algonkins of Massachusetts in the early 1630s: "Whole towns of them were swept away, in some not so much as one soul escaping Destruction."[4] William Bradford of Plymouth Plantation, a few miles south, provided a few more details on just how hard the Algonkins nearby were hit, and how the death rates could soar to such heights in these epidemics. Some of the victims, he wrote,

> fell down so generally of this disease as they were in the end not able to help one another, no not to make a fire nor fetch a little water to drink, nor any to bury the dead. But would strive as long as they could, and when they could procure no other means to make fire, they would burn the wooden trays and dishes they ate their meat from, and their very bows and arrows. And some would crawl out on all fours to get a little water, and sometimes die by the way and not be able to get in again.[5]

The disease raged through New England, on west into the St. Lawrence–Great Lakes region, and from there no one knows how much farther. Smallpox whipsawed back and forth through New York and surrounding areas in the 1630s and 1640s, reducing the populations of the Huron and Iroquois confederations by an estimated 50 percent.

After that, smallpox never seemed to stay away for more than two or three decades at a time. The missionaries, Jesuit and Mennonite, the traders from Montreal and Charleston – they all had the same appalling story to tell about smallpox and the indigenes. In 1738 it destroyed half the Cherokee, in 1759 nearly half the Catawbas, in the first years of the nineteenth century two-thirds of the Omahas and perhaps half the entire population between the Missouri River and New Mexico, in 1837–8 nearly every last one of the Mandans and perhaps half the people of the high plains.[6] Every European people to establish major settlements in North America – the English, French, Dutch, Spanish, and Russian – recorded, sometimes in gloom, sometimes in exultation, the horrors of smallpox running loose among Americans who had never known it before.

The disease often spread far beyond the European frontier, often to people who had barely heard of the white invaders. Smallpox probably reached the Puget Sound area on the northwest Pacific coast in 1782 or 1783, a part of the world then as distant from the main centers of human population as any place on earth. When the explorer George Vancouver sailed into the Sound in 1793, he found Amerindians with pockmarked faces, and human bones scattered along the beach at Port Discovery –

skulls, limbs, ribs, backbones – so many as to produce the impression that this was "a general cemetery for the whole of the surrounding country." He judged that "at no very remote period this country had been far more populous than at present." It was an assessment that he could accurately have extended to the entire continent.[7]

Smallpox may have reached the pampa as early as the 1520s or 1530s, as suggested earlier. In 1558 or 1560, smallpox appeared again (or for the first time) in the grasslands of the Río de la Plata and killed, says a hearsay account, "more than 100,000 Indians."[8] We have only one source for this, but the explosion of smallpox in Chile and Paraguay at about the same time and in Brazil from 1562 to 1565, killing masses of indigenes, provides strong support for this report of the disease afflicting the people of the lower reaches of the Río de la Plata.

From the last decades of the sixteenth century and into the second half of the nineteenth century, smallpox swept the southern steppes and adjacent areas again and again, seemingly arising whenever enough susceptibles had been born since the last epidemic to support a new one. The seventeenth century opened with the government at Buenos Aires asking the Spanish crown for permission to import more black slaves, because smallpox had struck down so many of the Amerindians. That city alone had at least four epidemics of smallpox in less than a hundred years (1627, 1638, 1687, and 1700), and many others followed in the next two centuries. The first solid reference to the disease in Rio Grande do Sul did not appear until 1695, but this firestorm of a disease must have swept that province, contiguous to both Portuguese and Spanish areas where epidemics blazed up again and again, long before the end of the seventeenth century.

The death rates could be very high. In 1729, two churchmen, Miguel Ximénez and a priest named Cattaneo, started out from Buenos Aires for the missions in Paraguay accompanied by 340 Guaraní. Eight days up the Río de la Plata, smallpox appeared among the latter. All but forty contracted the infection, and for two months the disease raged, at the end of which 121 were convalescing and 179 were dead. The Jesuits, a group more given to numerical precision than most, reckoned that 50,000 had died in the Paraguayan missions in the 1718 smallpox, 30,000 in the Guaraní villages in 1734, and 12,000 in 1765. Out of how many at risk? We shall have to leave that to the demographic historians.

We shall never know how many died among the tribes roaming the pampa. Their ability to flee at short notice must have saved them from some epidemics, but the longer they avoided the infection, the more pulverizing its impact when it did strike. For instance, there is the case of the Chechehets, in 1700 one of the more numerous of the peoples of the grasslands, and therefore probably a tribe that had dodged the worst epidemics. When this tribe acquired smallpox near Buenos Aires early in the eighteenth century, it suffered near obliteration. The Chechehets tried to fly from this danger, which this time only increased their losses: "During the journey they daily left behind them their sick friends and relations, forsaken and alone, with no other assistance than a hide reared up against the wind, and a pitcher of water." They even killed their own shamans "to see if by this means the distemper would cease." The Chechehets never recovered as an autonomous people. By the end of the century, even their language was gone. Today we have fifteen of their words and some place names, barely as much as we have of the language of the Guanches.[9]

This disease continued to periodically ravage the pampean tribes, terminating only with the spread of vaccination and the destruction, incarceration, or expulsion of the last peoples of the Argentine steppe. Doctor Eliseo Cantón, physician, scientist, and medical historian of Argentina, stated flatly that the extermination of the Amerindians as an effective force on the pampa was due not to the Argentinian army and its Remingtons, but to smallpox. . . .

The impact of smallpox on the indigenes of Australia and the Americas was more deadly, more bewildering, more devastating than we, who live in a world from which the smallpox virus has been scientifically exterminated, can ever fully realize. The statistics of demographic decline are cold, the eyewitness accounts at first moving, but eventually only macabre. The impact was so awesome that only a writer with the capabilities of a Milton at the height of his powers could have been equal to the subject, and there was no one like him on Española in 1519 or in New South Wales in 1789. . . .

Smallpox was only one of the diseases the *marinheiros* let loose on the native peoples overseas – perhaps the most destructive, certainly the most spectacular – but only one. We have not dealt at all with respiratory infections, the "hectic" fevers so often prevalent among the indigenes after contact with the strangers from over the horizon. To cite one piece of evidence, in the 1960s, 50 to 80 percent of central Australian Aborigines examined in one study had coughs and abnormal breath sounds, the higher percentages being among those most recently come in from the desert. We have said nothing of enteric infections, which unquestionably have killed more humans in the last few millennia than any other class of diseases, and still are doing so. Cabeza de Vaca, staggering lost and desperate across Texas circa 1530, unintentionally presented his Amerindian masters with some sort of dysenteric disease that killed half of them and elevated him and his comrades to the status of priestly physicians, ironically saving their lives. We have said nothing of the insect-borne diseases, though in the nineteenth century, malaria was the most important sickness in the entire Mississippi Valley. We have said nothing of the venereal infections, which depressed the indigenes' birth rates as they raised death rates from Labrador to Perth in western Australia. Old World pathogens in their dismal variety spread widely beyond the seams of Pangaea and weakened, crippled, or killed millions of the geographical vanguard of the human race. The world's greatest demographic disaster was initiated by Columbus and Cook and the other *marinheiros*, and Europe's overseas colonies were, in the first stage of their modern development, charnel houses. Afterward, mixed European, African, and indigene societies quite unlike any that had ever existed before grew up in the colonies in the torrid zone, with the single major exception of northern Australia. The temperate-zone colonies developed less distinctively; they became Neo-European, with only minorities of non-whites.

We accept that Mexico and Peru were full of indigenous peoples prior to European arrival, because their ancient monuments of stone are too huge to ignore and because their descendants still live in these lands in large numbers. But to imagine the Neo-Europes, now chock-full of Neo-Europeans and other Old World peoples, as once having had large native populations that were wiped out by imported diseases calls for a long leap of historical imagination. Let us examine one specific case of depopulation of a Neo-Europe.

Let us select a Neo-European region where indigenous agriculturalists of an advanced culture lived: the portion of the eastern United States between the Atlantic and the Great Plains, the Ohio Valley and the Gulf of Mexico. By the time Europeans had quartered that region, had traversed it up and down, back and forth, often enough in search of new Aztec Empires, routes to Cathay, and gold and furs to have acquainted themselves with its major features – by 1700 or so – the native inhabitants were the familiar Amerindians of the United States history textbooks: Cherokee, Creek, Shawnee, Choctaw, and so forth. These and all the others, with only one or two exceptions, were peoples without pronounced social stratification, without the advanced arts and crafts that aristocracies and priesthoods elicit, and without great public works comparable to the temples and pyramids of Meso-America. Their populations were no greater than one would expect of part-time farmers and hunters and gatherers, and in many areas less. Very few tribes numbered in the tens of thousands, and most were much smaller.

The scene in this part of North America had been very different in 1492. The Mound Builders (a general title for a hundred different peoples of a dozen different cultures spread over thousands of square kilometers and most of a millennium) had raised and were raising up multitudes of burial and temple mounds, many no more than knee or hip high, but some among the largest earthen structures ever created by humans anywhere. The largest, Monks Mound, one of 120 at Cahokia, Illinois, is 623,000 cubic meters in volume and covers six and a half hectares. Every particle of this enormous mass was carried and put into place by human beings without the help of any domesticated animals. The only pre-Columbian structures in the Americas that are larger are the Pyramid of the Sun at Teotihuacán and the great pyramid at Cholula. Cahokia, in its heyday, about 1200 A.D., was one of the great ceremonial centers of the world, served by a village with a population estimated by some archeologists as upward of 40,000. (The largest city in the United States in 1790 was Philadelphia, with a population of 42,000.) Graves at Cahokia and other such sites contain copper from Lake Superior, chert from Arkansas and Oklahoma, sheets of mica probably from North Carolina, and many art objects of superb quality. They also contain, in addition to the skeletons of the honored dead, those of men and women apparently sacrificed at the time of burial. One burial pit at Cahokia contains the remains of four men, all with heads and hands missing, and about fifty women, all between eighteen and twenty-three years of age. Surely this assemblage is evidence for a grim religion and a severely hierarchical class structure – this last a key factor in the origins of civilization everywhere.

When whites and blacks settled near the site of Cahokia and similar centers (Moundsville, Alabama; Etowah, Georgia) in the eighteenth and nineteenth centuries, the local Amerindian societies were relatively egalitarian, their population sparse, their arts and crafts admirable but no longer superb, their trade networks regional; these people knew nothing of the mounds and ceremonial centers, abandoned generations before. The whites credited them to Vikings, or to the lost tribes of Israel, or to prehistoric races now gone from the earth.

The builders of the mounds had been Amerindians, of course, in some cases, no doubt, the ancestors of the people who were living near the sites when the Old World settlers arrived. These ancestors had been alive in large numbers when the Europeans first approached the coasts of the Americas. They were the people through whose lands and bodies Hernando de Soto hacked a path from 1539 to 1542 in his search for wealth equal to what he had seen in Peru. His chroniclers give us a clear impression of regions of dense population and many villages in the midst of vast cultivated fields, of stratified societies ruled with an iron hand from the top, and of scores of temples resting on truncated pyramids, which though often stubby and made of earth rather than masonry, remind one of similar structures in Teotihuacán and Chichén Itzá.

Where in the images of North American native societies that we share today is there a place for De Soto's wily opponent, the "Señora of Cofachiqui," a province that probably contained the present site of Augusta, Georgia. She traveled by sedan chair borne by noblemen and was accompanied by a retinue of slaves. For a distance of a hundred leagues "she was greatly obeyed, whatsoever she ordered being performed with diligence and efficacy."[10] Seeking to deflect the greed of the Spaniards away from her living subjects, she sent the former off to sack a burial house or temple that was thirty meters long and twelve or so wide, with a roof decorated with marine shells and fresh-water pearls, which "made a splendid sight in the brilliance of the sun." Inside were chests containing the dead, and for each chest a statue carved in the likeness of the deceased. The walls and ceiling were hung with art work, and the rooms filled with finely carved maces, battle-axes, pikes, bows, and arrows inlaid with fresh-water pearls. The building and its contents were, in the opinion of one of the grave robbers, Alonso de Carmona, who had lived in both Mexico and Peru, among the finest things he had ever seen in the New World.

The Amerindians of Cofachiqui and of much of what is now the southeastern United States were impressive country cousins of the civilized Mexicans, perhaps comparable to the immediate predecessors of the Sumerians in general culture, and there were a lot of them. The latest scholarly work estimates that the population of one marginal area, Florida, may have been as high as 900,000 at the beginning of the sixteenth century. Even if we skeptically subtract half from that figure, the remainder is impressively large. The southeastern United States, relative to what it had been, was vacant circa 1700 when the French came to stay.

Something eliminated or drove off most of the population of Cofachiqui by the eighteenth century, as well as a number of other areas where heavy populations of people of similar cultural achievements had lived two centuries before: along the Gulf Coast between Mobile Bay and Tampa Bay, along the Georgia coast, and on the banks of the Mississippi above the mouth of the Red River. In eastern and southern Arkansas and northeastern Louisiana, where De Soto had found thirty towns and provinces, the French found only a handful of villages. Where De Soto had been able to stand on one temple mound and see several villages with their mounds and little else but fields of maize between, there was now wilderness. Whatever had afflicted the country through which he had passed may have reached far to the north as well. The region of southern Ohio and northern Kentucky, among the richest in natural food resources on the continent, was nearly deserted when whites first penetrated from New France and Virginia.

There had even been a major ecological change in the regions adjacent to the Gulf of Mexico and for tens of kilometers back from the coast, a change paralleling and probably associated with the decline in Amerindian numbers. In the sixteenth century, De Soto's chroniclers saw no buffalo along their route from Florida to Tennessee and back to the coast, or if they did see these wonderful beasts, they did not mention them – which seems highly improbable. Archeological evidence and examination of Amerindian place names also indicate that there were no buffalo along the De Soto route, nor between it and salt water. A century and a half later, when the French and English arrived, they found the shaggy animals present in at least scattered herds from the mountains almost to the Gulf and even to the Atlantic. What had happened in the interim is easy to explain in the abstract: An econiche opened up, and the buffalo moved into it. Something had kept these animals out of the expanses of parklike clearings in the forest that periodic Amerindian use of fire and hoe had created. That something declined or disappeared after 1540. That something was, in all likelihood, the Amerindians themselves, who naturally would have killed the buffalo for food and to protect their crops.

The cause of that decline and disappearance was probably epidemic disease. No other factor seems capable of having exterminated so many people over such a large part of North America. The dismal genocidal process had already begun before De Soto arrived in Cofachiqui. A year or two before, a pestilence had threshed through that province, killing many. Talomeco, where the Spanish raided the burial temple mentioned earlier, was one of several towns without inhabitants because an epidemic had killed and driven off so many. The intruders found four large houses there filled with the bodies of people who had perished of the pestilence. The Spanish judged Cofachiqui heavily populated, but its citizens said their number had been much greater before the epidemic. De Soto entered Cofachiqui on the heels of a medical disaster, just as he had with Pizarro in Peru. . . .

The epidemics continued to arrive and to do their work of extermination, as they did in every part of the Americas we know anything about in the sixteenth and seventeenth centuries. To cite but one, in 1585–6, Sir Francis Drake led a large fleet to the Cape Verdes, where his men picked up a dangerous communicable disease, and then sailed off to raid the Spanish Main, but so many of the English were sick and dying that the venture failed miserably. Seeking redress, he attacked the Spanish colony at St. Augustine, Florida, infecting the local people with the Cape Verde epidemic. The Amerindians, "at first coming of our men died very fast, and said amongst themselves, it was the English god that made them die so fast." Presumably the disease proceeded on into the interior.[11]

When the French penetrated into the hinterlands behind the coast of the Gulf of Mexico, where De Soto had fought so many battles with so many peoples, they found few to oppose their intrusion. And the decline in Amerindian numbers continued; indeed, it probably accelerated. In six years, the last of the Mound Builders, the Natchez, with their pyramid-top temples and their supreme leader, the Great Sun, diminished by a third. One of the Frenchmen wrote, unintentionally echoing the Protestant, John Winthrop, "Touching these savages, there is a thing that I cannot omit to remark to you, it is that it appears visibly that God wishes that they yield their place to new peoples."[12]

The exchange of infectious diseases – that is, of germs, of living things having geographical points of origin just like visible creatures – between the Old World and its American and Australasian colonies has been wondrously one-sided, as one-sided and one-way as the exchanges of people, weeds, and animals. Australasia, as far as science can tell us, has exported not one of its human diseases to the outside world, presuming that it has any uniquely its own. The Americas do have their own distinctive pathogens, those of at least Carrion's disease and Chagas' disease. Oddly, these very unpleasant and sometimes fatal diseases do not travel well and have never established themselves in the Old World. . . . *Niguas*, as Fernándo de Oviedo called the tropical American chigger causing barefoot Spaniards so much trouble in the sixteenth century, reached Africa in 1872 and spread across the continent as an epidemic of lost toes and fatal secondary infections of tetanus, but it has since retreated to the nuisance category and has never changed the Old World's demographic history. Europe was magnanimous in the quantity and quality of the torments it sent across the seams of Pangaea. In contrast, its colonies, epidemiologically impecunious to begin with, were hesitant to export even the pathogens they did have. The unevenness of the exchange . . . operated to the overwhelming advantage of the European invaders, and to the crushing disadvantage of the peoples whose ancestral homes were on the losing side of the seams of Pangaea.

Notes

1 Andrés Bernáldez, *Historia de los Reyes Católicos Don Fernando y Doña Isabel*, in *Crónicas de los Reyes de Castilla desde Don Alfonso el Sabio, Hasta los Católicos Don Fernando y Doña Isabel* (Madrid: M. Rivadeneyra, 1878), III, 668; *Journals and Other Documents of Columbus*, trans. Samuel Eliot Morison (New York: Heritage Press, 1963), 226–7.
2 Louis Becke and Walter Jeffery, *Admiral Philip* (London: Fisher & Unwin, 1909), 74–5.

3   I shall always be referring to the often fatal variola major smallpox. The mild variola minor did not appear until late in the nineteenth century. Donald R. Hopkins, *Princes and Peasants, Smallpox in History* (University of Chicago Press, 1983), 5–6.

4   John Duffy, "Smallpox and the Indians in the American Colonies," *Bulletin of the History of Medicine* 25 (July–August 1951): 327.

5   William Bradford, *Of Plymouth Plantation*, ed. Samuel Eliot Morison (New York: Knopf, 1952), 271.

6   Alfred W. Crosby, "Virgin Soil Epidemics as a Factor in the Aboriginal Depopulation in America," *William and Mary Quarterly*, 3rd series 33 (April 1976): 290–1.

7   Richard White, *Land Use, Environment, and Social Change. The Shaping of Island County, Washington* (Seattle: University of Washington Press, 1980), 26–7; Robert H. Ruby and John A. Brown, *The Chinook Indians, Traders of the Lower Columbia River* (Norman: University of Oklahoma Press, 1976), 80.

8   Juan López de Velasco, *Geografía y Descripción Universal de las Indias desde el Año de 1571 al de 1574* (Madrid: Establecimiento Tipográfico de Fortanet, 1894), 552.

9   Thomas Falkner, *A Description of Patagonia* (Chicago: Armann & Armann, 1935), 98, 102–3, 117; *Handbook of South American Indians*, ed. Julian H. Steward (Washington D.C.: United States Government Printing Office, 1946–59), VI, 309–10; see also Guillermo Fúrlong, *Entre las Pampas de Buenos Aires* (Buenos Aires: Talleres Gráficos "San Pablo," 1938), 59.

10 *Narratives of the Career of Hernando de Soto*, trans. Buckingham Smith (New York: Allerton Book Co., 1922), I, 65, 70–1.

11 Charles Creighton, *A History of Epidemics in Britain* (Cambridge University Press, 1891), I, 585–9; Julian S. Corbett, ed., *Papers Relating to the Navy During the Spanish War, 1585–1587* (Navy Records Society, 1898), XI, 26.

12 John R. Swanton, *Indian Tribes of the Lower Mississippi Valley and Adjacent Coast of the Gulf of Mexico* (Smithsonian Institution Bureau of American Ethnology, bulletin no. 43, 1911), 39. See also Henry F. Dobyns, *Their Number Become Thinned, Native American Population Dynamics in Eastern North America* (Knoxville: University of Tennesee Press, 1983), 247–90; George R. Milner, "Epidemic Disease in the Postcontact Southeast: A Reappraisal," *Mid-Continent Journal of Archeology* 5 (no. 1, 1980): 39–56. The archeologists are beginning to produce physical evidence that supports the hypothesis of fierce epidemics, swift population decline, and radical cultural change in the Gulf region in the sixteenth century. See Caleb Curren, *The Protohistoric Period in Central Alabama* (Camden, Ala.: Alabama Tombigbee Regional Commission, 1984), 54, 240, 242.

Documents

Frank Givens, "Saynday and Smallpox: The White Man's Gift"

Reprinted from Alice Marriott and Carol K. Rachlin, *American Indian Mythology*
(New York: Thomas Y. Cravell Co., 1968)

Understanding what it was like for Indians to undergo the calamity of smallpox
is very difficult. Few Indians possessed a written language. Most recorded the
formative events and developments of their history in stories passed from
generation to generation. "Saynday and Smallpox: The White Man's Gift"
reflects the experience of Kiowa Indians, a people of the southern Great Plains
who were decimated by smallpox in the nineteenth century. Frank Givens, a
Kiowa man, told this tale in the twentieth century. In it, the Kiowa's mythic
hero, Saynday, who always protects his people from harm and who is also
notoriously crafty, meets smallpox, a venomous mass-murderer who comes
from the world of white men. At first, this seems like a story scripted from a
simple good versus evil drama, with the Indian hero facing the white monster.
But pay careful attention to what happens here. Is smallpox a spiritual presence,
and if so, is it as powerful as the spirits of the Koyukon world which we read
about in chapter 1? How does Saynday protect his people from smallpox? How
does its deadly presence shape their relations with other Indians? Are whites
and their dreaded disease the only enemies of the Kiowa people? How does
Saynday think he will overcome smallpox in the long run?

* * *

Saynday was coming along, and as he came he saw that all his world had
changed. Where the buffalo herds used to graze, he saw white-faced cattle.
The Washita River, which once ran bankful with clear water, was soggy
with red mud. There were no deer or antelope in the brush or skittering
across the high plains. No white tipis rose proudly against the blue sky;
settlers' soddies dented the hillsides and the creek banks.

My time has come, Saynday thought to himself. The world I lived in is
dead. Soon the Kiowa people will be fenced like the white man's cattle,
and they cannot break out of the fences because the barbed wire will tear
their flesh. I can't help my people any longer by staying with them. My
time has come, and I will have to go away from this changed world.

Off across the prairie, Saynday saw a dark spot coming toward him
from the east, moving very slowly.

That's strange, too, Saynday thought to himself. The East is the place of birth and of new life. The things that come from the East come quickly; they come dancing and alive. This thing comes as slowly as death to an old man. I wonder what it is?

Almost absent-mindedly, Saynday started walking eastward. As he went the spot grew larger, and after a while Saynday saw that it was a man on a horse.

The horse was black, but it had been powdered to roan with the red dust that the plows had stirred up when they slashed open the plains. Red dust spotted the man's clothing – a black suit and a high hat, like a missionary's. Red dust blurred his features, but behind the dust Saynday could see that the man's face was pitted with terrible scars.

The stranger drew rein, and sat looking at Saynday. The black roan horse lifted one sore hoof and drooped its head as if it were too weary to carry its burden any farther.

"Who are you?" the stranger asked.

"I'm Saynday. I'm the Kiowas' Old Uncle Saynday. I'm the one who's always coming along."

"I never heard of you," the stranger said, "and I never heard of the Kiowas. Who are they?"

"The Kiowas are my people," Saynday said, and even in that hard time he stood up proudly, like a man. "Who are you?"

"I'm Smallpox," the man answered.

"And I never heard of *you*," said Saynday. "Where do you come from and what do you do and why are you here?"

"I come from far away, across the Eastern Ocean," Smallpox answered. "I am one with the white men – they are my people as the Kiowas are yours. Sometimes I travel ahead of them, and sometimes I lurk behind. But I am always their companion and you will find me in their camps and in their houses."

"What do you do?" Saynday repeated.

"I bring death," Smallpox replied. "My breath causes children to wither like young plants in spring snow. I bring destruction. No matter how beautiful a woman is, once she has looked at me she becomes as ugly as death. And to men I bring not death alone, but the destruction of their children and the blighting of their wives. The strongest warriors go down before me. No people who have looked on me will ever be the same." And he chuckled low and hideously. With his raised forearm, Smallpox pushed the dust off his face, and Saynday saw the scars that disfigured it.

For a moment Saynday shut his eyes against the sight, and then he opened them again. "Does that happen to all the people you visit?" he inquired.

"Every one of them," said Smallpox. "It will happen to your Kiowa people, too. Where do they live? Take me to them, and then I will spare you, although you have seen my face. If you do not lead me to your people, I will breathe on you and you will die, no matter whose Old Uncle you are." And although he did not breathe on Saynday, Saynday smelled the reek of death that surrounded him.

"My Kiowa people are few and poor already," Saynday said, thinking fast as he talked. "They aren't worth your time and trouble."

"I have time and I don't have to take any trouble," Smallpox told him. "Even one person whom I blot out, I can count."

"Oh," said Saynday. "Some of your ways are like the Kiowas', then. You count the enemies that you touch."

"I have no enemies," said Smallpox. "Man, woman, or child – humanity is all alike to me. I was brought here to kill. But, yes, I count those I destroy. White men always count: cattle, sheep, chickens, children, the living and the dead. You say the Kiowas do the same thing?"

"Only the enemies they touch," Saynday insisted. "They never count living people – men are not cattle, any more than women and children are."

"Then how do you know the Kiowas are so few and poor?" Smallpox demanded.

"Oh, anybody can see that for himself," Saynday said. "You can look at a Kiowa camp and tell how small it is. We're not like the Pawnees. They have great houses, half underground, in big villages by the rivers, and every house is full of people."

"I like that," Smallpox observed. "I can do my best work when people are crowded together."

"Then you'd like the Pawnees," Saynday assured him. "They're the ones that almost wiped out the Kiowas; that's why we're so few and so poor. Now we run away whenever we see a stranger coming, because he might be a Pawnee."

"I suppose the Pawnees never run away," Smallpox sneered.

"They couldn't if they wanted to," Saynday replied. "The Pawnees are rich. They have piles of robes, they have lots of cooking pots and plenty of bedding – they keep all kinds of things in those underground houses of theirs. The Pawnees can't run away and leave all their wealth."

"Where did you say they live?" Smallpox asked thoughtfully.

"Oh, over there," Saynday said, jerking his chin to the north.

"And they are rich, and live in houses, with piles of robes to creep into and hide?"

"That's the Pawnees," Saynday said jauntily. He began to feel better. The deathly smell was not so strong now. "I think I'll go and visit the Pawnees first," Smallpox remarked. "Later on, perhaps, I can get back to the Kiowas."

"You do that," directed Saynday. "Go and visit the Pawnees, and when you grow tired there from all the work you have to do, come back and visit my poor people. They'll do all they can for you."

"Good," said Smallpox. He picked up his reins and jerked his weary horse awake. "Tell your people when I come to be ready for me. Tell them to put out all their fires. Fire is the only thing in the whole world that I'm afraid of. It's the only thing in God's world that can destroy me."

Saynday watched Smallpox and his death horse traveling north, away from the Kiowas. Then he took out his flint and steel, and set fire to the spindly prairie grass at his feet. The winds came and picked up the fire, and carried it to make a ring of safety around the Kiowas' camps.

"Perhaps I can still be some good to my people after all," Saynday said to himself, feeling better.

And that's the way it was, and that's the way it is, to this good day.

Told to Alice Marriott by Frank Givens (Eagle Plume).

From Thomas James, *Three Years among the Indians and Mexicans*

Reprinted from *Three Years among the Indians and Mexicans*, 1846 edn (Philadelphia and New York: J. B. Lippincott Co., 1962)

While smallpox and other imported diseases were a pathogenic firestorm which made the conquest of the Americas easier for grasping colonists, not all invaders were so uniformly horrific for all Indians. In this regard, the horse was at least in part the counterpart of smallpox. The horse was a European import that revolutionized life for many Indians. There were few if any horses in Indian hands prior to the seventeenth century, when Indians took horses abandoned or lost by the Spanish and converted them to their own use. In many places, the horse made Indians much more difficult to conquer. It allowed many Indians to move out on the Great Plains to hunt buffalo as a primary means of subsistence, a way of life that was much less alluring before horses brought increased speed and mobility. The ways that horses conveyed power and strength to Indians are suggested in the following account. Thomas James spent three years in the far Southwest in the early nineteenth century, at a time when Spain's empire included a vast part of what would one day become most of the American Southwest. His encounter with Ute Indians, who had adapted the horse for their own hunting, raiding, and trading economy, suggests how tenuous Spanish control over this region actually was, and how much Ute success with horse breeding and horse rearing contributed to a powerful sense of autonomy from the Spanish empire.

After reading this account, it becomes clear that invading biota do not always displace indigenous peoples.

*   *   *

...In the latter part of February [1822] I received a deputation of fifty Indians from the Utah tribe on the west side of the mountains. They came riding into the city, and paraded on the public square, all well mounted on the most elegant horses I had ever seen. The animals were of a very superior breed, with their slender tapering legs and short, fine hair, like our best blooded racers. They were of almost every color, some spotted and striped as if painted for ornament. The Indians alighted at the Council House and sent a request for me to visit them. On arriving I found them all awaiting me in the Council House, with a company of Spanish officers and gentlemen led hither by curiosity. On entering I was greeted by the Chief and his companions, who shook hands with me. The Chief, whose name was Lechat, was a young man of about thirty and of a right Princely port and bearing. He told me in the Spanish language, which he spoke fluently, that he had come expressly to see me and have a talk with me. "You are Americans, we are told, and you have come from your country afar off to trade with the Spaniards. We want your trade. Come to our country with your goods. Come and trade with the Utahs. We have horses, mules and sheep, more than we want. We heard that you wanted beaver skins. The beavers in our country are eating up our corn. All our rivers are full of them. Their dams back up the water in the rivers all along their course from the mountains to the Big water. Come over among us and you shall have as many beaver skins as you want." Turning round and pointing to the Spaniards, in [a] most contemptuous manner and with a scornful look he said, "What can you get from these? They have nothing to trade with you. They have nothing but a few poor horses and mules, a little puncha, and a little tola (tobacco and corn meal porridge) not fit for any body to use. They are poor – too poor for you to trade with. Come among the Utahs if you wish to trade with profit. Look at our horses here. Have the Spaniards any such horses? No, they are too poor. Such as these we have in our country by the thousand, and also cattle, sheep and mules. These Spaniards," said he, turning and pointing his finger at them in a style of contempt which John Randolph would have envied, "what are they? What have they? They won't even give us two loads of powder and lead for a beaver skin, and for a good reason they have not as much as they want themselves. They have nothing that you want. We have every thing that they have, and many things that they have not." Here a Spaniard cried out: "You have no money." Like a true stump orator the Utah replied, "and you have very little. You are *depicca*." In other words you are poor miserable devils and we are the true capitalists of the country. With this and much more of the same purport, he concluded his harangue, which was delivered in the most independent and lordly manner possible. He looked like a King upbraiding his subjects for being poor, when they might be rich, and his whole conduct seemed to me like bearding a wild beast in his den. The "talk" being had, Lechat produced the *calama* or pipe, and we smoked together in the manner of the Indians. I sent to my store and procured six plugs of tobacco and some handkerchiefs, which I presented to him and his company, telling them when they smoked the tobacco with their Chiefs to remember the Americans, and treat all who visited their country from mine as they would their own brothers. The council now broke up and the Chief, reiterating his invitations to me to visit his country, mounted his noble steed, and with his company rode out of the city, singing and displaying the handkerchiefs I had presented them, from the ends of their lances as standards. They departed without the least show of respect for the Spaniards, but rather with a strong demonstration on the part of Lechat of contempt for them....

*   *   *

John C. Ewers, "Horse Breeding"

Reprinted from *The Horse in Blackfoot Indian Culture* (Washington, DC: Smithsonian Institute Press, 1955)

The adoption of horses by Indians required large cultural changes. As they turned this new organism to their own use, they also changed their cultures and their ways of interacting with nature. A common misconception is that horses "ran wild" for the most part, and that some of these might have been caught and tamed by Indians, who otherwise had no horses unless they stole them from their enemies. Although some Indians did specialize in catching wild horses, and horse theft was a common way of gaining new animals, breeding horses from Indian herds was also widespread. In fact, the propagation of the horse through-out the Americas came about in part because Indians developed ways of breeding and rearing horses. In Montana, horses could not survive the winters without Indian caretakers to feed them and provide minimal shelter. In the 1950s, anthropologist John C. Ewers explored traditions of horsecraft among the Blackfoot Indians of the northern Great Plains. Many of the men he interviewed were Piegan, a sub-tribe of the once-powerful Blackfoot Confeder-acy. Some of them had known the great horse trainers, horse catchers, and horse doctors of the 1850s–1870s. What steps did Blackfoot horsemen take to differentiate their horses from their neighbors' animals? How did they control horse breeding to maintain the best horse lines in their possession?

* * *

Important Role of Horse Breeding

So much emphasis has been given in the literature to the more exciting topic of horse raiding as a source of Plains Indian wealth in horses that the subject of breeding horses has been neglected. In reality animals bred from their own herds comprised a goodly proportion of the horses owned by the Blackfoot in 19th-century buffalo days. If the increase of the Indians' herds through breeding was not as great as that achieved by modern stockmen, we must remember that their herds were periodically reduced by destructive winter storms, diseases, animal predators, and other causes, as well as by theft on the part of enemy raiders. Had it not been for the breeding of their own herds, Blackfoot horse population surely would have shown a steady decrease during 19th-century buffalo days.

Blackfoot men differed markedly in the attention they gave to horse breeding and in the success they achieved in building up their herds thereby. It is noteworthy that those Piegan who were named by my informants as owners of the largest herds were also remembered as men who were especially successful in breeding horses. Stingy, the blind man, could not participate in horse raids, but he became one of the wealthiest Piegan horse owners through his skill in raising horses. Many Horses and Many-White-Horses were mentioned frequently in informants' discussions of breeding practices. The Blackfoot believed that those men who were very successful in raising horses possessed a secret power that insured their success in that enterprise.

Blackfoot efforts in breeding generally were directed toward producing one or more of three qualities in colts. These were (1) a certain color, (2) large size, and (3) swiftness of foot. Although many of their methods hardly can be considered scientific, they bear evidence of Blackfoot concern with problems of horse breeding.

Selection of Studs

There was little or no effort to mate certain stallions with selected mares. The studs were permitted to mate with any mare in a man's herd. However, the most successful breeders were careful in the choice of their stallions. A man who desired to raise colts of a certain color chose a stallion of that color for a stud. If he wished for large colts he selected a stallion of greater than average size. If he wanted fast animals above all else, he employed a stallion of demonstrated swiftness. Generally men with small herds possessed a single stallion. Owners of large herds kept four or more stallions. Usually all other males were castrated. The Blackfoot recognized that some stallions were poor breeders. If, after a period of trial, a stallion failed to produce colts in the number or quality desired, a man who could afford to do so replaced that stud with another one.

Three Calf, whose father owned a fine herd of 40 pinto horses, said his father had but one stallion, a large, black pinto, bred from his own herd. Many Horses owned a number of stallions, pintos of several varieties, which he used for no other purpose than breeding and on which he lavished great care. His stallions were never broken to the saddle. Stingy, who bred for size, used a large horse for a stud. He rode it, and kept it picketed at night in the spring breeding season to prevent other Indians from making use of it. When colts dropped, he herded them with the mares and colts. The Piegan sometimes called Stingy, "White Man," because he raised such large horses. Other breeders selected their stallions for swiftness regardless of their size or coloring. All careful breeders took pains to obtain the best horses they could get of the type they most desired for studs. However, most men were too poor or too careless to devote much thought to stallion selection. They were happy just to possess a stallion. "That is why there were so many scrub, no good horses around."

If a man owned one or more mares but no stallion he might go to his neighbor's herd at night and "borrow" his stud to mate with his own mare, without the knowledge of the stallion's owner. This is said to have been a rather common practice.

Careful breeders also took pains to prevent old, broken-down stallions of their neighbors from mingling with their mares. Where so many horse herds were pastured in the neighborhood of a camp this was a difficult task. However, boys caring for the herds of cautious owners were instructed to keep their herds separate in breeding season and to drive away undesirable stallions that came near them. If a poor old stallion was found bothering their mares, the boys caught him, threw him down, and tied a large buffalo rib or hip bone to his forelock. The frightened animal left on the run. If a stray stallion persisted in bothering a man's herd, the herd owner told the stallion's owner to take better care of his horses thereafter.

Maintenance of Color Lines

Some men tried to build up herds of a single color. Three Calf said that after his father possessed 40 pintos he made no attempt to add to his herd except by breeding. He gave away any horses given him, and disposed of any colts bred to his herd that were not pintos. Many-White-Horses, so named because all the horses in his herd were whites or grays, traded any dark-colored horses he obtained for white ones. Nevertheless, his horses were said to have been of rather poor quality. They were small, tender-hoofed animals. When the Government furnished large stallions to Piegan owners, Many-White-Horses refused to accept them. He feared the stallions would injure his small mares. So he continued to raise large numbers of little horses. They had more prestige than practical value.

Joseph Sherburne recalled that when he traveled the Blackfeet Reservation (in the first decade of the 20th century) making collections for his father's store, some Indian owners of large herds still specialized in horses of a particular color or conformation. He learned to recognize the peculiarities of the horses of different owners so that he could tell from a distance the ownership of many range horses by their appearance. There were 10 or 12 owners on the Blackfeet Reservation in Montana at that time whose horses were readily distinguishable by their physical appearance. Mr. Sherburne said the uniformity of these herds was maintained both by selection of studs and by swapping of horses which failed to exhibit the desired characteristics.

George Catlin, "Wild Horses at Play"

This 1830s painting by George Catlin depicts a herd of wild horses on the Great Plains. It might be perceived as an illustration of raw, frontier nature. But how does the environmental history of the horse shape your understanding of this image? A painting that at first seems to suggest untouched American nature at some level portrays Eurasian organisms transforming their adopted homeland. Are these wild horses in some measure the side effects of colonialism? Or is the image even more complicated? Some of these animals may have escaped from Indian camps. Might their physical characteristics, their coloring, and even their size, have been shaped by the influence of Indian horse breeders? Is the nature in this image more Eurasian or more American? Both? Neither?

Figure 2.1. Wild horses at play. From George Catlin, *Wild Horses at Play* (1834–7), Smithsonian American Art Museum.

3

Colonial Natures: Marketing the Countryside

The far-reaching environmental changes of the colonial period owe their origins in part to the organisms described above, but they also stem from the very distinctive goals Europeans had in their relations with nature. William Cronon, in an excerpt from his prize-winning book *Changes in the Land: Indians, Colonists, and the Ecology of New England*, reveals how many of the most significant changes resulting from the arrival of European colonists in the Americas came about because the colonists sought to sell products of American ecosystems as commodities in the transatlantic market. Among the pre-eminent commodities of the colonial economy was livestock. Settlers raised domesticated animals partly to make money. The spread of livestock across New England thus reflected the expansion of the market economy. It brought profound social and environmental developments, including wholesale shifts in property relations (suggested by the proliferation of the fence, a device for controlling livestock) and New England ecology. As you read this selection, keep your eye on the ways that market demand for livestock encouraged their propagation and attendant environmental changes.

A World of Fields and Fences

William Cronon

One must not exaggerate the differences between English and Indian agricultures. The two in many ways resembled each other in the annual cycles by which they tracked the seasons of the year. Although English fields, unlike Indian ones, were cultivated by men as well as women and contained a variety of European grains and garden plants which were segregated into single-species plots, their most important crop was the same maize grown by Indians. Like the Indians, the English began working their fields when the land thawed and cleared of snow sometime in March. They too planted in late March, April, and May, and weeded and hilled their corn – if rather more carelessly than the Indians – a month or two later. Summer saw colonists as well as Indians turning to a wide range of different food sources as they became available: fish, shellfish, migratory birds, foraging mammals, and New England's many wild berries. August through October was the season of harvest when corn was gathered, husked, and stored, and other crops were made ready for the winter months. November and December saw the killing of large mammals – albeit of different species than the Indians had hunted – from the New England woods, the meat and hides of which were then processed for use in the months to come. The rest of the winter was devoted to tasks any southern New England Indian would readily have recognized: making and repairing tools and clothing, looking after firewood, occasionally fishing or hunting, and generally living off the stored produce of the preceding year. As the days lengthened and became warmer, the cycle began again: Europeans as well as Indians were inextricably bound to the wheel of the seasons.[1]

What made Indian and European subsistence cycles seem so different from one another had less to do with their use of plants than their use of animals. Domesticated grazing mammals – and the tool which they made possible, the plow – were arguably the single most distinguishing characteristic of European agricultural practices. The Indians' relationships to the deer, moose, and beaver they hunted were far different from those of the Europeans to the pigs, cows, sheep, and horses they owned. Where Indians had contented themselves with burning the woods and concentrating their hunting in the fall and winter months, the English sought a much more total and year-round control over their animals' lives. The effects of that control ramified through most aspects of New England's rural economy, and by the end of the colonial period were responsible for a host of changes in the New England landscape: the seemingly endless miles of fences, the silenced voices of vanished wolves, the system of country roads, and the new fields filled with clover, grass, and buttercups.[2]

Livestock were initially so rare in Plymouth and Massachusetts Bay that both William Bradford and John Winthrop noted in their journals the arrival of each new shipment of animals. Plymouth was over three years old before it obtained the "three heifers and a bull" which Bradford described as "the first beginning of any cattle of that kind in the land." Massachusetts Bay had a larger number of livestock almost from the start, but there were by no means enough to satisfy colonial demand for more animals. One colonist explained to an English patron that cattle were "wonderful dear here," and another argued that the most profitable investment a merchant could make in New England would be "to venture a sum of moneys to be turned into cattle." As a result, ship after ship arrived laden with upward of fifty animals in a load. By 1634, William Wood was able to define the wealth of the Massachusetts Bay Colony simply by referring to its livestock. "Can they be very poor," he asked, "where for four thousand souls there are fifteen hundred head of cattle, besides four thousand goats and swine innumerable?"[3]

The importance of these various animals to the English colonists can hardly be exaggerated. Hogs had the great virtues of reproducing themselves in large numbers and – like goats – of being willing to eat virtually anything. Moreover, in contrast to most other English animals, they were generally able to hold their own against wolves and bears, so that they could be turned out into the woods for months at a time to fend for themselves almost as wild animals. They required almost no attention until the fall slaughter, when – much as deer had been hunted by Indians – they could be recaptured, butchered, and used for winter meat supplies. Cattle needed somewhat more attention, but they too were allowed to graze freely during the warmer months of the year. In addition to the meat which they furnished, their hides were a principal source of leather, and milch cows provided dairy products – milk, cheese, and butter – that were unknown to the Indians. Perhaps most importantly, oxen were a source of animal power for plowing, clearing, and other farmwork. The use of such animals ultimately enabled English farmers to till much larger acreages than Indians had done, and so produce greater marketable surpluses. When oxen were attached to wheeled vehicles, those surpluses could be taken to market and sold. Horses were another, speedier source of power, but they were at first not as numerous as oxen because they were used less for farmwork than for personal transportation and military purposes. Finally, sheep, which required special attention because of their heavy wear on pastures and their vulnerability to predators, were the crucial supplier of the wool which furnished (with flax) most colonial clothing. Each of these animals in its own way represented a significant departure from Indian subsistence practices.[4]

What most distinguished a hog or a cow from the deer hunted by Indians was the fact that the colonists' animal was owned. Even when it grazed in a common herd or wandered loose in woodlands or open pastures, a fixed property right inhered in it. The notch in its ear or the brand on its flanks signified to the colonists that no one other than its owner had the right to kill or convey rights to it. Since Indian property systems granted rights of personal ownership to an animal only at the moment it was killed, there was naturally some initial conflict between the two legal systems concerning the new beasts brought by the English. In 1631, for instance, colonists complained to the sachem Chickatabot that one of his villagers had shot an English pig. After a month of investigation, a colonial court ordered that a fine of one beaver skin be paid for the animal. Although the fine was paid by Chickatabot rather than the actual offender – suggesting the confusion between diplomatic relations and legal claims which necessarily accompanied any dispute between Indian and English communities – the effect of his action was to acknowledge the English right to own animal flesh. Connecticut went so far as to declare that Indian villages adjacent to English ones would be held liable for "such trespasses as shalbe committed by any Indian" – whether a member of the village or not – "either by spoilinge or killinge of Cattle or Swine either with Trappes, dogges or arrowes." Despite such statutes, colonists continued for many years to complain that Indians were stealing their stock. As late as 1672, the Massachusetts Court was noting that Indians "doe frequently sell porke to the English, and there is ground to suspect that some of the Indians doe steale and sell the English mens swine." Nevertheless, most Indians appear to have recognized fairly quickly the colonists' legal right to own animals.[5]

Ironically, legal disputes over livestock arose as frequently when Indians *acknowledged* English property rights as when they denied them. One inevitable consequence of an English agricultural system that mixed the raising of crops with the keeping of animals was the necessity of separating the two – or else the animals would eat the crops. The obvious means for accomplishing this task was the fence, which to colonists represented perhaps the most visible symbol of an "improved" landscape: when John Winthrop had denied that Indians possessed anything more than a "natural" right to property in New England, he had done so by arguing that "they inclose noe Land" and had no "tame Cattle to improve the Land by." Fences and livestock were thus pivotal elements in the English rationale for taking Indian lands. But this rationale could cut both ways. If the absence of "improvements" – fences – meant to the colonists that Indians could claim to own only their cornfields, it also meant that those same cornfields lay open to the ravages of English grazing animals. Indians were quick to point out that, since colonists claimed ownership of the animals, colonists should be responsible for any and all damages caused by them.[6]

Much as they might have preferred not to, the English had to admit the justice of this argument, which after all followed unavoidably from English conceptions of animal property. Colonial courts repeatedly sought some mechanism for resolving the perennial conflict between English grazing animals and Indian planting fields. In 1634, for instance, the Massachusetts Court sent an investigator "to examine what hurt the swyne of Charlton hath done amongst the Indean barnes of corne," and declared that "accordingly the inhabitants of Charlton promiseth to give them satisfaction." Courts regularly ordered payment of compensation to Indians whose crops had been damaged by stock, but this was necessarily a temporary solution, administered after the fact, and one which did nothing to prevent further incidents. Colonists for this reason sometimes found themselves building fences on behalf of Indian villages: in 1653, the town of New Haven promised to contribute sixty days of labor toward the construction of fences around fields planted by neighboring Indians. Similar efforts were undertaken by colonists in Plymouth Colony when Indians at Rehoboth complained of the "great dammage" caused to their crops by English horses. The fences built across the Indians' peninsula of land at Rehoboth did not, of course, prevent animals from swimming around the barrier, and so Plymouth eventually – for a short while – granted Indians the right to impound English livestock and demand payment of damages and a fine before animals were returned to their owners.[7]

Such solutions had the virtue – in principle – of giving Indians at least theoretical legal standing as they made their complaints to colonial courts, but the laws also forced Indians to conduct their agriculture in a new way. Indians wishing compensation for damages to their crops were required to capture wandering animals and hold them until they were claimed by their owners; moreover, the value of damages was to be "judged and levied by some indifferent man of the English, chosen by the Indians treaspased." Indians had no right to collect damages by killing a trespassing animal: as always, the rare occasions when colonists offered Indians legal protection were governed wholly by English terms. The long-run effect was to force Indians to adopt fencing as a farming strategy. When New Haven built fences for its neighbors, it was only on the understanding that the Indians would agree "to doe no damag to the English Cattell, and to secure their owne corne from damage or to require none." Indians, in other words, were eventually assumed to be liable for the maintenance of their own fences; if these were in disrepair, no damages could be collected for the intrusions of wandering animals. When Indians near Massachusetts Bay "promised against the nexte yeare, and soe ever after, to fence their corne against all kinde of cattell," they were making what would prove to be an irrevocable commitment to a new way of life.[8]

Indians were not alone among New England's original inhabitants in encountering new boundaries and conflicts as a result of the colonists' grazing animals. Native predators – especially wolves – naturally regarded livestock as potential prey which differed from the deer on which they had previously fed only by being easier to kill. It is not unlikely that wolves became more numerous as a result of the new sources of food colonists had inadvertently made available to them – with unhappy consequences for English herds. Few things irritated colonists more than finding valuable animals killed by "such ravenous cruell creatures." The Massachusetts Court in 1645 complained of "the great losse and damage" suffered by the colony because wolves killed "so great nombers of our cattle," and expressed frustration that the predators had not yet been successfully destroyed. Such complaints persisted in newly settled areas throughout the colonial period.[9]

Colonists countered the wolf threat in a variety of ways. Most common was to offer a bounty – sometimes twopence, sometimes ten shillings, sometimes a few bushels of corn, sometimes (for Indian wolf hunters) an allotment of gunpowder and shot – to anyone who brought in the head of a wolf. All livestock owners in a town were legally bound to contribute to these bounties. Their effect, like that of the fur trade, was to establish a price for wild animals, to create a court-ordered market for them, and so encourage their destruction. Indians especially were led to hunt wolves by these means. But bounties had several drawbacks. They occasionally tempted hunters to bring in the heads of wolves which had been killed many miles from English settlements and so forced towns to pay for predators that had never been a threat to English stock. Since neither wolves nor Indians respected the jurisdictional boundaries of English towns, it was difficult to distinguish which town should pay which hunter for which wolf. There was, moreover, a recurring problem of people trying to sell the same wolf's head twice, so that towns were forced to cut off the dead animal's ears and bury them separately from the skull in order to prevent repeated bounty payments for it.[10]

Whenever the wolf problem seemed especially severe, colonists supplemented the customary bounties with more drastic measures. Special hunters were occasionally appointed to leave poisoned bait or to set guns with tripwires as traps for wolves; domesticated animals killed by the traps were to be paid for by the town as a whole. Individual wolves that were particularly rapacious might have an unusually high bounty placed on their heads: thus, New Haven in 1657 offered five pounds to anyone who could kill "one great black woolfe of a more than ordinarie bigness, which is like to be more feirce and bould than the rest, and so occasions the more hurt." A number of settlements fought wild dogs with domesticated ones. In 1648, Massachusetts ordered its towns to procure "so many hounds as they thinke meete...that so all meanes may be improved for the destruction of wolves." Towns regularly ordered collective hunts of areas that were suspected of harboring wolves. Indeed, wolves became a justification for draining and clearing swamps. The anonymous "Essay on the Ordering of Towns" in 1635 suggested that towns hold every inhabitant responsible for clearing the "harboring stuffe" from the "Swampes and such Rubbish waest grownds" that sheltered wolves. That this was not merely a theoretical proposal is shown by Scituate's decision in the mid-seventeenth century to divide its five hundred acres of swampland into parcels of two to five acres and to require every landowner to clear one of them. Entire ecological communities were thus threatened because they represented "an annoyance and prejudice to the town...both by miring of cattle and sheltering of wolves and vermin." Whether the assault was conducted with bounties, hunting dogs, or the removal of the animals' habitats, wolves suffered much the same fate as the rest of New England's mammals. Although they were still found in northern New England at the end of the colonial period, Dwight reported that they were gone from the south. Because, unlike Indians, wolves were incapable of distinguishing an owned animal from a wild one, the drawing of new property boundaries on the New England landscape inevitably meant their death.[11]

Conflicts among Indians, wolves, and colonists over the possession and trespasses of grazing animals paralleled even more complicated conflicts among colonists themselves. Farmers accustomed to an English landscape hemmed in by hedges and by customs regulating the common grazing of herds found themselves forced to change their agricultural practices in unfenced New England. Whereas most livestock in England had been watched over by individual herders, labor was scarce enough in New England that only the most valuable animals – milch cows, sheep, and some horses and oxen – could generally be guarded in this way. Large numbers of swine and dry cattle in particular received less supervision than they would have gotten in England, and so presented a more or less constant threat to croplands. Fences could take the place of herders only where colonists built and maintained them, conditions that rarely applied in new settlements. Accordingly, towns and colonies alike were constantly shifting their regulations in an effort to control the relationship between domesticated animals and crops.

Cattle and horses, for instance, were valuable enough so that colonial laws usually held farmers responsible for protecting their crops from them rather than requiring that the animals be restrained. In 1633, the Plymouth Court ordered that no one should "set corne...without inclosure but at his perill." Massachusetts Bay tried in 1638 to spread the burden of this responsibility by requiring that "they that plant are to secure theire corne in the day time; but if the cattle do hurt corne in the night, the owners of the cattle shall make good the damages." But the new rule, not too surprisingly, proved impossible to enforce, and within two years the colony was again declaring that planters rather than animal owners must bear the responsibility for protecting crops. Unfenced property boundaries, in other words, did not give legal protection against trespass by cattle. According to the Massachusetts Court in 1642, "Every man must secure his corne and medowe against great cattell." If a property owner failed to do this, said the Court, and "if any damage bee done by such cattle, it shallbee borne by him through whose insufficient fence the cattle did enter."[12]

But this by no means solved all problems. Large animals were quite capable of destroying a sound fence if they put their minds to it, and so towns were eventually forced to appoint fence viewers, who regularly visited farms to "see that the fence be sett in good repaire, or else complaine of it." If a fence was declared sound by the fence viewers, its owner could collect damages from anyone whose animals broke into the field; if a fence was unsound, on the other hand, its owner not only was legally unprotected from damage by animals but might also be required to pay the costs borne by neighbors who repaired it. The competing claims of property in animals and property in lands were thus resolved in a way that in principle, seemed to reduce the absolute protection of the latter. In practice, however, cattle regulations had the opposite effect. Through the agency of the fence viewers and the formal litigation of the courts, towns took an increasing responsibility not only for enforcing the abstract boundaries between adjacent tracts of real estate but for guaranteeing that those boundaries were marked by the physical presence of fences. The fact that landed property received only conditional protection in law became a major impetus for fencing the countryside, and so redrawing the New England map.[13]

Not all English animals were equally protected by such fence laws. Swine were the weed creatures of New England, breeding so quickly that a sow might farrow twice in a year, with each litter containing four to twelve piglets. They so rapidly became a nuisance that, as early as 1633, the Massachusetts Court declared that "it shalbe lawfull for any man to kill any swine that comes into his corne"; the dead animal was to be returned to its owner only after payment had been made for damages to crops. The inadequacy of this solution is suggested by the proliferation of swine laws in the ensuing years. Colonists were glad to have swine reproducing and fattening themselves in forested areas distant from English settlements – where only Indians would have to deal with their depredations – but towns tried to restrain the animals whenever they wandered too near English fields. By 1635, Massachusetts had ordered towns to construct animal pounds to which untended swine could be taken whenever they were found within one mile of an English farm. A year later, the Court went so far as to declare an open season on any stray swine: unless pigs were restrained by fence, line, or pigkeeper, it was lawful "for any man to take them, either alive or dead, as hee may." Anyone so doing got one half the value of the captured animal, while the Commonwealth of Massachusetts claimed the other; the owner got nothing. Ownership rights to swine were thus much more circumscribed than similar rights to cattle. The law produced so much protest from pig-keeping colonists that it was repealed two years later, but the battle of the swine nevertheless continued for many years. Complaints against pigs were a near constant feature of colony and town court proceedings, where the animals were sometimes portrayed almost as a malevolent force laying siege to defenseless settlements. The Massachusetts Court in 1658, for instance, reported that "many children are exposed to great daingers of losse of life or limbe through the ravenousnese of swyne, and elder persons to no smale inconveniencies." To modern ears, such statements perhaps seem a little comic, but that reaction is surely one of ignorance: swine could indeed be vicious creatures, and no animal caused more annoyances or disputes among colonists.[14]

Ultimately, swine were relegated either to farmyard sties, where they could be fed corn, alewives, and garbage, or to relatively isolated areas, where they could feed as they wished and do little harm. Favorite swine-raising locations were coastal peninsulas and offshore islands, where the animals were free to do their worst without interfering with English crops. In the late 1630s, both Roger Williams and John Winthrop were moving swine onto islands in Narragansett Bay, and colonists elsewhere did likewise. Along the coast, the animals wreaked havoc with oyster banks and other Indian shelfish-gathering sites, but caused little trouble to the English. Roger Williams described how "the English swine dig and root these Clams wheresoever they come, and watch the low water (as the Indian women do)." In one important sense, then, English pigs came into direct competition with Indians for food: according to Williams, "Of all English Cattell, the Swine (as also because of their filthy dispositions) are most hateful to all Natives, and they call them filthy cut throats." Pigs thus became both the agents and the emblems for a European colonialism that was systematically reorganizing Indian ecological relationships.[15]

In the vicinity of English settlements, regulations were eventually passed requiring that hogs be yoked so that they would be unable to squeeze through fences, and ringed through the nose so that they would be prevented from rooting out growing plants. But the chief goal of swine regulations was to keep uncontrolled pigs away from settlements. At a heated New Haven town meeting in 1650, farmers declared that, if swine were allowed to forage freely, "they would plant no corne, for it would be eaten up." The compromise solution was an order that no pigs should run loose unless driven at least eight miles from town center. Other communities passed similar regulations. And yet driving swine to the edges of town was obviously a temporary solution that lasted only so long as a town had edges beyond which were unenclosed common lands where pigs could run. Moreover, this "solution" tended to provoke conflict *between* towns when swine crossed town boundaries to descend on other settlements. Massachusetts Bay in 1637 pointed to the long-term solution of this problem by disclaiming any direct responsibility for the regulation of swine and delegating that burden to individual towns. "If any damage bee done by any swine," it said, "the whole towne shalbee lyable to the parties action to make full satisfaction." By making the control of swine a community responsibility, the Court redefined the property boundaries that applied to this particular animal so as to ensure its proper regulation. As the landscape gradually became peopled with settlements, the effect of legal liabilities was increasingly to restrain the movements of wandering hogs, until finally the beasts were more or less entirely confined to fenced farmyards.[16]

What became true of swine also became true of horses, sheep, and cattle: each was allocated its separate section of a settlement's lands. The interactions among domesticated grazing animals, demographic expansion, and English property systems had the effect not only of bounding the land with relatively permanent fences but of segregating the uses to which that land was put. Even the earliest colonial towns had divided their territories according to intended function, and colonists had been granted land accordingly. Fences thus marked off, not only the map of a settlement's property rights, but its economic activities and ecological relationships as well. At the center of a family's holdings was its house lot, around which a host of activities revolved, most of them controlled by women: food processing, cloth and tool making, poultry keeping, vegetable and herb gardening, and domestic living generally. Nearby were the outbuildings where animals spent their winters and some of their summer nights, as well as the various lots in which sheep, horses, milch cows, and pigs could be fed when not free to graze. In order for such animals to survive the winter, hay had to be cut in mid- to late summer, dried, and rationed out to them from November through early spring. This necessitated reserving large tracts of land for mowing, an activity which generally took place along the banks of streams, in salt marshes, and anywhere else that grass could be found. Aside from grain fields, all other lands were committed to grazing, including the upland woodlots where families cut their fuel and lumber. The key functional boundary in an English settlement was always the one between pasture and nonpasture: it was because the barrier between these two had to be so rigid that colonial towns presented such a different appearance from that of earlier Indian villages.[17]

English colonists reproduced these broad categories of land use wherever and however they established farms. Early land divisions had been done communally, each town deciding what agricultural activity would take place in different parts of its territory. Later divisions were generally made through the abstract mechanism of land speculation and tended to ignore both the ecological characteristics of a given tract of land and its intended agricultural use in order to facilitate the buying and selling that brought profits to speculators. This marked an important new way of perceiving the New England landscape, one that turned land itself into a commodity, but from the point of view of ecological practices, it merely transferred land-use decisions from the town to the individual landowner. Every farm family had to have its garden, its cornfields, its meadows, and its pastures, no matter who decided where they would be located and how they would be regulated. In so dividing their lands, colonists began to create the new ecological mosaic that would gradually transform New England ecosystems.[18]

Livestock not only defined many of the boundaries colonists drew but provided one of the chief reasons for extending those boundaries onto new lands. Indian villages had depended for much of their meat and clothing on wild foraging mammals such as deer and moose, animals whose populations were much less concentrated than their domesticated successors. Because there had been fewer of them in a given amount of territory, they had required less food and had had a smaller ecological effect on the land that fed them. The livestock of the colonists, on the other hand, required more land than all other agricultural activities put together. In a typical town, the land allocated to them was from two to ten times greater than that used for tillage. As their numbers increased – something that happened quite quickly – the animals came to exert pressure even on these large amounts of land.[19]

Before examining the ecological relationships of domesticated animals, it is well to remember their economic relationships. Livestock very early came to play a role in the New England economy comparable to that of fish and lumber: they proved to be a most reliable commodity. By 1660, Samuel Maverick, who had been one of the earliest English settlers in Massachusetts Bay, could point to increased numbers of grazing animals as one of the most significant changes in New England towns since his arrival. "In the yeare 1626 or thereabouts," he said,

there was not a Neat Beast Horse or sheepe in the Countrey and a very few
Goats or hoggs, and now it is a wonder to see the great herds of Catle
belonging to every Towne.... The brave Flocks of sheepe, The great
number of Horses besides those many sent to Barbados and the other
Carribe Islands, And withall to consider how many thousand Neate Beasts
and Hoggs are yearly killed, and soe have been for many yeares past for
Provision in the Countrey and sent abroad to supply Newfoundland,
Barbados, Jamaica, and other places, As also to victuall in whole or in
part most shipes which comes here.

Maverick viewed New England with a merchant's eye, and regarded its
livestock as one of its most profitable productions.[20]

Whether sold fresh to urban markets or salted for shipment to Caribbean sugar plantations, grazing animals were one of the easiest ways for a
colonist to obtain hard cash with a minimum of labor. October and
November saw many colonial farmers make an annual pilgrimage to
coastal cities such as Boston, New Haven, and Providence, where fatted
animals could be sold or exchanged for manufactured goods. This
economic profitability contributed to the ecological consequences of
livestock raising. Besides intensifying pressure on grazing lands and
inviting more territorial expansion, it necessitated the construction of
roads connecting interior towns with urban centers. No small number of
trees were destroyed by the construction of these roads – they were
typically between 99 and 165 feet wide – but their seemingly excessive
size was more than justified since they facilitated moving large herds to
market. Roads were the link binding city and countryside into a single
economy. During the course of the colonial period, the opportunities
represented by that linkage encouraged farmers to orient more and more
of their production toward commercial ends. As one eighteenth-century
visitor to New England observed:

> Boston and the shipping are a market which enriches the country interest
> far more than the [trade in exports,] which, for so numerous a people, is
> very inconsiderable. By means of this internal circulation, the farmers and
> country gentlemen are enabled very amply to purchase whatever they want
> from abroad.

Almost from the start, port cities exemplified the different ways in which
Indians and colonists organized their economies, and no commodity
moved more readily from farm to city than did animals.[21]

Livestock production was tied to the markets of the ports by a web
of relationships that extended well beyond the fall drives. Whether
generating a surplus by their own reproduction, by their labor in working
crops, or by their contribution to lowering transportation costs in

bringing themselves and other goods to market, grazing animals were one of the linchpins that made commercial agriculture possible in New England. Without them, colonial surpluses would probably have been produced on much the same scale as Indian ones; with them, colonial agriculture had a more or less constant tendency to expand and to put increasing pressure on its surrounding environment. As the ecologist E. Fraser Darling has noted, "Pastoralism for commercial ends . . . cannot continue without progressive deterioration of the habitat."[22]

Signs that such deterioration was taking place, or at least that the number of animals was outrunning the available food supply, became apparent within four years of Boston's founding. In 1634, the inhabitants of Newtown (Cambridge) complained of "want of accommodation for their cattle," and asked the Massachusetts Court for permission to migrate to Connecticut. When colonists in Watertown and Roxbury put forward similar petitions a year later, John Winthrop explained that "the occasion of their desire to remove was, for that all towns in the bay began to be much straitened by their own nearness to one another, and their cattle being so much increased." Regions which had once supported Indian populations considerably larger than those of the early English settlements came to seem inadequate less because of *human* crowding than because of *animal* crowding. Competition for grazing lands – which were initially scarcer than they later became – acted as a centrifugal force that drove towns and settlements apart. In 1631, Bradford lamented the changes wrought by livestock in Plymouth Colony: "no man," he wrote,

> now thought he could live except he had cattle and a great deal of ground to keep them, all striving to increase their stocks. By which means they were scattered all over the Bay quickly and the town in which they lived compactly till now was left very thin and in a short time almost desolate.

Unlike tillage, whose land requirements were far lower, pastoralism became a significant force for expansion. Further, if Bradford is to be believed, it also contributed to the famous declension which helped drive New England towns from their original vision of compact settlements, communal orders, and cities upon hilltops.[23]

One reason that scarcity of grazing land so quickly became a problem in Massachusetts Bay had to do with the nature of New England's native grasses, which included broomstraw, wild rye, and the *Spartinas* of the salt marshes. Because most of the first English settlements were made on Indian village sites, the lands of which had been regularly cultivated and burned, there were extensive areas around them where only grass and shrubs grew. Animals could be turned loose to graze on these with virtually no preparation of the land, but often seemed to fare poorly on their new diet. Many colonists commented on the relative inferiority of New England hay in comparison with that of England, and one wrote in disgust that "it is so devoid of nutritive vertue, that our beasts grow lousy with feeding upon it, and are much out of heart and liking." More serious than the *quality* of the native grasses, however, was their inadequate *quantity*: domesticated animal populations quickly ran out of pasture, so that their owners had to clear land to create more.[24]

Curiously, many colonists claimed that the native grasses, although initially very "rank" and "coarse," seemed to improve the more they were mowed or eaten. "In such places where the cattle use to graze," wrote William Wood, "the ground is much improved in the woods, growing more grassy and less weedy." What in fact was happening was that a number of native grasses and field plants were slowly being destroyed and replaced by European species. Annual grasses were quickly killed off if grazed too closely, and the delicate crowns of some perennials fared little better. Not having evolved in a pastoral setting, they were ill prepared for their new use. That was why European grasses, which *had* adapted themselves to the harsh requirements of pastoralism, began to take over wherever cattle grazed. "English grasses," such as bluegrass and white clover, spread rapidly in newly settled areas. Initially carried to the New World in shipboard fodder, and in the dung of the animals which ate them, these European species were soon being systematically cultivated by colonists. By the 1640s, a regular market in grass seed existed in the Narragansett country, and within one or two generations, the plants had become so common that they were regarded as native.[25]

Grazing animals were among the chief agents in transmitting to America one of the central – albeit unapplauded – characters of European agriculture: the weed. Because Indians kept no cattle, and because their mixed-crop, hoe agriculture provided a relatively dense ground cover, they failed to develop as many of the plant species which in the Old World followed wherever human beings disturbed the soil. Like the "English grasses," weeds had evolved any of a number of adaptations that allowed them to tolerate grazing and to move quickly onto cleared agricultural land: they were able to germinate under a wide variety of environmental conditions, they grew rapidly, they might continuously produce huge quantities of seeds designed for widespread dispersal, and they were often brittle so that when broken off by cattle or farmers they could readily regenerate themselves from their remaining fragments. A few indigenous species had enough of these characteristics that they too became more common as a result of European settlement. Probably the most prolific of these was ragweed, which underwent such a population explosion in the colonial period that pollen scientists today, when studying the sediments in pond and lake bottoms, use the plant as a means of dating the arrival of the Europeans.[26]

Most weeds, however, were European. John Josselyn in 1672 listed no fewer than twenty-two European species which had become common in the area around Massachusetts Bay "since the English planted and kept Cattle in New England." Among these were such perennial favorites as dandelions, chickweeds, bloodworts, mulleins, mallows, nightshades, and stinging nettles. Because it seemed to crop up wherever the English walked, planted, or grazed animals, the Indians called plantain "Englishman's Foot," a name that suggests their awareness of the biological invasion going on around them. Not only Indians were affected by this invasion, since colonial grain crops – and, worse, the seeds used to plant them – were difficult to keep separate from the weeds that grew in their midst. As early as 1652, settlers in New Haven Colony were debating whether something could be done "to prevent the spreding of sorrill in the corne feilds," but did so to no avail. Many of these European weeds – to say nothing of grains, vegetables, and orchard trees – would eventually be among the commonest plants of the American landscape, their populations sustained in all places by the habitats human beings and domesticated animals created for them.[27]

Although the invasion of livestock was sustained by the parallel invasion of edible plants, the two were rarely in perfect balance, at least in the eyes of colonists who for economic reasons sought to raise more animals. Livestock production expanded throughout New England in the eighteenth century and brought with it regular complaints about pasture shortages. By 1748, the Connecticut agricultural writer Jared Eliot was commenting that "the scarcity and high price of hay and corn is so obvious, that there are few or none Ignorant of it." The shortage of hay, he said, had been "gradually increasing upon us for sundry Years past," and was the direct result of livestock populations outgrowing available meadowlands. If pastures were inadequate, old and new settlements alike had to follow the process of forest clearing described in the preceding chapter, planting corn and rye before the unplowed soil was finally ready to be seeded with English grasses. During the eighteenth century, the range of grasses which were raised for moving was extended to include such species as timothy, red clover, lucerne (alfalfa), and fowl-meadow grass, all of which rapidly became common throughout the colonies.[28]

Where mowing was unnecessary and grazing among living trees was possible, settlers saved labor by simply burning the forest undergrowth – much as the Indians had once done – and turning loose their cattle. But because English livestock grazed more closely and were kept in denser concentrations than the animals for whom Indians had burned the woods, English pastoralism had the effect of gradually shifting the species composition of any forest used for pasture. In at least one ill-favored area, the inhabitants of neighboring towns burned so frequently and grazed so intensively that, according to Peter Whitney, the timber "was greatly injured, and the land became hard to subdue. Hurtleberry and whitebush sprung up, together with laurel, sweetfern and checker-berry, which nothing but the plough will destroy." In the long run, cattle tended to encourage the growth of woody, thorn-bearing plants which they could not eat, and which, once established, were very difficult to remove. Such plants had to be cleared regularly with a scythe or grub hoe if they were not to take over a pasture entirely. The only other way of dealing with them was to graze sheep heavily in areas which the bushes had taken over; the flocks sometimes succeeded in reclaiming land that had otherwise become useless.[29]

The tree species of the uplands were also affected by grazing, espe-cially when exhausted fields were allowed to revert to wooded pastures. Hemlocks, whose shallow root systems were very sensitive to fire, tended to disappear from all woods that were burned for pasture. Where they were protected from fire, on the other hand, grazing encouraged their growth by destroying the more edible hardwood species that would otherwise have competed with them, so that hemlocks then became the dominant species of north-facing slopes. When land was initially cleared, whether for crops or pasture, the removal of existing trees had the effect of releasing the dormant seeds of certain species that preferred full sunlight and open growing conditions. Pin cherry was one of these. Timothy Dwight told of a farmer in Vermont in whose fields "there customarily sprung up ... an immense multitude of cherry trees," even though the surrounding forest was composed entirely of beech, hemlock, and maple. Red cedar also often acted as a pioneer on cleared lands.[30]

Which species invaded which fields depended primarily upon whether or not grazing animals were allowed on the land. The ecological effects of pasturing and clearing on forest composition could become quite com-plex. In oak and birch forests that were cut for lumber and fuel, for instance, these two tree species were able to regenerate themselves by sprouting from their roots and stumps, and could be cut again in as little as fourteen years. Cyclical cutting of this kind – known as a coppice system – was common among colonial farmers, and strongly favored hardwood species, which could sprout, over conifers, which could not. Coppice cutting was a major reason that chestnuts, which were prolific sprouters, increased their relative share of New England forests following European settlement. But if sprout hardwood forests were used for pasture after being cut, the sprouts were destroyed by being grazed, and the less edible white pine often came up instead. Conversely, white pines – which could not sprout but compensated for this by producing enormous quantities of airborne seeds – failed to regenerate themselves *unless* pasturing took place, because of their need for full sunlight and their inability to compete with hardwood species. The same was true of red cedar. In southern New England, abandoned croplands were more often than not invaded by gray birch; abandoned pastures, on the other hand, were taken over by red cedar and white pine.[31]

Livestock not only helped shift the species composition of New England forests but made a major contribution to their long-term deterioration as well. If colonial lumberers made sure that woods were stripped of their largest and oldest trees, grazing animals made sure that those trees were rarely replaced. Benjamin Lincoln wrote with some emotion when he argued:

> We suffer exceedingly at this day by the ill judged policy of permitting the cattle to run at large in the woods, especially in the full settled towns. Those tracts reserved for building, timber, fence-stuff, and fuel, are constantly thinning, and many of them are ruined as wood land, there are so large a proportion of cattle turned out, compared with the plants which come up in the spring, and the shoots which appear around the stumps of trees fallen the year before.

To Lincoln, allowing animals to graze in the woods was to let trees be "wantonly destroyed," and he sought to show that doing so was actually "more expensive and injurious to the common interest, than if lands were ploughed, and grain sowed, on which they might feed."[32]

Lincoln's concern was well-founded. Wherever the English animals went, their feet trampled and tore the ground. Because large numbers of them were concentrated on relatively small tracts of land, their weight had the effect of compacting soil particles so as to harden the soil and reduce the amount of oxygen it contained. This in turn curtailed the root growth of higher plants, lowered their ability to absorb nutrients and water, and encouraged the formation of toxic chemical compounds. Soil compaction, in other words, created conditions that were less hospitable to plant life and eventually lowered the soil's carrying capacity for water. (One of the things that distinguished European clover and timothy grass from other plants was precisely their ability to live on severely compacted soils containing little oxygen.) Ironically, then, an additional effect of woodland grazing was to kill many of the plants on which livestock depended for food, so that animals ran out of browse before their grazing season was over. Their survival in these circumstances depended on the colonists' efforts to open new pastures, create additional hay meadows, or cultivate more grain crops. Pasture deterioration was thus an incentive for still more intensive colonial deforestation.[33]

But the greatest effect of domesticated animals on New England soils came in the one area from which they were systematically excluded during most seasons of the year: croplands. Precolonial Indian women had had only their hoes and their own hands to turn the soil; the colonists, on the other hand, could use their oxen and horses to pull plows, which stirred the soil much more deeply. Plowing destroyed all native plant species to create an entirely new habitat populated mainly by domesticated species, and so in some sense represented the most complete ecological transformation of a New England landscape. Animals made it possible for a single colonial family to farm much larger areas than their Indian predecessors had done. Moreover, colonial farmers, because of their fixed notions of property ownership, continued to plow the same fields years after Indians would have abandoned them. The intimate connection between grazing animals, plows, and fixed property lay at the heart of European agriculture, with far-reaching ecological consequences.[34]

Whatever the causes that reduced the ground cover of New England soils, the long-term effect was to put those soils in jeopardy. The removal of the forest, the increase in destructive floods, the soil compaction and close-cropping wrought by grazing animals, plowing – all served to increase erosion. The naturalist John Bartram wrote to Jared Eliot in the mid-eighteenth century and spoke of a time

> above 20 years past when the woods was not pastured and full of high weeds and the ground light[,] then the rain sunk much more into the earth and did not wash and tear up the surface (as now). The rivers and brooks in floods would be black with mud but now the rain runs most of it off on the surface[,] is colected into the hollows which it wears to the sand and clay which it bears away with the swift current down to brooks and rivers whose banks it overflows.

Though he wrote of the mid-Atlantic colonies rather than New England, Bartram described processes which were unquestionably going on in both regions. Within a year or two after a forest was cleared, its soil began to lose the nutrients that had originally sustained (and been sustained by) its ecological community. Particles of inorganic matter in its runoff water increased perhaps five- or sixfold, and dissolved minerals also washed away more quickly. In pastures and meadows, both effects were aggravated by the presence of grazing animals; in planting fields, deeply stirred soils came into greater contact with both air and water, thus decomposing organic material and losing dissolved nutrients more rapidly. The result was to reduce still further the ability of soils to sustain plant life.[35]

Notes

1 Manasseh Minor, *The Diary of Manasseb Minor* (1915); Thomas Tusser, *Five Hundred Points of Good Husbandrie* (London, 1580); *The Husbandman's Guide*, 2nd ed. (New York, 1712), pp. 3–15; Edwin Stanley Welles, *The Beginnings of Fruit Culture in Connecticut* (Hartford, CT, 1936), pp. 30–2; Darrett B. Rutman, *Husbandmen of Plymouth* (Boston, 1967), pp. 50–2.

2 Conrad M. Arensberg, "The Old World Peoples," *Anthropological Quarterly*, 36 (1963), pp. 75–99.

3 Compare John Winthrop, *Winthrop's Journal*, James Kendall Hosmer, ed. (New York, 1908); and William Bradford, *Of Plymouth Plantation*, Samuel Eliot Morison, ed. (New York, 1952). (The quotation is on p. 141.) Other quotations are in Everett Emerson, ed., *Letters from New England* (Amherst, MA, 1976), pp. 110, 225; and William Wood, *New England's Prospect* (1634), Alden T. Vaughan, ed. (Amherst, MA, 1977), p. 69. Plymouth had other livestock before it first obtained cattle: in 1623, it possessed six goats, fifty swine, and a number of hens. Emmanuel Altham to Sir Edward Altham, September 1623, in *Three Visitors to Early Plymouth*, Sidney V. James, Jr., ed. (Plimoth Plantation, 1963), p. 24.

4 Carl Bridenbaugh, *Fat Mutton and Liberty of Conscience* (Providence, 1974), pp. 27–60; Percy Wells Bidwell and John I. Falconer, *History of Agriculture in the Northern United States* (Washington, D.C., 1925), pp. 18–32; Howard S. Russell, *A Long, Deep Farrow: Three Centuries of Farming in New England* (Hanover, NH, 1976), pp. 30–8, 151–69.

5 Winthrop, *Journal*, I, p. 64; J. Hammond Trumbull, ed., *The Public Records of the Colony of Connecticut* (Hartford, 1850), p. 19; Nathaniel B. Shurtleff, ed., *Records of the Governor and Company of the Massachusetts Bay in New England* (Boston, 1853), IV, Part 2, pp. 512–13.

6 John Winthrop, "Reasons to Be Considered," *Winthrop Papers*, Massachusetts Historical Society (1931), II, p. 141.

7 Shurtleff, *Massachasetts Records*, I, pp. 121, 133; Franklin Bowditch Dexter, ed., *New Haven Town Records, I, 1649–1662* (New Haven, CT, 1917), p. 193; Nathaniel B. Shurtleff, ed., *Records of the Colony of New Plymouth in New England* (Boston, 1855), III, pp. 21, 89, 106, 119, 132, 192; James P. Ronda, "Red and White at the Bench: Indians and the Law in Plymouth Colony, 1620–1691," *Essex Institute Historical Collections*, 110 (1974), pp. 208–9.

8 Shurtleff, *Plymouth Records*, III, p. 192; Dexter, *New Haven Records*, I, p. 193; Shurtleff, *Massachusetts Records*, I, p. 99.

9 I am indebted to Edmund Morgan for the suggestion that colonial wolf populations probably rose after the arrival of English live stock; the anonymous author of the "Essay on the Ordering of Towns" (in the *Winthrop Papers*, III, p. 185) corroborates this, but for different reasons, with the claim that "I have often hearde (by seemeing credible men) that Wolves are much more increased since our Nation came then when the Indians possessed the same, and a Reason rendred, that they were dilligent in destroying the Yonge." One

can doubt the "Reason rendred" by wondering whether a people who kept no livestock would have troubled themselves so much over predators who lived off the deer herds, but perhaps they did. Colonial wolf populations are impossible to estimate accurately. One gets the feeling that, for colonists, wolves were either "very common, and very noxious," or were nonexistent. There does not appear to have been any middle ground between these two conditions. Colonists, like many who keep cattle today, surely overestimated the damage done by wolves, and probably attributed to wolves livestock deaths which had nothing to do with the predators. On early responses to wolves, see Shurtleff, *Massachusetts Records*, III, pp. 10, 17; Winthrop, *Journal*, I, pp. 53, 67, III; Wood, *Prospect*, pp. 45–6.

10   On wolf bounties, see Shurtleff, *Massachusetts Records*, I, pp. 81, 102, 156, 218, 252, 304, 319; II, pp. 84–5, 103, 252; III, pp. 10, 17, 134, 319; IV, Part 2, pp. 2, 42; V, p. 453; Shurtleff, *Plymouth Records*, I, pp. 22, 31; III, pp. 50–1, 85–6; *Town Records of Salem* (Salem, 1868), pp. 107, 127. Most town records contain a number of entries similar to the ones I cite here.

11   John Josselyn, *New-England's Rarities Discovered* (1672), Edward Tuckerman, ed., in *Transactions and Collections of the American Antiquarian Society*, 4 (1860), pp. 150–1; Dexter, *New Haven Records*, pp. 73–4, 92, 309; Shurtleff, *Massachusetts Records*, II, pp. 252–3; M. Minor, *Diary*, pp. 32, 48, 53, 81, 98, 105, 113, 119, 120; Jeremy Belknap, *History of New Hampshire* (Dover, NH, 1812), III, pp. 108–9; Benjamin Trumbull, *A Complete History of Connecticut* (Hartford, CT, 1797), p. 26; Herbert B. Adams, "Village Communities of Cape Anne and Salem," *Johns Hopkins University Studies in Historical and Political Science*, ser. I, 9–10 (1883), p. 58; "Ordering of Towns," *Winthrop Papers*, III, p. 184; *Scituate Records*, I, p. 48, as quoted by John Robert Stilgoe, *Patterns on the Land: The Making of a Colonial Landscape, 1633–1800*, Ph.D. Thesis, Harvard University, 1976, p. 159; Timothy Dwight, *Travels in New England and New York* (1821), Barbara Miller Solomon, ed. (Cambridge, MA, 1969), I, p. 33.

12   Shurtleff, *Plymouth Records*, I, p. 6; Shurtleff, *Massachusetts Records*, I, pp. 215, 221, 272; II, pp. 14–15.

13   Charles J. Hoadly, ed., *Records of the Colony of New Haven* (Hartford, 1858), p. 579; Dexter, *New Haven Records*, pp. 65, 132, 234, 281; Shurtleff, *Massachusetts Records*, I, p. 333; III, p. 319; David Thomas Konig, "Community Custom and the Common Law: Social Change and the Development of Land Law in Seventeenth-Century Massachusetts," *American Journal of Legal History*, 18(1974), pp. 137–77. For a fine detailed discussion of how earlier English field practices fed into these colonial systems, see David Grayson Allen, *In English Ways* (Chapel Hill, 1981).

14   Rutman, *Husbandmen of Plymouth*, p. 49; Shurtleff, *Massachusetts Records*, I, pp. 106, 150, 157, 182, 219–20, 222, 238–9, 255, 265, 270; IV, Part 2, p. 322. It is quite likely that disputes over swine expressed a disguised class conflict. Because pigs were so cheap and easy to raise, they were favored by poorer colonists as a source of meat; wealthier colonists, who could afford to keep larger numbers of cattle, had less need of them. The evidence cited

above in Shurtleff suggests that a number of colonists were decidedly un-happy about the swine laws, and spoke against them so vociferously that the Massachusetts Court felt compelled to mete out stiff fines. No study of this issue has been done for colonial New England, but Steven Hahn's article on the nineteenth-century South is suggestive: "Hunting, Fishing, and Foraging: Common Rights and Class Relations in the Postbellum South," *Radical History Review*, 26 (October 1982), pp. 37–64.

15 Shurtleff, *Massachusetts Records*, I, pp. 188–9; Roger Williams, *The Letters of Roger Williams*, John Russell Bartlett, ed., *Publications of the Narragansett Club*, 6 (1874), pp. 71, 78, 104; "Leift Lion Gardener His Relation of the Pequot Warres," *Massachusetts Historical Society Collections*, 3rd ser., 3 (1833), p. 154; Roger Williams, *A Key into the Language of America* (1643), John J. Teunissen and Evelyn J. Hinz, eds. (Detroit, 1973), p. 182; Wood, *Prospect*, p. 57, Thomas Morton, *New English Canaan* (1637), Charles F. Adams, ed., *Pubs. of the Prince Society*, XIV (Boston, 1883), p. 227.

16 *Salem Records*, pp. 130, 137, 143, 152; Dexter, *New Haven Records*, pp. 19–20; Shurtleff, *Massachusetts Records*, I, p. 215.

17 On these land divisions, see the general list of town studies and histories of New England agriculture in William Cronon, *Changes in the Land: Indians, Colonists and the Ecology of New England* (New York: Hill and Wang, 1983), pp. 228–30.

18 On speculation, see ibid., pp. 234–5.

19 George Perkins Marsh, *Man and Nature* (1864), David Lowenthal, ed. (Cambridge, MA, 1965), p. 74; Allen, *In English Ways*, p. 231; Hugh M. Raup and Reynold E. Carlson, "The History of Land Use in the Harvard Forest," *Harvard Forest Bulletin*, 20 (1941), p. 25.

20 Richard Bushman, *From Puritan to Yankee* (Cambridge, MA, 1967), pp. 31–2; Bridenbaugh, *Fat Mutton*, pp. 27–60; Bidwell and Falconer, *Northern Agriculture*, pp. 26–32, 40–8; Darrett B. Rutman, "Governor Winthrop's Garden Crop: The Significance of Agriculture in the Early Commerce of Massachusetts Bay," *William and Mary Quarterly*, 3rd ser., 20 (1963), pp. 396–415; Samuel Maverick, "A Briefe Discription of New England," *Massachusetts Historical Society Proceedings*, 2nd ser., I (1884–85), p. 247; Joseph Hadfield, *An Englishman in America*, 1785, Douglas S. Robertson, ed. (Toronto, 1933), p. 198.

21 M. Minor, *Diary*, pp. 31, 42, 49, 50, 56, 57, 74, etc.; Carl Bridenbaugh, "Yankee Use and Abuse of the Forest in the Building of New England, 1620–1666," *Massachusetts Historical Society Proceedings*, 89 (1977), pp. 34–5; *American Husbandry* (1775), Harry J. Carman, ed. (New York, 1939), pp. 44–5; Gary B. Nash, *The Urban Crucible* (Cambridge, MA, 1979).

22 E. Fraser Darling, "Man's Ecological Dominance through Domesticated Animals on Wild Lands," in William L. Thomas, ed., *Man's Role in Changing the Face of the Earth* (Chicago, 1956), p. 781.

23 Winthrop, *Journal*, I, pp. 132, 151; Emerson, *Letters*, p. 154; Bradford, *Plymouth Plantation*, p. 253.

24   Thomas Hutchinson, *The History of the Colony and Province of Massachusetts-Bay* (1765), Lawrence Shaw Mayo, ed. (Cambridge, MA, 1936), I, p. 405; John Smith, "Advertisements for the Unexperienced Planters of New-England" (1631), *Massachusetts Historical Society Collections*, 3rd ser., 3 (1833), p. 37; Emerson, *Letters*, pp. 214, 227.

25   Wood, *Prospect*, p. 34; James, *Plymouth Visitors*, p. 67; Everett Edwards, "The Settlement of Grasslands," in *USDA Yearbook, Grass* (1948), p. 17; Bidwell and Falconer, *Northern Agriculture*, p. 20; Lyman Carrier, *The Beginnings of Agriculture in America* (New York, 1923), pp. 239–43; Bridenbaugh, *Fat Mutton*, pp. 31–3; Roger Williams, *Letters*, John R. Bartlett, ed. (Providence, 1874), pp. 146–7; Robert R. Walcott, "Husbandry in Colonial New England," *New England Quarterly*, 9 (1936), pp. 239–40. At least one New England town – New Haven – made an effort to protect its English grasses during the early years of settlement. The town voted in 1654: "All men were desired to take notice that if any cut up any English grass which growes about the markit place, the streets, or other commons, to plant in their owne ground, they must expect to receive due punishment for the same." Dexter, *New Haven Records*, p. 204.

26   Alfred J. Crosby, "Ecological Imperialism: The Overseas Migration of Western Europeans as a Biological Phenomenon," *Texas Quarterly*, 30 (1978), pp. 18–19; Hutchinson, *History of Massachusetts-Bay*, I, p. 403; Herbert G. Baker, "The Evolution of Weeds," *Annual Review of Ecology and Systematics*, 5 (1974), p. 4; Margaret B. Davis, "Phyto-geography and Palynology of Northeastern United States," in H. E. Wright, Jr., and David G. Grey, eds., *The Quaternary of the United States* (Princeton, NJ, 1965), p. 396; Richard B. Brugam, "Pollen Indicators of Land-Use Change in Southern Connecticut," *Quaternary Research*, 9 (1978), pp. 349–62.

27   John Josselyn, *New-England's Rarities Discovered* (1672), Edward Tuckerman, ed., *Transactions and Collections of the American Antiquarian Society*, 4 (1860), pp. 216–19; Asa Gray, "The Flora of Boston and Its Vicinity, and the Changes It Has Undergone," in Justin Winsor, ed., *The Memorial History of Boston* (Boston, 1880), pp. 17–22; Gray, "The Pertinacity and Predominance of Weeds," *American Journal of Science and Arts*, 3rd ser., 18: 105 (September 1879), pp. 161–7; Dexter, *New Haven Records*, p. 132. I have relied throughout on Merritt L. Fernald, *Gray's Manual of Botany*, 8th ed. (New York, 1950), to determine whether a plant is of European or American origins. An interesting popular account of plant migrations is Claire S. Houghton, *Green Immigrants: The Plants That Transformed America* (New York, 1978).

28   Jared Eliot, *Essays upon Field Husbandry in New England* (1748–62), Harry J. Carman and Rexford G. Tugwell, eds. (New York, 1934), pp. 27–9, 61–6; Carrier, *Beginnings of Agriculture*, pp. 239–42; Bidwell and Falconer, *Northern Agriculture*, pp. 103–5; Samuel Deane, *The New-England Farmer* (Worcester, MA, 1790), pp. 28–9, 285–6.

29   Peter Whitney, *History of the County of Worcester* (Worcester, MA, 1793), p. 203; Harold J. Lutz, "Trends and Silvicultural Significance of Upland Forest Successions in Southern New England," *Yale School of Forestry*

Bulletin, 22 (1928), p. 22; Stanley W. Bromley, "The Original Forest Types of Southern New England," *Ecological Monographs*, 5 (1935), pp. 79–80; Eliot, *Essays*, p. 19.

30 Lutz, "Trends of Upland Forest Succession," p. 22; H. I. Winer, *History of the Great Mountain Forest, Litchfield County, Connecticut*, Ph.D. Thesis, Yale University, 1955, p. 255; Bromley, "Original Forest Types," p. 80; Timothy Dwight, *Travels in New England and New York* (1821), Barbara M. Solomon, ed. (Cambridge, MA, 1969), II, pp. 309–10; P. L. Marks, "The Role of Pin Cherry *(Prunas pensylvanica* L.) in the Maintenance of Stability in Northern Hardwood Ecosystems," *Ecological Monographs*, 44 (1974), pp. 73–88.

31 Dwight, *Travels*, I, p. 75; Bromley, "Original Forest Types," pp. 75, 80; E. Lucy Braun, *Deciduous Forests of Eastern North America* (New York, 1950), p. 253; G. E. Nichols, "The Vegetation of Connecticut, II, Virgin Forests," *Torreya*, 13 (1913), pp. 199–215; Lutz, "Trends of Upland Forest Succession," p. 15.

32 B[enjamin] Lincoln, "Remarks on the Cultivation of the Oak," *Massachusetts Historical Society Collections*, 2nd ser., I (1814), p. 193.

33 E. A. Johnson, "Effects of Farm Woodland Grazing on Watershed Values in the Southern Appalachian Mountains," *Journal of Forestry*, 50 (1952), pp. 109–13; Harry O. Buckman and Nyle C. Brady, *The Nature and Property of Soils*, 7th ed. (New York, 1969), pp. 249–53; Eugene P. Odum, *Fundamentals of Ecology*, 3rd ed. (Philadelphia, 1971), pp. 418–19.

34 Gottfried Pfeifer, "The Quality of Peasant Living in Central Europe," in Thomas, *Man's Role in Changing the Earth*, pp. 249–53.

35 Eliot, *Essays*, p. 204; Angus McDonald, *Early American Soil Conservationists* (1941), *USDA Miscellaneous Publications*, #449 (Washington, D.C., 1971), pp. 3–19; F. H. Bormann, *et al.*, "The Export of Nutrients and Recovery of Stable Conditions Following Deforestation at Hubbard Brook," *Ecological Monographs*, 44 (1974), pp. 255–77. The literature about Hubbard Brook, on which much of the argument of this paragraph relies, is quite large; see Cronon, *Changes in the Land*, pp. 212–13.

Documents

Robert Cushman, "Reasons and Considerations Touching the Lawfulness of Removing out of England into the Parts of America" (1622)

Reprinted from, *Remarkable Providences 1600–1760*, ed. with Introduction and notes by John Demos (New York: Braziller, 1972).

Since prior occupancy gave Indians a title to North America in the minds of many European thinkers, various colonial writers tried to rationalize such rights away.

In this justification for English claims to Indian land, note the ways in which Robert Cushman, a colonist, regards Indians as nomadic wanderers who do not farm the land or "order" it. In fact, as William Cronon pointed out, New England Indian villages were often farming communities. Why did colonists like Cushman refuse to recognize them as such? Is there a connection between these early colonial understandings of Indians as rootless wanderers and popular perceptions of all Indians as nomadic hunters? What other reasons does Cushman give for seizing Indian land? Is there a connection between Cushman's religious enthusiasm and his understanding of Indians and the New England countryside?

* * *

Letting pass the ancient discoveries, contracts, and agreements which our Englishmen have long since made in those parts, together with the acknowledgment of the histories and chronicles of other nations who profess [that] the land of America from the Cape de Florida unto the Bay Canado (which is, south and north, three hundred leagues and upwards; and east and west, further than yet hath been discovered) is proper to the king of England, yet letting that pass – lest I be thought to meddle further than it concerns me or further than I have discerning – I will mention such things as are within my reach, knowledge, sight, and practice, since I have travailed in these affairs.

And first, seeing we daily pray for the conversion of the heathens, we must consider whether there be not some ordinary means and course for us to take to convert them, or whether prayer for them be only referred to God's extraordinary work from heaven. Now it seemeth unto me that we ought also to endeavor and use the means to convert them; or they [ought to] come to us. To us they cannot come, [for] our land is full; to them we may go, [since] their land is empty.

This then is a sufficient reason to prove our going thither to live lawful: their land is spacious and void, and they are few and do but run over the grass, as do also the foxes and wild beasts. They are not industrious, neither have [they] art, science, skill or faculty to use either the land or the commodities of it; but all spoils, rots, and is marred for want of manuring, gathering, ordering, etc. As the ancient patriachs therefore removed from straiter places into more roomy [ones], where the land lay idle and wasted and none used it, though there dwelt inhabitants by them (as in Gen. 13: 6, 11, 12, and 34: 21, and 41: 20), so is it lawful now to take a land which none useth and make use of it.

And as it is common land or unused and undressed country, so we have it by common consent, composition, and agreement, which agreement is double: First, the imperial governor, Massasoit, whose circuits in likelihood are larger than England and Scotland, hath acknowledged the king, majesty of England, to be his master and commander, and that once in my hearing, yea, and in writing under his hand to Captain Standish – both he and many other kings which are under him, [such] as Pamet, Nauset, Cummaquid, Narrowbiggonset, Namaschet, etc., with diverse others that dwell about the bays of Patuxet and Massachusetts. Neither hath this been accomplished by threats and blows or [by] shaking of sword and sound of trumpet; for as our faculty that way is small and our strength less, so our warring with them is after another manner, namely, by friendly usage, love, peace, honest and just carriages, good counsel, etc. – that so we and they may not only live in peace in that land, and they yield subjection to an earthly prince, but [also] that as voluntaries they may be persuaded at length to embrace the prince of peace, Christ Jesus, and rest in peace with Him forever.

Secondly, this composition is also more particular and applicatory, as touching ourselves there inhabiting; [for] the emperor [of the Indians] by a joint consent hath promised and appointed us to live at peace where [ever] we will in all his dominions, taking what place we will and as much land as we will, and bringing as many people as we will, and that for these two causes. First, because we are the servants of James, King of England, whose the land (as he confesseth) is; second, because he hath found us just, honest, kind, and peaceable, and so loves our company. Yea, and that in these things there is no dissimulation on his part, nor fear of breach (except our security engender in them some unthought of treachery, or our incivilities provoke them to anger) is most plain in other relations, which show that the things they did were more out of love than out of fear.

It being then, first, a vast and empty chaos, secondly, acknowledged the right of our sovereign king, [and] thirdly, by a peaceable composition in part possessed of diverse of his loving subjects, I see not who can doubt or call in question the lawfulness of inhabiting or dwelling there. But [it is clear] that it may be as lawful for such as are not tied upon some special occasion here to live there as well as here; yea, and as the enterprise is weighty and difficult, so the honor is more worthy, to plant a rude wilderness, to enlarge the honor and fame of our dread sovereign, but chiefly to display the efficacy of power of the gospel both in zealous preaching, [and in] professing, and [in] wise walking under it, before the faces of these poor blind infidels. . . .

Lion Gardener, "Livestock and War in Colonial New England"

Reprinted from "Leift Lion Gardener: this Relation of the Pequot Warres," *Massachusetts Historical Society Collections*, 3rd ser. 3 (1833), 154–5

The second document in this section illuminates some of the surprising ways that Indians responded to environmental changes in the New England landscape. Lion Gardener was a New England colonist who took part in the Pequot War, during which most of the Pequot Indians of the region were massacred by a colonial militia. Gardener's account is of course full of his own biases, and his relating of the Indians' perspective on these events is questionable since he relied on hearsay for much of it. Nonetheless, this excerpt from his history of the Pequot War is instructive for its environmental context. Here, he recounts what he was told about the reasons for Indian hostility to settlers. Among the Indians battling the settlers were the Naragansetts. A Naragansett leader, Miantanomo, has journeyed to a neighboring village and invited its inhabitants to join a war against the settlers. You will have to make allowance for Gardener's spelling: 'Naraganset' for Naragansett, and 'Miantenomie' for Miantanomo. Note how, in this account, Indians recognized the changes in the land around them and had a good understanding of the reasons for those changes. Although we tend to think of environmental change as non-violent, how are war and biotic shift entangled in the story of colonialism? Was Miantonomo interested only in expelling settlers and returning to old ways? Or was he hoping to innovate, combining new alliances with older Indian traditions and the new "technology" of livestock? Indians often saw the advantages of owning livestock, and many would have owned more themselves except for the continual encroachment on their lands by expanding and aggressive colonial settlements.

What possibility was there for Indian success without secure Indian title to large grazing parcels?

*   *   *

A while after this came Miantenomie from Block-Island to Mantacut with a troop of men, Waiandance being not at home; and instead of receiving presents, which they used to do in their progress, he gave them gifts, calling them brethren and friends, for so are we all Indians as the English are, and say brother to one another; so must we be one as they are, otherwise we shall be all gone shortly, for you know our fathers had plenty of deer and skins, our plains were full of deer, as also our woods, and of turkies, and our coves full of fish and fowl. But these English having gotten our land, they with scythes cut down the grass, and with axes fell the trees; their cows and horses eat the grass, and their hogs spoil our clam banks, and we shall all be starved; therefore it is best for you to do as we, for we are all the Sachems from east to west, both Moquakues and Mohauks joining with us, and we are all resolved to fall upon them all, at one appointed day; and therefore I am come to you privately first, because you can persuade the Indians and Sachem to what you will, and I will send over fifty Indians to Block-Island, and thirty to you from thence, and take an hundred of Southampton Indians with an hundred of your own here; and when you see the three fires that will be made forty days hence, in a clear night, then do as we, and the next day fall on and kill men, women, and children, but no cows, for they will serve to eat till our deer be increased again. – And our old men thought it was well. So the Sachem came home and had but little talk with them, yet he was told there had been a secret consultation between the old men and Miantenomie, but they told him nothing in three days. So he came over to me and acquainted me with the manner of the Narragansets being there with his men, and asked me what I thought of it; and I told him that the Narraganset Sachem was naught to talk with his men secretly in his absence, and I bid him go home, and told him a way how he might know all, and then he should come and tell me; and so he did, and found all out as is above written, and I sent intelligence of it over to Mr. Haynes and Mr. Eaton; but because my boat was gone from home it was fifteen days before they had any letter, and Miantenomie was gotten home before they had news of it. And the old men, when they saw how I and the Sachem had beguiled them, and that he was come over to me, they sent secretly a canoe over, in a moon-shine night, to Narraganset to tell them all was discovered; so the plot failed, blessed be God, and the plotter, next Spring after, did as Ahab did at Ramoth-Gilead. – So he to Mohegin, and there had his fall. . . .

Spanish priests Joseph Antonio Murguía and Thomás de la Peña explain Indian frustration with settler livestock in colonial California, 1782

Reprinted from *Writings of Junípero Serra*, ed. Antonine Tibesar, vol. 4 (Washington, DC: Academy of American Franciscan History, 1966)

The final document in this section takes us across the continent to the Spanish colony on the West Coast of North America, in the area that eventually became the state of California. Here, Catholic priests were in charge of converting Indians to Christianity and, to some degree, protecting them from the predations of other Spanish settlers, especially soldiers. Indians were settled at mission complexes, where priests oversaw their education as farmers. (Unlike Indian peoples in New England, California Indians for the most part did not farm prior to the arrival of the Spanish, but instead made a very good living from gathering wild foodstuffs and hunting.)

In this document, two priests explain to their superior how Indians in their region are becoming increasingly angry about the ways in which settler livestock and settler encroachments on their land are making their lives more difficult at the mission. They appeal for the colonial settlement to be removed. The letter mentions a "reduction," the term for placing Indians in a mission. The letter also refers to "gentiles," Indians who lived outside of missions, in traditional villages. Did settler possession of livestock in California make peaceful relations with Indians less likely? Was livestock, in some sense, a weapon for the dispossession of Indians?

Reverend Father President Fray Junípero Serra.
Venerable Father in Christ and Sir:
... Over and above the fact that the land belongs to the Indians since they were born on it – they, and their fathers and forebears – and have for generations lived on the berries in the woods, which they gathered in proper season; in addition, there is the fact that His Majesty distinctly lays down in Law 9, Book 6, Section 1, as found in the *Nueva Recopila-ción*, that they should still retain possession of it just as before the reduction. Furthermore, His Majesty similarly decrees in Law 8, Section 3, Book 6 that wherever sites are located for pueblos or reductions, they should be provided with the conveniences of water, land, mountains, entrances and exits, and tillage land and common land for a full league around, suitable for the Indians to pasture their flocks, and that this should not be mixed up with others belonging to Spaniards. . . .

Now the townspeople here under discussion have, as everyone knows, quantities of livestock, both large and small. And recent history has shown that, besides getting mixed up with the livestock belonging to the Indians from the mission, the animals, both large and small, belonging to the townsfolk have caused unceasing damage to the crops put in by the Indians. Now all this took place before they were in formal possession even of the land on this side of the river – and the boundary line comes right up to the ground which the Indians have placed under cultivation – it is evident that the damages – and nobody can deny it – will be far greater. The consequence will be, perhaps, that the Indians will have to stop their field work, so as not to labor in vain; and they will have to rely for their food on the herbs and acorns they pick in the woods – just as they used to do before we came. This source of food supply, we might add, is now scarcer than it used to be, owing to the cattle; and many a time the gentiles living in the direction of the pueblo have complained to us about it. . . .
Kissing the hand of Your Reverence,
      Your devoted subjects and servants,
  Fray Joseph Antonio Murguía
                    Fray Thomás de la Peña

4

Forest and Plantation in Nineteenth-Century America

This chapter includes two essays about the US in the nineteenth century, one on the North and the other on the South. It also includes two sets of documents, which together take us to the North, the South, and the Far West, as we explore diverse developments in American environmental history during this period.

Section I: Clearing the Forest

The prodigality of American settlers is legendary: game hunted to extinction, cathedral forests laid low, soil plowed to exhaustion. Where William Cronon argues that colonists often denuded forests for profit, Alan Taylor, a Pulitzer prize-winning historian, suggests that another influence played a strong role as well. He contends that early Americans were often hostile to forests because they underscored settler poverty and, in very real ways, threatened death and destruction.

Does this essay make early American hostility towards the natural world more comprehensible to you? How were the natural perceptions of early American settlers different from the natural perceptions of Buffalo Bird Woman, or Koyukon hunters? Do you think they felt more *in* control of nature or more controlled *by* it? And how does this affect your perception of their wastefulness and hostility to the natural environment? Alan Taylor begins his essay with a discussion of a famous novel by James Fenimore Cooper, *The Pioneers*. Our documents for this section will allow you to examine the section of the novel that Taylor is referring to, and to compare it to similar, factual accounts.

"Wasty Ways": Stories of American Settlement

Alan Taylor

In his 1823 novel *The Pioneers, or The Sources of the Susquehanna*, James Fenimore Cooper recalls his childhood world: Otsego County in central New York during the 1790s, when settlers remade the local forest into farms. Cooper depicts the settlers as possessed by an irrational, emotional lust to decimate nature. Their slaughter of the wild plants and animals exceeds all considerations of economic need and interest. In two especially vivid scenes, the settlers of Templeton (the fictional version of the Otsego village of Cooperstown) festively muster to massacre a flock of passenger pigeons and a school of Otsego bass. At the pigeon hunt, "None pretended to collect the game, which lay scattered over the fields in such profusion, as to cover the very ground with the fluttering victims." Similarly, the settlers are "Inflamed beyond the bounds of discretion" at "the sight of the immense piles of fish, that were slowly rolling over on the gravelly beach." They leave most to die and rot, unwanted and unneeded. Otsego's dominant landlord, Judge Marmaduke Temple (modeled on the novelist's father, Judge William Cooper) sadly assures his daughter, "The poor are always prodigal, my child, where there is plenty, and seldom think of a provision against the morrow." He especially laments the rapid decline of the local fish: "like all the other treasures of the wilderness, they already begin to disappear, before the wasteful extravagance of man." Another character, the canny old hunter Natty Bumppo, shares this distress: "I call it sinful and wasty to catch more than can be eat."[1]

Raised in wealth and comfort, Cooper offered an elitist explanation for settler profligacy with nature – abundance brought out the worst in the human nature of common folk. Incapable of restraint, the vulgar settlers despoiled nature as an unthinking sport. In contrast to explanations that emphasize the short-term rationality of profit maximization, Cooper insisted that the "profit" settlers sought was primarily psychic and emotional: the sheer thrill of killing and wasting. In the early American republic, where the unrestrained transformation of the wilderness was the essence of egalitarian opportunity, Cooper's argument was literally uncommon. But his distrust of the common man more often echoes in this century's writings by environmentalists and environmental historians appalled at the consequences of the settler past.

Like Cooper, environmental historians write after the fact of transform-ation, and most cannot help but be impressed by the settlers' destructive mastery over nature, at least in the short term. Environmental historical narratives of North American settlement often open with a nostalgic description of a natural abundance now lost: towering forests, immense flocks of waterfowl, majestic game animals, a boundless, diverse tangle of wild plants, and native peoples who manage their environment with restraint (but never without effect). Then the powerful Euro-American settlers appear to attack and subdue the wild. Only later do their succes-sors experience the harsh consequences, as a nature scorned counter-attacks with severe erosion, dust storms, shrinking aquifers, and salinized soil. In sum, a tripartite structure characterizes the classic envir-onmental histories: initial abundance, transforming settlers, and a legacy of diminished nature. Such narratives are powerful and persuasive because, from our contemporary vantage point, they convey a truth: we do live in an altered nature of diminished diversity and painful dilemmas that derive from the settlement past.

By making so much of settlers' power over nature, however, our envir-onmental narratives make too little of settlers' initial weakness and suffering. In fact, their eventual power derived from their initial pain. This essay locates the settlers' assault on the wild within their often harsh initial experiences with a new land and within the stories they told one another about the meaning of their experiences. The focus will be on Otsego County, the setting for *The Pioneers*, during its period of intense settlement and deforestation, from 1785 to 1820. . . .

The drastic consumption of nature had its roots in the prolonged and previous period when early settlers felt threatened and often over-matched by their new environmental setting. The forest's abundant and diverse plant and animal life was simultaneously alluring and threatening to new settlers coming from older communities. The "wil-derness" contained both resources that were scarce at home *and* dan-gerous beings that had been exterminated further east. The vast forest was a valuable storehouse of firewood, potash, and lumber, *and* a haven for wild, dangerous predators, as well as an encumbrance that ob-structed sunlight where settlers intended to plant crops. Pigeons and deer were windfall sources of food *and* a menace to newly planted crops. Settlers valued bears for their meat and hides, but dreaded their attacks on orchards and livestock. In settler experience, the abundance of nature was often either fleeting or complicated with hidden menace. The scenes of slaughter remembered by Cooper were particular moments of transi-tion when settlers felt a new power to impose their will upon the wilder-ness – moments of perverse but joyous revenge. Only by restoring settlers' fears and sufferings can we adequately explain the excesses of their assault upon nature. This does not justify their actions, but it does render comprehensible patterns of behavior that modern sensibilities and perfect hindsight too easily dismiss as simple irrationality and greed.

Settlers' behavior emerged from a dialectic between their experiences and their own environmental storytelling. They entered into Otsego County informed by the stories heard at home and in childhood about their parents' and grandparents' struggles to make their own farms in a similar landscape of rocky soil, heavy timber, and howling wolves. Repeating the harsh experiences of their predecessors, Otsego's settlers added to a stock of stories about environmental conflict. On the one hand, their stories of endurance in the face of daunting hardships asserted that they were worthy heirs, replicating the environmental ordeals and triumphs of their venerable ancestors. On the other hand, their stories also built up an animus against the wild as the source of their pain and anxiety. Small wonder then that they could delight in opportunities to kill trees, birds, or fish by the thousands. Their stories shaped their behavior, which generated new experiences of both hardship and conquest. In turn, these became the substance of their own narratives, shaping the environmental expectations and behavior of the next generation, who tended to move westward to make their own farms in the forests and prairies of Michigan, Ohio, Illinois, Wisconsin, and Iowa.

Hardships

Upstate New York's settlers were farming people who ventured onto tracts recently wrested from the Iroquois during the American Revolution. Migrating primarily from western New England, these settlers quadrupled New York's population from 340,120 in 1790 to 1,372,812 in 1820. At the same time, the Iroquois population shrank under the pressures of disease, war, and dispossession to only about 3,500 in 1794. The victors confined the vanquished to shrinking reservations on fractions of their prewar domain.

Compared to their Iroquois predecessors, the settlers used more land more intensively because they came in vastly greater numbers and because they sought a marketable surplus as well as family subsistence from their agriculture. The Indians had confined their horticulture to subsistence and had restricted their settlements to the fertile riverine floodplains, reserving the extensive uplands as a forest for hunting and gathering. After 1783, the victorious settlers seized the riverine villages of the Indians and expanded up onto the forested hills and ridges, pushing their multiplying farms into almost every corner of the new state. In contrast to the Indians, who obtained most of their meat from fishing and hunting, the settlers relied primarily on domesticated live-stock kept as private property. While no Indian family owned any par-ticular deer or bear until the animal had been killed, settlers regarded their living cattle, horses, sheep, and pigs as private, individual posses-sions. The newcomers hoped to render the landscape safe and product-ive for their livestock and for their more extensive fields of grain by clearing the forest and destroying most of the wild mammals. In their drive to create more property, to produce grains for external markets (as well as for their own subsistence), and to maximize the number of privately owned animals, settler families cleared and fenced much more land, and built more and larger buildings, than did the Indians.

Disregarding the signs of prior Indian use, the new settlers called the forested uplands of New York a "wilderness" – by which they meant a land-scape that they had not yet reworked to fit their needs and expectations. No romantics, the settlers did not celebrate the American forest as a paradise, as an escape from corrupt society into a presocial innocence. On the con-trary, they regarded the wilderness as threatening and unproductive. . . .

The settlers regarded their farm-building as "improvements" that refined the so-called "wilderness" into a more productive and secure version of nature. . . . Settlers meant to replace a nature that they called wilderness with another nature called pastoral.

During that long process of transformation, however, the settlers were vulnerable to natural forces beyond their control. At the end of the eighteenth century, upstate New York was abundantly endowed with the wild life that settlers needed to subdue. A heavy, tangled forest of large oak, beech, maple, chestnut, pine, and hemlock trees covered the hills and sheltered numerous carnivorous mammals – bears, panthers, and wolves – who threatened the domesticated livestock and plants introduced by the settlers. Remaking this dense forest into productive farms was a long, laborious process for people armed only with hand tools – axes and saws, hammers and hoes, guns and knives – and assisted by oxen and fire. . . . At first, nature seemed too powerful; the settlers appeared overmatched by the forest and its denizens. Consequently, new settlements meant severe hardships, intense labor, sudden dangers, and frequent hunger. In 1798, Isaac Lyman explained that his fellow settlers disliked missionaries: "They say they wish not to have them preach of Hell & Damnation, for let any Person come into a New Settlement & see how they fare, [he] will say the Inhabitants suffer all those torments of Hell and Damnation to a perfection."[2]

Poorer folk, with limited prospects at home in eastern New York and western New England, bore the shocks of early settlement in upstate New York. After touring the New York settlements, Judge James Kent (who came from downstate) confided that

I am wholly cured of (if I ever had) any disposition for living in a new Country. There are very few Comforts in poor log Houses in the wilderness at a great Distance from Markett & the Conveniences of Life. They are totally detached from all Elegance & Luxury & surrounded by [a] harsh & rugged natural Landscape, by rude woods & dreary naked Trees & Stumps, by a poor & rude race of the first Settlers, by muddy & impassable roads – In short by Poverty & hard labor.[3]

Because prosperous people felt little pressure and less inducement to forsake the comforts of an old community for the rigors of a new settlement, most early settlers came from relatively poor families. . . .

The early newcomers struggled within a vicious cycle: their initial poverty increased their vulnerability to hardships, and those hardships prolonged their poverty. In nearby northern Pennsylvania, John Lorain remarked that

[The settlers] have been driven, either by folly or unmerited misfortunes, to seek refuge in the forests, without sufficient funds to meet the expenditures, actually necessary to accomplish a better mode of management, and are doomed, by the stern hand of adversity, to deprivations, hardships, and sufferings, which could have been readily avoided, had they possessed a capital commensurate with their undertaking.

This interplay of prolonged poverty and frontier hardship was manifest in the grim experiences of the Beach family, who emigrated from Connecticut during the 1780s to settle beside the Susquehanna River in the Otsego country. Their grandson, Josiah Priest, reported that after two years of hard labor their new homestead produced a promising crop. It seemed "that the period of their privations was near its close." But on October 6, 1787, a heavy rainstorm drenched the hills, filled the creeks, and swelled the Susquehanna into a flood that carried away the newly cut harvest: sheaves of wheat and rye and heaps of pumpkins and flax. For want of capital, the family had not built a barn to store their crop. The following June, another flood swamped Timothy Beach's canoe, drowning him and sentencing his widow and children to "wretched poverty."[4]

During their first two years on the land, few Otsego settlers could clear and cultivate enough land to feed themselves. Hunger was common during the late spring and early summer, after the previous harvest had been consumed and before the next ripened. Near-famine conditions prevailed in localities where crop parasites or early frosts cut short the harvest in their small clearings. When shaded by the large, surrounding forest, grains, especially corn, might not ripen before the mid-September frost. And the settlers unwittingly brought "the blast" (or "black stem rust") with them from New England; this fungal parasite could destroy an entire field of wheat, or at least render the grain unpleasantly dark and moldy.... Even when the settlers could raise sufficient crops, they suffered from a lack of bridges and roads to carry produce to gristmills and to market. To make flour, isolated settlers had to pound their corn by hand with a mortar and pestle – long, tedious, back-numbing labor.[5]

Early settlers also had to fight an often losing battle to defend orchards, poultry, and livestock from marauding bears and wolves, and to protect grain and garden plants from pigeons, squirrels, and grasshoppers. In July 1786, Benjamin Gilbert of Otsego complained to his diary that "The bears have deprived me of a hope of making one Barrel [of] Cider. This year Wolves are very plenty and have injured me much." In August 1798, the *Otsego Herald* reported that grasshoppers had devastated the county's grasses and crops: "Many fine meadows appear as if a fire had passed through them." That summer the grasshoppers had consumed "more grass, than all the cattle, sheep, &c. in the county."[6]

When their produce ran short, settlers relied upon hunting, gathering, and fishing for sustenance. Ironically, during the seasons of early hardship the settlers found relief by tapping the wild abundance that they were ultimately determined to conquer. Josiah Priest later recalled that the "wild woods . . . afforded buds, roots, berries and nuts, upon which human life might possibly subsist, and of the first settlers, many were compelled to live upon them or starve.... Because the wild leek was abundant and the earliest plant to mature in the spring, it was an essential food source for settlers and their cattle. . . .

Fishing was the primary recourse for starving settlers. In the spring of 1785, Priest's family "learned of the Indians how to catch fish.... Without this relief, they must have finally perished." Fish abounded in "those early times before the Susquehannah was interrupted by milldams, and its lucid waters beclouded with sawdust." Settlers caught fish, especially trout, with baited hooks or lured them within spearing range at night by placing a burning pine knot in an iron basket that projected from the bow of a boat or canoe. Thousands of fish – especially shad, herring, and Otsego bass – could be taken at once with a seine net set into the lake or river waters by a boat and drawn ashore by cooperating settlers. Settlers also learned from the Indians to build weirs, elaborate V-shaped traps of tightly interwoven branches held in place by stakes driven into the river bottom and extending from one bank to the other. Whether employing nets or weirs, cooperating settlers threw the trapped fish onto the dry beach to die and then formed them into equal-sized piles, one per fisherman. The piles were "cried off" to particular fishermen in a manner intended to ensure a fair distribution without wrangling. One settler stood or sat with his back to the fish and answered with a man's name the question posed by another who went from pile to pile: "Who shall have this [heap]?" Cooperative labor culminated in an egalitarian distribution of the fish as private property.[7]

Dangers

In addition to their endemic poverty and seasonal hunger, the first settlers were also prone to sudden and violent accidents. The dangers emerged, in part, from the raw power of nature's extremes, but also in part from the inadequate contrivances the settlers made to try and contain that energy. By emigrating into the forest, settlers placed themselves in harm's way, gambling their subsistence and health on their eventual success in the arduous transformation of the forest into farms. In the short term, they compounded their vulnerability by entrusting their lives and livestock to hastily built dams, roads, bridges, and barns that often collapsed with crippling and fatal consequences. By claiming the life or health of a laboring boy or man, an accident could deal a disastrous blow to a frontier family already struggling to make ends meet. . . .

Traveling could turn deadly in a land where the forest dwarfed the new clearings, the rivers flowed rapidly over hidden logs and rocks, and the roads, bridges, and ferries were few and precarious. Sometimes the winter ice gave way beneath traveling parties, and the dark, frigid waters swallowed sleighs, horses, oxen, and humans. Winter blizzards could trap and disorient travelers and hunters, bringing death from exposure. Caught by "the great snowstorm" of December 1796 while out hunting, sixteen-year-old Samuel Thornton of Otsego County was found dead the following April after the snow melted. In the spring, heavy rains combined with melting snow and ice to swell rivers and streams into raging torrents. In April 1796, a canoe carrying a settler family overturned in the Susquehanna River after striking a heavy log. The four adults struggled to safety on the banks, but the river swept away and drowned their four children. Josiah Priest had good reason to dread the spring floods in the Susquehanna. In 1788, a freshet killed his grandfather by a overturning his canoe; six years later, another flood claimed his father, who died of pneumonia contracted while rescuing others from the cold, swollen river.[8]

Traveling overland became even more dangerous as settlers began to thin out the forest. Before the settlers had arrived, the dense forest buffered individual trees from direct gusts of wind, permitting tall, straight growth without deep roots. As settlers cut into the groves, remaining trees that were weakly anchored by shallow roots were exposed to wind storms that toppled trunks and branches onto cattle and people below. One Sunday, young brothers George and Andrew Peck stole away from their cabin to collect beechnuts in the woods. On their way home, they were overtaken by a furious windstorm tearing "through the forest, the trees falling in all directions." The boys barely escaped death when, in George Peck's words, "an immense hemlock blew down with a crash and buried us with its foliage, the massy trunk striking the earth within three or four feet of me, and the great branches stretching all around us."[9]

Felling trees with an axe was dangerous, as well as hard and dirty work. According to the *Otsego Herald*, the Cooperstown newspaper, on April 7, 1797, Silas Shoemaker, "a hearty man about 27 years of age," was chopping down trees when one fell upon him. "He was a poor, hard laboring man, and left a disconsolate widow, three small children, and an old helpless decrepid mother, to lament his death – which demands the attention of all good charitable people." Returning to Cooperstown from a foray into the forest to cut firewood, Timothy Johnson died suddenly when a vengeful tree dropped a heavy limb onto his skull.[10]

Lightning or careless settlers frequently caused extensive forest fires that imperiled their farms, lives, and livestock. These fires broke out in times of summer drought and fed upon all the dead, drying trunks, branches, and brush that littered the forest floor as the settlers cut into the wilderness. Consequently, fires that escaped from settler control produced more intense, widespread, and destructive blazes than the smaller fires that Indians had annually set to consume the underbrush. Unlike Indian fires, settler fires raged up into the forest canopy to consume mature trees.

Settlers had to build all the infrastructure they had taken for granted in their former communities: stores, roads, bridges, mills, schools, and meetinghouses. Hastily and sloppily built by unskilled labor, these structures frequently failed, with catastrophic consequences. As with their partial clearings, the settlers' buildings increased, rather than reduced, their danger in the short term. In 1804, John Williams Jr. approached Cooperstown on his return from Albany with a wagonload of rum. On the eastern edge of the village, his wagon struck a deep rut, pitching Williams forward onto the road and under rolling wheels that crushed out his life. Henry Clarke Wright recalled the collapse of a sawmill dam on Otsego Stream: "such a rush and roar of waters! sweeping fences, bridges, pigs, sheep and cattle away and spreading wide the desolation." ... On a hot July day in 1801, Micaiah Bennet took a break from his field work and sought out the shade beside a large leach tub filled with acidic potash. "The instant he sat down the tub fell on him, and confined him," the local newspaper reported, "with one of his knees doubled directly against his breast, nearly four hours, when he was discovered by his father in the most horrid torture." Pulled free, he died two hours later. "He was the eldest son of his father, who severely feels the heavy stroke. *How uncertain is life!*" lamented the *Otsego Herald*. At a barn raising in Otsego Township four years later, the improperly stayed frame collapsed, killing three men and crippling two others.[11]

Of course, the great majority of settlers survived the swirling blizzards, swollen rivers, falling trees, forest fires, poisonous plants, collapsing leach tubs and house frames, runaway wagons, bursting dams, and grinding waterwheels. But such episodes were sufficiently common to remind frontier dwellers that they led a harsher and more unpredictable life than did their friends and relatives back home in old Connecticut and Massachusetts. And those who did not directly encounter danger felt its proximity as they heard hearthside stories of harsh environmental experience. Henry Clarke Wright recalled hearing such tales as a boy in Otsego:

> Stories of Indian tortures and burnings; of Indian tomahawks and scalping-knives; stories of encounters with wild beasts, of dark nights spent in the woods, and of hair-breadth escapes from the wild dangers of wading and swimming rivers, and crossing mountain torrents; stories of children strayed or lost, or torn to pieces, or starved to death in the woods.

Similarly, in the *Otsego Herald*, tales of accidental mayhem dominated the local news. By dwelling on the grim and horrific, local stories and reportage magnified the impact of fatal or crippling accidents on settler minds.[12]

Grim episodes and tales of a harsh and capricious nature promoted morbid reflections.... George Peck had nearly died beneath a falling hemlock tree while traveling on a Sunday. He later recalled that "for weeks the affair harrowed up my soul.... The idea of being [nearly] killed in the act of breaking the Sabbath made my very bones shake, and many were the vows I made to lead a new life."... The terrifying tales of lurking dangers and sudden deaths led the young Henry Clarke Wright to associate "the Deity with soul-crushing mysteries."[13]

Some brooding settlers went beyond somber reflection to fatal melancholy. Three sudden accidents – a toppling tree, a raging river, and a fall from a cart – claimed three men who were the friends of Luther Peck of Middlefield. "These sad events, following each other in swift succession, deeply affected him," recalled his son George. Luther Peck experienced morbid dreams and dreaded that this own death was imminent. "Such was his mental distress that he wasted away under it, and his kind neighbors were alarmed lest he should lose his reason or die." Peck found relief through an evangelical rebirth as a devout Methodist. Abigail Beach of Unadilla was not so fortunate. Returning home after her father's death by drowning, young Deborah Beach found her mother Abigail afflicted by paralyzing grief. "She only gazed with a sort of vacant stare, not seeming to know me" because "a settled melancholy had seized her for its victim." Abigail Beach never fully recovered. On a Sunday in 1804, Uriah Luce of Cooperstown entered his barn to find twelve-year-old Timothy Johnson "hanging by a rope fastened to the great beam." The coroners ruled his death a suicide. "It is remarkable," Elihu Phinney noted, "that his father was killed suddenly about four years ago, by the falling of a limb of a tree, which fractured his skull, and that his mother died very suddenly soon after and that a sister a few years since fell into a well and was drowned."[14]

Endurance

Given these often grim conditions, why did settler families venture into the forest to make farms? They persisted through hardships and dangers because they anticipated that their labor would ultimately prevail in the creation of a new nature that would provide a secure prosperity. Settlers were, in the words of one frontier missionary, "all under the influence of a hope of better times," if they could but endure the early hardships to make substantial farms. Through persistence, settlers meant to amass the property that endowed independence, with all its promises of material comfort, social respectability, and political rights. They also found encouragement in the precedent of their parents and grandparents, who had persevered through similar travails in order to build successful farms on an earlier frontier.[15]

The Otsego settlers also found inspiration in their Protestant Christian faith, which taught that conquering the forest and its wild animals was service to God.... On one Sabbath day, a congregation gathered in Richfield to hear the Reverend Daniel Nash, the Episcopal missionary to the Otsego country. When one congregant looked out the window and bellowed that he saw a bear, all the men seized their rifles and bolted from the meeting. After a great scramble through the forest culminated in the bear's death and butchering, the settlers returned to the service. Resuming his sermon, Nash "rather admitted that it was a good christian act to destroy the dangerous animal on the sabbath." In 1811, the Reverend Whiting Griswold dedicated a new church in Otsego County with this announcement: "A number of you can look back to the time when this place *began* to settle; you ventured yourselves and families into a dreary wilderness. . . . Where but a few years since little could be heard but the noise of wild beasts, now a sanctuary of Jehovah is erected, where his gospel shall be preached, *his* praises sung, and his name invoked." By transforming the forest into a landscape of farms, stores, roads, bridges, and churches, the settlers believed that they secured their eternal, as well as their temporal, interests.[16]

In addition to their hopes of future prosperity and salvation, settlers endured frontier hardships and dangers because some of their stories celebrated extraordinary exertions against the wild. Although some frontier stories promoted dread, and even a morbid resignation, others exhorted action by heroicizing the people (usually men, sometimes boys, occasionally women) who dared the most to confront and transform their dangerous world. The stories especially honored those who destroyed wolves, panthers, and bears. . . . Accounts of battles with wild carnivores were second only to tales of heroism in fighting Indians. Settlers defined themselves as civilized by hating and killing all other carnivorous beings – human and nonhuman alike – who preyed upon the herbivores of the North American forest.

The *Otsego Herald* published some of these tales of wild animal killers. . . . In September 1799, John King of Butternuts followed the "howling of a large herd of wolves" that had "torn to pieces" seven sheep belonging to a neighbor. Overtaken, the nine wolves turned to attack King. He shot the lead wolf and his dog charged into the midst of the others. The pack killed the dog, but King benefitted from the delay to recharge his gun and fire, mortally wounding a second wolf. The other wolves fled. After skinning and decapitating the two dead wolves, King "returned home in triumph," the hero of his settlement. In August 1805, William Shaw of Delhi, in neighboring Delaware County, tracked a she-bear to her den,

> entered the subterraneous haunt of the ferocious animal, and descending to her very seat, there, fearless of the consequences, placed a rope round her neck, and she was dragged forth to the astonishment of all present. – This is the second feat of the kind we believe on record; and for cool resolution and determined courage, elevates the name of SHAW of Delhi, to a rank second only to the intrepid [Israel] PUTNAM of former days.

The newspaper boasted that a settler of their own generation and county was as worthy as a celebrated mid-eighteenth-century predecessor in the dangerous work of killing the wild. Such stories celebrated the victors as the most brave and cunning representatives of a courageous and clever people – proper heroes for emulation.[17]

Devastation

Encouraged by their expectations, faith, and stories – and empowered by their swelling numbers and sustained labor – settlers eventually gained the upper hand over the forest and its beasts. They then assailed the wild plant and animal life with a vengeance born, in part, from the memory of recent sufferings. The English traveler Isaac Weld marveled that Americans hated trees and "cut away all before them without mercy; not one is spared; all share . . . in the general havoc." In 1794, another Englishman, William Strickland, observed that all Americans "agree in this; that trees are a nuisance and ought to be destroyed by any, and every means." Farmers disdained even preserving a few shade trees around their homes, for deforestation was a mark of pride and status.[18] . . .

Coming from a continent where forests had become preciously rare, European visitors were horrified by the massive destruction of the trees in New York. Julian Niemcewicz of Poland lamented the "sorry sight, to see for mile after mile, these enormous skeletons, these gigantic cadavers, shorn of their bark and half-burnt, lying about wasted." In 1794, English visitor William Strickland raged that "The barbarous backwoodsman has got possession of the soil, and fire and the axe are rapidly levelling the woods." After devastating the local forest, "it is then left to him only to sally forth and seek on the frontiers, a new country which he may again devour." He characterized New York's settlers as "the most destructive race that ever disfigured and destroyed a beautiful and luxuriant country." The deforestation was so rapid and thorough that by 1800 leading New Yorkers worried about a looming fuel crisis in the Hudson River valley and began to call, in vain, for conservation measures.[19]

As they filled the land and felled the forest, the settlers also destroyed the larger mammals – beavers, deer, bears, panthers, and wolves. Most hunting was carried out by individuals or by pairs of men, but sometimes settlers in a neighborhood united in a group hunt. Hunting parties manifested the medley of the competitive and the communal, the laborious and the festive, that characterized rural culture. Hunters simultaneously worked together to drive game into a narrowing circle and competed with one another (or with a rival team) to kill the greatest number of animals. At a predetermined day and time, the men gathered, elected captains, strung themselves apart in a semicircle, then advanced to close the circle, trapping and killing the animals within. After counting up the dead and recognizing the victors, the hunters ended the day with festive eating and drinking. Such hunts protected crops and asserted humanity's supremacy over other life, sustained bonds between neighbors, established a local pecking order of male prowess, celebrated republican principles, and reaffirmed a male monopoly over weapons and public gatherings. . . .

The population of large wild mammals rapidly declined under the gunfire of the growing number of settlers, as well as from the transformed habitat wrought by deforestation. In 1850, an old hunter in upstate New York calculated that in his lifetime he had killed 77 panthers, 214 wolves, 219 bears, and 2,550 deer. Many hunters ignored with impunity the rarely enforced state law against killing deer in winter. James Macauley lamented that "In the winter the hunters in the new countries often avail themselves of crusts, when these animals break through, and are unable to fly, and destroy whole flocks. The destruction on these occasions, is wanton, since neither their meat nor skins are [then] worth much." In 1794, in the upper Hudson River valley, William Strickland remarked that

> In this vast tract of country no deer, or other useful animal or next to none exist; and scarce a living creature is to be seen. Thus has a country, once abounding in animated nature, for want of Laws to protect, or sense in the people to kill with moderation and in seasonable times, in the short space of 20 years become still as death.

William Cooper estimated that settlers could count on harvesting deer only during the first ten years of a settlement. In 1791, just five years after his settlement began, Cooper boasted that wolves had already retreated from the vicinity of Cooperstown: "those Swamps that four years ago was a safe retreat for those devouring animals are now become plentiful Pastures." . . . By 1810, major mammals had virtually disappeared from Otsego County, save for a few in the mountains on the southern fringe.[20]

Edible fish also began to dwindle under the pressure of a growing settler population and the accompanying changes in the land and rivers. . . . Mill dams built in the Susquehanna River obstructed the ascent of shad and herring from Chesapeake Bay to Lakes Otsego and Canadarago. In turn, the loss of this food supply undercut the trout and bass, already under relentless pressure from fishermen. The discharge of sawdust from mills and acids from tanneries into the streams and lakes reduced the oxygen in the waters, afflicting the fish. Deforestation along the streams exposed their waters to direct sunlight and to an increased burden of eroded soil, raising water temperatures and diminishing clarity, all to the detriment of cold-water fishes. Because the forest canopy and roots combined to retain moisture in the soil, the local streams had enjoyed a relatively constant flow through the year; deforestation meant greater springtime surges and a diminished flow in the summer drought, extremes that stressed the traditional fishes. The one species that adapted well to the changes, the pickerel, aggressively expanded at the expense of the more docile and fleshier fishes preferred by humans.[21]

Settlers' treatment of wild animals and plants derived from their antici-
pation of a future landscape deforested, depleted of wildlife, and dedicated to agriculture. Rather than seek an equilibrium with wild animal and
plant populations, most settlers killed as much and as often as they could in
order to claim the largest possible share in a bounty that they regarded
as inevitably short-lived. Emigrating from districts already deforested
and depleted of wildlife, the settlers considered the wilderness as a
temporary place and condition where an unconquered nature imposed
special hardships and compensated with unusual windfalls. By exploiting
nature's bounty, settlers meant to transform the conditions that entailed
their hardships. Destroying the forest and its denizens brought immediate
excitement and sustenance while advancing development of the agricultural landscape necessary for long-term prosperity. . . .

William Cronon argues that narration is not simply the long-after-the-
fact imposition of historians on a receding past. Narratives were woven
into the fabric of settlers' lives. Stories shaped their self-image, framed
their expectations, and motivated their actions. In turn, their own
experiences revised and added to the stock of narratives passed on to
their children. By telling tales of their endurance and heroism in the face
of a cruel nature, Otsego's settlers ensured that their children would
perpetuate, on new frontiers farther west, their way of life as relentless
transformers of a forested land.[22]

Epilogue

Success in environmental transformation eventually altered the perception of nature by later generations who lived in Otsego County. By the
mid-nineteenth century, they enjoyed more security and comfort
because there was so little left that their predecessors had called wild.
Some could even begin to regret that their ancestors had so thoroughly
cleared the forest, exterminating locally the larger mammals and tastier
fish. While they lamented the loss of those animals that seemed attractive
and useful, like deer or Otsego bass, no one yet openly mourned for
destroyed wolves and panthers.

In the late 1840s, Susan Fenimore Cooper, daughter of the novelist, told
the revealing story of the last deer then surviving in the vicinity of Cooperstown. Kept in the village as the pet of a local woman (probably Susan's
mother), this deer "became a great favorite, following the different
members of the family about, caressed by the neighbors, and welcome
everywhere." One morning the fawn was sunning itself upon the steps of a
store when a stranger and his hound strode into the village. Spooked, the
fawn bolted, with the hound and some village dogs in pursuit. The men of

Cooperstown ran after their dogs, hoping to save the fawn. Alas, the deer swam across part of the nearby lake and plunged into a wood where a stray rabbit hunter – not privy to the animal's history and ownership – was so surprised to see a fawn that he reflexively shot it dead. Discovering a collar bearing the owner's name, the hunter hastened into the village to return the item to the grieving family. In honor of the dead deer, the villagers renamed the bay it had swum across as "Fawn Bay" and the site of its death as "Fawn Spring."[23]

The scramble to save the deer, and the mourning and memorialization that its death evoked, reveals how thoroughly the times and nature had changed in Otsego by the 1840s. In contrast to their settler grandfathers, who had competed to kill the largest number of deer, the villagers of the 1840s raced to rescue the last, local survivor of the species. As private property, the fawn had enjoyed protection from the guns and dogs of the other villagers. As a rarity, the fawn had attracted sentimental affection and nostalgic curiosity from the local people. They cherished the fawn as a symbol of the wild that had become newly precious because their grandparents had rendered it so scarce. Indeed, they anthropomorphized the fawn into a sort of neighbor and mourned when it died. Unwilling to let the deer go, they memorialized the fawn's last moments in place names. As the settlers' ordeal faded in time and memory, their heirs began to regret the conquest of the wild that had left them such a tamed landscape.

Notes

I am grateful to Gregory Nobles and Richard White for their thoughtful criticism and generous suggestions that helped prepare this essay for publication.

1   James Fenimore Cooper, *The Pioneers, or The Sources of the Susquehanna* (crit. ed. of New York, 1823; reprint, Albany: State University of New York Press, 1980), 244–52, 259–66.

2   Isaac Lyman (who had moved to central New York), quoted in Chilton Williamson Jr., *Vermont in Quandary: 1763–1825* (Montpelier, Vt.: n.p., 1949), 256.

3   James Kent, "Journal of a Northern Tour," June 1803, Reel 6, James Kent Papers, Library of Congress. . . .

4   John Lorain, "Observations on the Comparative Value of Soils, &c.," Philadelphia Society for Promoting Agriculture, *Memoirs*, vol. 3 (1814): 101; Henry Clarke Wright, *Human Life Illustrated in My Individual Experience as a Child, a Youth, and a Man* (Boston: Bela Marsh, 1849), 26; Josiah Priest, *Stories of Early Settlers in the Wilderness; Embracing the Life of Mrs. Priest, Late of Otsego County, N. Y.* (Albany, N.Y.: J. Munsell, 1837), 4, 16, 35, 38.

5   Beardsley, *Reminiscences*, 55; William Cooper, *Guide in the Wilderness*, 14; Willard V. Huntington, "Old Time Notes," New York State Historical Association, Cooperstown, N.Y. (hereafter NYSHA), 707; Priest, *Stories*

of the Early Settlers, 36; Benjamin Gilbert to Daniel Gilbert, 18 July 1786, in *A Citizen-Soldier in the American Revolution: The Diary of Benjamin Gilbert in Massachusetts and New York*, ed. Rebecca D. Symmes (Cooperstown: New York State Historical Association, 1980), 81; Benjamin Gilbert, "Diary," 12 May 1786, 18 May 1786, NYSHA.

6   Benjamin Gilbert to Daniel Gilbert, 18 July 1786, in Symmes, *Citizen-Soldier*, 81; Benjamin Gilbert, "Diary," 12 May 1786, 18 May 1786, NYSHA; *Otsego Herald*, 30 August 1798.

7   Priest, *Stories of Early Settlers*, 20, 22–23, 35; Huntington, "Old Time Notes," 1064; J. F. Cooper, *The Pioneers*, 251–66, 274; Edmund E. Lynch, "Fishing on Otsego Lake" (Master's thesis, State University of New York at Oneonta, 1965), 20; De Witt Clinton, *Account of the Salmo Otsego, Or the Otsego Basse, In a Letter to John W. Francis, M. D.* (New York: C. S. Van Winkle, 1822), 3–4.

8   William Cooper to Henry Drinker, 11 February 1790, Correspondence Box 1741–1792, Henry Drinker Papers, Historical Society of Pennsylvania, Philadelphia; *Otsego Herald*, 17 April 1797; 4 May 1797; Priest, *Stories of Early Settlers*, 20, 27; Susan Fenimore Cooper, *Rural Hours*, 18, 20, 31–32; J. F. Cooper, *Pioneers*, 242–43; Ralph Birdsall, *Fenimore Cooper's Grave and Christ Churchyard* (New York: privately printed, 1911), 53–54.

9   Isaac Weld Jr., *Travels Through the States of North America . . . During the Years 1795, 1796, and 1797*, vol. 1 (London, 1807; reprint, New York: Johnson Reprint Corp., 1968), 40; Metchie J. E. Budka, ed., "Journey to Niagara, 1805: From the Diary of Julian Ursyn Niemcewicz," *New York Historical Society Quarterly* 44 (1960): 86; George Peck, *The Life and Times of Rev. George Peck, D. D., Written by Himself* (New York: Carleton and Porter, 1874), 34.

10   *Otsego Herald*, 4 May 1797; 25 December 1800; 24 April 1806.

11   J. F. Cooper, *Pioneers*, 41–45, 100–101; Wright, *Human Life*, 25; *Otsego Herald*, 23 July 1801; 18 October 1804; 19 September 1805.

12   Wright, *Human Life*, 44; *Otsego Herald*, 12 May 1796; 17 April 1797; 4 May 1797; 10 April 1800; 25 September 1800; 25 December 1800; 23 July 1801; 18 October 1804; 19 September 1805; 24 April 1806.

13   *Otsego Herald*, 10 April 1800; Peck, *Life and Times of Rev. George Peck*, 35; Wright, *Human Life*, 44.

14   Peck, *Life and Times of Rev. George Peck*, 24, 26; Deborah Beach, quoted in Priest, *Stories of Early Settlers*, 27; *Otsego Herald*, 27 September 1804.

15   Reverend John Taylor, quoted in David M. Ellis, *Landlords and Farmers in the Hudson-Mohawk Region, 1790–1850* (Ithaca: Cornell University Press, 1946), 17; William Strickland, *Journal of a Tour in the United States of America, 1794–1795* (New York: New York Historical Society, 1971), 96; Michel-Guillaume St. Jean de Crevecoeur, *Journey Into Northern Pennsylvania and the State of New York*, ed. Clarissa Spencer Bostelmann (Ann Arbor: University of Michigan Press, 1964), 486.

16   Beardsley, *Reminiscences*, 42–45; Rev. Whiting Griswold, *A Sermon Delivered January 1st, 1811, at the Dedication of the Presbyterian Meeting-House, in Hartwick, Otsego County* (Cooperstown, N.Y.: J. H. Prentiss, 1815), 20–21.

17   "Bear Battle," *Otsego Herald,* 22 June 1797; "Defeat of the Wolves," *Otsego Herald,* 19 September 1799; "Daring Feat," *Otsego Herald,* 9 June 1803; "A Second Putnam," *Otsego Herald,* 3 October 1805.

18   Strickland, *Journal of a Tour,* 139.

19   Budka, "Journey to Niagara, 1805," 91; Strickland, *Journal of a Tour,* 138, 146, 170; Simon Desjardins, "Castorland Journal," trans. Franklin B. Hough, New York State Library, 46; Samuel L. Mitchell, "Address," Society for the Promotion of Agriculture, Arts, and Manufactures, Instituted in the State of New York, *Transactions,* vol. 1 (Albany, 1801), 213.

20   Jeptha R. Simms, *Trappers of New York, or a Biography of Nicholas Stoner & Nathaniel Foster* (Albany, N.Y.: J. Munsell, 1850), 255; Macauley, *The Natural... History of the State of New-York,* vol. 1, 449; Strickland, *Journal of a Tour,* 147; William Cooper, *Guide in the Wilderness,* 44; William Cooper to Henry Drinker, 3 November 1791, Correspondence Box 1741–1792, Henry Drinker Papers, Historical Society of Pennsylvania, Philadelphia; ...James Fenimore Cooper, *Notions of the Americans, Picked Up by a Travelling Bachelor,* vol. 1 (Philadelphia, 1828; reprint, New York: Frederick Ungar, 1963), 241.

21   Priest, *Stories of Early Settlers,* 23; Macauley, *The Natural... History of the State of New York,* vol. 1, 109; Clinton, *Account of the Salmo Otsego,* 4–5; Shaw T. Livermore, *A Condensed History of Cooperstown* (Albany, N.Y.: J. Munsell, 1862), 125; David Starr Jordan and Barton Warren Evermann, *The Fishes of North and Middle America* (Washington, D.C.: GPO, 1896), 465; Elihu Phinney, "Fish and Fishing in Otsego Lake," in *A Centennial Offering, Being a Brief History of Cooperstown,* ed. S. M. Shaw (Cooperstown, N.Y.: Freeman's Journal Press, 1886), 185; Jay Bloomfield, ed., *Lakes of New York State,* vol. 3 (New York: Academic Press, 1978–1980), 119–23; New York (State) Conservation Department, *A Biological Survey of the Delaware and Susquehanna Watersheds: Supplemental to the Twenty-Fifth Annual Report, 1935* (Albany: State of New York, 1936), 49–53, 113–18.

22   William Cronon, "A Place for Stories: Nature, History, and Narrative," *Journal of American History* 78 (1992): 1349–79; David Carr, "Narrative and the Real World: An Argument for Continuity," *History and Theory* 25 (1986): 117.

23   Susan Fenimore Cooper, *Rural Hours,* 240–44.

Documents

James Fenimore Cooper on the Wasty Ways of Pioneers

Reprinted from *The Leatherstocking Saga,* ed. Allan Nevins (New York: Pantheon, 1954)

Our first document is excerpted from James Fenimore Cooper's *The Pioneers.* Although the novel is fictional, the account of passenger pigeon slaughter is drawn from Cooper's personal experience, and scenes like it were repeated across America in the nineteenth century. Towns often declared holidays – "Pigeon Days" – to allow residents to take part in a kind of secular community ritual of taking pigeons. This kind of document is especially helpful in understanding the outlook of its author, who was one of the foremost cultural figures of his age. Cooper was from an elite rural family. His father, William, was the founder of Cooperstown, New York.

Does the writing of James Fenimore Cooper show more sympathy for the pigeons or the settlers? In this excerpt, do you detect any trace of the settler fear and resentment of wild animals that Alan Taylor describes? Does Cooper have any more sympathy for poor settlers than for wealthy ones?

* * *

If the heavens were alive with pigeons, the whole village seemed equally in motion with men, women, and children. Every species of firearms, from the French ducking-gun, with a barrel near six feet in length, to the common horseman's pistol, was to be seen in the hands of the men and boys; while bows and arrows, some made of the simple stick of a walnut sapling, and others in a rude imitation of the ancient crossbows, were carried by many of the latter. . . .

So prodigious was the number of the birds, that the scattering fire of the guns, with the hurling of missiles and the cries of the boys, had no other effect than to break off small flocks from the immense masses that continued to dart along the valley, as if the whole of the feathered tribe were pouring through that one pass. None pretended to collect the game, which lay scattered over the fields in such profusion as to cover the very ground with the fluttering victims.

Leatherstocking was a silent but uneasy spectator of all these proceedings, but was able to keep his sentiments to himself until he saw the introduction of the swivel into the sports.

"This comes of settling a country!" he said; "here have I known the pigeons to fly for forty long years, and, till you made your clearings, there was nobody to skear or to hurt them. I loved to see them come into the woods, for they were company to a body; hurting nothing; being, as it was, as harmless as a garter snake. But now it gives me sore thoughts when I hear the frighty things whizzing through the air, for I know it's only a motion to bring out all the brats in the village. Well! the Lord won't see the waste of His creaters for nothing, and right will be done to the pigeons as well as others, by and by. There's Mr. Oliver, as bad as the rest of them, firing into the flocks, as if he was shooting down nothing but Mingo warriors."

Among the sportsmen was Billy Kirby, who, armed with an old musket, was loading, and without even looking into the air, was firing and shouting as his victims fell even on his own person. He heard the speech of Natty, and took upon himself to reply –

"What! old Leatherstocking," he cried, "grumbling at the loss of a few pigeons! If you had to sow your wheat twice and three times as I have done, you wouldn't be so massyfully feeling'd towards the divils. Hurrah, boys! scatter the feathers! This is better than shooting at a turkey's head and neck, old fellow."

"It's better for you, maybe, Billy Kirby," replied the indignant old hunter, "and all them that don't know how to put a ball down a rifle barrel, or how to bring it up again with a true aim; but it's wicked to be shooting into flocks in this wasty manner; and none do it who know how to knock over a single bird. If a body has a craving for pigeon's flesh, why! it's made the same as all other creaters, for man's eating; but not to kill twenty and eat one. When I want such a thing I go into the woods till I find one to my liking, and then I shoot him off the branches, without touching a feather of another, though there might be a hundred on the same tree. You couldn't do such a thing, Billy Kirby – you couldn't do it if you tried."

"What's that, old cornstalk! you sapless stub!" cried the wood chopper. "You've grown wordy, since the affair of the turkey; but if you're for a single shot, here goes at that bird which comes on by himself."

The fire from the distant part of the field had driven a single pigeon below the flock to which it belonged, and, frightened with the constant reports of the muskets, it was approaching the spot where the disputants stood, darting first from one side, and then to the other, cutting the air with the swiftness of lightning, and making a noise with its wings not unlike the rushing of a bullet. Unfortunately for the wood chopper, notwithstanding his vaunt, he did not see this bird until it was too late to fire as it approached, and he pulled his trigger at the unlucky moment when it was darting immediately over his head. The bird continued its course with the usual velocity.

Natty lowered the rifle from his arm when the challenge was made, and, waiting a moment until the terrified victim had got in a line with his eye, and had dropped near the bank of the lake, he raised it again with uncommon rapidity and fired. It might have been chance, or it might have been skill, that produced the result; it was probably a union of both; but the pigeon whirled over in the air, and fell into the lake with a broken wing. At the sound of his rifle both his dogs started from his feet, and in a few minutes the slut brought out the bird, still alive.

The wonderful exploit of Leatherstocking was noised through the field with great rapidity, and the sportsmen gathered in to learn the truth of the report.

"What!" said young Edwards, "have you really killed a pigeon on the wing, Natty, with a single ball?"

"Haven't I killed loons before now, lad, that dive at the flash?" returned the hunter. "It's much better to kill only such as you want, without wasting your powder and lead, than to be firing into God's creaters in this wicked manner. But I come out for a bird, and you know the reason why I like small game, Mr. Oliver, and now I have got one I will go home, for I don't relish to see these wasty ways that you are all practysing, as if the least thing wasn't made for use, and not to destroy."

"Thou sayest well, Leatherstocking," cried Marmaduke, "and I begin to think it time to put an end to this work of destruction."

"Put an ind, Judge, to your clearings. An't the woods His work as well as the pigeons? Use, but don't waste. Wasn't the woods made for the beasts and birds to harbor in? and when man wanted their flesh, their skins, or their feathers, there's the place to seek them. But I'll go to the hut with my own game, for I wouldn't touch one of the harmless things that cover the ground here, looking up with their eyes on me, as if they only wanted tongues to say their thoughts."

With this sentiment in his mouth, Leatherstocking threw his rifle over his arm, and followed by his dogs, stepped across the clearing with great caution, taking care not to tread on one of the wounded birds in his path. He soon entered the bushes on the margin of the lake, and was hid from view. . . .

Edwin Bryant, *What I Saw in California* (1846)

Reprinted from *A World Transformed: Firsthand Accounts of California before the Gold Rush* (Berkeley: Heyday Books, 1999)

James Fenimore Cooper described the profligate extermination of wildlife in upstate New York. But did other settlers in other parts of North America behave the same way? Our second document is an account by Edwin Bryant, who toured California when it was still a province of Mexico, in 1845. At this time, a small number of Americans had settled in the region, including one of Bryan's acquaintances on this trip, Robert Livermore, and the man Bryan refers to as Dr. Marsh. Many of these Americans joined with the elite of California's Mexican society in the ranching industry.

Pay close attention, and you can learn a good deal about California's environmental history and how poverty and international trade influenced the ways settlers interacted with nature there. Note how widespread cattle ranching has become, and the changes it has brought to the land (wild oats, which Bryant mentions, are exotic to California). As Bryant reveals, Californians of the 1840s traded cattle hides to firms in New York and Boston, where, California leather provided vital materials like machine belts and shoes for the Industrial Revolution. In what ways has the absence of a manufacturing industry in California made her settlers more dependent on merchants from New York and Boston? And how much has this motivated California ranchers to produce ever more cattle?

* * *

... The horned cattle of California that I have thus far seen are the largest and the handsomest in shape that I ever saw. There is certainly no breed in the United States equaling them in size. They, as well as the horses, subsist entirely upon the indigenous grasses at all seasons of the year; and such are the nutritious qualities of the herbage, that the former are always in condition for slaughtering, and the latter have as much flesh upon them as is desirable, unless (which is often the case) they are kept up at hard work and denied the privilege of eating, or are broken down by hard riding. The varieties of grass are very numerous, and nearly all of them are heavily seeded when ripe and are equal if not superior, as food for animals, to corn and oats. The horses are not as large as the breeds of the United States, but in point of symmetrical proportions and in capacity for endurance, they are fully equal to our best breeds. The distance we have traveled today I estimate at thirty-five miles.

September 17. The temperature of the mornings is most agreeable, and every other phenomenon accompanying it is correspondingly delightful to the senses. Our breakfast consisted of warm bread, made of unbolted flour; stewed beef, seasoned with *chile colorado*, a species of red pepper; and *frijoles*, a dark colored bean; with coffee. After breakfast I walked with Dr. Marsh to the summit of a conical hill, about a mile distant from his house, from which the view of the plain on the north, south, and east, and the more broken and mountainous country on the west is very extensive and highly picturesque. The hills and the plain are ornamented with the evergreen oak, sometimes in clumps or groves, at others standing solitary. On the summits and in the gorges of the mountains, the cedar, pine, and fir display their tall, symmetrical shapes; and the San Joaquín, at a distance of about ten miles, is belted by a dense forest of oak, sycamore, and smaller timber and shrubbery. The herds of cattle are scattered over the plain – some of them grazing upon the brown but nutritious grass; others sheltering themselves from the sun, under the wide-spreading branches of the oaks. The *toute ensemble* of the landscape is charming.

Leaving Dr. Marsh's about three o'clock p.m., we traveled fifteen miles over a rolling and well-watered country, covered generally with wild oats, and arrived at the residence of Mr. Robert Livermore just before dark. We were most kindly and hospitably received and entertained by Mr. L. and his interesting family. After our mules and baggage had been cared for, we were introduced to the principal room in the house, which consisted of a number of small *adobe* buildings, erected apparently at different times and connected together. Here we found chairs and, for the first time in California, saw a sideboard set out with glass tumblers and chinaware. A decanter of *aguardiente*, a bowl of loaf-sugar, and a pitcher of cold water from the spring were set before us; and being duly honored, had a most reviving influence upon our spirits as well as our corporeal energies. Suspended from the walls of the room were numerous coarse engravings – highly-colored with green, blue, and crimson paints – representing the Virgin Mary and many of the saints. These engravings are held in great veneration by the devout Catholics of this country. In the corners of the room were two comfortable-looking beds with clean white sheets and pillowcases, a sight with which my eyes have not been greeted for many months.

The table was soon set out and covered with a linen cloth of snowy whiteness, upon which were placed dishes of stewed beef – seasoned with *chile colorado* – *frijoles*, and a plentiful supply of *tortillas*, with an excellent cup of tea, to the merits of which we did ample justice. Never were men blessed with better appetites than we are at the present time.

Mr. Livermore has been a resident of California nearly thirty years; and having married into one of the wealthy families of the country, is the proprietor of some of the best lands for tillage and grazing. An *arroyo*, or small rivulet fed by springs, runs through his *rancho* in such a course that, if expedient, he could, without much expense, irrigate one or two thousand acres. Irrigation in this part of California, however, seems to be entirely unnecessary for the production of wheat or any of the small grains. To produce maize, potatoes, and garden vegetables, irrigation is indispensable. Mr. Livermore has on his *rancho* about 3,500 head of cattle. His horses, during the late disturbances, have nearly all been driven off or stolen by the Indians. I saw in his *corral* a flock of sheep numbering several hundred. They are of good size, and the mutton is said to be of an excellent quality, but the wool is coarse. It is, however, well adapted to the only manufacture of wool that is carried on in the country – coarse blankets and *serapes*. . . .

California, until recently, has had no commerce in the broad signification of the term. A few commercial houses of Boston and New York have monopolized all the trade on this coast for a number of years. These houses have sent out ships freighted with cargoes of dry goods and a variety of knick-knacks saleable in the country. The ships are fitted up for the retail sale of these articles, and trade from port to port, vending their wares on board to the *rancheros* at prices that would be astonishing at home. For instance, the price of common brown cotton cloth is one dollar per yard, and other articles in this and even greater proportion of advance upon home prices. They receive in payment for their wares, hides and tallow. The price of a dry hide is ordinarily one dollar and fifty cents. The price of tallow I do not know. When the ship has disposed of her cargo, she is loaded with hides and returns to Boston, where the hides bring about four or five dollars, according to the fluctuations of the market. Immense fortunes have been made by this trade; and between the government of Mexico and the traders on the coast, California has been literally skinned, annually, for the last thirty years. Of natural wealth the population of California possesses a superabundance and are immensely rich; still, such have been the extortionate prices that they have been compelled to pay for their commonest artificial luxuries and wearing apparel, that generally they are but indifferently provided with the ordinary necessaries of civilized life. For a suit of clothes, which in New York or Boston would cost seventy-five dollars, the Californian has been compelled to pay five times that sum in hides at one dollar and fifty cents; so that a *caballero*, to clothe himself genteelly, has been obliged, as often as he renewed his dress, to sacrifice about 200 of the cattle on his *rancho*. No people, whether males or females, are more fond of display; no people have paid more dearly to gratify this vanity; and yet no civilized people I have seen are so deficient in what they most covet. . . .

Section II: Nature and Slavery

Slavery was a defining institution of nineteenth-century America. For historians, the subject often leads to discussions of power, who had it, how much they had, and how they exercised it. What can the methods of environmental history reveal to us about such questions? Mart Stewart argues that slave peoples exercised considerable control over the local landscape of the rice plantation, and that within it they found degrees of autonomy not available to slaves in other places.

How did slave perceptions of nature differ from the perceptions of masters? How does the engineered environment of the rice plantation differ from other environments we have already examined, such as the New England forest or the California coast?

Rice, Water, and Power: Landscapes of Domination and Resistance in the Lowcountry, 1790–1880

Mart A. Stewart

The production of one of the American antebellum South's chief export commodities, rice, which was grown on plantations in tidewater South Carolina and Georgia, required the large-scale manipulation of the low-country environment. The well-engineered rice plantation, one South Carolina planter explained, was a "huge hydraulic machine." "The whole apparatus of levels, floodgates, trunks, canals, banks, and ditches is of the most extensive kind," he said, "requiring skill and unity of purpose to keep in order."[1] The "machines," in their most developed form, were massive engineering achievements that reshaped portions of the tidewater environment and required enormous investments of well-organized labor to make and maintain.

Water by its very nature imposes specific social, economic, and political necessities upon those who would control it, Karl Wittfogel has argued in *Oriental Despotism*, his provocative analysis of the great hydraulic civilizations in the ancient Middle and Far East. As many scholars who have tested Wittfogel's ideas through specific case studies of both past and present hydraulic cultures have discovered, each culture has distinctive features that are not predicted by Wittfogel's model. Yet this basic insight, that in societies that channel water for productive purposes, the flow of power and the control of water become harnessed together, applies to all studies of these cultures. Water and power converged in the tidewater, also, in a unique set of relationships. When rice planters and their slaves wrenched these "hydraulic machines" out of the river-swamp muck of the tidewater and operated them to produce this commodity, rice, they followed and further bound up and refined their relationships with each other. They imposed an orderly design on specific sections of the coastal plain environment and created a landscape within which crops, labor, and plantation communities were organized. Planters rationalized nature in the plantations to an extent that was unsurpassed on any agricultural enterprise in North America previous to the late nineteenth century.

Space is shaped in characteristic ways by every society; it is a social construct and an economic production, but can also be a means of production as well as a political instrument. Humans shape the land according to social, economic, and political agendas, within the constraints and limits of the particular environment in which they live. Planters coerced slaves into constructing systems to harness the flow of the tides to increase the production of rice for the market, and then used these systems to extend their domination and control over both environment and laborers. The landscapes they created expressed and reinforced at the same time the basic social and economic values of lowcountry society.

The planters' landscape of rice, water, and power was not constructed on unshakable ground. Slaves lived differently than their masters in this landscape and differently than their masters expected them to live. Power in the tidewater moved with the manipulation and control of the flow of water on the land, but the waterways were open to African-Americans who could move about on them. The unique feature of rice production work regimens – the task system – gave slaves in the lowcountry their "own time" within which they could moderate or modify the usual order of the plantation. At the same time, they moved in a different perceptual environment than their masters, both within and beyond the plantation banks.

The landscape they created was not as permanently marked as the one planters made. It moved between, rather than along, the inscriptions of property ownership and control. Planters always sought to order the movements of their slaves, and the African-American landscape was shaped on contested terrain. Nonetheless, it was deeply etched into the region. The rich estuarine environments filled subsistence needs and yielded up small commodities to the African-Americans whose movements around the locale were closer to the ground than their masters. Culture and nature were not so sharply distinguished from each other for slaves; the African-American experiences on the land and water were also intricately woven into the cultural fabric of the communities they created.

Two landscapes evolved in the lowcountry. One was clearly marked, and expressed the attempts of planters to manipulate water and dominate labor in the interest of production and profit. The other moved along quarterdrains and canals on the rice plantations but also on the waterways beyond the banks, and followed the attempts of slaves to mark out small spheres of autonomy. In the long duration, this latter, the landscape of African-Americans, became the prevalent one. After the Civil War and Emancipation, as the highly-structured plantation landscape began to erode, freedmen made more visible the landscape they had begun to shape as slaves.

Several scholars have described the development of the lowcountry rice
agriculture regimen, and a summary sketch will be adequate here. Rice
planters in the area first used an impoundment method to grow rice in
freshwater swamps. In the mid-eighteenth century they began experi-
menting with the use of tide-powered hydraulic systems. The development of these systems involved considerable trial and error on the part of
the planters and their slaves. By the nineteenth century, methods for
growing rice became increasingly standardized in the lowcountry.
Planters had an ideal in mind in the 1820s and 1830s when they wrote
articles about "rice culture" for agricultural journals. They acknowledged
local variations in the application and practice of the system, but regarded
fewer and fewer of these as the consequences of chance. By 1850, planters
talked about the system being "perfected."

The efforts to install the necessary system of drainage ditches and
banks that would allow the planters and their managers and overseers
a rational control of water flow required large, well-organized slave
forces and were constrained by several environmental imperatives. In
the first place, the disease environment of the lowcountry made year-
round habitation dangerous to whites; Africans who were partially
immune to malaria and yellow fever acquired a demographic edge in
the lowcountry plantation belt.

Planters also had to observe certain environmental conditions when
they decided on the location of their plantations within the tidewater.
The sites had to be near the mouth of a river and at a sufficient "pitch of
tide," with enough difference between the water levels of high and low
tides to facilitate easy flooding and draining of the fields. If the plantation was too close to the sea, the tides could push salt or brackish water
into the fields. A location too far upriver would remove the plantation
from tidal influence. Such a location, above the floodplain, would also
expose the plantation to the undiminished force of freshets coming down
the river. Rivers with long watersheds and deep channels – in Georgia,
the Savannah and the Altamaha, and in South Carolina, the Combahee
and Santee, for example – made the best locations (Map 4.1). Rivers that
did not have an adequate freshwater discharge to maintain a freshwater
current above the heavier incoming salt current, and estuaries that
resembled salt lagoons or that had turbulent currents and considerable
mixing of fresh and salt water did not make good environments for tidal
plantations.

Once planters, probably with the assistance of skilled slaves, established
a proper site for a wet-culture rice plantation, the procedure they used to
take in the area that was to be cultivated was usually the same in most
places in the tidewater. Plantation-making required a strong slave force to
put up the outer banks, construct the "check" banks, and install trunks

and floodgates in the banks. These systems required massive investments of labor. An eighth-square-mile plantation had two-and-a-quarter miles of exterior, interior, and "check" banks, and twelve or thirteen miles of canals, ditches, and quarterdrains. In other words, slaves working with axes and shovels had to move well over 39,000 cubic yards of fine-grained river-swamp muck to construct an eighty-acre plantation, in addition to clearing the land and leveling the ground. The regular maintenance of the system also required large applications of labor, especially when freshets or gales damaged the systems. Because of the labor requirements alone, then, the landscape developed and expanded slowly.

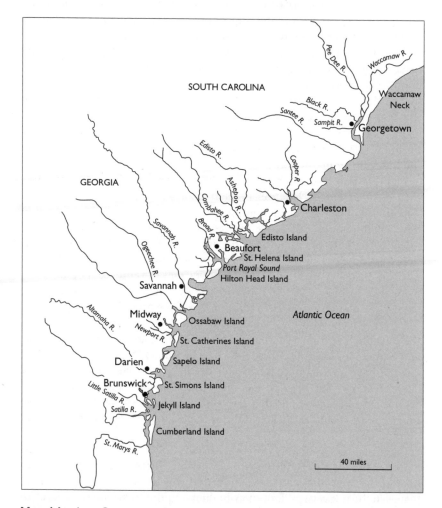

Map 4.1. Low Country rice rivers.

The grid of irrigation, drains, ditches, and canals, and of squares enclosed by check banks, all enclosed within an outer embankment, ordered the environment and provided a framework for crop production (Map 4.2). Both crop culture and labor were organized within this grid on the rice plantation. The various steps of rice cultivation were delegated to the different hands by task; the standard size of each task from the beginning was the quarter acre, marked off by quarterdrains.

The nature of the task system and its difference from the gang system used on upland cotton plantations is fairly well-known. What is significant here was that the task system and the physical grid within which it was organized became intertwined. By the early antebellum period, a "task" had become a unit of measurement, about 105 feet long, or a quarter acre, that planters and slaves applied to other situations. They perceived space and time in different ways through the "task." Most significantly, as slaves began to make distinctions between their own time and the time spent completing their daily tasks for the planter, they also began to distinguish between the space marked out by the task, the planter's space, and the space outside the banks and in the interstices of the grid that was their own.

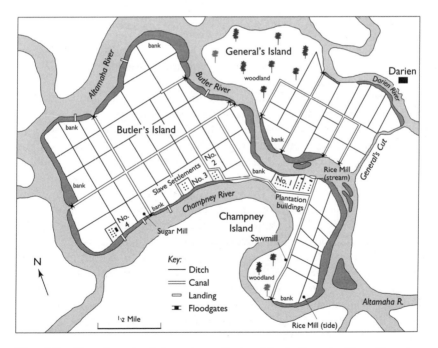

Map 4.2. Rice plantation infrastructure: Butlers Island, Altamaha River, Georgia, c 1855.

The development by planters and slaves of a hydraulic grid, a rational system with which tidal energy could be manipulated, and within which the crop and labor systems were organized, was not a deliberate attempt by them to structure resources and labor in an industrial model, to make a factory in the field. Such a model may have been expressed by this arrangement, but the arrangement itself was merely a system to manipulate water and to organize the land and the work upon the land. Once in place, however, the grid became a frame through which both planters and slaves organized their perceptions of the land and labor on the land. As the system became "perfected," planters organized the environment on an industrial model and the slave force in a highly-disciplined manner. Slaves, for their part, perceived space and time organized by this framework as not their own, and sought to articulate their own landscape in the gaps between tasks and in the space beyond the banks.

Rice does not require an extensive irrigation system and intensive use of the land to produce a crop. Natives grew it in parts of Indonesia, Malaysia, India, and the highlands of Vietnam on swidden plots in forests. Along the Inland Delta of the Niger River in West Africa, Africans grew rice on floodplains with only an occasional alteration of the environment. More significantly, West Africans grew different kinds of rice in different floodplain conditions and manipulated crops and agricultural practices to suit the environment, rather than vice versa. When high yields are crucial, however, wet rice culture utilizing an extensive irrigation system makes an enormous difference in the amount of rice that can be produced.

Tidewater rice-growing, then, expanded with the development of an economy that made this agricultural commodity profitable and was pushed into its fullest development by planters who were interested in maximizing production and profits. Planters simplified nature on the plantations, and created an artificial ecosystem with a massive application of human energy. The creators and managers of this system continued to redefine nature by conceiving of water in the surrounding environment as a source of energy. The raw flow of the coastal rivers and the Atlantic tides became a resource to command for flooding the fields. For planters who installed water mills on their plantations, water also became so many tons per minute of energy to extract for driving plantation machinery. South Carolina and Georgia rice planters selected out certain tidewater resources and amplified them by channeling them into the plantations' production process. With each successful step they took in the direction of channeling and dominating nature, they increased their belief in their power to control it.

The rice plantation landscape appeared to be a successful adaptation to nature. The efficient operation of this hydraulic machine, however, masked a fundamental reality. In order for the simplified and fragile ecological equilibrium of the rice plantation to be constructed and maintained, the equally fragile social equilibrium of the plantation community had to be stabilized through firm managerial authority and strict discipline. A quick repair of damage to the system was necessary, as when Roswell King, the manager of a large plantation on Butlers Island in the Altamaha River, in March 1807 took forty hands, a rice flat full of straw, and a boatload of timber, and shored up a fifty-foot breach – caused by a freshet – in the outer bank of the plantation in six hours. This kind of authority and disciplined organization was a social development, one that went hand-in-hand with the development of the natural environment. The engineering of nature and the engineering of one group of humans by another developed mutually. The slaves, subject to the discipline and order imposed by their owner, became instruments of environmental manipulation. The environment – especially the flow of water – then became an instrument to control the slaves. Slaves on the plantations became subject not only to the authority of the master and his hired managers, but also to the demands of the artificial ecosystem they had labored to establish. The environment did not determine this structure of authority and discipline, but once planters and their managers and overseers created this system, they used the shaped environment to consolidate it.[2]

Neither nature nor enslaved humans were so tractable, easy to regulate, and amenable to discipline, however, and challenges to the domination of masters were common. Some disordering forces blasted the foundations of social and environmental stability on the plantations. Several hurricanes caused such serious damage that some planters had to rebuild portions of their plantations. When British forces left several Georgia sea island plantations after a brief occupation in early 1815, over a thousand lowcountry slaves followed their promise of freedom and left with them. Their flight, in this rehearsal for emancipation, knocked a large hole in the labor forces of some planters and forced them to reduce their production. These were major challenges that temporarily swamped the exertions of some planters to maintain regular operations, and that required extensive salvage efforts, innovative management, and the coerced labor of a large force of slaves to overcome.

To control and prevent smaller perturbations in the usual stream of activity on a well-regulated rice plantation, planters used various means to manipulate and coerce the slaves: bribes and incentives, whippings, extra work as punishment, close supervision by a hierarchy of drivers, overseers, and managers, and the extensions of various "privileges." Though these methods were largely successful in maintaining order on the plantations, slaves were seldom as disciplined and as dependent on their masters as masters imagined or wanted them to be. Not only did they have time, after their tasks were completed in mid- or late-afternoon, to pursue their own interests, but their intimate knowledge of the environment both on and off the plantation allowed them to pass through it with ease and to procure from it plants and animals to supplement their provisions and small commodities for their own profit.

On the plantation, their work accustomed them to a much closer view of the cultivated environment than the managers' or masters'. When a storm came they went out on the banks to repair breaches; sometimes the slave settlements themselves were immersed. They were responsible for cleaning out the small but destructive imperfections of the cultures, for ridding the fields of the pests, the weeds and insects, that periodically have population explosions in single-crop environments. If caterpillars or grasshoppers attacked the cotton, the hands had to make an attempt to clean the fields. "About ten days past those large, black and red winged Grasshoppers was so numerous I ordered them picked from the Cotton," Roswell King reported on one occasion. He could describe them at arm's length only because he counted the bushels of grasshoppers – about forty – the hands picked from the plants.[3]

At the same time, they were aware, from row to row, of the progress of the plants during the growing season. They put seeds in the ground and covered them with their feet, stirred and tilled the earth when hoeing, and bent down over rice stalks or moved slowly down rows of cotton (cotton was sometimes grown in rotation with rice) during harvest. The hands experienced the crop cultures from the ground up.

Perceptions and behavior went hand-in-hand. Slaves translated this keen awareness and precise knowledge of the environment into a landscape of subsistence and small profit. They commonly planted in the interstices of the plantation grid, in the hours after they completed their tasks. They raised small crops of corn, sweet potatoes, benne seed, sugar cane, red peppers, okra, groundnuts, and rice around their cabins, on the canal banks, and in ponds and "bottom places" in the undeveloped portions of the plantations. Lowcountry slaves also commonly owned a variety of barnyard fowl and ran cattle and hogs in the nearby woods and marshes.

They also used to advantage their understanding of the swamps and woods beyond the banks. There they found firewood, logs to make canoes, and Spanish moss to sell for mattress stuffing. They gathered, hunted, and fished the rich resources of the estuarine environment. White-tailed deer, opossum, rabbits, raccoons, alligators, and waterfowl, as well as a wide variety of shellfish, crustaceans, and fish provided them with supplements to their plantation rations. Tidewater and sea island slaves may have procured nearly half the meat in their diets from wild sources.

Masters encouraged slaves to provide for themselves, to reduce plantation expenses, but they wanted slaves to depend on them for the core of their diets. But slaves who had time of their own, could move about easily in good weather on the network of waterways that laced the region, and had the skills to exploit the rich estuary and coastal environments for both sustenance and trade, had access to unique opportunities that were often threatening to plantation order.

Technically the slaves on the coast were subject to the state slave codes, which restricted all movements without a permission ticket. But unregulated movement on the waterways beyond the immediate environs of the coastal plantations was a common accomplishment for slaves, though they had to go and return "between two days." Their success in exploiting estuarine resources in the surrounding environment provided incentives for continued exploitation, as did close ties with African-Americans on neighboring plantations. Masters often extended certain "privileges" for excursions beyond the banks, including trips to nearby towns, yet they sought to monitor movement carefully within circumscribed limits. When they were unable to restrict the movements of slaves with regulations, they destroyed or locked up their canoes. Slaves simply made new ones. Canoes, knowledge of the waterways, and the slaves' movements beyond the banks in their "own time" made one of the larger gaps through which plantation order and discipline leaked.[4]

Planters worried that slaves who traveled beyond the banks and beyond plantation regulations were doing much more than gathering moss. In 1829, when Roswell King, Jr., attempted to stop the trade the Butlers Island slaves conducted in Darien, a mile away from the plantation by water, he was worried not about the trade, but the other kinds of activities he associated with it. Along with the trade, he wanted to end, he said, ". . . indiscriminate intercourse with other plantations, having wives abroad or strangers having wives here, introducing disease and contention, leaving homes on Saturday night, & returning on Monday morning, all of which tend to produce drunkenness, idleness, thievery, & indisposition."[5] For King, as with others who sought to grow rice in the tidewater, the movements of slaves beyond the banks brought disorder of every kind. Planters saw order in the environment and the regulations of the slaves as intertwined, and sought to manage both. They bound up plantation order and the grid of discipline with their authority and attempted to maintain control, as best they could, over both the actions and the environments of their slaves.[6]

What was "disorder" to planters – they also called challenges to plantation order "contamination" or "pollution" – was a limited autonomy to slaves. When slaves moved beyond the grid of discipline on the plantation, they were not skulking around the waterways with no purpose other than to make trouble. They were creating a community of their own that had its own coherence and that was closely tied to the environment where they lived and labored. The slaves also generalized their unique perceptions of and interaction with the natural environment of the tidewater and their knowledge of its functions into cultural forms that bound up self, community, and nature in specific locales (such as folk tales that reflected their precise understanding of the natural environment and social relations together, and family networks that were closely tied to the locale). And though their culture was hemmed in by the constraints of slavery, it provided them some insulation against the efforts of their masters to control their lives.

As several scholars have explained, after the Civil War and Emancipation planters retained the dominant hand in the control of land along the coast, but they could no longer coerce labor to keep the rice plantations going. If laborers were to work in the rice fields, they had to be bargained with. Freedmen and women whose understanding of the cycles of rice production had been passed down for at least two generations and who had the skills to exploit the tidewater environments to meet subsistence needs had a bargaining edge when contracting for labor with their old masters. Though South Carolina and Georgia planters were able to coax former slaves to labor for them in the rice fields, they often had to make concessions to them.

Planters also attempted to confront new labor shortages and to maintain the rice plantation regimen by reducing the formidable labor needs of rice culture. They used mules to pull drags to clean the ditches, plows and harrows to prepare the ground, rice drills to plant, horse-hoes to weed the crops, and carts to carry harvested rice from the fields to the rice barns. Previously most of these tasks had been done exclusively by hand. Planters also built elevated platforms on the banks for the bundles of recently-harvested rice, to protect them from freshets and to eliminate possible salvage costs. Some also changed the growing regimen to circumvent the necessity of certain kinds of labor.

In the 1880s, the development of a modern, more mechanized rice industry on fresh land in Louisiana, Arkansas, and East Texas added to the troubles of the Georgia and South Carolina tidewater planters and put them in a competitive bind. Though most were able to reduce labor costs, it became still more difficult for many of them to maintain the necessary profit margin to keep the hydraulic infrastructure of the plantations in good order.

Planters especially struggled with the high costs of maintaining the banks, drains, and ditches. Every freshet and gale challenged the functioning of the hydraulic system and the commitment of planters to continue operations. The planters' illusion of domination dissolved completely at this point, and the effectiveness of the "hydraulic machine" was challenged conclusively at the same time. The freedmen refused to get into the ditches and go out on the banks altogether. When planters were no longer able to coerce them, ditch and bank maintenance was the one kind of plantation work they refused to do. Rice planters throughout the lowcountry experimented with imported laborers – Irish, English, Italian and Chinese – for the necessary ditch and embankment maintenance, but failed to find a long-term solution to this perennial problem.

This was the strongest sign of the vulnerability of the rice plantation hydraulic system to forces beyond the banks. The War permanently upset the equilibrium of social relations on tidewater plantations. With a change in social relations came a change in environmental ones. This increasingly exposed the vulnerability of the rice plantation landscape to both human and natural forces. What one rice plantation manager in 1880 called the "two essentials" of a rice harvest, good weather and "plenty of labor offering," were needed for maintaining the means of production as well as for production. When the weather was not good, the second "essential" became even more important.[7]

Rice plantations and the culture for which they provided the material foundation were deeply entrenched in the lowcountry. Planters had structured society and economy in the tidewater with the hydraulic infrastructures of the rice plantations; these required large commitments of capital, labor, and other resources. Once in place, the system carried powerful incentives for further commitment. In spite of the dependence of the system on the market and the vulnerability of it to environmental and social challenges, tidewater planters continued producing rice for another thirty or forty years.

Finally, planters proved unable to persist with the illusion of economic viability. Low profits, strong competition, and labor and environmental problems combined to destroy the economy and the landscape that structured it. A series of devastating storms along the Georgia and South Carolina coasts in the 1890s sealed the fate of this kind of land use in the lowcountry. Planters could no longer bear the high cost of maintaining the rice production infrastructure and of producing rice in a restricted labor market. Though a few rice plantations continued to operate into the twentieth century, this hydraulic landscape, which had dominated the tidewater for over a century and had provided the material foundation for a society that had already faded, eroded beyond repair.

In the meantime, tidewater African-Americans shaped their antebellum landscape more freely and in more visible terms, in a patchwork of landholdings that became hubs of their movements around the locale for occasional wage or sharecropping labor and for fishing, hunting, and gathering. They were unusually successful, compared to freedmen elsewhere, in acquiring small parcels of land of their own. The demise of staple-crop agriculture, declining prices for land, and the availability of wage-paying jobs combined to provide conditions that freedmen exploited extensively to purchase land, to acquire some measure of self-sufficiency, and to achieve independence from the supervision and domination of their old masters. The rice plantation landscape was no longer contested terrain, as freedmen either gained some leverage to work as they wished or removed themselves from the plantations altogether.

Though the economy lowcountry African-Americans were able to create and negotiate remained a poor one and occupied a peripheral position to the larger American economy, freedmen in the tidewater were on the whole able to remain more independent of white supervision and domination – to be more "free" – than freedmen and women in other plantation areas in the South after the Civil War and the failure of Reconstruction. They did so by using the land in their own ways and then by working for wages or for a share of the crop on a daily, weekly, or seasonal basis. In effect, they expanded the "own time" they had as slaves to fill most of their days. Coastal freedmen founded an economy and community life on perceptions of and relationships with the natural environment they had cultivated most intensively as slaves, after they had completed their tasks. When some researchers from the U.S. Bureau of Soils observed in 1910 that the only labor available for agriculture in coastal Glynn County was from the black population, but that these hands were "unskilled and scarce for farm work, owing to the fact that a living can be made easily in fishing and oystering or by working intermittently at turpentine gathering or lumbering," they were recognizing work patterns, perceptions of the environment, and a land use behavior that had its origin in the area over a century before. The planters' hydraulic landscape of power and profitability had disintegrated, and this, the landscape of the African-Americans they dominated, became the dominant one in the tidewater.

Acknowledgment

The author thanks Jane Haraway-Stewart for drawing the maps.

Notes

1 David Doar, *Rice and Rice Planting in the South Carolina Low Country* (Charleston, S.C.: The Charleston Museum, 1970), 8.
2 Roswell King to Pierce Butler, March 28, 1807, Butler Family Papers (hereinafter BFP), Historical Society of Pennsylvania (hereinafter HSP).
3 Roswell King to Pierce Butler, August 2, 1818, July 23, 1808, BFP, HSP.
4 Act for ordering and governing Slaves within this Province, May 10, 1770, in Howell Cobb, comp., *General and Public Statutes of the State of Georgia* (N.Y.:

Edward O. Jenkins, 1859), 596; Roswell King to Pierce Butler, July 20, 1817, BFP, HSP.
5   Roswell King, Jr., to Thomas Butler, August 9, 1828, BFP, HSP.
6   Roswell King, Jr. to Thomas Butler, August 9, September 27, 1835, WFP, HSP.
7   James Couper to P. C. Hollis, April 10, August 26, 1880, BFP, HSP.

Documents

Map of Doboy and Altamaha Sounds (1856)

Maps can be very useful tools for environmental history. Our first document is a map of Doboy and Altamaha Sounds in the rice district. This is an area that is central to Stewart's analysis. You can see the grid pattern of canals that

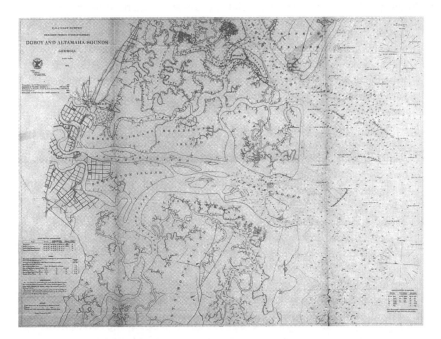

Map 4.3.   Doboy and Altamaha Sounds, Georgia, prepared by the U.S. Coast Survey in 1850. Hydraulic waterways, as the map shows, connect to natural ones. Depictions of rice fields and works adjacent to Darien, on Broughton Island, Generals Island, the south bank of the Altamaha, and on portions of Butlers Island and Champneys Island can be seen at left. Courtesy, Hargrett Rare Book and Manuscript Library, University of Georgia Libraries.

water the rice plantations at the left, and how they join up to the curving waterways of lowland rivers such as the Altamaha. Without having read Stewart's article, it would be easy to speculate that the change in the shape of waterways across the map – from free-flowing river to regimented grid – represented a decline in the freedom of people who lived there. But Mart Stewart suggests that the situation was more complicated than that, and that slaves and masters had very different perceptions of the canals and the surrounding landscape.

As an exercise in mapping slave autonomy and economy, try the following. On a piece of notebook paper, draw a sample grid of canals and natural waterways. Then add other features to your map, such as slave gardens, cabins, and livestock. Point out where slaves might have wanted to gather mussels, fish, and other wildlife. What other economic activities of slaves does Stewart discuss that you can put on your map? Once you have mapped out how slaves might have lived in this area, ask yourself what features of this mapped landscape owners would have approved of? Which ones did they seek to limit or eliminate? And how did the slaves' intimate knowledge of this environment make it more difficult for masters to exploit them as laborers during the time of slavery and after? In what ways did the environment of this area assist in the downfall of slavery as a labor system?

Frederick Law Olmsted, "The Rice District"

Reprinted from *The Cotton Kingdom: A Selection*, ed. David Freeman Hawke (New York: Bobbs-Merrill Company, Inc., 1971)

Our last document in this chapter is a description of a rice and cotton plantation in Georgia, written by the landscape architect (and northerner) Frederick Law Olmsted in the 1850s. Slaves assigned to different duties valued the relative autonomy available to them, ways that should make us question whether the freedom of the open waterways in the rice districts was preferred by all slaves. Note also the prevalence of malaria.

This connects this chapter to the Alfred Crosby reading in Chapter 2. Malaria is a plasmodium carried by mosquitoes. It is endemic to Africa, and was carried to the Americas by the clouds of mosquitoes hovering over water barrels in the holds of ships. It devastated Indian peoples, and took a heavy toll among white settlers in the Americas, too. Because Africans have developed limited resistance to the plasmodium over millennia of exposure to it, the expansion of the malarial frontier in the southern lowland districts (where winters are mild enough for mosquitoes to survive) helped to make Africans the preferred labor force of plantation owners there. Thus, we must ask: does the biological advantage of disease immunity always imply a political advantage? Or were African and African-American slaves in part the victims of their own biological success?

* * *

Plantation, February. – I left [Savannah] yesterday morning, on horse-back, with a letter in my pocket to Mr. X., under whose roof I am now writing.

Mr. X. has two plantations on the river, besides a large tract of poor pine forest land, extending some miles back upon the upland, and reaching above the malarious region. In the upper part of this pine land is a house, occupied by his overseer during the malarious season, when it is dangerous for any but Negroes to remain during the night in the vicinity of the swamps or rice fields. Even those few who have been born in the region, and have grown up subject to the malaria, are said to be generally weakly and short-lived. The Negroes do not enjoy as good health on rice plantations as elsewhere; and the greater difficulty with which their lives are preserved, through infancy especially, shows that the subtle poison of the miasma is not innocuous to them; but Mr. X. boasts a steady increase of his Negro stock, of five per cent per annum, which is better than is averaged on the plantations of the interior.

The plantation which contains Mr. X.'s winter residence has but a small extent of rice land, the greater part of it being reclaimed upland swamp soil, suitable for the culture of Sea Island cotton. The other plantation contains over five hundred acres of rice land, fitted for irrigation; the remainder is unusually fertile reclaimed upland swamp, and some hundred acres of it are cultivated for maize and Sea Island cotton.

There is a "Negro settlement" on each; but both plantations, although a mile or two apart, are worked together as one, under one overseer – the hands being drafted from one to another as their labor is required. Some-what over seven hundred acres are at the present time under the plow in the two plantations: the whole number of Negroes is two hundred, and they are reckoned to be equal to about one hundred prime hands – an unusual strength for that number of all classes. The overseer lives, in winter, near the settlement of the larger plantation, Mr. X. near that of the smaller.

It is an old family estate, inherited by Mr. X.'s wife, who, with her children, was born and brought up upon it in close intimacy with the Negroes, a large proportion of whom were also included in her inherit-ance, or have been since born upon the estate. Mr. X. himself is a New England farmer's son, and has been a successful merchant and manu-facturer.

The patriarchal institution should be seen here under its most favorable aspects; not only from the ties of long family association, common traditions, common memories, and, if ever, common interests, between the slaves and their rulers, but, also, from the practical talent for organization and administration, gained among the rugged fields, the complicated looms, and the exact and comprehensive counting houses of New England, which directs the labor.

The house servants are more intelligent, understand and perform their duties better, and are more appropriately dressed, than any I have seen before. The labor required of them is light, and they are treated with much more consideration for their health and comfort than is usually given to that of free domestics. They live in brick cabins, adjoining the house and stables, and one of these, into which I have looked, is neatly and comfortably furnished. Several of the house servants, as is usual, are mulattoes, and good looking. The mulattoes are generally preferred for indoor occupations. Slaves brought up to housework dread to be employed at field labor; and those accustomed to the comparatively unconstrained life of the Negro settlement, detest the close control and careful movements required of the house servants. It is a punishment for a lazy field hand, to employ him in menial duties at the house, as it is to set a sneaking sailor to do the work of a cabin servant; and it is equally a punishment to a neglectful house servant, to banish him to the field gangs. All the household economy is, of course, carried on in a style appropriate to a wealthy gentleman's residence – not more so, nor less so, that I observe, than in an establishment of similar grade at the North.

5

Urban Nature and Urban Reforms

Many people think of environmental history as rural history, in part because we tend to believe that cities are somehow outside nature. In fact, urban settlements are as intimately entwined with the natural world as any wilderness or farm field. Their concentrations of people, animals, energy, and resources often lead to unprecedented environmental changes, including new relationships between organisms. The growth of American cities in the eighteenth and nineteenth centuries entailed new relations between people, space, and resources such as water, shelter, and food. One result of this was a new environment for disease. In 1832, Asiatic cholera arrived in the United States. A bacterium conveyed largely by unsanitary water, it became to the nineteenth century what bubonic plague had been to the fourteenth century. It killed half the people who caught it. It knocked people dead in the streets, almost without warning. Its virulence was so great that it threatened the very existence of urban America, and it spread from cities into the countryside in devastating ways. In 1849, for example, cholera spread from cities to rural settlements and along the Oregon Trail, where it killed many Gold Rush emigrants and devastated Indian tribes of the Great Plains.

In important ways, the ongoing story of pathogenic evolution and transmission in America's cities takes us back to the virgin soil epidemics described in chapter 2. Without radical changes to deliver fresh water for drinking, cleaning, and sewage disposal, cholera might well have made the great cities of modern America merely a dream. The cholera epidemics of the 1830s motivated civic leaders and their constituents to support construction of aqueducts. In New York City, the Croton aqueduct would bring a plentiful supply of fresh water from the Croton watershed some 40 miles away. Charles Rosenberg explains how cholera changed Americans' perception of nature and disease, and galvanized support for civic projects to build new delivery systems for that vital natural resource, water. Although Americans in 1832 did not know that cholera was caused by bacteria, or that it was carried in contaminated water, they intuitively sensed that cleanliness would protect them from its terrors. In a way, they were right.

How much do changes in nature lead to changes in our perceptions of how to organize our settlements and our human relations? How does changing nature lead to shifts in perceived needs for new relations between peoples and their governments?

From *The Cholera Years: The United States in 1832, 1849, and 1866*

Charles E. Rosenberg

Introduction

Cholera was the classic epidemic disease of the nineteenth century, as plague had been of the fourteenth. When cholera first appeared in the United States in 1832, yellow fever and smallpox, the great epidemic diseases of the previous two centuries, were no longer truly national problems. Yellow fever had disappeared from the North, and vaccination had deprived smallpox of much of its menace. Cholera, on the other hand, appeared in almost every part of the country in the course of the century. It flourished in the great cities, New York, Cincinnati, Chicago; it crossed the continent with the forty-niners; its victims included Iowa dirt farmers and New York longshoremen, Wisconsin lead miners and Negro field hands.

Before 1817, there had probably never been a cholera epidemic outside the Far East; during the nineteenth century, it spread through almost the entire world. Of all epidemic diseases, only influenza in the twentieth century has had a more extensive odyssey.

Cholera could not have thrived where filth and want did not already exist; nor could it have traveled so widely without an unprecedented development of trade and transportation. The cholera pandemics were transitory phenomena, destined to occupy the world stage for only a short time – the period during which public health and medical science were catching up with urbanization and the transportation revolution. Indeed, cholera was to play a key role in its own banishment from the Western world; the cholera epidemics of the nineteenth century provided much of the impetus needed to overcome centuries of governmental inertia and indifference in regard to problems of public health.

It was not easy for survivors to forget a cholera epidemic. The symptoms of cholera are spectacular; they could not be ignored or romanticized as were the physical manifestations of malaria and tuberculosis. One could as easily ignore a case of acute arsenical poisoning, the symptoms of which are strikingly similar to those of cholera. The onset of cholera is marked by diarrhea, acute spasmodic vomiting, and painful cramps. Consequent dehydration, often accompanied by cyanosis, gives to the sufferer a characteristic and disquieting appearance: his face blue and pinched, his extremities cold and darkened, the skin of his hands and feet drawn and puckered. "One often," recalled a New York physician, "thought of the Laocoön, but looked in vain for the serpent." Death may intervene within a day, sometimes within a few hours of the appearance of the first symptoms. And these first symptoms appear with little or no warning. He felt no premonition of cholera at all, reported a New Yorker in 1832, until he pitched forward in the street, "as if knocked down with an axe."[1]

The abrupt onset and fearful symptoms of cholera made Americans apprehensive and reflective – as they were not by the equally deadly, but more deliberate, ravages of tuberculosis or malaria. "To see individuals well in the morning & buried before night, retiring apparently well & dead in the morning is something which is appalling to the boldest heart."[2] It is not surprising that the growing public health movement found in cholera an effective ally.

It was not until 1883 that Robert Koch, directing a German scientific commission in Egypt, isolated the organism that causes cholera – *Vibrio comma*, a motile, comma-shaped bacterium. Once they find their way into the human intestine, these vibrios are capable of producing an acute disease which, if untreated, kills roughly a half of those unfortunate enough to contract it. Cholera, like typhoid, can be spread along any pathway leading to the human digestive tract. Unwashed hands or uncooked fruits and vegetables, for example, are frequently responsible for the transmission of the disease, though sewage-contaminated water supplies have been the cause of the most severe, widespread, and explosive cholera epidemics.

Though never endemic in this country, cholera returned to the United States four times after its initial appearance in 1832–34. After this two-year visit, North America was free of the disease until the winter of 1848–49. Between 1849 and 1854, however, no twelve-month period passed without cholera appearing in some part of the United States. Then the disease disappeared as abruptly as it had in 1834; it was not to return until 1866.

Thirty-four years are a short time in man's history. Yet few historians would question the significance or magnitude of the changes effected in American society between 1832 and 1866....

Perhaps most striking of the changes in America between 1832 and 1866 was the dissipation of the piety still so characteristic of many Americans in the Age of Jackson. The evangelical fervor of this earlier generation had been eroded by a materialism already present in 1832, but seemingly triumphant by 1866.... Cholera, a scourge of the sinful to many Americans in 1832, had, by 1866, become the consequence of remediable faults in sanitation. Whereas ministers in 1832 urged morality upon their congregations as a guarantor of health, their forward-looking counterparts in 1866 endorsed sanitary reform as a necessary prerequisite to moral improvement. There could be no public virtue without public health.

The means of improving the public health seemed clear enough. Clean streets, airy apartments, a pure supply of water, were certain safeguards against epidemic disease. And by 1866, advocates of sanitary reform could in justification of their programs point to the discovery of John Snow, a London physician, that cholera was spread through a contaminated water supply. The matter-of-fact, empirical approach to epidemiology which enabled Snow to confirm his theory of the disease's transmission would have been rare a century before. He had, as well, new theories of disease causation, of the very nature of disease, available to him. Cholera in 1849, for example, was assumed by the great majority of physicians to be a specific disease, whereas in 1832, most practitioners had still regarded cholera as a vague atmospheric malaise and had vigorously disavowed the very existence of specific disease entities.

In 1832, most Americans regarded the United States as a land of health, virtue, and rustic simplicity. Cities seemed often unnatural and perhaps ultimately undesirable excrescences in our otherwise green and pleasant realm. By 1866, this was no longer the case. America's cities had grown immensely in size and significance; they could be deplored, but no longer ignored. But though the existence of the city might be inevitable, its evils were not. The willingness to accept the city and its continued growth was an indispensable step in the finding of appropriate solutions to the problems such growth created. Flight to the country was no longer in 1866, as it had been to many in 1849, an acceptable solution to urban problems. A pure water supply, adequate sanitation, and a reliable police force were necessary if the dangerous and unhealthful conditions of city life were to be ameliorated.

When in the spring of 1832 Americans awaited cholera, they reassured themselves that this new pestilence attacked only the filthy, the hungry, the ignorant. There seemed few such in the United States. In the spring of 1866, when Americans again prepared themselves for an impending cholera epidemic, they expected no such exemption. North America had nurtured slums as squalid as any of those festering in the Old World. Their inhabitants, moreover, were not the pious, cleanly, and ambitious Americans of an earlier generation. Filthy, illiterate peasants could expect no greater exemption from cholera in Boston than that which they had received in Ireland. America was no longer a city set upon a hill. The piety which sustained such a belief and the confidence which this belief engendered were both disappearing. Americans were adjusting to life on the plain.

The Epidemic: 1832

It had been an unhealthy winter and the dry spring promised a sickly summer. But New York, a vigorous city of almost a quarter of a million, had other concerns in the spring of 1832. She was the greatest port of the continent, one of the greatest in the world, and her leaders were busy at wharves and in counting rooms ensuring her continued eminence. It was an election year, and the readers of New York's score of newspapers were not allowed to forget the Indian troubles, the tariff controversy, or the bank question.

Like Boston, Philadelphia, and Baltimore, New York was a city which faced Europe, and there was disquieting news from across the Atlantic. Cholera had broken out in England; a *cordon sanitaire* – enforced by heavily armed troops – had failed to halt the spread of the disease westward from Poland and Russia. Quarantine restrictions seemed to be of no avail, and as the summer of 1832 approached, it appeared more than likely that America, like Russia, France, and England, would be visited by this newest judgment. Only the Atlantic Ocean continued to protect the United States.

This, the first invasion of Europe by cholera, had not gone unnoticed in America. Throughout the fall and winter of 1831–32, newspapers, magazines, and pamphlets reported in alarming detail its westward spread. Most dismaying, because most dispassionate, were the reports of the French and English medical commissions sent to study the disease in Russia and Poland. American medical men turned to the treatises of East India Company physicians, familiar for decades with this pestilence new to the medical world of Europe, in hopes of finding some remedy. By July of 1832, it seemed questionable whether a single periodical had appeared in the past six months without "something on this all engrossing subject."

Private citizens were not alone in their concern. On September 6, 1831, the New York City Board of Health had resolved that three of the city's most prominent physicians be requested to form a committee of correspondence to gather information.[3] . . .

Collecting information could not alone prevent disease. Stringent quarantines were immediately invoked against Europe's cholera-ridden ports. In the past, restrictions had been applied only during the summer months. But cholera, unlike yellow fever, seemed to show no preference for warm climates, and quarantine regulations were maintained in America's Atlantic ports throughout the winter of 1831–32. . . .

With the spring of 1832 and the recrudescence of the epidemic in Europe, only the most sanguine remained confident that America would continue to be spared. . . . Even the common folk began to sense omens. All that year, one Washingtonian recalled: "The Sun Rised and Set Red . . . and two Black Spots could be discovered disstint in the Sun."[4]

But Americans were not without consolation. Cholera did not attack all, nor did it seem to be an arbitrary imposition of God. It was subject to natural laws and acted through second causes, attacking only those who had somehow weakened or "predisposed" themselves. Filth, misery, vice, and poverty conspired to produce its unfortunate victims. Few such could be found in a land enjoying those unique blessings granted the United States. . . .

Americans, as they readily acknowledged, were the best educated, the freest, and the most pious of people. . . . The history of cholera seemed to demonstrate clearly that those countries with fewest Christians had been scourged most severely. America's chastisement would certainly be light, the pious hopefully predicted, for fully one half of the world's evangelical Christians lived within her boundaries.

It did not seem, moreover, that a nation predominately rural could be severely tried. Only in the densely populated cities of the Old World had cholera raged uncontrolled. Rural communities were assured that their pure atmosphere, uncrowded streets, and isolation guaranteed exemption from the disease. Even America's great eastern cities seemed cleaner and their inhabitants of better character than their counterparts in Europe. . . .

Nevertheless, few pious Americans dared deny that their nation, despite the great favors granted it by the Lord, still harbored a great many of the sinful and vicious – more than enough to provoke divine judgment. New York seemed especially vulnerable, the largest and filthiest, the most crowded and vice-disfigured of American cities.

Apprehensive New Yorkers took stock of their city and were not reassured by what they saw and smelled. New York was dirty, and dirt seemed to breed disease – not only cholera, but yellow fever, malaria, and every other sort of pestilence. Boston and Philadelphia seemed immaculate country villages by comparison.

The thousands of swine that roamed its streets were the city's shame, but, nevertheless, its only efficient scavengers. The indifference of the Common Council to the problem of sanitation almost necessitated the lenience, if not affection, with which the pigs were treated. Ordinances to control them were passed from time to time, but never enforced. Respectable folk were continually exasperated by the sight of the beasts, some even threatening to shoot them on sight.

Pigs, goats, and dogs did not provide the only street cleaning apparatus. Citizens were required by law to sweep in front of their houses on certain specified days. Dust and rubbish were to be gathered into a pile in the middle of the gutter from which place they were to be collected by the municipality. An item of Tammany graft or inefficiency, this collection was usually neglected; and appropriately, the decomposing mass of filth which adorned the middle of the streets was called "corporation pie" (New Yorkers, it should be noted, ordinarily referred to their municipal government as the Corporation). In any case, most informed citizens agreed, the streets could never be cleaned properly unless an adequate supply of water was introduced into the city.

Four decades of agitation for a municipal water system had failed to bring results. Few travelers failed to comment on the poor quality of New York water. A standing joke maintained that city water was far better than any other, since it served as a purgative as well as for washing and cooking. Most people were sensible enough not to drink it, except when forced by poverty or betrayed through inadvertence. Only the poor used the city pumps. Those who could afford the expense had their water supplied in hogsheads from the "pure" springs and wells of the countryside.

Foreigners regarded dyspepsia as America's national malady, and an American dinner could easily be an unnerving experience. Filthy and adulterated food was prepared with little care or cleanliness in kitchens swarming with flies and then bolted as rapidly as possible – perhaps in self-defense. Although cleanliness was appreciated as an abstract virtue, its observance in practice left much to be desired. A New England physician remarked that not one in five of his patients bathed or washed their bodies in water once a year.[5] And this was the wholesome New England countryside. For the city poor, maintaining any kind of cleanliness was almost impossible. Most lived in tiny unventilated apartments, often with whole families – and perhaps a few boarders – occupying the same room, a condition deplored by physicians and moralists alike. The most miserable and degraded lived in unfinished cellars, their walls a mat of slime, sewage, and moisture after every rain. Houses adjoined stables, abattoirs, and soap factories; their front yards were the meeting place of dogs, swine, chickens, and horses.

Their city a seemingly foreordained stopping place for cholera, New Yorkers naturally questioned the powers which their municipal government would be able to call upon should there be an epidemic.... The day-to-day business of keeping a city of a quarter of a million healthy was the responsibility of only three men, the health officer of the port, the resident physician, and the city inspector.

The health officer, appointed by the state and working in conjunction with the Board of Health, was responsible for enforcing the quarantine regulations. The duty of the resident physician, a municipal appointee, was to diagnose and report any communicable diseases which might exist in the city. This was a peculiarly vulnerable position, for premature diagnosis of an epidemic disease would mean severe loss to the city's business. The resident physician in 1819 who had had the temerity to diagnose a case of yellow fever was bestowed with "every abusive epithet which could degrade or disgrace" and threatened with personal injury. (The board itself was, as William Dunlap remarked to his friend Dr. John W. Francis, "more afraid of the merchants than of lying."[6]) The city inspector, another municipal officer, was more strictly an administrator, charged with the keeping of vital statistics and the enforcement of sanitary regulations.

The weaknesses of the board were apparent to even the most casual observer. Composed of laymen, it was dependent for advice upon the city's physicians, while as an executive committee, it was dependent upon the Board of Assistant Aldermen for financial and legislative support. The board had only three regular employees, a secretary and two assistants. It had no office, no dispensary, not even a library. It hibernated each winter. Its membership was undistinguished, and as events were to show, slow to act on professional advice when it seemed to endanger the financial well-being of the city.

As spring warmed into summer, the inactivity of the Corporation began to provoke more and more criticism. Nothing, it seemed, had been done to protect the city. Cholera would rage uncontrollably should it arrive "at this moment," one critic warned early in June, "in the midst of the filth and stench with which our streets are filled."[7] But the authorities had not been completely supine. Walter Bowne, the mayor, had hastened to proclaim a blanket quarantine against almost all of Europe and Asia. On June 4, a new act to regulate the cleaning of the city's streets was introduced into the Board of Assistants. The act, which was signed by the Mayor on Wednesday, June 13, completely reorganized New York's sanitation system.

Two days later, on the fifteenth, the threat became more real and more imminent. The Albany steamboat which docked that Friday afternoon brought word that cholera had broken out in Quebec and Montreal. The Atlantic had been forded – America's last great defense had failed, and it hardly seemed possible that she could be spared. . . .

The news from Canada was uniformly discouraging. The mortality rate in Quebec and Montreal had not been surpassed in any part of the world, and there was little dissent when Mayor Bowne proclaimed an unprecedentedly severe quarantine. Without the permission of the Board of Health, no ship could approach closer than three hundred yards to the city; no vehicle closer than a mile and a half.[8]

It seemed on Sunday that every minister in the city had chosen cholera as his text. "The consternation in the city is universal," a young artist noted in his journal, "Wall Street and the Exchange are crowded with eager groups waiting for the latest intelligence."[9] . . .

The medical profession was particularly conscious of the danger and of its responsibility should there be an epidemic. Accordingly, the Medical Society, which represented two-thirds of the city's licensed physicians, formed a special committee of fifteen to study the problem. At their first meeting, this committee formulated a program of public and individual hygiene for the days ahead. It was most important, they urged, that the streets be kept clean throughout the coming summer. To help accomplish this, and to purify the atmosphere, water should be run from the hydrants several times a week. The streets themselves, as well as private sinks, yards, and cesspools should be disinfected with chloride of lime or quicklime. Individuals were urged to be calm, to be temperate in dining and drinking, and to be especially scrupulous in washing. Learned in a generation of yellow fever epidemics and gleaned from accounts of cholera in Europe, these recommendations represented the best medical opinion of the time.[10]

Despite such excellent and reassuring advice, many New Yorkers were already leaving or planning to leave the city. Those who stayed stocked up, if they could afford to, on the cholera specifics which were being hurriedly concocted, bottled, and labeled by apothecaries and free-lance quacks. Even the more irreverent were sobered by the threat of this "pestilence that walketh in darkness."[11] . . .

Cholera appeared in Montreal on June 6. By June 14, it was in Whitehall, New York; by June 18, at Mechanicsville and Ogdensburg. . . .

New Yorkers anxiously noted the filth accumulating in their streets, the decaying garbage and stagnant pools in vacant lots, and grew even more alarmed as cholera moved steadily south from Montreal and Quebec. Their fears and conjectures were soon to become reality.

Late Monday night, June 26, an Irish immigrant named Fitzgerald came home violently ill. The pain in his stomach grew worse during the night, and in the morning he called a doctor. When the doctor arrived, Fitzgerald was already feeling better, but his two children were sick, complaining of agonizing cramps in their stomachs. The children died on Wednesday, but not before they were seen by many physicians, all of whom agreed upon a diagnosis of Asiatic cholera.[12] Mrs. Fitzgerald died on Friday, and the next few days brought a scattering of similar cases: patients suffering with intestinal spasms, diarrhea, and vomiting. Most of them died.

By the end of the week, the Board of Health had received several reports of cholera cases. On Friday (June 30), Dr. James Manley, the resident physician responsible for the diagnosis of contagious disease, reported two "undoubted cases."[13] Despite such convincing evidence, the Board of Health and the mayor were still reluctant to make these reports public....

By the end of the first week in July, almost everyone who could afford to had left the city. Farm houses and country homes within a thirty-mile radius were completely filled. Roads leading from the city were crowded not only with carts, horses, and carriages, but with "oceans" of pedestrians, trudging in the mid-summer heat with packs on their backs. A merchant living on one of the principal residential streets recalled that his and one other family were the only ones on the street to remain. The young wife of another merchant baked all the bread and cake eaten in her house during the epidemic – at the end of the summer even making the yeast. Visitors to the city were struck by the deathly silence of the streets, unaccustomedly clean and strewn with lime. Even on Broadway, passers-by were so few that a man on horseback drew curious faces to upper windows. One young woman recalled seeing tufts of grass growing in the little-used thoroughfares....

Nevertheless, the epidemic increased. On Thursday, July 5, the Court of Sessions discharged on their own recognizance all prisoners confined in the almshouse for misdemeanors. Cholera had broken out at the almshouse, and it seemed unjust to expose petty offenders to probable death. The felons in the penitentiary and the bridewell were soon sent to temporary shelters on Blackwells Island....

At last the Board of Health began to take action, outfitting five special cholera hospitals, one in the Hall of Records, another in a school, a third in an old bank, and a fourth in an abandoned workshed. These tardy measures could not still a growing criticism. Had the lives of the city's humble artisans and mechanics been sacrificed to the commercial interests which seemed to have paralyzed the board into inactivity? Editorials urged that the Board of Health be forced to resign if it could not fulfil its duties.[14] The Board itself was becoming desperate: one member –

Alderman Meigs – proposed a reward of twenty dollars for any licensed physician who cured a case of cholera (July 14).

Fortunately, the disorganization of the city was never to become complete. Respectable persons of regular habits reassured themselves that they had little to fear. Only the dirty, the intemperate, those who had somehow predisposed themselves, were cholera's intended victims. The Special Medical Council announced on July 10, a day on which there had been forty-five deaths, "that the disease in the city is confined to the imprudent, the intemperate, and to those who injure themselves by taking improper medicines."[15]

Obviously then, the most important task in preventing the spread of cholera was to safeguard the common people against their dangerous habits of life. Accordingly, the Special Medical Council drew up the following recommendations, which were distributed in handbills and published prominently in all of the city's newspapers.

Notice

Be temperate in eating and drinking,

avoid crude *vegetables* and *fruits*;

abstain from *cold water*, when heated;

and above all from *ardent spirits* and

if habit have rendered it indispensable, take much less than usual.

Sleep and clothe warm

Avoid labor in the heat of day.

Do not sleep or sit in a draught of air when heated.

Avoid getting wet

Take no medicines without advice.

As business in the city stagnated, even the most deserving among the poor were soon penniless. . . .

. . . Cartloads of coffins rumbled through the streets, and when filled, returned through the streets to the cemeteries. Dead bodies lay unburied in the gutters, and coffin-makers had to work on the Sabbath to supply the demand. Charles G. Finney, the evangelist, recalled having seen five hearses drawn up at the same time at different houses within sight of his door. Harsh smoke from burning clothes and bedding filled the air, mingling with the acrid fumes of burning tar, pitch, and other time-tested preventives. Houses stood empty, prey to dust, burglary, and vandalism. By August, many of the churches were closed – especially those with wealthier congregations. St. George's shut its doors for almost the entire month; its pastor wrote that three-quarters of his flock were absent anyway.

The deserted houses and shops were a constant temptation to the criminal and near-criminal elements of the city, and the Board of Health soon authorized the mayor to employ additional watchmen. Even this did not seem to have been too effective in checking what one newspaperman spoke of as an "epidemic of burglaries."[16] . . . Breaking and entering was not the only means of taking advantage of the city's disorganization. Swindlers attempted to defraud the Savings Bank by presenting falsified passbooks, while businessmen were accused of using the epidemic as an excuse for defaulting on their obligations.

The poor, deserving and undeserving, resented the unwonted intrusion of authority into their affairs. As had been the case in epidemics since the Middle Ages, the lower classes forcibly discouraged attempts to take their sick to hospitals, which were regarded as little more than charnel houses. Physicians and city officials were attacked and brutally beaten. Mobs opposed the precipitate burial of the dead that had been dictated by the Special Medical Council. The inmates of one tenement, "a miscellaneous mob of men and women," blocked the hallways of their building, forcing the authorities to lower a coffin out of a window. When it reached the ground, the women of the building stood upon it to prevent its being taken away. They had planned to wake the corpse, and a sizable number of black eyes and bloody noses on both sides testified to the fervor of their convictions.[17]

The Five Points, the city's red-light district, had always been an object of distaste for the respectable, but at no time was their indignation greater than during the epidemic. The case rate was highest in this moral slough, and the disease soon spread to respectable citizens unfortunate enough to live in the vicinity.

> The Five Points . . . are inhabited by a race of beings of all colours, ages, sexes, and nations, though generally of but one condition, and that . . . almost of the vilest brute. With such a crew, inhabiting the most populous and central portion of the city, when may we be considered secure from pestilence. Be the air pure from Heaven, their breath would contaminate it, and infect it with disease.[18]

William A. Caruthers, a young Virginia physician and novelist-to-be, helping to treat the poor in the Five Points was shocked at the misery he saw – far worse, he later wrote, than that to be found among the most ill-used of slaves in his native South. The inhabitants of the Five Points seemed to the young physician no longer human. Dead at heart, they endured cholera like "a flock of sheep swept off suddenly by some distemper." Rum was their only anodyne. Loaves of bread distributed by the benevolent had to be cut into quarters, for intact loaves were pawned for drink.[19]

By July 20, the cholera epidemic had reached its height. August brought with it a gradual but steady decline in the number of new cases, and though the epidemic smouldered on throughout that fall, it had completely disappeared by Christmas.

The factors causing its subsidence can, in retrospect, only be guessed at, even by the trained epidemiologist. Almost certainly, however, an important reason was the disappearance of dense concentrations of susceptible persons living in crowded and filthy conditions. Those of the poor who had not died either had some sort of immunity or had been removed by the authorities to less exposed quarters. Changes in the temperature and humidity may have affected either the cholera vibrio or the ability of the water supply to act as a carrier. In any case, cholera's stay in New York was short and left behind no endemic foci from which new epidemics might originate.

... On August 28, the Special Medical Council pronounced New York safe, and two days later issued its last cholera report. As early as August 20, the Board of Health had begun to close the cholera hospitals, displaying an alacrity conspicuously absent in its preparations for the epidemic. On August 27, the board began to make provisions for the storage and inventory of its remaining supplies. By the end of the month, only one hospital remained open.

With the last days of August, the city began to come fully alive.... But the epidemic had not become a memory for all New Yorkers. William Dunlap wrote on September 3 that more people were dying than when the Corporation reported.[20] And the winter promised to be a severe one: there were hundreds of widows and orphans to be provided for, and beggars could be found in every busy street.

Americans prided themselves on their railroads, canals, and steamboats. Before the end of 1832, cholera was to travel on them all. Few communities, however remote, escaped its visits; and hastily dug graves in every state between Maine and Wisconsin bore witness to the extent of cholera's wanderings. It followed the army of General Scott against Blackhawk, killing white and Indian alike and spreading to Wisconsin and Illinois. So terrifying was the disease that settlers deserted the shelter of Chicago, where it had broken out, preferring to take their chances with the scalping knives of the savages....

The larger cities established cholera hospitals, instituted feverish clean-ups, and continued their quarantines. Despite these efforts, only Boston and Charleston among America's larger cities were to escape; New Orleans was probably the most severely visited. Cholera claimed five thousand lives in the Crescent City.

The South was spared until August and September. Some sections, escaping lightly even then, were to be visited with greater severity in the spring of 1833, when the disease, quiescent during the cold of winter, broke out with undiminished virulence in the West and South. Small villages, even isolated farms, were stricken. And here the disease was most terrifying: it had to be faced alone, often without friend, minister, or physician. The appearance of cholera in even the smallest hamlet was the signal for a general exodus of the inhabitants, who, in their headlong flight, spread the disease throughout the surrounding countryside.

Unswayed by the arguments of physicians, common folk insisted that the disease must be contagious. In Chester, Pennsylvania, several persons suspected of carrying the pestilence were reportedly murdered, along with the man who had sheltered them. Armed Rhode Islanders turned back New Yorkers fleeing across Long Island Sound. At Ypsilanti, the local militia fired upon the mail stage from cholera-infested Detroit. Everywhere there were stringent quarantines. The newly arrived foreign immigrants were particularly feared. Even if they did not carry the disease, the dirty and crowded conditions in which they lived and moved provided the perfect soil in which to germinate the seeds of pestilence.

Those who could deserted cities for the pure air and waters of the countryside. Those who could not experimented with other means of prevention. Many dosed themselves with the "cholera preventives" which enriched apothecaries and quacks throughout the country. A greater number took refuge in alcohol; French brandy and port were held in particularly high esteem for their bracing qualities. The more temperate enveloped themselves in camphor vapors, hoping to neutralize the cholera influence which tainted the atmosphere, while many communities hoped to achieve the same end with the fumes of burning tar or pitch. In New Orleans, such clouds of smoke covered whole blocks. No chances could be taken, no possibility ignored. On one Louisiana plantation, the main house was fumigated morning and evening with burning sugar and vinegar, while its inhabitants were enveloped at all times in clouds of dense smoke from tar burning in the yard. Meats were served smothered in garlic, and no one ventured abroad without camphor somewhere on his person.

The epidemic provoked anxiety even in those places fortunate enough to have escaped its effects.[21] . . . Mothers feared for their young children, even those seemingly healthy. In cholera times, the slightest malaise might be a premonitory symptom of the disease. The country, especially clean and elevated places, seemed to offer the only security against the disease.

Despite many pious hopes, cholera was no converting ordinance. The vicious seemed merely to have been hardened in their depravity, though the spiritually minded Christian was confirmed in his faith. Deserted streets and desolate towns returned to life with almost indecent haste. . . .

Cholera returned again in 1833 and 1834, then vanished as abruptly as it had come. It was to be fifteen years before it was again to find root in American soil.

Notes

1   Edward H. Dixon, *Scenes in the Practice of a New York Surgeon* (New York, 1855), p. 15; John Stearns to the New York City Board of Health, July 19, 1832, Filed Papers of the Common Council, File Drawer T-592, Municipal Archives and Records Center.

2   Diary of a Young Man in Albany, July 18, 1832, Manuscript Division, New York Historical Society.

3   New York City Board of Health, Minutes, September 6, 1831, Municipal Archives and Records Center (cited hereinafter as Minutes). Massachusetts Medical Society, *A Report on Spasmodic Cholera*...(Boston, 1832), p. I.

4   Diary of Michael Shiner, p. 49, Manuscript Division, Library of Congress.

5   [A Physician], *A Rational View of the Spasmodic Cholera*...(Boston, 1832), p. 17.

6   William Dunlap, *Diary of William Dunlap (1766–1839)* (New York, 1930), III, 814.

7   *Truth Teller* (New York), June 2, 1832.

8   *Evening Post* (New York), June 16, 1832.

9   Diary of Thomas Kelah Wharton, June 17, 1832, Manuscript Division, New York Public Library.

10 *Truth Teller* (New York), June 23, 1832.

11 *Observer (New York)*, June 30, 1832.

12 N.Y.C. Board of Health, *Reports of Hospital Physicians and Other Documents in Relation to the Epidemic Cholera of 1832*, edited by Dudley Atkins (New York, 1832), pp. 9–10.

13 City Clerk's Papers, File Drawer U-58, Municipal Archives and Record Center, New York.

14 *Cholera Bulletin*, July 9, 13, 1832. This publication was issued twice weekly during the epidemic by "an association of physicians."

15 Minutes, July 10, 1832.

16 *Evening Post* (New York), July 23, 1832.

17 *Commercial Advertiser* (New York), July 3, August 14, 1832.

18 *Evening Post* (New York), July 23, 1832.

19 William A. Caruthers, *The Kentuckian in New-York*...(New York, 1834), II, 28–29.

20 Dunlap, *op. cit.*, IV, 617.

21 Diary of Lucretia Mott Hall, August 12, 1832, Manuscript Division, New York Historical Society.

Documents

San Francisco fire, 1850s

In addition to the threat of cholera, fire was another constant source of civic disruption. Since America's forests remained abundant for most of the

Figure 5.1. Fire in San Francisco, 1850s. From L. Beebe and C. Clegg, *The American West: The Pictorial Epic of a Continent* (New York: E. P. Dutton & Co., 1955), p. 140.

nineteenth century, most buildings were wooden. Thus towns and cities represented large piles of dry lumber, organized into living space for people, effectively stacked and ordered to allow plenty of oxygen to flow over it. Until the end of the century, most lighting and heating came from open-flame lanterns and fireplaces. Disastrous unions between flame and wood were all too frequent, and fires could spread with terrible speed. The litany of urban fire disaster was long: San Francisco burned four times in the 1850s, and several times thereafter (most famously in 1906, after the great earthquake of that year); much of Chicago burned to the ground in 1871, and there were huge fires in virtually every other city in this period. A reliable and plentiful water supply was the first requirement for combating urban fire.

Figure 5.2. The crowd celebrating at the Owensmouth Cascades, near Sylmar, on November 5, 1913. Courtesy of Los Angeles Department of Water and Power.

Crowd with empty aqueduct

Dynamited portion of LA aqueduct

The disasters of cholera and fire in the nineteenth century ensured that by the twentieth century, Americans associated adequate water supplies with civic success. In the early 1900s, the city of Los Angeles, located in arid southern California, was desperate for more water to provide for its population and

Figure 5.3.   A dynamited portion of the Los Angeles Aqueduct, 1927. Courtesy of Security Pacific Historical Photograph Collection, Los Angeles Public Library.

ensure future growth. Like New York officials before them, city officials in LA looked to distant rural water supplies for their solution. Working with state and federal authorities, they constructed an aqueduct across the desert to the Owens Valley, on the far side of the Sierra Nevada. Traditionally, the opening of a major aqueduct was cause for civic celebration. New York City threw a party when the Croton aqueduct opened in 1842. In figure 5.2, a crowd gathers to cheer the arrival of water in the Los Angeles aqueduct, in 1913.

But in arid California, the aqueduct also met opposition. Water flowing to Los Angeles meant less water for farmers and ranchers along the Owens River. As the city grew, the rural settlements of the Owens Valley dried up, shrank, and began to disappear. Rural opponents of the water transfer protested, occupied, and occasionally bombed the Los Angeles aqueduct. In figure 5.3, inspectors examine the scene of a dynamite attack on the aqueduct in 1927. Such efforts were mostly in vain. The aqueduct was quickly restored, and the water continued to flow to the city.

The images shown in Figures 5.2 and 5.3 suggest the need to explore how cities reorganize relations between rural people and rural resources. Environmentally, what *is* a city? Is it merely a concentration of people and economic connections? Or does it also extend to the furthest reaches of its environmental needs? Does New York extend to the Croton watershed, where its vital water supply still comes from? Were farmers of the Croton watershed actually, in some way, New York City residents? Does Los Angeles actually stretch across California, from the coast to the eastern side of the state, where so much of its water originates? How do we describe the boundaries of urban environments? Given the demands that modern cities make on the countryside, is it even possible to separate them conceptually into different environments?

6
Markets, Nature, and the Disappearing Bison

For a lesson in how new technologies and consumer demand can drastically alter a natural system, it is hard to beat the story of the buffalo. But what is the real history of the bison's near-extinction?

For many years, historians have attributed the decline of the bison largely to one cause: white buffalo hunters, who, after the Civil War, began to answer the market's demand for buffalo robes (to make winter coats and, beginning in the early 1870s, leather) and tongues (considered a delicacy among white consumers). In a short period of time, these hunters annihilated millions of buffalo. The animals were all but extinct by the 1880s.

In recent years, environmental historians have re-examined the evidence. In his famous article, Dan Flores argues that our old ideas of the bison's near-demise are too simple, and that the bison herds were on their way to destruction before most white hunters arrived. A variety of factors were involved, including drought, competition for forage between bison and horses (wild and Indian-owned), Indian decisions to supply robes for Eastern markets well before the Civil War, and exotic cattle diseases which infected wild buffalo.

Make a list of the causes that Flores enumerates for the bison decline prior to 1850, and then rate them as to which is most important. Could Indians have continued to hunt bison indefinitely if Euro-Americans had not become established in the New World? Which is the greater cause of bison decline, the market for robes or Indian subsistence? How much of a responsibility for the near-extinction of the bison do non-Indian consumers, the people who actually *bought* the robes, have? Flores's argument is not universally accepted, and in the document section you will have the chance to consider the older theory which places more blame on white hunters.

Bison Ecology and Bison Diplomacy Redux: Another Look at the Southern Plains from 1800 to 1850

Dan Flores

Like some tremendous, crashing sound that ceased abruptly just at the moment we turned to listen but whose reverberations ricochet around in the topography yet – that's how more than a thousand centuries of buffalo moving across the landscape of the West strikes many of us at the beginning of the new century. . . .

While this [essay] focuses on the first half of the nineteenth century, when all the necessary patterns fell into place for the great herds' subsequent crash, I feel an obligation to add that the years from 1800 to 1850 on the Plains shouldn't constitute an apologia for the period that followed. By no means does the Indian robe trade exonerate the white hide hunt that delivered the knockdown flurry, or make the federal government's refusal to implement a conservation policy for buffalo during the 1870s any easier to condone. Far from it. . . .

The new buffalo story relies much more on Indian sources than was the case in the past, but we all ought to keep in mind that the intent of history is not to make one group look better, or worse, than another now. The intent is to use as wide an array of evidence as possible to figure out what happened in the past. Native people who remain convinced that bison and Indians have had a special relationship for centuries shouldn't see in the following story an argument that over the long term this was not the case. I in fact would insist that more than eight thousand years of bison hunting on the Great Plains constitutes the longest-sustained human lifeway in North American history.

Yet virtually all Plains Indians have in their tribal lore stories of past times when, as a result of human hubris or miscalculation, bison went away. My argument is that as a result of their capture by the global market economy, Plains people experienced another such time in the nineteenth century. In any case, that all our ancestors – irrespective of their cultures, worldviews, or religions – were as humanly fallible then as we all are now ought not to stun us. That idea is essential to compassionate history.

What I actually advocate here, as will be evident by the end of the story, is not so much an environmental history based purely on the market or even human nature – nothing quite so materialist or universalist – but biocultural history. The following events were unique to their time and place. And as always, it was in the realm of religious and spiritual beliefs that culture unfurled most strikingly into the ecological world. . . .

Environmental historians, and ethnohistorians whose interests have been environmental topics, have in the two past decades been responsible for many of our most valuable recent insights into the history of Native Americans since their contact with Euro-Americans. Thus far, however, modern scholarship has not reevaluated the most visible historic interaction, the set piece if you will, of Native American environmental history. On the Great Plains of the American West during the two centuries spanned by 1680 and 1880, almost three dozen Native American groups adopted horse-propelled, bison-hunting cultures that literally defined "Indianness" for Americans and most of the world. It is the end of this process that has most captured the popular imagination: the military campaigns against and the brutal incarceration of the horse Indians, accompanied by the astonishingly rapid elimination of bison, and of an old ecology that dated back ten thousand years, at the hands of commercial hide hunters. This dramatic end, which occurred in less than fifteen years following the end of the Civil War, has by now entered American mythology. Yet our focus on the finale has obscured an examination of earlier phases that might shed new light on the historical and environmental interaction of the horse Indians and bison herds on the plains.

In the nineteenth-century history of the Central and Southern Plains, there have long been some perplexing questions for which environmental history seems well suited to suggest answers. Why, for example, were the Comanches able to replace the Apaches on the bison-rich Southern Plains? Why did the Kiowas, Cheyennes, and Arapahos gradually shift southward into the Southern Plains between 1800 and 1825? And why, after fighting each other for two decades, did these Southern Plains peoples effect a rapprochement and alliance in the 1840s? What factors were operating to bring on such an escalation of Indian raids into Mexico and Texas in the late 1840s that the subject assumed critical importance in the Treaty of Guadelupe-Hidalgo? If the bison herds were so vast in the years before the hide hunters, why are there so many reports of starving Indians on the Plains by 1850? And finally, given our standard estimates of bison numbers, why is it that the hide hunters are credited with only some 10 million market hides, including no more than 3.5 million from the Southern Plains in the 1870s?

Apposite to all of these questions is a central issue: how successful were the horse Indians at creating a dynamic ecological equilibrium between themselves and the vast bison herds that grazed the Plains? That is, had they developed sustainable hunting practices that would maintain the herds and so permit future generations of hunters to follow the same way of life? This is not to pose the "anachronistic question" (the term is Richard White's) of whether Indians were ecologists.[1] But how a society or a group of peoples with a shared culture makes adjustments to live within the carrying capacity of its habitat is not only a valid question to ask of the historical record, it may be one of the salient questions to ask about any culture.... The answers are complex and offer a revision of both Plains history and Western Indian ecological history.

Working our way through to them requires some digression into the large historical forces that shaped the Southern Plains over the last hundred centuries. The perspective of the *longue durée* is essential to environmental history. What transpired on the Great Plains from 1800 to 1850 is not comprehensible without taking into account the effect of the Pleistocene extinctions of ten thousand years ago, or the cycle of droughts that determined the carrying capacity for animals on the grasslands. Shallower in time than these forces but just as important to the problem are factors that stemmed from the arrival of Europeans in the Americas. Trade was an ancient part of the cultural landscape of the continent, but the Europeans altered the patterns, the goods, and the intensity of the trade. And the introduction of horses and horse culture accomplished a technological revolution for the Great Plains. The horse was the chief catalyst of an ongoing remaking of the tribal map of western America, as new Indian groups moved onto the plains and incessantly shifted their ranges and alliances in response to a world where accelerating change seemed almost the only constant.

At the beginning of the nineteenth century, the dominant groups on the Southern Plains were the two major divisions of the Comanches: the Texas Comanches, primarily Kotsotekas, and the great New Mexico division, spread across the country from the Llano Estacado Escarpment west to the foothills of the Sangre de Cristo Mountains, and comprising Yamparika and Jupe bands that only recently had replaced the Apaches on the high plains. The Comanches' drive to the south from their original homelands in southwestern Wyoming and northwestern Colorado was a part of the original tribal adjustments to the coming of the horse to the Great Plains. There is reason to believe that the eastern Shoshones, from whom the Comanches were derived before achieving a different identity on the Southern Plains, were one of the first intermountain tribes of historic times to push onto the plains. Perhaps as early as 1500 these proto-Comanches were hunting bison and using dog power to haul their mountain-adapted four-pole tipis east of the Laramie

Mountains. Evidently this movement was a response to a wetter time on the Central Plains and larger bison concentrations than earlier.

These early Shoshonean hunters may not have spent more than three or four generations among the thronging Plains bison herds, because by the late seventeenth century they had been pushed back into the mountains and sagebrush deserts by various tribes, especially the Assiniboines and Blackfeet, newly armed with European guns, that were filtering westward from the region around the Great Lakes. If so, they were among a complex of tribes southwest of the lakes that over the next two centuries would be displaced by a massive Siouan drive to the west, an imperial expansion for domination of the prize buffalo range of the Northern Plains and a wedge that sent ripples of tribal displacement across the Plains.

. . . Pressed back toward the mountains as Shoshones, they thus turned in a different direction and emerged from the passes through the Front Range as the same people but bearing a new name given them by the Utes: Komantcia. They still lacked guns, but now began their intimate association with the one animal, aside from the bison, inextricably linked with Plains life. The Comanches began acquiring horses from the Utes within a decade or so after the Pueblo Revolt of 1680 sent horses and horse culture diffusing in all directions from New Mexico. Thus were born the "hyper-Indians," as one scholar has called the Plains people.[2]

The Comanches became, along with the Sioux, the most populous and widespread of all the peoples that now began to ride onto the vast sweep of grassland to participate in the hunter's life. They began to take possession of the Southern Plains by the early 1700s. By 1800 they were in full control of all the country east of the mountains and south of the Arkansas River clear to the Texas Hill Country. . . . What everyone seems to agree on is that when the Comanches began to move onto the Southern Plains with their new horse herds, their culture was adapting in interesting ways to the wealth of resources now available to them.

For the Comanches, the Southern Plains must have seemed an earthly paradise. The Pleistocene extinctions nine thousand years earlier had left dozens of grazing niches vacant on the American Great Plains. Nature's solution was to evolve a dwarf species of bison that had a higher reproductive capability than any of its ancestors and to flood most of those vacant niches with an enormous biomass of one grazer. In an ecological sense, bison were a weed species that had proliferated as a result of a major disturbance. That disturbance still reverberated, making it easy for Spanish horses, for example, to reoccupy their old niche and rapidly spread across the plains. And it made the horse Indians a group of humans who throve on a unique environmental situation that has few parallels elsewhere in world history.

The dimensions of the wild bison population on the Southern Plains, and the Great Plains in general, have been much overstated in popular literature. For one thing, pollen analysis and the archeological data indicate that for the Southern Plains there were intervals, some spanning centuries, others decades, when bison must have been almost absent. Two major times of absence occurred between 5000 and 2500 B.C. and between A.D. 500 and 1300. These times when bison bones disappear from the archeological sites correspond to pollen data indicating droughts. The severe Southwest drought that ended early in the fourteenth century was replaced by a five-hundred-year cycle of more mesic conditions and a return of bison in large numbers to the Southern Plains from their drought refugia to the east and west. . . .

More important, our popular perception of bison numbers based on the estimates of awed nineteenth-century observers is probably too high. There very likely were never anything like 100 million or 60 million bison on the Plains during the present climate regime because the carrying capacity of the grasslands was not that high. The best technique for determining bison carrying capacity on the Southern Plains is to extrapolate from U.S. census data for livestock, and the best census for the extrapolation is that of 1910, after the industry crashes of the 1880s had reduced animal numbers to something realistic, but before the breakup of ranches and the Enlarged Homestead Act of 1909 resulted in considerable sections of the Southern Plains being broken out by farmers. Additionally, dendrochronological data seem to show the turn of the century as median, between-droughts-years for rainfall on the Southern Plains, rendering the census of 1910 particularly suitable as a baseline for carrying capacity and animal populations.

The 1910 agricultural census indicates that in the 201 counties that then comprised the 240,000 square miles of the Southern Plains, the nineteenth-century carrying capacity during periods of median rainfall would have been about seven million cattle – equivalent grazers, specifically for 1910, about 5,150,000 cattle and 1,890,000 horses and mules. This does not translate directly into a bison population figure, since their migratory grazing patterns and coevolution with the native grasses made bison as a wild species about 18 percent more efficient on the Great Plains than domestic cattle. And varying climate conditions during the nineteenth century, as I will demonstrate, noticeably affected grassland carrying capacity so that the ecological reality was a dynamic cycle that could swing considerably from decade to decade. But if the Great Plains' bovine carrying capacity of 1910 expresses a median reality, then during prehorse times the Southern Plains might have supported an average of about 8.2 million bison, the entire Great Plains perhaps 28–30 million.

Eight million bison on the Southern Plains may not be so many as we've been led to believe, but to the Comanches the herds probably seemed limitless. Whether the Comanches came to the Southern Plains because of horses or because of bison, bison availability through horse culture caused a specialization that resulted in the loss of two thirds of their former plant lore and to a consequent loss of status for Comanche women, an intriguing development that seems to have been true to a greater or lesser extent among all the tribes that moved onto the plains during this period. . . .

The Comanches, as is well known, were not the only people on the Southern Plains during the horse period. The New Mexicans, both Pueblo and Hispanic, continued to hunt on the wide-open Llanos, as did the Prairie Caddoans, although the numbers of the latter were dwindling rapidly by 1825. The New Mexican peoples and the Caddoans of the middle Red and Brazos Rivers played major trade roles for the Southern Plains, and the Comanches in particular. Although the Comanches did engage in the classic Plains exchange of bison products for horticultural produce and European trade goods, and did trade horses and mules with a series of little-known Anglo-American traders from Missouri, Arkansas, and Louisiana, they were never a high-volume trading people until relatively late in their history. Early experiences with American traders and disease led them to distrust trade with Euro-Americans, and on only one or two occasions did they allow short-lived posts to be established in their country. Instead, peace with the Prairie Caddoans by the 1730s, and with New Mexico in 1786, sent Comanche trade both east and west, but often through Indian middlemen.

In this classic period between 1800 and 1850, the most interesting Southern Plains development was the cultural interaction between the Comanches and surrounding Plains Indians to the north. The Kiowas were one of those groups.

The Kiowas are and have long been an enigma. . . . [They] believe that they started their journey to Rainy Mountain on the Oklahoma plains from the north. And indeed, in the eighteenth century we do find them on the Northern Plains, near the Black Hills. . . .

Displaced by the wars for the buffalo ranges in the north, the Kiowas began to drift southward again – or perhaps, since the supply of horses was the Southwest, simply began to stay longer on the Southern Plains. Their rapprochement with the Comanches came between 1790 and 1806, and thereafter they were so closely associated with the northern Comanches that they were regarded by some as merely a Comanche band, although in many cultural details the two groups were dissimilar. Spanish and American traders and explorers of the 1820s found them most closely associated with the two forks of the Canadian River and on the various headwater streams of the Red.

The other groups that increasingly began to interact with the Comanches during the 1820s and thereafter were also Northern Plains in origin. These were the Arapahos and the Cheyennes, who by 1825 were beginning to establish themselves on the Colorado buffalo plains from the North Platte all the way down to the Arkansas River.

The Algonkian-speaking Arapahos and Cheyennes had once been farmers living in earth lodges on the upper Mississippi. By the early 1700s both groups were in present North Dakota, occupying villages along the Red and Sheyenne Rivers, where they first began to acquire horses, possibly from the Kiowas. Fur wars instigated by the Europeans drove them farther southwest and more and more into a plains, bison-hunting culture, one. . . . that the women of these farming tribes probably resisted as long as possible. But by the second decade of the nineteenth century, the Teton Sioux wedge had made nomads and hunters of the Arapahos and Cheyennes.

Their search for prime buffalo grounds and for ever larger horse herds, critical since both tribes had emerged as middlemen traders between the villagers of the Missouri and the horse reservoir to the south, first led the Cheyennes and Arapahos west of the Black Hills into Crow lands and then increasingly southward along the mountain front. . . .

Three factors seem to have drawn the Arapahos and Cheyennes so far south. Unquestionably, the vast horse herds of the Comanches and Kiowas was one, an unending supply of horses for the trade, which by 1825 the Colorado tribes were acquiring through daring raids. Another was the milder winters south of the Arkansas, which made horse pastoralism much easier. The third factor was the abnormally rich wildlife bounty of the early nineteenth-century Southern Plains, the direct result of an extraordinary series of years between 1815 and 1846 when, with the exception of a minor drought in the early 1820s, rainfall south of the Arkansas was considerably above average. . . .

Thus, at the outset of the period from 1825 to 1850, the Comanches and Kiowas found themselves at war with Cheyennes, Arapahos, and other tribes to the north. Meanwhile, the Colorado tribes opened another front in a naked effort to seize the rich buffalo range of the upper Kansas and Republican Rivers from the Pawnees. These wars produced interesting ecological developments, developments that seem to have been typical across most of the continent. Where the boundaries of warring tribes met, buffer zones of various sizes that neither side occupied became established where some hunting was allowed but was usually light. One such buffer zone on the Southern Plains was along its northern perimeter, between the Arkansas and North Canadian Rivers.

Another was in present western Kansas, between the Pawnees and the main range of the Colorado tribes, and a third seems to have existed during this time from the forks of the Platte to the mountains. The importance of these buffer zones is that they left game within them relatively undisturbed and allowed the buildup of herds that later might be exploited when tribal boundaries or agreements changed.

The appearance of American traders like Bent and Ceran St. Vrain marked the Southern Plains tribes' growing immersion in a market economy increasingly tied to world-wide trade networks that were dominated by Euro-Americans. Like all humans, Indians had always altered their environments. But as most modern historians of Plains Indians and the Western fur trade have realized, Western tribes during the nineteenth century not only had become technologically capable of pressuring their resources, they were becoming less "ecosystem people" year after year.[3] ...

The crux of the problem in studying Southern Plains Indian ecology and bison is to determine whether the Plains tribes had established a society in ecological equilibrium, one where population does not exceed the carrying capacity of its habitat and so maintains a healthy, functioning ecology that can be sustained over the long term. Resolving such a question involves an effort to come to grips with the factors affecting bison populations, those affecting Indian populations, and the cultural aspects of Plains Indian utilization of bison. None of these puzzles is easy to resolve.

Studies done on the fertility of modern, protected bison herds on the Plains indicate that bison are a prolific species that increase their numbers by an average of 18 percent a year, assuming a normal (51/49) sex ratio with breeding cows amounting to 35 percent of the total. In other words, if the Southern Plains supported 8.2 million bison in years of median rainfall, the herds would have produced about 1.4 million calves a year. To maintain an ecological equilibrium with the grasses, the Plains bisons' natural mortality rate would have had to approach 18 percent as well.

Today the several protected bison herds in the West have a natural mortality rate, without predation, ranging between 3 percent and 9 percent. The Wichita Mountains herd, the only large herd left on the Southern Plains, falls midway between with a 6 percent mortality rate. Despite a search for it, no inherent naturally regulating mechanism has yet been found in bison populations, necessitating active culling programs at all the Plains bison refuges. The kind of starvation-induced population crashes that affect ungulates like deer seemingly were mitigated on the wild, unfenced Plains by the bison's tendency – barring any major impediments – to shift its range great distances to better pasture.

Determining precisely how the remaining annual mortality in the wild herds was affected is not easy, because the wolf/bison relationship on the Plains was never studied. Judging from dozens of historical documents attesting to wolf predation of bison calves, including accounts of the Indians, wolves do seem to have played a critical role in Plains bison population dynamics and not just as culling agents of diseased and old animals.

Human hunters were the other source of mortality. For nine thousand years Native Americans had hunted bison without exterminating them, perhaps building into their gene pool an adjustment to human predation. But there is archeological evidence that beginning about A.D. 1450, with the advent of "mutualistic" trade between new Puebloan communities recently forced by drought to relocate on the Rio Grande and a new wave of Plains hunters (probably the Athapaskan-speaking Apaches), human pressures on the southern bison herd had accelerated, evidently dramatically if the archeological record in New Mexico is an accurate indication. That pressure would have been a function of both Indian population size and their cultural utilization of bison. The trade of bison-derived goods for the produce of the horticultural villages fringing the Plains meant, of course, that bison would be affected by changes in human populations periphery to as well as on the Great Plains. . . .

The cultural utilization of bison by horse Indians has been studied by Bill Brown in an article published in 1986.[4] Adapting a sophisticated formula worked out first for caribou hunters in the Yukon, Brown has estimated Indian subsistence (caloric requirements plus the number of robes and hides required for domestic use) at about forty-seven animals per lodge per year. At an average of eight people per lodge, that works out to almost six bison per person in a year's time. Brown's article is not only highly useful in getting us closer to a historic Plains equation than ever before, it is also borne out by at least one historic account. In 1821 trader Jacob Fowler camped for several weeks with seven hundred lodges of Southern Plains tribes on the Arkansas River. Fowler was no ecologist; in fact, he could hardly spell. But he was a careful observer, and he wrote that the big camp was using up a hundred bison a week. In other words, seven hundred lodges were using bison at a rate of about fifty-two per lodge per year, or six and a half animals per person.[5] These are important figures. Not only do they give us some idea of the mortality percentage that can be assigned to human hunters, by extension they help us fix a quadruped predation percentage as well.

Estimates of the number of Indians on the Southern Plains during historic times are not difficult to find, but do tend to vary widely. . . . If the historic Southern Plains hunting population did reach as high as

30,000, then even that level of human pressure would have accounted for only 195,000 bison per year at an estimate of 6.5 animals per person.

But another factor must have played a significant role. While quadruped predators concentrated on calves and injured or feeble animals, human hunters had different criteria. Historical documents attest to the horse Indians' preference for and success in killing two- to five-year-old bison cows, which were preferred for eating and for their thinner, more easily processed hides and their luxurious robes. Studies done on other large American ungulates indicate that removal of breeding females at a level that exceeds 7 percent of the total herd will initiate the onset of population decline. With 8.2 million bison on the Southern Plains, this critical upper figure for cow selectivity would have been about 574,000 animals. Reduce the total bison number to 6 million and the yearly calf crop to 1.08 million, probably more realistic median figures for the first half of the nineteenth century (see below), and the critical mortality for breeding cows would still have been 420,000 animals. As mentioned, thirty thousand horse-mounted bison hunters, hunting for subsistence, would have harvested bison at a yearly rate of fewer than two hundred thousand. Hence I would argue that, theoretically, on the Southern Plains during favorable climate episodes (like that of 1550 to 1850), the huge biomass of bison left from the Pleistocene extinctions would have supported the subsistence needs of more than sixty thousand Plains hunters.

All of which raises some serious questions when we look at the historical evidence of 1800 to 1850. By the end of that period, despite an effort on the part of many Plains tribes at population growth, the population estimates for most of the Southern Plains tribes were down, and many of the bands seemed to be starving. . . . Bison were becoming less reliable, and the evolution toward a raiding/true horse pastoralism economy was well underway. Clearly, by 1850 something had altered the situation on the Southern Plains. The "something," in fact, was a whole host of ecological alterations that historians with a wide range of data at their disposal are only now, more than a century later, beginning to understand.

As early as 1850 the bison herds had been weakened in a number of ways. The effect of the horse on Indian culture has been much studied, but for the purpose of working out a Southern Plains ecological model, it is important to note that horses had requirements of their own that directly affected bison numbers. By the second quarter of the nineteenth century the horse herds of the Southern Plains tribes must have ranged as high as a quarter million animals (at an average of five to ten horses per person), with an estimated two million wild mustangs overspreading the country between south Texas and the Arkansas River. That many animals of a species with an 80 percent dietary overlap with bovines and, perhaps more critically, similar water requirements, must have had an adverse impact on bison carrying capacity, especially since Indian horse herds concentrated the tribes in the moist canyons and river valleys that bison also used for watering. Judging from the 1910 Agricultural Census discussed earlier, two million or more horses would have reduced the median grassland carrying capacity for the southern bison herd to fewer than six million animals.

Another factor that may have already started to diminish overall bison numbers was the effect of exotic bovine diseases. Anthrax seems to have been introduced into the bison herds from a sourcepoint in Louisiana around 1800; its effect is most pronounced on animals whose immune systems have been weakened by droughts or harsh winters. Bovine tuberculosis apparently was brought to the Plains by feral and stolen Texas cattle and by stock on the overland trails. It quite likely was one of these diseases that accounted for inexplicable masses of dead buffalo, like those Charles Goodnight saw along the Concho River in 1867. Brucellosis perhaps arrived too late on the continent (the 1880s) to have had an impact on wild bison ecology, although if it were present then Indian women butchering buffalo would have been at risk for contracting the human version of the disease, undulant fever.

Earlier I mentioned modern natural mortality figures for bison of 3 percent to 9 percent of herd totals. On the wilderness Plains, events like fires, floods, drowning, droughts, and stress-related die-offs may have increased this percentage considerably. But if we hold to the upper figure, then natural mortality might have taken an average of 50 percent of the annual bison increase of 18 percent. Since thirty thousand subsistence hunters would have accounted for only 18 percent of the bison's yearly increase (based on a herd of six million), then the long wondered-at wolf predation perhaps was the most important of all the factors regulating bison populations, with a predation percentage of around 32 percent of the annual bison increase. (Interestingly, this dovetails closely with the Pawnee estimate that wolves got three to four of every ten calves born.) Canids are known for their ability to adjust their litter sizes to factors like mortality and resource abundance. Thus, while mountain men and traders who poisoned wolves for their pelts may not have significantly reduced wolf populations, their tactics may have inadvertently killed thousands of bison, for poisoned wolves drooled and vomited strychnine over the grass in their convulsions. Many Indians lost horses in this way.

The nineteenth-century climate cycle, strongly linked correlatively with bison populations in the archeological data for earlier periods, must have simultaneously interacted with these other factors to produce a decline in bison numbers between 1840 and 1850. Except for a dry period in the mid-to-late 1820s, the first four decades of the nineteenth century had been a time of above-normal rainfall on the Southern Plains. With the carrying capacity for bison and horses high, the country south of the Arkansas sucked tribes to it as into a vortex. But beginning in 1846, rainfall plunged as much as 30 percent below the median for nine years of the next decade. On the Central Plains, six years of this same time span were dry. These droughts, in fact, marked the end of the three-century-long wet cycle known as the Little Ice Age. But now the growth of human populations and settlements in Texas, New Mexico, and the Indian Territory blocked the bison herds from migrating to their traditional drought refugia on the periphery of their range. Thus, a normal climate swing combined with unprecedented external pressures to produce an effect unusual in bison history – a core population, significantly reduced by competition with horses and by drought, that was quite susceptible to human hunting pressure.

Finally, alterations in the historical circumstances of the Southern Plains tribes between 1825 and 1850 undoubtedly had serious repercussions for Plains ecology. Some of these circumstances were indirect and beyond the tribes' ability to influence. Traders along the Santa Fe Trail shot into, chased, and disturbed the southern herds. New Mexican Ciboleros continued to take fifteen thousand to twenty-five thousand bison a year from the Llano Estacado. The U.S. government's removal of more than eighty thousand Eastern Indians into Oklahoma accelerated the pressure on the bison herds at a level impossible to estimate. . . .

Insofar as the Southern Plains tribes had an environmental policy, then, it was to protect the bison herds from being hunted by outsiders. The Comanches could not afford to emulate their Shoshonean ancestors and limit their own population. Beset by enemies and disease, they had to try to keep their numbers high, even as their resource base diminished. For the historic Plains tribes, warfare and stock raids addressed ecological as well as cultural needs and must have seemed far more logical solutions than consciously reducing their own populations as the bison herds became less reliable.

For those very reasons, after more than a decade of warfare among the buffalo tribes, in 1840 the Comanches and Kiowas adopted a strategy of seeking peace and an alliance with the Cheyennes, Arapahos, and Kiowa-Apaches. From the Comanche point of view, it brought them allies against Texans and Eastern Indians who were trespassing on the Plains. The Cheyennes and Arapahos got what they most wanted: the chance to hunt the grass- and bison-rich Southern Plains, horses and mules for trading, and access to the Spanish settlements via Comanche lands. But the peace meant something else in ecological terms. Now all the tribes could freely exploit the Arkansas Valley bison herds. This exploitation of a large, prime bison habitat that had been a boundary zone for Indian hunters may have been critical. . . .

One other advantage the Comanches and Kiowas derived from the peace of 1840 was freedom to trade at Bent's Fort. Although the data to prove it are fragmentary, this conversion of the largest body of Indians on the Southern Plains from subsistence/ecosystem hunters to a people intertwined in the European market system may have added catalyst stress to a bison herd already being eaten away on a variety of fronts. How serious the market incentive could be is indicated by John Whitfield, agent at Bent's second fort in 1855, who wrote that 3,150 Cheyennes were killing 40,000 bison a year.[6] That is just about twice the number the Cheyennes would be expected to harvest through subsistence hunting alone. (It also means that every Cheyenne warrior was killing forty-four bison a year, and Cheyenne women each were processing robes at the rate of almost one a week.) With the core bison population seriously affected by the drought of the late 1840s, the additional, growing robe trade of the Comanches likely brought the Southern Plains tribes to a critical level in their utilization of bison. Drought, coupled with Indian market hunting and cow selectivity, must stand as the critical element – albeit augmented by more minor factors such as white disturbance, new bovine diseases, and increasing grazing competition from horses – that explains the bison crisis of the mid-century Southern Plains. . . .

To the question, did the Southern Plains Indians successfully work out a dynamic, ecological equilibrium with the bison herds?, I would argue that the answer remains ultimately elusive because the relationship was never allowed to play itself out. The trends, however, seem to suggest that a satisfactory solution was improbable. One factor that worked against the horse tribes was their short tenure. It may be that two centuries was too brief a time for them to have created a workable system around horses, the swelling demand for bison robes generated by the Euro-American market, and the expansion of their own populations so as to hold their territories. Some of those forces, such as the tribes' need to expand their numbers and the advantages accruing from participation in the robe trade, worked in opposition to their creating an equilibrium with the bison herds. Too, many of the forces that shaped their world were beyond the power of the Plains tribes to influence. Indeed, from the modern vantage, it is clear that the ecology of the Southern Plains by the mid-nineteenth century had become so complicated that neither Indians nor Euro-Americans of those years could have grasped how it all worked.

Finally, and ironically, it seems that the Indian religions, so effective at calling forth awe and reverence for the natural world, may have actually inhibited the Plains Indians from completely understanding bison ecology and their role in it. True, native leaders such as Yellow Wolf, the Cheyenne whom James Abert interviewed and sketched at Bent's Fort in 1845, surmised the implications of market hunting. As he watched the bison disappearing from the Arkansas Valley, Yellow Wolf asked the whites to teach the Cheyenne hunters how to farm, never realizing that he was reprising a Plains Indian/Euro-American conversation that had taken place sixty years earlier in that same country.[7] But Yellow Wolf was marching to his own drummer, for it remained a widespread tenet of faith among most Plains Indians through the 1880s that bison were supernatural in origin. As a first-hand observer and close student of the nineteenth-century Plains reported, "Every Plains Indian firmly believed that the buffalo were produced in countless numbers in a country under the ground, that every spring the surplus swarmed like bees from a hive, out of great cave-like openings to this country, which were situated somewhere in the great 'Llano Estacado' or Staked Plain of Texas."[8]

This religious conception of the infinity of nature's abundance was poetic and on one level also empirical: bison overwintered in large numbers in the protected canyons scored into the eastern escarpment of the Llano Estacado, and Indians had no doubt many times witnessed the herds emerging to overspread the high plains in springtime. But such a conception did not aid the tribes in their efforts to work out an ecological balance amidst the complexities of the nineteenth-century Plains.

In a real sense, then, the more familiar events of the 1870s only delivered the *coup de grace* to the free Indian life on the Great Plains. The effects of exotic diseases and wars with the encroaching whites caused Indian numbers to dwindle after 1850 (no more than fourteen hundred Comanches were enrolled at Fort Sill in the 1880s). This combined with bison resiliency to preserve a good core of animals until the arrival of the hide hunters, who nonetheless can be documented with taking only about 3.5 million animals from the Southern Plains.

But the great days of the Plains Indians, the primal poetry of humans and horses, bison and grass, sunlight and blue skies, and the sensuous satisfactions of a hunting life on the sweeping grasslands was a meteoric time indeed. And the meteor was already fading in the sky a quarter century before the Big Fifties began to boom.

Notes

1   Richard White, "American Indians and the Environment," *Environmental Review* 9 (Summer 1985): 101–3; and Richard White and William Cronon, "Ecological Change and Indian–White Relations," in *Indian–White Relations*, vol. 4 of *Handbook of North American Indians*, ed. William C. Sturtevant (Washington, D.C.: Smithsonian Institution Press, 1978–89), 417–29.

2 William Brandon, *Indians* (Boston: Houghton Mifflin, 1987), 340.

3 Raymond Dasmann, "Future Primitive," *Coevolution Quarterly* 11(1976): 26–31.

4 Bill Brown, "Comancheria Demography, 1805–1830," *Panhandle-Plains Historical Review* 59 (1986): 8–12.

5 Jacob Fowler, *The Journal of Jacob Fowler: Narrating an Adventure from Arkansas through the Indian Territory, Oklahoma, Kansas, Colorado, and New Mexico, to the Sources of the Rio Grande del Norte*, ed. Elliott Coues (New York: F. P. Harper, 1898), 59, 61.

6 James Whitfield, "Census of the Cheyenne, Comanche, Arapaho, Plains Apache, and the Kiowa of the Upper Arkansas Agency, 15 August 1855," U.S. Department of the Interior, Bureau of Indian Affairs, Letters Received by the Office of Indian Affairs, 1824–1881. National Archives, RG 75, M234.

7 James W. Abert, *The Journal of Lieutenant J. W. Abert from Bent's Fort to St. Louis in 1845*, ed. H. Bailey Carroll (Canyon, TX: West Texas Historical Association, 1941), 15–16; Whitfield, "Census," 5–6.

8 Richard I. Dodge, *Our Wild Indians* (1883; repr. Freeport, NY: Books for Libraries Press, 1970), 286.

Documents

Billy Dixon, "Memories of buffalo hunting"

Reprinted from Olive K. Dixon, *Life of "Billy" Dixon: Plainsman, Scout and Pioneer* (Austin, TX: State House Press, 1987), pp. 80–3

Billy Dixon was a market hunter on the Southern Plains in the 1870s. To what causes does he attribute the bison's destruction? What drove white men to hunt buffalo in the 1870s, according to Dixon? Some might say greed is a factor. But do Dixon and his assistant, or other hunters he writes about, seem greedy? Why is Dixon's account of bison destruction so different from that of the environmental historian, Flores? While reading Dixon's account, take note of how Indian hostility to white hunters helped keep whites out of Indian hunting lands. Dan Flores reminds us that Indians also participated in the robe market. But is it possible that the bison would have disappeared faster without Indian warriors to hold the droves of white hunters at bay?

* * *

When the [Atchison, Topeka, and Santa Fe railroad] construction was stopped at Granada, hundreds of men were thrown out of employment, and found it necessary to make some kind of shift for work, or leave the country. Right here is where the rapid extermination of the buffalo began. All of these men who could rustle a team and a wagon and get hold of an outfit went out on the Plains to kill buffalo. During the fall and winter of 1872 and 1873 there were more hunters in the country than ever before or afterwards. Thus came the high tide of buffalo-hunting. More were killed that season than in all subsequent seasons combined. I feel safe in saying that 75,000 buffalo were killed within sixty or seventy-five miles of Dodge City during that time. The noise of the guns of the hunters could be heard on all sides, rumbling and booming hour after hour, as if a heavy battle were being fought. There was a line of camps all the way from Dodge City to Granada.

Throughout the time since 1871 Jack Callahan and I had worked together. Perkins and Donnelly were still with us. "Cranky" McCabe, his good humor having revived, came back to work for me. A single night at the card table in Dodge City generally wound up McCabe's ball of yarn, and at once he was ready to return to the buffalo range without complaint. Apparently, there was something he had to get out of his system, and after he had been purged he was ready to resume his old ways. There was not a lazy bone in his body, and I never had a better hand. I was very much attached to Jack Callahan. He was always in good humor, which is a fine quality for a man to have in a hunting camp. A bad temper can spoil the pleasure of an entire camp. Some mornings we would sleep late. When the sun got in his eyes, Jack would jump up, exclaiming "By George, this will never do! It will never buy my girl a dress nor pay for the one she has."

After we had been at Dodge City a few days, taking in the sights, we grew tired of loafing, and decided to strike out and go to new hunting grounds. So we went up the Arkanas River, along the north side, to what was known as Nine Mile Ridge, where we crossed to the south side of the river.

The increasing numbers and destructiveness of the buffalo-hunters had been making the Plains Indians more and more hostile. The danger to hunters was increasing day by day. All that region south of the Arkansas was forbidden ground, the Indians insisting that the white men should obey the terms of the Medicine Lodge treaty. If the killing of the buffalo should continue unabated, the Indians would soon be facing starvation; at least, their old freedom would be at an end, as they could no longer roam the country at will, confident of finding meat in abundance wherever they might go.

The Arkansas was called the "dead line," south of which no hunter should go. The river was patrolled at intervals by Government troops, as a feeble indication that the Medicine Lodge treaty had not been forgotten, but their vigilance was so lax that there was no difficulty in crossing back and forth without detection. The danger of attack by Indians was a far more potent obstacle to the buffalo-hunter, but as buffalo grew fewer in number and the price of hides advanced, even this did not deter hardy hunters from undertaking forays into the forbidden country. The troops were supposed to prevent the passing of the Indians to the north side of the river. This patrol also failed to work.

We gazed longingly across the sandy wastes that marked the course of the Arkansas. The oftener we looked the more eager we became to tempt fate. Even the sky looked more inviting in that direction, and often after a flurry of cold weather the wind from the south was mild, balmy and inviting. As a matter of fact, the possible danger of encountering hostile Indians added spice to the temptation.

So we crossed over. Finding a pleasant stretch of bottom land, where the grass grew tall and thick, we cut and stacked a lot of prairie hay for our teams and saddle horses. The grass waved above our horses' backs as we rode along. Later, we found Indians too numerous in this vicinity for us to devote much time to hunting and we abandoned this camp.

Figure 6.1. "Curing Hides and Bones," Paul Frenzeny and Jules Tavernier drawing, from *Harper's Weekly*, April 4, 1874. Courtesy Kansas State Historical Society.

"Curing Hides and Bones" *Harper's Weekly*, April 4, 1874

Dan Flores argues that trade in buffalo robes depleted bison populations in the early nineteenth century. Later developments were still worse for the animals. In the early 1870s, eastern tanneries found a way to turn bison hides to leather. Robes were still profitable, but now any bison hide, even one with a thin summer coat, was worth money. The new marketability of hides, combined with the extension of the railroad onto the Great Plains, made the buffalo range a more attractive destination for thousands of white hunters, who stalked the region in competition with the thousands of Indians who yet depended on buffalo for sustenance. Figure 6.1 is from a popular magazine of the 1870s. What you see here is a staging area for shipping buffalo products to the market. Note the hides drying, pegged to the ground. Buffalo bones were gathered to make fertilizer for farmers and gardeners in the East. The telegraph and railroad are visible in the background, reminding us that Billy Dixon and other market hunters were connected to urban centers in the East (and on the West Coast). In earlier times, Indian hunters and white traders on the Plains had used riverboats and rafts to transport their goods to markets downriver, especially in St Louis and New Orleans. Without transportation links to the cities, especially the railroad, white market hunters like Dixon could not have got their hides to market without losing money on the exchange.

Which was most important in ensuring the bison's decline: the robe trade, new tanning methods, or the railroad? Is it even possible to separate the causes in this manner?

Drake Hotel, Thanksgiving Menu, 1886

Reprinted from Peter Matthiessen, *Wildlife in America* (New York: Viking Press, 1959), p. 166

Finally, we should keep in mind that hunting for the market went far beyond bison. Virtually every game animal was hunted and sold for consumption, and as the urban population of the United States expanded in this period, demand for game soared, with the result that wildlife populations frequently declined to dangerously low levels. From 1855 to 1893 John B. Drake, proprietor of the Drake Hotel in Chicago, gave an annual game dinner at Thanksgiving. This was the menu for 1886.

How many different game species do you count on this menu? Who was eating this food? Who was hunting it? Assuming that most of the hunters were like Billy Dixon, scrambling to make a living, how were they different from the clientele of the Drake Hotel? Why would a hotel make game the chief offering

for a holiday dinner? How was it different from beef, pork, or chicken, which
were readily available (and no more expensive) at the time? What is special
about game meat that made it highly sought after by Americans?

PROCESSION OF GAME

Soup
Venison (Hunter Style)   Game Broth

Fish
Broiled Trout, Shrimp Sauce
Baked Black Bass, Claret Sauce

Boiled
Leg of Mountain Sheep, Ham of Bear
Venison Tongue, Buffalo Tongue

Roast
Loin of Buffalo, Mountain Sheep, Wild Goose, Quail, Redhead Duck,
Jack Rabbit, Blacktail Deer, Coon, Canvasback Duck, English Hare,
Bluewing Teal, Partridge, Widgeon, Brant, Saddle of Venison, Pheasants,
Mallard Duck, Prairie Chicken, Wild Turkey, Spotted Grouse, Black
Bear, Opossum, Leg of Elk, Wood Duck, Sandhill Crane, Ruffed
Grouse, Cinnamon Bear

Broiled
Bluewing Teal, Jacksnipe, Blackbirds, Reed Birds, Partridges, Pheasants,
Quails, Butterballs, Ducks, English Snipe, Rice Birds, Red-Wing Starling,
Marsh Birds, Plover, Gray Squirrel, Buffalo Steak, Rabbits, Venison Steak

Entrees
Antelope Steak, Mushroom Sauce; Rabbit Braise, Cream Sauce; Fillet of
Grouse with Truffles; Venison Cutlet, Jelly Sauce; Ragout of Bear, Hunter
Style; Oyster Pie

Salads
Shrimp, Prairie Chicken, Celery

Ornamental Dishes
Pyramid of Game en Bellevue, Boned Duck au Naturel, Pyramid of
Wild-Goose Liver in Jelly, The Coon out at Night, Boned Quail in
Plumage, Red-Wing Starling on Tree, Partridge in Nest, Prairie Chicken
en Socle

7

The Many Uses of Conservation

The conservation movement represents one of the most far-reaching and influential developments in American environmental history. By the late 1880s, the rapid decline in various wildlife species, widespread deforestation, and continuing concerns about rapid urbanization led to a widespread sense of anxiety in the United States. A consensus emerged, especially among the middle and upper classes, that both nature and society needed to be better managed to ensure America's traditional abundance of natural resources. These perspectives found expression in the conservation movement.

Many of conservation's earliest supporters were sportsmen, recreational hunters who sought to maintain adequate game populations for hunting. But there was much more to the conservationist movement than a ubiquitous appreciation for wildlife. In fact, different people understood nature and wild animals in very different ways, and as a result the conflicts over conservation were many. Conserving resources was more complicated than just avoiding "greed." It meant constraining other people from using them. Who was constrained, and how, were volatile questions which often fell out along lines of race and class. Benjamin Johnson explores how strikers in the iron mines of Minnesota became the target of corporate owners and conservationists alike in the early twentieth century.

Johnson explains how mine owners and merchants in Minnesota sought to enforce conservation laws, particularly hunting regulations, against striking workers, particularly immigrants, during labor troubles at the region's lead mines in the early 1900s. His analysis suggests that conservation could be a tool for forcing people back to wage work, and that more generally its supporters sought to reorder nature in ways that would make it accessible as a recreational resource, but not for subsistence purposes. This was typical of conservation across the country. For all its accomplishments, conservation generally benefited the urban middle classes and rural elites at the expense of the rural poor. The documents in this section will suggest some of the broader implications of conservation, and its hotly contested history.

Conservation, Subsistence, and Class at the Birth of Superior National Forest

Benjamin Heber Johnson

In the United States today, anti-environmentalism – broadly defined as opposition to state regulation of natural resources and management of public lands – is a powerful political sentiment. Its proponents range from libertarians and corporate board members to grassroots organizations and workers in extractive industries. Its targets include national environmental legislation, environmentalist legislators, and local environmental activity. Anti-environmentalism finds some of its strongest support in communities on the edges of federal wilderness areas. Many residents of such communities, like their counterparts in developing nations, resent what they perceive as the control of outsiders through environmental regulations and public land bureaucracies. Contemporary U.S. anti-environmentalism is conservative in that it defines itself in opposition to the ideology and programs of the liberal state. Like other conservatives, anti-environmentalists argue that, rather than serving the interests of society as a whole, liberalism's expansion of the power of the state has in fact been used by elites for their own ends and in ways that conflict with the desires and needs of communities and "ordinary people."

Historians have paid conservatism far less attention than its power and importance in U.S. history warrant. Environmental historians are no exception to this pattern. Scholars have been understandably too interested in environmentalism to spend much energy on detailing the motives and sources of its opponents; thus, the history of environmental politics has generally been told from the point of view of environmentalists and their conservationist predecessors. In his history of the concept of wilderness in U.S. thought, Roderick Nash laid the foundation for this approach in the early stages of environmental history. Nash writes as though the history of the wilderness aesthetic were synonymous with the history of appreciation of nature.[1] Such is also the case with major studies of conservationist and environmentalist efforts to create parks and wilderness areas. Most historians present these places as self-evident "wilderness areas," largely unaffected by humans and appealing precisely because of their distance from the pressures of modern life. From this perspective, rapacious exploitation is the always-present counterpart of the altruistic desire to protect them. Such accounts rely heavily on the documents of environmental and conservation groups, and as a result, are often triumphal accounts of the victory of environmentalism in which enlightened nature lovers do battle with their shortsighted, provincial, or merely greedy opponents.

Recent scholarship provides some of the tools and information necessary to tell histories of environmentalism and protected areas that take anti-environmentalism seriously. Rather than assuming that a wilderness ethos is an obvious and "natural" way of expressing appreciation for nature, historians can now avail themselves of much more nuanced and contextual understandings of the intellectual history of the concept of *wilderness*. In U.S. culture, as William Cronon argues, the mystique of wilderness emerged from the Romantic notion of the sublime and from the nineteenth-century belief in the frontier as the breeding ground for democracy and national character. Despite its key role in rallying environmental sentiment, wilderness can be seen as an escapist fantasy better suited for individual therapeutic experience than for the daunting social task of making a living from nature in a sustainable and respectful fashion. Scholars have done a particularly good job demonstrating how wilderness ideology made it all too easy to overlook the long history of Indian inhabitation, and how it often clashed with native understandings and subsistence uses of nature.[2]

Recent accounts of conservation, more focused on social history, also avoid environmentalist triumphalism. They instead tell more complex and less moralistic stories of how state conservation created landscapes administered by experts on behalf of the bureaucratic state and the modern economy. Beginning in the late nineteenth century, game bureaucracies sought to replace a set of local commons with a national commons in which wildlife was the property of the state or federal government, an effort which enlisted the support of some locals, generally elite factions. More intensive management in an area directly under government control, such as the Adirondacks preserve, did not maintain a wilderness apart from the modern world, but rather created landscapes managed by professional bureaucrats in the interests of visiting tourists and national economic power.

While much remains to be explored in the social history of American conservation, it is already clear that such studies will help to explain the sources, motives, and ideologies of anti-environmentalism. This essay reconsiders the history of environmental conflict in Northeastern Minnesota in light of the impact of Superior National Forest's establishment in 1909, specifically by examining the effects of state conservation on local resource use and economic hierarchies in the nearby town of Ely. Local elites in Ely were the critical clients and beneficiaries of the expansion of state power that conservation embodied. The ability of the town's merchant elite to implement state conservation in its own interest posed a threat to important subsistence uses by the area's poorer residents. The result was a deepening of the gap between the way these two groups perceived the natural world around them and the bureaucracies that were increasingly regulating it. These early conflicts helped contribute to widespread local opposition to the management of the forest, an opposition that lasts to this day.

Today, Ely, Minnesota, is a town of about four thousand people sixty miles north of Duluth, and just twenty miles south of the Canadian border. It is known to most outsiders as the major jumping-off point to Ontario's Quetico Park and the Boundary Waters Canoe Area Wilderness (BWCAW) of Superior National Forest, the most heavily visited wilderness in the United States and the largest such protected area east of the Mississippi.

Nowhere in the United States have the effects of environmentalism been more dramatic. Since the 1920s, an organized wilderness protection lobby has been remarkably successful in protecting and restoring what it perceives as the area's pristine qualities. A series of federal laws and land purchases transformed the forests and lakes which surround Ely from a patchwork of state, federal, and private lands devoted primarily to commercial timber production to a larger national forest originally devoted to a variety of uses, and today dominated by a national wilderness area devoted to recreation and wilderness preservation. This transformation produced enormous local animosity toward the environmental and conservation groups responsible for it. As the timber harvest declines and more and more of the region's iron mines close, tourism increasingly dominates the town's economy, forcing Ely to cater to outdoor enthusiasts – the very outsiders whose support for wilderness protection engendered so much local resentment.

In the 1870s, the rich deposits of the Vermilion Iron Range drew large numbers of Americans and Europeans to Northeastern Minnesota, previously home to the Ojibway, some scattered European-stock and mixed-blood traders, and subsistence farmers. By 1884, an operating iron mine existed in Tower, twenty miles to the west of Ely. The mine was connected to the Lake Superior ports of Twin Harbors and Duluth by the Duluth and Iron Range Railroad. In 1883, prospectors discovered a rich vein of iron ore next to Long Lake. A township was platted nearby in 1887, a village organized in 1888, and a formal city charter signed in 1891.

Iron deposits near Ely, on the east end of the Vermilion Iron Range, gave rise to five mines – the Sibley, Zenith, Pioneer, Chandler, and Section 30. The mines required large workforces, which meant that by 1900 Ely's population had risen to 3,717 from only 901 a decade before. The population remained small until 1910, when it reached 3,972, then climbed to 4,902 by 1920. The first settlers in Ely were native-born Americans and some skilled Cornish and English miners and engineers, but most who followed them in the 1890s were men from Finland and Slovenia (then an Austrian province). The labor requirements of mining and timbering and the overwhelmingly immigrant population meant that the sex ratio was heavily skewed toward men. The town quickly took on a distinctive ethnic geography, most of it divided between Finns and a few Swedes on one side, and Slovenes and a few Italians on the other.

Ely's boisterous ethnic diversity impressed itself upon residents and visitors alike. Each group had its own secret and fraternal societies, churches, marching bands, and even sports teams. Ties of ethnicity pervaded every aspect of life. Interethnic marriages provoked controversy and lasting animosity. As one resident who grew up in the 1910s remembered, "They used to have to be real careful about the football team in high school and the cheerleaders. So many had to be Slovenian and so many had to be Finn or else there'd be a big ruckus."[3] One native Pennsylvanian wrote his family with the disparaging remark that "One Austrian, a cousin Jack, a Finlander, a Russian Jew, and one white man are running for mayor."[4]

Ely's heavily masculine and working-class public culture could offend the sensibilities of Anglo-American visitors. . . . Many visitors commented on the large number of saloons and the frequent barroom brawls and streetfights. The visiting evangelist Billy Sunday put the matter succinctly with his comment that "the only difference between Ely and Hell is that there is a railroad out of Ely."[5]

The apparent disorder and debauchery of Ely's social life contrasted sharply with the rigid political and economic control of the mining interests. The residents of Ely lived both literally and figuratively in the shadow of the iron mines. Company property accounted for about 90 percent of Ely's assessed property values. The town newspaper was called the *Ely Miner*. John Pengilly, the superintendent of the Chandler mine, won the village's first presidency in 1888. Many of the recent immigrants lived in company houses, and many more on land owned by mining companies.[6] Most of their modest homes were simple shacks "built by nailing boxboards to upright timbers with tarpaper to cover them . . . they had flat roofs and were not much over six feet high with a dirt floor."[7]

Mining work provided the core of life in Ely. Virtually all Finnish and Slovenian men worked in the mines, and almost all of Ely's women worked in boarding houses or took boarders into their own homes. Working conditions in the mines were grim at best. One resident who grew up in the 1910s recalled that the older men in his family would "leave in the morning in the dark and come home in the dark. They used to work there for twelve hours...."[8] Hardly a week went by without some mention in the paper of a mining fatality, usually caused by a cave-in, flooding, improperly set explosives, or a long fall. In the early twentieth century, the annual death rate in Minnesota's iron mines was about 7.5 per thousand employees; from 1905 to 1909, St. Louis County saw 277 workers die in the mines. Nonlethal hazards also abounded. High levels of carbon dioxide produced by workers and draft animals accumulated in the mines, causing "dizziness, headaches, and shortness of breath." Miners often returned to the surface drenched in perspiration and water after working in hot, wet mines; pneumonia and other respiratory ailments could result from exposure to frigid winter air. Finally, epidemic diseases like typhoid arose from unclean drinking water and unsanitary bathroom facilities in the mines.

Because of such working conditions, the iron mines of northeastern Minnesota were the sites of major strikes and labor agitation. In 1907, a strike on the ore-loading docks at Duluth and Two Harbors spread to the iron fields. Workers demanded an end to the arbitrary power of foremen, the replacement of the piece-rate system with a flat daily wage, and an eight-hour day. Violence and the mass importation of strikebreakers, often Slovenians, defeated the strike after several months. A 1916 strike on the more southerly Mesabai Iron Range, partially under the auspices of the Industrial Workers of the World (IWW), also resulted in sporadic work stoppages in Ely's mines.

The strikes exposed a local political dynamic that would play a critical role in the implementation of state conservation. Company officials relied upon the support of local merchants, predominantly Anglo and German, to force the miners back to work. Shortly before the 1907 strike, the superintendent of the Oliver Iron Mining Company in Ely assured the general manager that the "business men of the city are very much opposed to any strike at this time and all say that wages are good. They also state that in case of any strike, they will all operate on a strictly cash basis."[9] Local merchants were given blacklists of labor agitators and strikers, who were then denied credit. In both 1907 and 1916, the mining companies successfully pressured Duluth-based wholesalers to force retailers in striking districts to operate on a cash-only basis (under ordinary circumstances, local grocers paid their wholesalers only once a month, which enabled them to extend credit to the miners, who were themselves paid monthly). "When the strikers retaliated by opening their own co-operative stores," historian Robert Eleff notes, "pressure from the mining companies on Duluth wholesalers soon prevented them from receiving any goods."[10]

In the wake of their 1907 defeat, many of the blacklisted union leaders and strikers, overwhelmingly Finnish, were forced into the countryside to make a living. As one observer noted, "Finns were blacklisted, and many of them, unable to get work, drifted back into the woods, to chop out a clearing in the boulder-strewn cutover land."[11] Townships adjacent to mining communities, often known as "little Finlands," grew rapidly after 1907. The Oliver Iron Mining Company, whose holdings produced more than three quarters of the iron from Minnesota's mines, reduced its workforce from 18 percent Finnish to 8 percent in the wake of the strike.

Blacklisted miners turned to the land for good reason. While wages paid by logging and mining companies provided a foundation for Ely's market economy, most area residents supplemented their income through direct access to the material necessities of life in the woods and waterways. Hunting, fishing, and trapping became especially critical during hard economic times. . . . The land could be abundant despite the harshness of the climate. Nearly all families harvested wood to heat their homes during the long winters. Most families kept livestock and raised their own vegetables. . . . In fact, keeping livestock in and near town was so common that in 1908 the city council passed a law holding owners liable for damage to property and gardens caused by animals. . . .

Needing more room for their livestock and gardens, many residents availed themselves of clearings in the surroundings woods. . . . Ida Erickson . . . remembers that "gardens were out somewhere else, you know, because at the time you could build your gardens anywhere. You didn't have to rent them from anybody."[12] Residents extended much of the ethnic geography of Ely into the countryside. Groups of families that built their homes together in town would often work the land together: "this family would help with that family and maybe three, four families would get together to get one area fixed up till everybody had all his stuff in for the winter."[13] The very high price of produce and other foodstuffs in northeastern Minnesota – contemporary observers estimated that food costs were 50 to 100 percent higher than downstate – bolsters the anecdotal evidence from oral histories that self-provisioning was economically critical.

Some locals relied on farming for their principal source of both income and subsistence. Despite newspaper claims that properly drained land would yield twenty times the wheat harvest of the prairie states, the

land did not lend itself to agriculture. The soil was terribly thin, so thin
that trees often toppled over because their roots could not support their
trunks and branches. Very few naturally open places existed, and stump
removal required time-consuming and backbreaking labor. Once a field
was cleared, the would-be farmer still had to face a growing season of
under one hundred days, much of which came with enough rain to
waterlog fields. Soil fertility usually declined sharply after the first
crop. Still, some managed to make a substantial part of their living
from farming. . . . Homesteaders generally raised "the necessary staples
like potatoes, other vegetables, eggs, milk, butter and so on."[14] Most
produce seems to have been for direct consumption, but there was a
substantial market for it in Ely, created by the very remoteness which
made so much farm produce expensive to buy.

Homesteading was enormously difficult work, but for at least some
residents staking out a claim was a viable option when economic down-
turns or personal misfortune struck. . . . The modest success of some in
homesteading endeavors led one observer to suggest homesteading as a
logical response to mining slowdowns across the Iron Range.[15]

But even those who lived out in the country had to turn to sources
of income and subsistence besides farming. According to one local
historian, "Homesteaders augmented their income by selling cordwood
and timber from their land, worked in lumber camps and were trappers
of fur bearing animals. For food, they supplied themselves with fish,
moose, and deer meat, both in and out of the legal season."[16] Homesteaders and townspeople alike turned to timber, which they sold to
neighbors as firewood and to merchants as Christmas trees. Most importantly, residents turned to the region's game and fish. "A home-
steader brought into court for illegally taking fish with a net, was asked
by the judge as to why he committed the act. The reply was, 'You can't
farm this country without a net and a 30-30 caliber rifle.'"[17] Townspeople also availed themselves of game with little regard for formal
legalities. As August Stromberg remembers, "When we run short [of
food] we just run out an' get another one . . . we salted down a lot of
moose and fish."[18] Netting and dynamiting for fish was a common way
to obtain food. In 1906, the *Miner* complained that "Parties returning
from trips up the lakes report that the netting and blasting of fish was
being carried on in almost every creek and river."[19] Game was useful not
only for meat, but also for the cash value of fur. Stromberg recalls that
"We trapped our own clothes. We kids, from the time we was ten years
old we used to trap for our clothes, weasels, muskrats, like that . . .
Maybe you got three dollars for a mink or fifty cents for a weasel, but
that was good money them days. We trapped enough to buy our
clothes."[20]

Conservation and Class Conflict

The 1909 establishment of Superior National Forest would challenge the subsistence practices so important to many of Ely's residents. The state of Minnesota's subsequent declaration that the forest would also be a state game preserve meant that subsistence activities on most of the least-used and least-populated lands were now either illegal or subject to restriction by state agents at will. Possession of any meat, fur, or weapons on the game reserve subjected one to immediate arrest and seizure of property; hunting of any animal, except for the state-supported extermination of wolves, was illegal. As the *Miner* opined shortly after the forest's establishment, "All of the officials and employees of the national government will be commissioned as deputy game wardens of the state, and will wage an active campaign against the useless and criminal slaughter of game and the illegal blasting and netting of fish."[21]

Concern over rapid deforestation by timber companies provided the primary impetus for the establishment of the forest. Widespread timber harvesting began near Ely in 1891, at first to supply the mines with timber supports, but soon with the express purpose of turning the forests into marketable lumber. By 1900, numerous logging companies were operating sawmills, small dams, sluiceways, and private railroads in the area that would eventually be encompassed by the national forest. Large stands of white and red pine – especially abundant to the northeast of Ely, but nearly logged out in the rest of the state – attracted the companies to the area. They cut some of the trees at mills near Ely, but shipped most by rail to Duluth or the Twin Cities for processing. The speed of this operation was both breathtaking and frightening to any who cared to ponder the future of the nation's forests and lumber supply. The harvest reached its peak in 1899 when Minneapolis sawmills cut more than 492 million board-feet of lumber. The yield subsequently declined, and most mills were shut down by the early 1920s. . . .

One obvious response to such unsustainable and chaotic private harvesting was state ownership and management of some of the remaining public domain. Minnesota's forestry commissioner, Christopher Andrews, first pursued such a course of action in the Quetico-Superior area in 1902, when he convinced the General Land Office to withdraw 500,000 acres of recently burned-over land from sale. In 1905, he secured the withdrawal of 141,000 acres of valuable timberland. In 1909, President Theodore Roosevelt formally made the withdrawals permanent with the establishment of Superior National Forest. The provincial government of Ontario, facing similar pressures and concerns, established a forest preserve just to the north of the U.S. forest; four years later, it was declared a provincial park.

For the commercial elite of Ely, which was sympathetic to the mining companies and interested in furthering the region's economic development, the establishment of the forest was both a threat and an opportunity. On one hand, state ownership of the land threatened to allocate resources to other interests and to funnel profits elsewhere. As the *Miner* complained of the 1905 land withdrawal, "Northern Minnesota is much too earnest in her building up an empire out of a wilderness to be patient with silly schemes or forest reserves, parks and hunting grounds that will block her efforts to make something out of herself."[22] ... Most historians of national forests emphasize these sorts of conflicts between local, development-minded interests and the usually distant supporters of state conservation. But in the early years of Superior National Forest, this sort of conflict was overshadowed by the cooperation of Ely business leaders with state bureaucracies and their outside constituents. Although aimed at conserving timber resources, the establishment of the forest inadvertently provided Ely's leading citizens with new ways to make money and to cement their local economic hegemony. Conservation and game laws transformed the previously common property of deer, fish, timber, furs, and other forest products into property owned, or at least allocated, by the state. Because the commercial elites of Ely were able to control state implementation, they benefited from this change in property tenure, while Ely's working people had to pay a higher and higher price for maintaining their access to critical material resources.

One of the primary motives that local merchants had for taking an interest in state conservation was the recent creation of a tourist industry, a business whose use of local natural resources could conflict with those of subsistence users. In 1910, one year after the establishment of Superior National Forest, some of the Ely residents who stood to benefit most from the visits of sportsmen organized themselves into a chapter of the American Game Protective Association. The organization's officers were some of the most prominent members of Ely's commercial and political elite. Mayor Louis Eisenach was the chair, and other directors included the aptly named Judge Thomas Jury, alderman and state game warden Fred James, banker and Burntside Lodge co-owner Lewis J. White, and several store owners. The association's first act was to assist in the placement of 600,000 pike and lake trout in Long Lake in June 1910.

An increasing number of outside organizations and interests also established tourist facilities in and around Ely and began patronizing local retail establishments. In 1910, a YMCA camp relocated to Long Lake, directly north of the town, and in 1911 the local hardware store started advertising the fact that it sold camping and fishing equipment.[23]

... Economically, tourists were important enough that the *Miner* began running front page pictures of beautiful lakes to enthrall outsiders. One outdoor magazine referred to Ely as the "gate of the nation's playground."[24] In 1914, the Ely-Burntside Outing Company finished construction of the Burntside Lodge and boasted of "reservations made from all over the United States." The lodge's proprietors were key members of the Ely commercial elite – the editor of the *Miner*, two store owners, a doctor, and the town's main banker. On the same lake, the "Oliver mining company had just completed a $10,000 clubhouse near the lake and a Minneapolis outdoors club had erected a camp to be used during the hunting seasons."[25]

In 1910, the state hired a new game warden, Fred James, to patrol out of Ely, with special attention to hunting on the game preserve. James was an influential resident. In 1886, he had come to Ely across the ice from Tower. He was the first postmaster, a signer of the petition for village incorporation, a longtime alderman, and a founding member of the local Game Protective Association. James Street was named after him, and the family business, the James Drug Store, operates to this day on Ely's main street. James's wardenship was soon to be a flash point for local conflicts over resource use.

In a sense, game laws were inherently at odds with the needs of subsistence use, quite apart from the actions of Ely's mercantile leaders. The setting of strict seasons and maximum quantities of certain fish species, as well as the setting of legitimate means of taking game – no fishing with nets, spears, or explosives, and no hunting with dogs or lights – served the needs and aesthetic values of sports hunters, but often directly conflicted with the methods of subsistence hunting. In Ely, game law enforcement consistently operated to the detriment of subsistence users and to the advantage of outside sports hunters and their local support network. Wardens would often sell seized game and equipment to Ely merchants, an ironic practice given that confiscation was originally made as a result of the illegal sale of venison. At a time when bitter strikes were fought for a daily wage of $3, venison and moose meat would fetch almost $20 per animal, rifles would be resold for $5 or $6, mink furs for about $5, and more common furs for $1 or $2. Not only were the lost proceeds a significant blow to local hunters, but the destruction, confiscation, or selling of canoes, traps, and guns deprived locals of equipment necessary to engage in common subsistence activities. Moreover, fines for violations were often onerous: approximately $25 plus court costs for possession of untagged venison, $10 for netting fish, and $100 for hunting deer out of season.

What must have made the enforcement of game laws especially galling to many locals was that wardens often made gifts of confiscated materials to the town's political and commercial elite. Fred James was particularly fond of this tactic. Over a period of several years, he gave partridge to the sheriff; forty pounds of moose meat to a butcher's shop; split a whole moose between the sheriff, police captain, justice of the peace, and several other friends; and kept a gasoline launch for his own use. . . .

Wardens and forest rangers generally exempted themselves from the very laws that they were sworn to enforce. Charles Cecil, a forest ranger, wrote home of the oddity of official poaching in Superior National Forest: "It's funny; everybody lives on wild meat here [at the Ranger Station] all the year round and they serve moosemeat to Forest supervisors and game wardens when they stop. . . ."[26] After several months in the service, Cecil's disquiet vanished from his letters home, only to be replaced with a menu-like description of the illegal fish, fowl, and meat that filled the rangers' stomachs. Cecil also revealed that this disregard for game laws extended all the way to the top. In 1911, he wrote home about a telling incident: "Carlos Avery, fish and game commissioner of the state, came down the lake with a game warden as a guide. They had a sack of trout which they kept out of sight and the warden said in explanation that they had captured some nets. They had ice for the fish, however, which I suppose they took up to make lemonade with? A little fishy in the telling."[27]

Conservation enforcement most obviously curtailed subsistence hunting and fishing, but it cut into other uses as well. Transforming much of the forest around Ely into state and federal property, to be sold to the most efficient timber companies, meant that the common practice of taking timber for firewood and construction became illegal. As the state forester made clear in 1912, the "law requires Forest officers to report cases of timber trespass on state lands and a number of instances have been reported by the Rangers."[28] Helmi Gawboy, a longtime resident of an Ojibway reservation on nearby Lake Vermilion, clearly remembered the effects of this regulation:

> If you didn't have a woodpile by your house, they'd tell you you were lazy. You didn't cut wood. If you had a pile of wood then they'd say you was commercializing in wood or where did you cut it from and that's the wrong type . . . They'd look at your fence posts that you'd put around your garden and you weren't supposed to cut cedar posts. And then everybody had been selling wood. Cutting wood and selling it to the school. And when we did it, then they'd come after us and said that we were commercializing in wood and we should pay for the stumpage. And if he didn't pay up they'd put him in jail.[29]

Ely's ethnic and class divisions conditioned both elite and common understandings of the contested access to natural resources. The editor of the *Miner* never tired of pointing out that immigrant workers were the chief users of the woods for subsistence. The *Miner* reflected the attitude of Ely's business elite in its contempt for how labor radicalism was bound up with subsistence use. In the aftermath of the 1907 miners' strike, the editor crowed that "the readers of the red-flag outfit have taken off their best clothes and have gone to the woods, in all probability to use some of the dynamite in blasting fish to fill their aching voids. The lay-off at the mines has been a hard blow to those laid off as well as those who agitated a living from the working-man."[30]

The *Miner*'s editorial stance reflected the alliance between local elites and outside sports hunters. Each year, the paper printed the game regulations in large print on the front page; in some years, it accompanied them with a lead editorial warning locals to "Read them over carefully and see that you do not run afoul of the game warden." In 1909, the editor ran a front-page reprint of a diatribe against "Pot Hunters" written by a Duluth sportsman. The *Miner*'s editor praised the author for laying "particular stress on the actions of the foreign born residents." The sportsman made clear that much of his contempt for these "foreigners" derived from the fact that "They do not hunt for the sport of it, but merely for a certain class of aliens, when employed on railroad and mining work, to board themselves... It is meat, even if bad meat, and that is all they are after. In many sections of Northern Minnesota and Wisconsin more game is killed by these people than by Americans who shoot during the closed season."[31]

... Almost all complainants to the game wardens or state officials went out of their way to make it clear that immigrants were the primary violators of game laws....

An ideological as well as social congruence existed between the state conservation bureaucracies and Ely's merchant elite. Conservation's emphasis on state-led economic modernization – as opposed to the waste, fraud, and chaos of the unregulated private timber companies – dovetailed nicely with the desire of local elites to curtail subsistence uses. Conservation can be understood, as historian Samuel P. Hays argues, as an effort by scientists and technicians to use their expertise to most efficiently manage state property and material production. From the perspective of conservation bureaucrats, less efficient uses of the landscape had to be curtailed, and clearly the single most important use of the forests around Ely was commercial timber production. As the state forester asserted, the "best interests of the state, as well as the settler, requires that this rocky land be used as our woodlot, to produce timber for ourselves and for the future."[32] From this conservationist perspective, the forests were an essential part of a modern economy in which each segment of society performed a specialized role: "The radiating influence of the standing forests is repeated when they are cut and utilized. The *producers* of the raw materials which supply the *factories*, which sell to the *wholesalers*, distributing to the *retailers*, who sell their wares to the *wage-earners* in forest and mill – are, with their employees, and the lumber companies and their employees, all more or less dependent upon the forests."[33] Although many urban elites saw sports hunting as a way of getting in touch with the primitive and manly virtues besieged by industrial society, state officials saw even sports hunting as an important part of their Progressive economic vision:

> The sportsman, too, is a medium, together with the lumber companies and the railroads, through which the forests exert an economic influence upon the country. They furnish cover for the game which calls him out. In pursuit of that game he expends quantities of ammunition. He buys guns, tents, canoes and endless other paraphernalia, in the production of which countless citizens gain their living. The ammunition bought from the retailer means renewed activities all along the line back to the charcoal burner.[34]

Ironically, even the antimodern aspects of early-twentieth-century nature tourism could be reconciled with the desire to curtail subsistence uses. Throughout the 1910s, an increasing number of visitors came to Ely in order to experience a wilderness that they wanted as far removed from civilization as possible. The desire for such a refuge logically implied the need to erase the record of extensive human use. A Minneapolis sporting magazine said that a trip to Superior National Forest "takes you into the heart of the wilderness and far beyond the last outposts of civilization."[35] A 1919 Forest Service publication underscored the area's remoteness, even as it asserted its accessibility: "Fine camping sites are abundant, and the voyageur can always pitch his tent wherever night overtakes him – at places others have camped before, or perhaps where the ring of the woodsman's ax has never broken the forest silence."[36] . . .

If the wealthy of Ely saw the curtailment of subsistence uses as part of a broader plan for orderly economic development, some evidence indicates that more plebeian locals perceived the landscape as a place for the enactment of their own, different, social vision. Such attitudes are hard to recover; working-class people did not write books and were more preoccupied with avoiding law enforcement officials than with leaving a cohesive record of their thoughts and actions. Nevertheless, oral histories provide a glimpse into this hidden world. They suggest that for lower-class European immigrants, as for the Ojibway, the woods were a distinctly human place in the sense that their wood, fish, berries, rice, fur, and meat were bound up in the struggle to make a living. When describing the lakes and woods around them, local subsistence users were far more likely to orient themselves by referring to nearby home-steads or familiar trapping grounds than by reference to natural land-marks. One labor radical clearly remembers that many homesteaders were forced back onto the land by labor conflicts in the mines: "But those old time pioneers who came here before and after the turn of the century, many of them settled out here in the woods because they were blackballed because they were forced out here in the woods because of their political activity on behalf of the working class."[37] . . .

World War I heightened the extent to which the woods became a place of refuge for radicals, particularly those of Finnish descent. In April 1917, aliens were banned from owning or carrying firearms. The same year, across the Iron Range, "home guards" were formed to support the war effort and halt draft-dodging. The membership of the board of Ely's home guard reflected a familiar pattern, being comprised of the Oliver Mining Company's Ely superintendent, his assistant, and their clerk; the chief of the Oliver Company's police; the supervisor of Superior National Forest; another local mine owner; and the editor of the *Miner*. For their part, many labor radicals, including the leadership of the IWW, opposed U.S. entry into the war. Large portions of Ely's working class dodged the draft, and the efforts of the home guard made the woods a scene of further social conflict along class lines. As Andy Johnson remembers, "there was quite a few of the young fellows who used to work in the woods who were dodging the draft here, and the home guards used to come down and hunt them down." Johnson's recollection suggests the extent to which the woods were home territory for the dodgers and more of a foreign place for their pursuers. The home guards "seldom ever went into the forest for their man," and when they did, "Sometimes they'd find him and most of the time they didn't."[38]

Perhaps the contrast between the freedom of the woods and the controlled work of the mines – and even the extension of the companies' power into town – helped to form plebeian attitudes toward nature. Andy Johnson's recollections may reveal just such an influence. Born in Finland in 1899 with the name Anti Hiltunen, Johnson began living on a homestead outside of Ely at age 11. After recounting the hard lot of miners and lumberjacks, as well as his own blacklisting for labor mili-tancy, Johnson's description of the pleasure he took in seeing nature seems all the more poignant. "Is there anything as beautiful as a spring morning in the Minnesota North Woods," he once wrote, "where tall pines are reflected on the calm surface of a pond; where ducks lazily bask in the sunshine; where birch and poplar leaves are brighter green than anywhere else?"[39] And even if it was not an incipient appreciation for untouched wilderness that travelers brought with them to Ely, Johnson's sensibility could take on quasi-environmental overtones: "This area was a terrible looking mess half a century ago when the timber barons got through with it. Everything was burnt down to the ground, but Mother Nature repaired the damage and the timber has grown back in so it is beautiful again. Of course, we miss the tall virgin pine."[40]

One incident in particular suggests the importance of local class divisions in the implementation of state conservation. In April 1910, state game warden Fred James shot Andrew Metsapelto on Long Lake. James alleged that Metsapelto and several other Finns had been illegally net fishing, an especially common practice on Long Lake, and that he had meant to fire a shot over the men's heads to frighten them into obeying his orders to come ashore. Metsapelto's companion, Otto Nykkanen, claimed that he and Metsapelto were returning from a pleasure outing and had neither fish nor net. According to Nykkanen, James, whom he did not recognize, had beckoned to them and then aimed and shot his friend after their canoe hit a rock that had turned them away from shore.[41]

Whatever story one believed, Andrew Metsapelto was killed by a .38 caliber bullet wound to the forehead. As the *Miner* made clear, the shooting quickly threatened to turn into a larger conflict: "News of the shooting spread like wildfire and in a remarkably short time a large crowd had congregated in the street near the jail [where James was being held after he had turned himself in] and mutterings were freely indulged in. The restlessness was more marked after it became known the man had died."[42] The crowd's rapid gathering outside the jail can be understood as a reflection of the ethnic and class tensions inherent in the efforts to curtail subsistence use and to open the woods to outside sportsmen. The members of what may well have become a lynch mob were drawn together because they knew that Andrew Metsapelto's shooting, whether accidental or deliberate, was part of a larger threat against their livelihoods and independence.

Not surprisingly, the elite of Ely rallied around Fred James: "A large force of deputies was sworn in and the crowd gradually dispersed. Mayor Eisenach [also the president of the Ely Game Protective Association] had ordered the saloons closed early in the evening thus removing a considerable incentive to lawlessness."[43] The *Miner*, whose editor was part-owner of a sportsmen's lodge on Lake Burntside, almost frantically defended James, insisting that "he has been an efficient game warden and has done much for the protection of game and fish . . . The personal opinion of the majority here is that the shooting was purely accidental." The newspaper's extensive coverage of James contrasted with its terse mention that "the unfortunate victim of the shooting" was survived by his mother and two siblings, "his father having died suddenly at the Pioneer mine about a month ago."[44]

James was subsequently charged with murder in the first degree. Five days after the shooting, George Bradley, the proprietor of the Vermilion Hotel, wrote to the state game commissioner requesting a shipment of trout eggs and offering information about James's prospects: "He has retained Baldwin and Baldwin of Duluth to defend him and I am told they are the best criminal lawyers up here. His friends are raising funds at Ely to pay for the defense – so I take it he will be looked after."[45]

Fred James was indeed looked after. Charges were reduced from murder to second-degree manslaughter. At the trial, held sixty miles away in Virginia, the judge read James's request for jury instructions, which began with the assertion that "the evidence in this case is undisputed that the defendant has always born a good reputation in the neighborhood in which he lived." The instructions emphasized that "if you find from the evidence that the deceased was engaged at the time . . . he was shot, in setting a fish net," then the jury had to consider that it was James's legal duty to arrest Metsapelto. After a thirty-minute deliberation, the jury found James innocent.[46]

Conclusion

It is difficult to fully ascertain the legacy of the conflicts which the James case reflects. Despite the severe consequences of being arrested for illegal resource use, it is not clear to what extent conservation policies were successful in curtailing the local subsistence economy, nor is it clear whether or not this pushed members of Ely's working class to identify themselves as wage-earners, thus turning them toward unionization as a viable way of improving their lot in life.

The intersection between local power structures and state conservation bureaucracies changed significantly in the 1920s. The naturalization of much of the immigrant population altered the local political dynamic and the composition of the juries that tried game law violators. The rise of a smaller merchant class tightly linked to specific immigrant groups – evident in some Iron Range towns by the time of the 1916 strike – decreased the propensity of merchants to ally themselves with outside forces such as mining companies and conservation bureaucracies. It seems reasonable to assume that subsistence practices declined in importance once locals found that unions (successfully organized in 1938) and social benefits like unemployment insurance granted them a more secure footing in the market economy.

Although the early tourist infrastructure was one motive for the local elite's receptiveness to state conservation, the increasing power of an outside wilderness protection lobby eventually drove a wedge between the forest service and its former supporters. An extensive road-building plan in the 1920s stirred boosters' hopes for widespread economic development, but it was scaled back after opposition from groups such as the Izaak Walton League. A subsequent proposal for waterpower and pulpwood logging development provoked even more opposition from regional and national environmental groups, who feared that the plan meant the end of the Quetico-Superior wilderness. Indeed, by the 1940s, local elites found that they had been all too successful in marketing the area as an untouched wilderness. As the populations and political clout of urban areas overshadowed places like Ely, environmentalists became increasingly successful in converting the area into a wilderness. In the 1940s, they secured appropriations for the addition of land to the National Forest and for the buy-out of resorts; by 1955, they had banned airplane landings and flights over the forest's roadless areas; and in the 1960s, they curtailed area logging and subsumed the roadless areas under the 1964 Wilderness Act, albeit with grandfather clauses allowing for continued logging and operation of resorts. In 1978, they secured the passage of federal legislation authorizing the purchase of numerous resorts and reserving much of the area for the exclusive use of canoe and kayak travel. As a result, since the 1950s virtually all outfitters and resort owners have resented national environmental groups and the U.S. Forest Service (which enforces the wilderness restrictions) with the fury of a scorned lover.

Contemporary anti-environmental rhetoric in Ely portrays this string of environmentalist victories as the betrayal of the town and its history to outside forces. Where environmentalists invoke the area's remote and rugged qualities to argue for the area's protection, anti-environmentalists tell a story of how outsiders – and the few locals who joined them – disrupted a once-harmonious relationship between people and nature. Although it obscures the complicity of local powers in the arrival of state conservation in places like Ely, this argument suggests that place – Ely as a community – became as important for anti-environmentalists as did place – the boundary waters as a wilderness – for environmentalists. This congruence is fitting, for both environmentalism and anti-environmentalism raise fundamental questions about the place of humans and nature in a modern economy. Ninety years after the establishment of Superior National Forest, these issues are still with us, in Ely, the United States, and the world.

Notes

1   Roderick Nash, *Wilderness and the American Mind*, 3d ed. (New Haven, Conn.: Yale University Press, 1982), esp. 208, 241–42.

2   William Cronon, "The Trouble with Wilderness; or, Getting Back to the Wrong Nature," in *Uncommon Ground: Toward Reinventing Nature*, ed. William Cronon (New York: W. W. Norton, 1995), 80–81; Mark David Spence, "Crown of the Continent, Backbone of the World: The American Wilderness Ideal and Blackfeet Exclusion from Glacier National Park," *Environmental History* 1 (1996): 29–49.

3   Joseph Pryatel, interview by Lynn Laitala, 21 November 1976, transcript, Minnesota Historical Society [hereafter MHS], 7.

4   Charles Cecil to Family, 28 March 1915, Letter 198, Box 2, Charles Cecil Papers, MHS.

5   Charles Cecil Papers, MHS, *passim*; the quote is found in John W. Somrock, *History of Incredible Ely* (Ely, Minn.: Cyko Art Print-Craft, 1976), 29.

6   *Ely Miner*, 15 February 1907, 1; Somrock, *History of Incredible Ely*, 10, 14.

7   Andy Johnson, "Reminiscences," n.d., Andy and Hannah Johnson Papers, MHS.

8   Pryatel, interview, 4.

9   Charles Trezona, correspondence, 18 July 1907, "Labor: Organizations and Disputes, 1892–1919 (no.1)" Folder, Papers Relating to Oliver Iron Mining Company, MHS.

10   Michael G. Karni, "The Founding of the Finnish Socialist Federation and the Minnesota Strike of 1907," in *For the Common Good: Finnish Immigrants and the Radical Response to Industrial America* (Superior, Wis.: Tyomies Society, 1977), 76; Clayton Videen Research Files, "The Finn-Liberal or Radical Extract" Folder, MHS, 141; Robert M. Eleff, "The 1916 Minnesota Miners' Strike Against U.S. Steel," *Minnesota History* 51 (1988): 70.

11   Clayton Videen Research Files, "The Finn-Liberal or Radical Extract" Folder, MHS, 142.

12   Ida Portham Erickson, interview by Lynn Laitala, 26 February 1976, transcript, MHS, 7.

13   Pryatel, interview, 21.

14   *Ely Miner*, 15 February 1907, 1; Emily Maki, interview by Lynn Laitala, n.d., transcript, MHS, 2.

15   Hannah and Andy Johnson, interview, 6; *Ely Miner*, 21 February 1908, 1.

16   Somrock, *History of Incredible Ely*, 27.

17   *Ely Miner*, 18 December 1908, 1; the quote is found in Somrock, *History of Incredible Ely*, 27.

18   August Stromberg, quoted in Hannah and Andy Johnson interview, 67.

19   *Ely Miner*, 4 May 1906, 1.

20   August Stromberg, quoted in Hannah and Andy Johnson interview, 68.

21   *Ely Miner*, 30 April 1909, 1.

22   *Ely Miner*, 17 November 1905, 1.

23   *Ely Miner*, 19 August 1910, 1, 4; 9 June 1911, 1.

24   "The Gate of the Nation's Playground: Ely, Minnesota Makes a Bid for the Real Sportsman," *Western Magazine* 7 (1915): 284–91.

25   *Milt Stenlund, Burntside Lake: The Early Days, 1880–1920* (Ely, Minn.: The Ely-Winton Historical Society, 1986), 17.

26   Charles Cecil to family, 7 September 1911, Letter 66, Box 1, Charles Cecil Papers, MHS.

27 Charles Cecil to family, 23 August 1911, Letter 64, Box 1, Charles Cecil Papers, MHS.

28 Minnesota Forestry Board, *Second Annual Report of the State Forester* (St. Paul, Minn.: n.p., 1912), 14.

29 Helmi Gawboy, interview by Lynn Laitala, 6 December 1975, transcript, MHS, 38. Gawboy was a Finnish woman married to an Ojibway man.

30 *Ely Miner*, 15 May 1908, 4.

31 *Ely Miner*, 3 September 1909, 4; 28 May 1909, 1.

32 Samuel P. Hays, *Conservation and the Gospel of Efficiency: The Progressive Conservation Movement, 1890–1920* (Cambridge, Mass.: Harvard University Press, 1959), esp. 265; Minnesota Forestry Board, *First Annual Report of the State Forester* (St. Paul, Minn.: n.p., 1911), 86.

33 Minnesota Forestry Board, *First Annual Report*, 90.

34 Ibid., 91.

35 "Gate of the Nation's Playground," 289.

36 U.S. Forest Service, *A Vacation Land of Lakes and Woods: The Superior National Forest* (n.p., 1919), 3.

37 Hannah and Andy Johnson, interview, 47.

38 *Ely Miner*, 27 April 1917, 1; 5 May 1917, 1; Johnson, interview, 81; Johnson, "Reminiscences." For an account of the anti-IWW rhetoric used by Minnesota's elite in the 1910s and its similarity to images of Indian savagery, see Gerald Roning, "Liquor, Wobblies, and Native Americans," paper presented at the 1997 Western History Association Conference, St. Paul, Minnesota.

39 Andy Johnson, unpublished manuscript, 1976, Andy and Hannah Johnson Papers, MHS.

40 Johnson, "Reminiscences."

41 *Ely Miner*, 8 April 1910, 1, 4.

42 Ibid.

43 Ibid.

44 Ibid.

45 George A. Bradley to Samuel Fullerton, 9 April 1910, Fish and Game Commission Correspondence, MHS.

46 *State v. Fred James*, case file, St. Louis County Court House, Virginia, Minnesota.

Documents

Gifford Pinchot, "The Meaning of Conservation"

Reprinted from Gifford Pinchot, *The Fight for Conservation* (New York: Doubleday, Page & Company, 1910)

Conservation involved more than wildlife protection. Management of forests was arguably its central concern. Gifford Pinchot was one of America's foremost conservationists, an early advocate of treating forestry as a kind of agriculture. He served as head of the new U.S. Forest Service under Theodore Roosevelt, and became the president's leading advisor on natural resource issues. The modern system of national forest administration owes much to his leadership. As you will see in this excerpt from his 1910 manifesto, *The Fight for Conservation*, his philosophy of resource management was not intended to stop forests, rivers, or land from being used, but rather to *control* exploitation through government action. In this way, forests and wildlife populations could replenish themselves, and provide vital resources to the nation in perpetuity.

As you read this excerpt from Pinchot's book, ask yourself how the imposition of government control over the landscape was likely to be received in America's rural communities. How did residents in Ely, Minnesota, respond to it in Benjamin Johnson's article? Were some people more likely to support conservation than others? Who were its most likely opponents?

*   *   *

The first great fact about conservation is that it stands for development. There has been a fundamental misconception that conservation means nothing but the husbanding of resources for future generations. There could be no more serious mistake. Conservation does mean provision for the future, but it means also and first of all the recognition of the right of the present generation to the fullest necessary use of all the resources with which this country is so abundantly blessed. Conservation demands the welfare of this generation first, and afterward the welfare of the generations to follow. . . .

Conservation stands emphatically for the development and use of water-power now, without delay. It stands for the immediate construction of navigable waterways under a broad and comprehensive plan as assistants to the railroads. More coal and more iron are required to move a ton of freight by rail than by water, three to one. In every case and in every direction the conservation movement has development for its first principle, and at the very beginning of its work. The development of our natural resources and the fullest use of them for the present generation is the first duty of this generation. So much for development.

In the second place conservation stands for the prevention of waste. There has come gradually in this country an understanding that waste is not a good thing and that the attack on waste is an industrial necessity. I recall very well indeed how, in the early days of forest fires, they were considered simply and solely as acts of God, against which any opposition was hopeless and any attempt to control them not merely hopeless but childish. It was assumed that they came in the natural order of things, as inevitably as the seasons or the rising and setting of the sun. To-day we understand that forest fires are wholly within the control of men. So we are coming in like manner to understand that the prevention of waste in all other directions is a simple matter of good business. The first duty of the human race is to control the earth it lives upon. . . .

In addition to the principles of development and preservation of our resources there is a third principle. It is this: The natural resources must be developed and preserved for the benefit of the many, and not merely for the profit of a few. We are coming to understand in this country that public action for public benefit has a very much wider field to cover and a much larger part to play than was the case when there were resources enough for every one, and before certain constitutional provisions had given so tremendously strong a position to vested rights and property in general. . . .

The conservation idea covers a wider range than the field of natural resources alone. Conservation means the greatest good to the greatest number for the longest time. One of its great contributions is just this, that it has added to the worn and well-known phrase, "the greatest good to the greatest number," the additional words "for the longest time," thus recognizing that this nation of ours must be made to endure as the best possible home for all its people.

Conservation advocates the use of foresight, prudence, thrift, and intelligence in dealing with public matters, for the same reasons and in the same way that we each use foresight, prudence, thrift, and intelligence in dealing with our own private affairs. It proclaims the right and duty of the people to act for the benefit of the people. Conservation demands the application of common-sense to the common problems for the common good.

The principles of conservation thus described – development, preservation, the common good – have a general application which is growing rapidly wider. The development of resources and the prevention of waste and loss, the protection of the public interests, by foresight, prudence, and the ordinary business and home-making virtues, all these apply to other things as well as to the natural resources. There is, in fact, no interest of the people to which the principles of conservation do not apply.

. . . The application of common-sense to any problem for the Nation's good will lead directly to national efficiency wherever applied. In other words, and that is the burden of the message, we are coming to see the logical and inevitable outcome that these principles, which arose in forestry and have their bloom in the conservation of natural resources, will have their fruit in the increase and promotion of national efficiency along other lines of national life.

The outgrowth of conservation, the inevitable result, is national efficiency. In the great commercial struggle between nations which is eventually to determine the welfare of all, national efficiency will be the deciding factor. So from every point of view conservation is a good thing for the American people.

The National Forest Service, one of the chief agencies of the conservation movement, is trying to be useful to the people of this nation. The Service recognizes, and recognizes it more and more strongly all the time, that whatever it has done or is doing has just one object, and that object is the welfare of the plain American citizen. . . .

The Natural Forests are in the West. Headquarters of the Service have been established throughout the Western country, because its work cannot be done effectively and properly without the closest contact and the most hearty coöperation with the Western people. It is the duty of the Forest Service to see to it that the timber, water-powers, mines, and every other resource of the forests is used for the benefit of the people who live in the neighborhood or who may have a share in the welfare of each locality. It is equally its duty to coöperate with all our people in every section of our land to conserve a fundamental resource, without which this Nation cannot prosper.

"Mr. A. A. Anderson, Special Supervisor of the Yellowstone and Teton Timber Reserves, Talks Interestingly of the Summer's Work"

Wyoming Stockgrower and Farmer, October 3, 1902

The second document is from a newspaper article by a superintendent for the federal Bureau of Forestry in 1902, A. A. Anderson was in charge of enforcing federal regulations on the forest reserves (now called national forests) in northwest Wyoming. He and officials like him were responsible for implementing Pinchot's policies. His understanding of the natural systems of the region, and the need to regulate their use, was typical of conservationists in this period. Notice how he sees the region's natural systems as a connected system essential to the region's economic development: the forests must be preserved to prevent erosion of the soil; this will keep streams and rivers from silting up and drying out, thereby guaranteeing water to the valleys below, which in turn will ensure adequate irrigation for new farms and towns. To Superintendent Anderson, as to other conservationists, regulation of the countryside was vital to the progress of civilization.

But are some people more likely to be regulated than others? Notice his special condemnation of Indian hunters, and market hunters (called "head hunters" because of their practice of hunting for trophy heads to sell to collectors), while he maintains special exemptions to the law for sheep owners. Who benefits from the conservationists' new rural order? And who suffers from it? What evidence is there in this report that not all Wyoming residents supported Superintendent Anderson?

* * *

I have been constantly in the field since July... I found affairs in the Teton Forest Reserve in a most unsatisfactory and inefficient condition. Sheep, and forest fires, mostly caused by the carelessness of men in charge of the sheep on the reserve, were destroying without hindrance from those whose duty it was to restrain and protect the timber, underbrush and grass which it is the policy of the government to keep intact as conservatories of the water supplies, upon which the agricultural enterprises in the valley below depend. Game was being killed without regard to existing game laws. I found in one place the carcasses of seven elk, from which nothing but the tusks had been removed. These teeth under the stimulus given to them by their use as emblems by the fast growing order of Elks has made them (but two of which are found in each animal), worth from five to fifty dollars per pair, according to the beautiful and peculiar markings upon them....

I found that upon the Teton Reserve the Indians had been allowed to hunt without regard to the restraining laws of the general government, or the state. They had been killing indiscriminately and in great numbers. I advised the department of the facts and have information from the Department of the Interior that in future Indians will not be allowed to hunt upon the reserves....

I have had each reserve ranger made a state game warden, I have changed the local supervisor in the Teton, and most of the rangers, and feel confident that I have succeeded in establishing there a strict enforcement of all government and state laws, rules, and regulations, for the protection of the reserve and the protection the laws give the game therein....

I have found that there have been fires on the heads of the Grey Bull [River] that should have been looked after by the employe[e]s of the government, and were not. It is my business to see that every man drawing pay for the care of government property does his duty, and I shall surely see that he does it. Any one in the present service found incapable or inefficient will be succeeded by a better man.

Every law, every rule, and every instruction, shall be carried out to the letter. I believe the care of these reserves should be as speedily as possible reduced to the discipline of the army, and the rangers uniformed. I think the game laws should be changed; the season is too long; the animals are chased, harrassed, and shot at. . . . [B]y the close of the open season they are so thin in flesh that they cannot stand the rigors of the winter in high altitudes which are the only place of any safety left for them.

I think certain sections should be closed entirely; regions affording feed in winter where the game could winter undisturbed, and be allowed to propagate in peace, the head-hunters have killed the bull big horns, elk, deer, and antelope until propagation has in great measure been arrested. This should by remedied by statute.

The Stock Situation

On my arrival here in July, I found more or less anxiety and apprehension on this question [of whether livestock would be allowed to graze on the forest reserves], especially on the point of the policy to be pursued in the regions lately added to the reserves. . . . I found about 110,000 sheep upon the reserves without the required grazing permits from the Department of the Interior. It was too late to enable their owners to find other feeding ground and their removal would evidently have caused great inconvenience, if not actual loss, so I wrote the Department asking that all stock at present on the reserve or accustomed to range there might be allowed to remain there without obtaining the necessary permit.

That policy has been pursued, and no sheep has been removed from the late extensions of the reserves.

It is the intention of the government to follow the most liberal policy in regard to granting grazing privileges upon the reserves.

Permits will be issued to all those living upon or near the reserves to place upon the reserves as much stock as the ranges will support.

To overstock, and thereby injure the ranges, is not to the interest of anyone. Especially is it an injury to those desiring to use the ranges from year to year.

The mountains set aside as timber reserves are most necessary to the entire state as a watershed. The denuding of the mountains by overgrazing and the destruction of the timber by fires will lessen the supply of water, and will, therefore, work injury to all settlers. It is the intention of the government to prevent this and thus facilitate the building of productive homes in the arid valleys tributary to these reservoirs which nature has provided.

The people of Wyoming have much to thank nature and Uncle Sam for. Nature has provided on this backbone of the continent, this birthplace of waters, protection for the embr[y]o Mississippis, Missouris,

Columbias; protection, from the trickling rill just released from its snowy bed, to the roaring torrent fighting its way through [the] rocky canyon.

Every tiny blade of grass, every shrub, every tree, and every rock, invites the running waters to loiter, to linger yet in their mountain birthplace. This flirtation of the waters with nature's obstructions, retards and conserves, with the results that the waters' reluctant departure from their mountain home makes fat streams throughout three or four months of spring and summer, just when needed by the crop growers. If these wise provisions are destroyed by stock grazing, by fires, by the denudation of timber, by carelessness, negligence, or the cupidity of men, the result will be felt in every valley along every stream, from the snow-clad peaks of the Rockies to the muddy mouth of the Mississippi and the wide estuary of the Columbia, and nature's wise provisions thus balked. It is to prevent this, to restrain, and hold in check the cupidity of a few stockmen, lumbermen, railroad tie contractors, careless campers, and thoughtless tourist[s], that Uncle Sam, at his own expense, has policed this region that he has so wisely reserved for the millions to come, for their prosperity, their pleasure.

These snow-clad peaks and timber-clothed mountain sides have been forever set aside sacred to the birthplace of waters, and a home for wild things seeking a refuge from man.

The wisdom and necessity of this protection has been demonstrated in the Adirondacks, in the hills of New England. Dry gullies, flooded to the point of destruction in wet weather, dry in dry weather, have taught the people of that region the lesson learned by the destruction of these forests, the obligation of nature's reservoirs that once held in check the waters that came in gentle flows throughout the early years of their occupation.

States in these regions are now by the enactment of protective laws, and vast expenditure of their own money, seeking to stay this destruction, and repair the damage done.

I fear not many in Wyoming appreciate the privilege they are enjoying by having Uncle Sam look after this most important and expensive matter for them. Every man who respects the law, every one who has the welfare of our great, grand, and beautiful region at heart, who appreciates the blessings we have, and would hold on to and cherished [sic] them, should hold out a helping hand to this great work. Vigilance in the right, and fearless exposure of all lawbreakers on these reserves by those who seek the benefits sought to be conferred by the government in this matter will soon result in the cessation of the wanton destruction of timber and the wicked and unlawful obliteration of game. I have spent the summer in the saddle, seeking to preserve to this well-loved region some of the charms that attracted me to it a dozen years ago, and to be instrumental by my best endeavors, to carry out the wise and benificent plans of the government for the preservation of our natural storage reservoirs. Without the work we are doing the irrigation laws lately passed by congress would be useless. Why storage reservoirs without water to store in them?

Charles Askins Describes Game and Hunting Conditions in the South

Reprinted from William Hornaday, *Our Vanishing Wildlife: Its Extermination and Preservation* (New York: New York Zoological Society, 1913)

Our last two documents suggest the ways in which conservation could reinforce racial hierarchies. The first is by Charles Askins, a white conservationist who writes about the supposed threat to southern wildlife from African-American hunters in the South in the early twentieth century. Apart from Askins's obvious racial prejudices, what can you learn about how black hunters might have viewed conservation in this period? In what ways could white southern landowners use hunting restrictions to better guarantee a compliant class of black laborers for southern plantations?

* * *

In the beginning not so much damage to southern game interests could be accomplished by our colored man and brother, however decided his inclinations. He had no money, no ammunition and no gun. His weapons were an ax, a club, a trap, and a hound dog; possibly he might own an old war musket bored out for shot. Such an outfit was not adapted to quail shooting and especially to wing shooting, with which knowledge Dixie's sportsmen were content. Let the negro ramble about with his hound dog and his war musket; he couldn't possibly kill the quail. And so Uncle Ike's grandson loafed and pottered about in the fields with his ax and his hound dogs, not doing so much harm to the quail but acquiring knowledge of the habits of the birds and skill as a still-hunting pot-hunter that would serve him well later on. The negro belongs to a primitive race of people and all such races have keener eyes than white men whose fathers have pored over lines of black and white. He learned to see the rabbit in its form, the squirrels in the leafy trees, and the quails huddled in the grass. The least shade of gray in the shadow of the creek bank he distinguished at once as a rabbit, a glinting flash from a tree top he knew instantly as being caused by the slight movement of a hidden squirrel, and the quiver of a single stem of sedge grass told him of a bevy of birds hiding in the depths. The pot-hunting negro has all the skill of the Indian, has more industry in his loafing, and kills without pity and without restraint. . . .

The time came when cotton went up to sixteen cents a pound and single breech-loading guns went down to five dollars apiece. The negro had money now, and the merchants – these men who had said let the nigger alone so long as he raises cotton and corn – sold him the guns, a gun for every black idler, man and boy, in all the South. Then shortly a wail went up from the sportsmen, "The niggers are killing our quail." They not only were killing them, but most of the birds were already dead. On the grounds of the Southern Field Club where sixty bevies were raised by the dogs in one day, within two years but three bevies could be found in a day by the hardest kind of hunting; and this story was repeated all over the South. Now the negro began to raise bird dogs in place of hounds, and he carried his new gun to church if services happened to be held on a week day. Finally the negro had grown up and had compassed his ambition: he could shoot partridges flying just the same as a white man, was a white man except for a trifling difference in color; and he could kill more birds, too, three times as many. . . .

There comes a time toward the spring of the year after the quail season is over when the average rural darky is "between hay and grass." The merchants on whom he has depended for supplies make it a practice to refuse credit between January first and crop time. The black has spent his cotton money, his sweet potato pile has vanished, the sorghum barrel is empty, he has eaten the last of his winter's pork, and all that remains is a bit of meal and the meat his gun can secure. He is hunting in grim earnest now, using all the cunning and skill acquired by years of practice. He eats woodpeckers, jaybirds, hawks and skunks, drawing the line only at crows and buzzards. At this season of the year I have carried chicken hawks up to the cabins for the sake of watching the delight of the piccaninnies who with glowing eyes would declare, "Them's mos' as good as chicken." What happens to the robins, doves, larks, red birds, mocking birds and all songsters in this hungry season needs hardly to be stated.

It is also a time between hay and grass for the rabbits and the quail. The cornfields are bare and the weed seeds are exhausted. A spring cold spell pinches, they lose their vitality, become thin and quite lack their ordinary wariness. Then the figure-four trap springs up in the hedgerow and the sedge while the work of decimation goes more rapidly along. The rabbits can no longer escape the half-starved dogs, the thinning cover fails to hide the quail and the song birds betray themselves by singing of the coming spring.

With the growing scarcity of the game now comes the season of sedge and field burning. This is done ostensibly to prepare the land for spring plowing, but really to destroy the last refuge of the quail and rabbits so that they can be bagged with certainty. All the negroes of a neighborhood collect for one of these burnings, all their dogs, and of course all the boys from six years old up. They surround the field and set it on fire in many places, leaving small openings for the game to dash out among the motley assembly. I have seen quail fly out of the burning grass with flaming particles still attached to them. They alight on the burnt ground too bewildered to fly again and the boys and dogs pick them up. Crazed rabbits try the gauntlet amidst the barking curs, shouting negroes and popping guns, but death is sure and quick. The few quail that may escape have no refuge from the hawks and nothing to eat, so every battue of this kind marks the absolute end of the birds in one vicinity; and the next day the darkies repeat the performance elsewhere. . . .

Not every white man in the South is a sportsman or even a shooter; many are purely business men who have said let the "nigger" do as he likes so long as he raises cotton and buys our goods. But Dixie has her full share of true men of the out-of-doors and they have sworn in downright Southern fashion that this thing has got to end. Nevertheless their problem is deep and puzzling. In Alabama they made an effort and a beginning. They asked for a law requiring every man to obtain written permission before entering the lands of another to hunt and shoot; they asked for a resident license law taxing every gun not less than five dollars a year; for a shortened season, a bag limit, and a complete system of State wardens. Unfortunately, a lot of white farmers were in the same range as the blacks, and being hit, too, they raised a great outcry. The result was that the Alabama sportsmen got everything they asked for except the foundation of the structure they were trying to build, the high resident license or gun tax which alone could have shut out three dollar guns and saved the remnant of the game. Under the new law the sale of game was forbidden, neither could it be shipped out of the State alive or dead; the ever popular non-resident license was provided for; the season was shortened and the bag limited; the office of State game warden was created with deputies to be paid from fines; hunting upon the lands of another without written permission became a misdemeanor; and then the whole thing was nullified by reducing the resident license to nothing where a man shot upon his own land, one dollar in his own county, and two dollars outside of it. In its practical workings the new law amounts to this: A few northern gunners have paid the non-resident license fee, and enough resident licenses have been taken out by the city sportsmen to make up the handsome salary of the State warden. The negro still hunts upon his own land *or upon the land of the man who wants corn and cotton raised*, with perfect indifference to the whole thing. Who was to enforce the law against him? Not the one disgusted deputy with three big counties to patrol who depended for his salary upon the fines collected from the negroes. It would take one man to every three miles square to protect the game in the South.

The one effective way of dealing with the situation in Alabama was to have legislated three dollar guns out of existence with a five dollar tax, adding to this nearly a like amount on dogs. Hardly a sportsman in the South will disagree with this conclusion. But sportsmen never had a majority vote either in the South or in the North, and the South's grave problem is yet unsolved.

. . . If only for selfish reasons, we of the North should reach to southern sportsmen a helping hand, for by and by the last of our migratory song birds will go down into Dixie and never return.

Ben Senowin testifies about being apprehended for game law violations

Annual Report of the Commissioner of Indian Affairs (Washington: Government Printing Office, 1896)

The final document in this section returns us to Wyoming. Throughout the West, Indians were often the targets of early conservationist legislation. Ben Senowin was a Bannock Indian who led a group of Bannock families on a hunting trip to Jackson Hole, a traditional Bannock hunting ground, in the mid-1890s. While there, they were surrounded and arrested by a white posse intent on enforcing regulations against elk hunting. Later investigation of these events revealed that the posse was trying to force Indians out of the hunting grounds so that they could make money guiding wealthy tourists during fall elk hunts of their own. After marching Senowin and his companions a full day out of the hunting grounds, the white posse attempted to massacre the Indians. Two Indians, an infant and an old man, were killed. The rest escaped. This is a copy of Senowin's affidavit to the courts, explaining his version of what happened. For the Bannock people, who were often desperately poor in this period, what was the impact of conservation?

Personally appeared before me Ben Senowin, a Bannock Indian, who, being duly sworn, deposeth and says: That he is the head of a clan, and that on or about July 15, 1895, while hunting on unoccupied Government lands east of Jacksons Hole, in the county of Uinta, State of Wyoming, under a pass from the U.S. Indian agent at Fort Hall Agency, and provisions of article 4 of the treaty with the Shoshones (Eastern band) and Bannock Indians, dated July 3, 1868, and ratified February

16, 1869, in company with Nemuts, Wa ha she go, Ya pa ojo, Poo dat, Pah goh zite, Mah mout, Se we a gat, Boo wah go, thirteen women and five children, all Bannock Indians, were, while in camp, feloniously assaulted and by force of arms attacked by a party of twenty-seven white men, and having been made under threat of death to give up all of their arms, consisting of seven rifles and ammunition, were marched thirty miles, more or less, in the direction of the white settlement; that during the afternoon of the aforesaid date, while passing through a belt of timber, the deponent saw several of the white men placing cartridges in their rifles and believing his own life and the lives of the members of his party to be in danger, called upon his people to run and escape, whereupon the white men, without just cause or provocation, commenced to fire with rifles loaded with ball cartridges upon him, the deponent, and his people; that he, the deponent, saw one Indian named Se we a gat fall dead, killed by said fire, and one Nemuts wounded, and that one infant was lost while they were escaping and has not since been found; and deponent further saith himself and his party were by force of arms of said party of white men and by threats of instant death feloniously deprived and robbed of the following articles of personal property, to wit: Seven rifles, twenty saddles, twenty blankets, one horse, nine packs of meat, and nine tepees, more or less; and deponent further saith that neither he or any of his people were told why or by what authority they were assaulted; that he is not aware that either he or any of his party had committed any offense against the laws of any State or the United States; or that he or any of his party ever attempted or offered any violence, or had made any threats against the life or property of any white man; that the white man never gave him or his party any hearing, or asked him or his party any questions through an interpreter or otherwise; that neither he or any of his party were ever called upon to answer or plead in any court of justice or make answer to any charge whatsoever.

BEN (his x mark) SENOWIN.

Witness:

RAVENEL MACBETH.

Sworn and subscribed to before me this 1st day of September, 1895.

P. H. RAY,
Captain, Eighth Infantry, Summary Court Officer.

CAMP UNITED STATES TROOPS,
Fort Hall Agency, Idaho.

I certify on honor that the following names were given me by Frank H. Rhoads, J. P., as the names of the men who committed the assault put forth in the foregoing affidavit: J. G. Fisk, Ham Wort, Steve Adams, Joe Calhoun, William Crawford, Ed. Crawford, Martin Nelson, Joe Enfinger, W. Munger, Ed. Hunter, Frank Woods, Frank Peterson, Jack Shive, George Madison, Andrew Madison, M. V. Giltner, Charles Estes, James Estes, Tom Estes, George Wilson, John Wilson, Erv Wilson, Victor Gustavse, Steve Leek, William Bellvue and John Cherrey, and William Manning.

THOS. B. TETER, *U. S. Indian Agent.*

COUNTY OF BINGHAM, *State of Idaho, ss.*

Personally appeared before me Nemuts, Boo wah go, Ya pa ojo, Mah mout, Wa ha she go, Poodat, and Pah goh zite, Bannock Indians; who, being duly sworn, deposeth and say that they have heard the interpreter read to them the foregoing affidavit of Ben Senowin; that they were there present and know of their own knowledge the statement set forth is true to the best of their knowledge and belief.

NEMUTS (his x mark).
BOO WAH GO (his x mark).
YA PA OJO (his x mark).
MAH MOUT (his x mark).
WA HA SHE GO (his x mark).
POO DAT (his x mark).
PAH GOH ZITE (his x mark).

Witnesses:

RAVENEL MACBETH.

TOMMY COSGROVE.

Sworn and subscribed to before me this 1st day of September, 1895.

P. H. RAY,
Captain, Eighth Infantry, Summary Court Officer.

CAMP UNITED STATES TROOPS,
Fort Hall Agency, Idaho.

Witness:

DAN'L T. WELLS,
Captain, Eighth Infantry.

8

National Parks and the Trouble with Wilderness

By the end of the nineteenth century, Americans had fallen in love with wilderness. They have continued to love it ever since. But the relationship has been a difficult one.

Where the term "wilderness" once invited Americans to make a landscape over into a farm field or town square, by the latter nineteenth century Americans had come to value certain unsettled landscapes in new ways, and many sought to preserve them from "improvement," or development. The reasons for this were complex. One was that by the 1880s, almost all of the most arable land in America, and even large parts of its marginal territories, had been fenced and plowed. Cities had grown at an astounding pace, and many wondered if the virtuous rural life which Americans had so long idealized would survive the mass migration to the cities that was under way.

But the cult of wilderness that emerged in this period had as much to do with American longings for a unique national identity to explain themselves to one another and the world. During the nineteenth century, American artists, writers, and political leaders frequently lamented the absence of long historical traditions in the new nation. Whereas the English, French, and Italian peoples could point to ancient ruins, cathedrals that were hundreds of years old, and traditions of arts and letters that went back almost to the dawn of Christianity, American culture was, by comparison, very new. Many found the material to fill this gap in America's monumental landscapes, the huge mountains and craggy peaks which dominated parts of the country, particularly in the West. By the late nineteenth century, there was widespread popular sentiment for the preservation of monumental wilderness landscapes as "national parks," where they would be protected for the American people to enjoy. Congress created Yellowstone National Park in 1872, and dozens of other national parks, including Yosemite, the Grand Canyon, and Mesa Verde in subsequent decades. Wilderness preservation has become a hallmark of American environmentalism since then.

You are about to read a historical examination of the American wilderness idea by William Cronon. This is one of the most controversial essays ever written by an American historian. Cronon illuminates the deep roots of the wilderness ethic, and suggests many reasons to doubt its viability as a way to structure our relations with nature. He has various objections to the wilderness idea, and you should keep a list of them as you read this provocative piece. But one continuing refrain is worth mentioning here, and it is that if "wilderness" means "untouched landscape," then it is doubtful that any real wilderness exists. Many wilderness areas that have become beloved to modern people were in fact frequented by Indians who shaped them through hunting, gathering, and occasional firing to clear underbrush. The creation of national parks at Yosemite, Glacier, Yellowstone, Grand Canyon, and other places entailed the expulsion of Indians, thereby creating an "uninhabited wilderness" to protect as a park. Although Cronon remains an advocate of wilderness protection, he has some new ways of thinking about nature that he would like us to consider. What are the problems and weaknesses of the wilderness idea? Do Cronon's suggestions offer a necessary revolution in the ways we think about nature? Or is the old wilderness idea still historically defensible? The documents in this section will introduce us to one of the greatest defenders of wilderness and one of the opponents of the wilderness idea, and will allow us a chance to examine some key wilderness legislation.

The Trouble with Wilderness, or, Getting Back to the Wrong Nature

William Cronon

The Time has Come to Rethink Wilderness

This will seem a heretical claim to many environmentalists, since the idea of wilderness has for decades been a fundamental tenet – indeed, a passion – of the environmental movement, especially in the United States. For many Americans wilderness stands as the last remaining place where civilization, that all too human disease, has not fully infected the earth. It is an island in the polluted sea of urban-industrial modernity, the one place we can turn for escape from our own too-muchness.

Seen in this way, wilderness presents itself as the best antidote to our human selves, a refuge we must somehow recover if we hope to save the planet. As Henry David Thoreau once famously declared, "In Wildness is the preservation of the World."[1]

But is it? The more one knows of its peculiar history, the more one realizes that wilderness is not quite what it seems. Far from being the one place on earth that stands apart from humanity, it is quite profoundly a human creation – indeed, the creation of very particular human cultures at very particular moments in human history. It is not a pristine sanctuary where the last remnant of an untouched, endangered, but still transcendent nature can for at least a little while longer be encountered without the contaminating taint of civilization. Instead, it is a product of that civilization, and could hardly be contaminated by the very stuff of which it is made. Wilderness hides its unnaturalness behind a mask that is all the more beguiling because it seems so natural. As we gaze into the mirror it holds up for us, we too easily imagine that what we behold is Nature when in fact we see the reflection of our own unexamined longings and desires. For this reason, we mistake ourselves when we suppose that wilderness can be the solution to our culture's problematic relationships with the nonhuman world, for wilderness is itself no small part of the problem.

To assert the unnaturalness of so natural a place will no doubt seem absurd or even perverse to many readers, so let me hasten to add that the nonhuman world we encounter in wilderness is far from being merely our own invention. I celebrate with others who love wilderness the beauty and power of the things it contains. Each of us who has spent time there can conjure images and sensations that seem all the more hauntingly real for having engraved themselves so indelibly on our memories. Such memories may be uniquely our own, but they are also familiar enough to be instantly recognizable to others. Remember this? The torrents of mist shoot out from the base of a great waterfall in the depths of a Sierra canyon, the tiny droplets cooling your face as you listen to the roar of the water and gaze up toward the sky through a rainbow that hovers just out of reach. Remember this too: looking out across a desert canyon in the evening air, the only sound a lone raven calling in the distance, the rock walls dropping away into a chasm so deep that its bottom all but vanishes as you squint into the amber light of the setting sun. And this: the moment beside the trail as you sit on a sandstone ledge, your boots damp with the morning dew while you take in the rich smell of the pines, and the small red fox – or maybe for you it was a raccoon or a coyote or a deer – that suddenly ambles across your path, stopping for a long moment to gaze in your direction with cautious indifference before continuing on its way. Remember the feelings of such moments, and you will know as well as I do that you were in the presence of something irreducibly nonhuman, something profoundly Other than yourself. Wilderness is made of that too.

And yet: what brought each of us to the places where such memories became possible is entirely a cultural invention. Go back 250 years in American and European history, and you do not find nearly so many people wandering around remote corners of the planet looking for what today we would call "the wilderness experience." As late as the eighteenth century, the most common usage of the world "wilderness" in the English language referred to landscapes that generally carried adjectives far different from the ones they attract today. To be a wilderness then was to be "deserted," "savage," "desolate," "barren" – in short, a "waste," the word's nearest synonym. Its connotations were anything but positive, and the emotion one was most likely to feel in its presence was "bewilderment" or terror.[2]

Many of the word's strongest associations then were biblical, for it is used over and over again in the King James Version to refer to places on the margins of civilization where it is all too easy to lose oneself in moral confusion and despair. The wilderness was where Moses had wandered with his people for forty years, and where they had nearly abandoned their God to worship a golden idol.[3] "For Pharaoh will say of the Children of Israel," we read in Exodus, "They are entangled in the land, the wilderness hath shut them in."[4] The wilderness was where Christ had struggled with the devil and endured his temptations: "And immediately the Spirit driveth him into the wilderness. And he was there in the wilderness for forty days tempted of Satan; and was with the wild beasts; and the angels ministered unto him."[5] The "delicious Paradise" of John Milton's Eden was surrounded by "a steep wilderness, whose hairy sides / Access denied" to all who sought entry.[6] When Adam and Eve were driven from that garden, the world they entered was a wilderness that only their labor and pain could redeem. Wilderness, in short, was a place to which one came only against one's will, and always in fear and trembling. Whatever value it might have arose solely from the possibility that it might be "reclaimed" and turned toward human ends – planted as a garden, say, or a city upon a hill. In its raw state, it had little or nothing to offer civilized men and women.

But by the end of the nineteenth century, all this had changed. The wastelands that had once seemed worthless had for some people come to seem almost beyond price. That Thoreau in 1862 could declare wildness to be the preservation of the world suggests the sea change that was going on. Wilderness had once been the antithesis of all that was orderly and good – it had been the darkness, one might say, on the far side of the garden wall – and yet now it was frequently likened to Eden itself. When

John Muir arrived in the Sierra Nevada in 1869, he would declare, "No description of Heaven that I have ever heard or read of seems half so fine."[7] He was hardly alone in expressing such emotions. One by one, various corners of the American map came to be designated as sites whose wild beauty was so spectacular that a growing number of citizens had to visit and see them for themselves. Niagara Falls was the first to undergo this transformation, but it was soon followed by the Catskills, the Adirondacks, Yosemite, Yellowstone, and others. Yosemite was deeded by the U.S. government to the state of California in 1864 as the nation's first wildland park, and Yellowstone became the first true national park in 1872.

By the first decade of the twentieth century, in the single most famous episode in American conservation history, a national debate had exploded over whether the city of San Francisco should be permitted to augment its water supply by damming the Tuolumne River in Hetch Hetchy valley, well within the boundaries of Yosemite National Park. The dam was eventually built, but what today seems no less significant is that so many people fought to prevent its completion. Even as the fight was being lost, Hetch Hetchy became the battle cry of an emerging movement to preserve wilderness. Fifty years earlier, such opposition would have been unthinkable. Few would have questioned the merits of "reclaiming" a wasteland like this in order to put it to human use. Now the defenders of Hetch Hetchy attracted widespread national attention by portraying such an act not as improvement or progress but as desecration and vandalism. Lest one doubt that the old biblical metaphors had been turned completely on their heads, listen to John Muir attack the dam's defenders. "Their arguments," he wrote, "are curiously like those of the devil, devised for the destruction of the first garden – so much of the very best Eden fruit going to waste; so much of the best Tuolumne water and Tuolumne scenery going to waste."[8] For Muir and the growing number of Americans who shared his views, Satan's home had become God's own temple.

The sources of this rather astonishing transformation were many, but for the purposes of this essay they can be gathered under two broad headings: the sublime and the frontier. Of the two, the sublime is the older and more pervasive cultural construct, being one of the most important expressions of that broad transatlantic movement we today label as romanticism; the frontier is more peculiarly American, though it too had its European antecedents and parallels. The two converged to remake wilderness in their own image, freighting it with moral values and cultural symbols that it carries to this day. Indeed, it is not too much to say that the modern environmental movement is itself a grandchild of romanticism and post-frontier ideology, which is why it is no accident that so much environmentalist discourse takes its bearings from the wilderness these intellectual movements helped create. Although wilderness may today seem to be just one environmental concern among many, it in fact serves as the foundation for a long list of other such concerns that on their face seem quite remote from it. That is why its influence is so pervasive and, potentially, so insidious.

To gain such remarkable influence, the concept of wilderness had to become loaded with some of the deepest core values of the culture that created and idealized it: it had to become sacred. This possibility had been present in wilderness even in the days when it had been a place of spiritual danger and moral temptation. If Satan was there, then so was Christ, who had found angels as well as wild beasts during His sojourn in the desert. In the wilderness the boundaries between human and nonhuman, between natural and supernatural, had always seemed less certain than elsewhere. This was why the early Christian saints and mystics had often emulated Christ's desert retreat as they sought to experience for themselves the visions and spiritual testing He had endured. One might meet devils and run the risk of losing one's soul in such a place, but one might also meet God. For some that possibility was worth almost any price.

By the eighteenth century this sense of the wilderness as a landscape where the supernatural lay just beneath the surface was expressed in the doctrine of the *sublime*, a word whose modern usage has been so watered down by commercial hype and tourist advertising that it retains only a dim echo of its former power. In the theories of Edmund Burke, Immanuel Kant, William Gilpin, and others, sublime landscapes were those rare places on earth where one had more chance than elsewhere to glimpse the face of God. Romantics had a clear notion of where one could be most sure of having this experience. Although God might, of course, choose to show Himself anywhere, He would most often be found in those vast, powerful landscapes where one could not help feeling insignificant and being reminded of one's own mortality. Where were these sublime places? The eighteenth century catalog of their locations feels very familiar, for we still see and value landscapes as it taught us to do. God was on the mountaintop, in the chasm, in the waterfall, in the thundercloud, in the rainbow, in the sunset. One has only to think of the sites that Americans chose for their first national parks – Yellowstone, Yosemite, Grand Canyon, Rainier, Zion – to realize that virtually all of them fit one or more of these categories. Less sublime landscapes simply did not appear worthy of such protection; not until the 1940s, for instance, would the first swamp be honored, in Everglades National Park, and to this day there is no national park in the grasslands.

Among the best proofs that one had entered a sublime landscape was the emotion it evoked. For the early romantic writers and artists who first began to celebrate it, the sublime was far from being a pleasurable experience. The classic description is that of William Wordsworth as he recounted climbing the Alps and crossing the Simplon Pass in his autobiographical poem *The Prelude*. There, surrounded by crags and waterfalls, the poet felt himself literally to be in the presence of the divine – and experienced an emotion remarkably close to terror:

> The immeasurable height
> Of woods decaying, never to be decayed,
> The stationary blasts of waterfalls,
> And in the narrow rent at every turn
> Winds thwarting winds, bewildered and forlorn,
> The torrents shooting from the clear blue sky,
> The rocks that muttered close upon our ears,
> Black drizzling crags that spake by the way-side
> As if a voice were in them, the sick sight
> And giddy prospect of the raving stream,
> The unfettered clouds and region of the Heavens,
> Tumult and peace, the darkness and the light –
> Were all like workings of one mind, the features
> Of the same face, blossoms upon one tree;
> Characters of the great Apocalypse,
> The types and symbols of Eternity,
> Of first, and last, and midst, and without end.[9]

This was no casual stroll in the mountains, no simple sojourn in the gentle lap of nonhuman nature. What Wordsworth described was nothing less than a religious experience, akin to that of the Old Testament prophets as they conversed with their wrathful God. The symbols he detected in this wilderness landscape were more supernatural than natural, and they inspired more awe and dismay than joy or pleasure. No mere mortal was meant to linger long in such a place, so it was with considerable relief that Wordsworth and his companion made their way back down from the peaks to the sheltering valleys.

Lest you suspect that this view of the sublime was limited to timid Europeans who lacked the American know-how for feeling at home in the wilderness, remember Henry David Thoreau's 1846 climb of Mount Katahdin, in Maine. Although Thoreau is regarded by many today as one of the great American celebrators of wilderness, his emotions about Katahdin were no less ambivalent than Wordsworth's about the Alps.

> It was vast, Titanic, and such as man never inhabits. Some part of the beholder, even some vital part, seems to escape through the loose grating of his ribs as he ascends. He is more lone than you can imagine. . . . Vast, Titanic, inhuman Nature has got him at disadvantage, caught him alone,

and pilfers him of some of his divine faculty. She does not smile on him as in the plains. She seems to say sternly, why came ye here before your time? This ground is not prepared for you. Is it not enough that I smile in the valleys? I have never made this soil for thy feet, this air for thy breathing, these rocks for thy neighbors. I cannot pity nor fondle thee here, but forever relentlessly drive thee hence to where I *am* kind. Why seek me where I have not called thee, and then complain because you find me but a stepmother?[10]

This is surely not the way a modern backpacker or nature lover would describe Maine's most famous mountain, but that is because Thoreau's description owes as much to Wordsworth and other romantic contemporaries as to the rocks and clouds of Katahdin itself. His words took the physical mountain on which he stood and transmuted it into an icon of the sublime: a symbol of God's presence on earth. The power and the glory of that icon were such that only a prophet might gaze on it for long. In effect, romantics like Thoreau joined Moses and the children of Israel in Exodus when "they looked toward the wilderness, and behold, the glory of the Lord appeared in the cloud."[11]

But even as it came to embody the awesome power of the sublime, wilderness was also being tamed – not just by those who were building settlements in its midst but also by those who most celebrated its inhuman beauty. By the second half of the nineteenth century, the terrible awe that Wordsworth and Thoreau regarded as the appropriately pious stance to adopt in the presence of their mountaintop God was giving way to a much more comfortable, almost sentimental demeanor. As more and more tourists sought out the wilderness as a spectacle to be looked at and enjoyed for its great beauty, the sublime in effect became domesticated. The wilderness was still sacred, but the religious sentiments it evoked were more those of a pleasant parish church than those of a grand cathedral or a harsh desert retreat. The writer who best captures this late romantic sense of a domesticated sublime is undoubtedly John Muir, whose descriptions of Yosemite and the Sierra Nevada reflect none of the anxiety or terror one finds in earlier writers. Here he is, for instance, sketching on North Dome in Yosemite Valley:

No pain here, no dull empty hours, no fear of the past, no fear of the future. These blessed mountains are so compactly filled with God's beauty, no petty personal hope or experience has room to be. Drinking this champagne water is pure pleasure, so is breathing the living air, and every movement of limbs is pleasure, while the body seems to feel beauty when exposed to it as it feels the campfire or sunshine, entering not by the eyes alone, but equally through all one's flesh like radiant heat, making a passionate ecstatic pleasure glow not explainable.

The emotions Muir describes in Yosemite could hardly be more different from Thoreau's on Katahdin or Wordsworth's on the Simplon Pass. Yet all three men are participating in the same cultural tradition and contributing to the same myth: the mountain as cathedral. The three may differ in the way they choose to express their piety – Wordsworth favoring an awe-filled bewilderment, Thoreau a stern loneliness, Muir a welcome ecstasy – but they agree completely about the church in which they prefer to worship. Muir's closing words on North Dome diverge from his older contemporaries only in mood, not in their ultimate content:

> Perched like a fly on this Yosemite dome, I gaze and sketch and bask, oftentimes settling down into dumb admiration without definite hope of ever learning much, yet with the longing, unresting effort that lies at the door of hope, humbly prostrate before the vast display of God's power, and eager to offer self-denial and renunciation with eternal toil to learn any lesson in the divine manuscript.[12]

Muir's "divine manuscript" and Wordsworth's "Characters of the great Apocalypse" were in fact pages from the same holy book. The sublime wilderness had ceased to be a place of satanic temptation and become instead a sacred temple, much as it continues to be for those who love it today.

But the romantic sublime was not the only cultural movement that helped transform wilderness into a sacred American icon during the nineteenth century. No less important was the powerful romantic attraction of primitivism, dating back at least to Rousseau – the belief that the best antidote to the ills of an overly refined and civilized modern world was a return to simpler, more primitive living. In the United States, this was embodied most strikingly in the national myth of the frontier. The historian Frederick Jackson Turner wrote in 1893 the classic academic statement of this myth, but it had been part of American cultural traditions for well over a century. As Turner described the process, easterners and European immigrants, in moving to the wild unsettled lands of the frontier, shed the trappings of civilization, rediscovered their primitive racial energies, reinvented direct democratic institutions, and thereby reinfused themselves with a vigor, an independence, and a creativity that were the source of American democracy and national character. Seen in this way, wild country became a place not just of religious redemption but of national renewal, the quitessential location for experiencing what it meant to be an American.

One of Turner's most provocative claims was that by the 1890s the frontier was passing away. Never again would "such gifts of free land offer themselves" to the American people. "The frontier has gone," he declared, "and with its going has closed the first period of American history."[13] Built into the frontier myth from its very beginning was the notion that this crucible of American identity was temporary and would pass away. Those who have celebrated the frontier have almost always looked backward as they did so, mourning an older, simpler, truer world that is about to disappear forever. That world and all of its attractions, Turner said, depended on free land – on wilderness. Thus, in the myth of the vanishing frontier lay the seeds of wilderness preservation in the United States, for if wild land had been so crucial in the making of the nation, then surely one must save its last remnants as monuments to the American past – and as an insurance policy to protect its future. It is no accident that the movement to set aside national parks and wilderness areas began to gain real momentum at precisely the time that laments about the passing frontier reached their peak. To protect wilderness was in a very real sense to protect the nation's most sacred myth of origin.

Among the core elements of the frontier myth was the powerful sense among certain groups of Americans that wilderness was the last bastion of rugged individualism. Turner tended to stress communitarian themes when writing frontier history, asserting that Americans in primitive conditions had been forced to band together with their neighbors to form communities and democratic institutions. For other writers, however, frontier democracy for communities was less compelling than frontier freedom for individuals. By fleeing to the outer margins of settled land and society – so the story ran – an individual could escape the confining strictures of civilized life. The mood among writers who celebrated frontier individualism was almost always nostalgic; they lamented not just a lost way of life but the passing of the heroic men who had embodied that life. Thus Owen Wister in the introduction to his classic 1902 novel *The Virginian* could write of "a vanished world" in which "the horseman, the cow-puncher, the last romantic figure upon our soil" rode only "in his historic yesterday" and would "never come again." For Wister, the cowboy was a man who gave his word and kept it ("Wall Street would have found him behind the times"), who did not talk lewdly to women ("Newport would have thought him old-fashioned"), who worked and played hard, and whose "ungoverned hours did not unman him."[14] Theodore Roosevelt wrote with much the same nostalgic fervor about the "fine, manly qualities" of the "wild rough-rider of the plains." No one could be more heroically masculine, thought Roosevelt, or more at home in the western wilderness:

There he passes his days, there he does his life-work, there, when he meets death, he faces it as he has faced many other evils, with quiet, uncomplaining fortitude. Brave, hospitable, hardy, and adventurous, he is the grim pioneer of our race; he prepares the way for the civilization from before whose face he must himself disappear. Hard and dangerous though his existence is, it has yet a wild attraction that strongly draws to it his bold, free spirit.[15]

This nostalgia for a passing frontier way of life inevitably implied ambivalence, if not downright hostility, toward modernity and all that it represented. If one saw the wild lands of the frontier as freer, truer, and more natural than other, more modern places, then one was also inclined to see the cities and factories of urban-industrial civilization as confining, false, and artificial. Owen Wister looked at the post-frontier "transition" that had followed "the horseman of the plains," and did not like what he saw: "a shapeless state, a condition of men and manners as unlovely as is that moment in the year when winter is gone and spring not come, and the face of Nature is ugly."[16] In the eyes of writers who shared Wister's distaste for modernity, civilization contaminated its inhabitants and absorbed them into the faceless, collective, contemptible life of the crowd. For all of its troubles and dangers, and despite the fact that it must pass away, the frontier had been a better place. If civilization was to be redeemed, it would be by men like the Virginian who could retain their frontier virtues even as they made the transition to post-frontier life.

The mythic frontier individualist was almost always masculine in gender: here, in the wilderness, a man could be a real man, the rugged individual he was meant to be before civilization sapped his energy and threatened his masculinity. Wister's contemptuous remarks about Wall Street and Newport suggest what he and many others of his generation believed – that the comforts and seductions of civilized life were especially insidious for men, who all too easily became emasculated by the femininizing tendencies of civilization. More often than not, men who felt this way came, like Wister and Roosevelt, from elite class backgrounds. The curious result was that frontier nostalgia became an important vehicle for expressing a peculiarly bourgeois form of antimodernism. The very men who most benefited from urban-industrial capitalism were among those who believed they must escape its debilitating effects. If the frontier was passing, then men who had the means to do so should preserve for themselves some remnant of its wild landscape so that they might enjoy the regeneration and renewal that came from sleeping under the stars, participating in blood sports, and living off the land. The frontier might be gone, but the frontier experience could still be had if only wilderness were preserved.

Thus the decades following the Civil War saw more and more of the nation's wealthiest citizens seeking out wilderness for themselves. The elite passion for wild land took many forms: enormous estates in the Adirondacks and elsewhere (disingenuously called "camps" despite their many servants and amenities), cattle ranches for would-be rough riders on the Great Plains, guided big-game hunting trips in the Rockies, and luxurious resort hotels wherever railroads pushed their way into sublime landscapes. Wilderness suddenly emerged as the landscape of choice for elite tourists, who brought with them strikingly urban ideas of the countryside through which they traveled. For them, wild land was not a site for productive labor and not a permanent home; rather, it was a place of recreation. One went to the wilderness not as a producer but as a consumer, hiring guides and other backcountry residents who could serve as romantic surrogates for the rough riders and hunters of the frontier if one was willing to overlook their new status as employees and servants of the rich.

In just this way, wilderness came to embody the national frontier myth, standing for the wild freedom of America's past and seeming to represent a highly attractive natural alternative to the ugly artificiality of modern civilization. The irony, of course, was that in the process wilderness came to reflect the very civilization its devotees sought to escape. Ever since the nineteenth century, celebrating wilderness has been an activity mainly for well-to-do city folks. Country people generally know far too much about working the land to regard *un*worked land as their ideal. In contrast, elite urban tourists and wealthy sportsmen projected their leisure-time frontier fantasies onto the American landscape and so created wilderness in their own image.

There were other ironies as well. The movement to set aside national parks and wilderness areas followed hard on the heels of the final Indian wars, in which the prior human inhabitants of these areas were rounded up and moved onto reservations. The myth of the wilderness as "virgin," uninhabited land had always been especially cruel when seen from the perspective of the Indians who had once called that land home. Now they were forced to move elsewhere, with the result that tourists could safely enjoy the illusion that they were seeing their nation in its pristine, original state, in the new morning of God's own creation. Among the things that most marked the new national parks as reflecting a post-frontier consciousness was the relative absence of human violence within their boundaries. The actual frontier had often been a place of conflict, in which invaders and invaded fought for control of land and resources. Once set aside within the fixed and carefully policed boundaries of the modern bureaucratic state, the wilderness lost its savage image and became safe: a place more of reverie than of revulsion or fear. Meanwhile, its original inhabitants were kept out by dint of force, their earlier uses of the land redefined as inappropriate or even illegal. To this day, for instance, the Blackfeet continue to be accused of "poaching" on the lands of Glacier National Park that originally belonged to them and that were ceded by treaty only with the proviso that they be permitted to hunt there.

The removal of Indians to create an "uninhabited wilderness" – uninhabited as never before in the human history of the place – reminds us just how invented, just how constructed, the American wilderness really is. To return to my opening argument: there is nothing natural about the concept of wilderness. It is entirely a creation of the culture that holds it dear, a product of the very history it seeks to deny. Indeed, one of the most striking proofs of the cultural invention of wilderness is its thoroughgoing erasure of the history from which it sprang. In virtually all of its manifestations, wilderness represents a flight from history. Seen as the original garden, it is a place outside of time, from which human beings had to be ejected before the fallen world of history could properly begin. Seen as the frontier, it is a savage world at the dawn of civilization, whose transformation represents the very beginning of the national historical epic. Seen as the bold landscape of frontier heroism, it is the place of youth and childhood, into which men escape by abandoning their pasts and entering a world of freedom where the constraints of civilization fade into memory. Seen as the sacred sublime, it is the home of a God who transcends history by standing as the One who remains untouched and unchanged by time's arrow. No matter what the angle from which we regard it, wilderness offers us the illusion that we can escape the cares and troubles of the world in which our past has ensnared us.

This escape from history is one reason why the language we use to talk about wilderness is often permeated with spiritual and religious values that reflect human ideals far more than the material world of physical nature. Wilderness fulfills the old romantic project of secularizing Judeo-Christian values so as to make a new cathedral not in some petty human building but in God's own creation, Nature itself. Many environmentalists who reject traditional notions of the Godhead and who regard themselves as agnostics or even atheists nonetheless express feelings tantamount to religious awe when in the presence of wilderness – a fact that testifies to the success of the romantic project. Those who have no difficulty seeing God as the expression of our human dreams and desires nonetheless have trouble recognizing that in a secular age Nature can offer precisely the same sort of mirror.

Thus it is that wilderness serves as the unexamined foundation on which so many of the quasi-religious values of modern environmentalism rest. The critique of modernity that is one of environmentalism's most important contributions to the moral and political discourse of our time more often than not appeals, explicitly or implicitly, to wilderness as the standard against which to measure the failings of our human world. Wilderness is the natural, unfallen antithesis of an unnatural civilization that has lost its soul. It is a place of freedom in which we can recover the true selves we have lost to the corrupting influences of our artificial lives. Most of all, it is the ultimate landscape of authenticity. Combining the sacred grandeur of the sublime with the primitive simplicity of the frontier, it is the place where we can see the world as it really is, and so know ourselves as we really are – or ought to be.

But the trouble with wilderness is that it quietly expresses and reproduces the very values its devotees seek to reject. The flight from history that is very nearly the core of wilderness represents the false hope of an escape from responsibility, the illusion that we can somehow wipe clean the slate of our past and return to the tabula rasa that supposedly existed before we began to leave our marks on the world. The dream of an unworked natural landscape is very much the fantasy of people who have never themselves had to work the land to make a living – urban folk for whom food comes from a supermarket or a restaurant instead of a field, and for whom the wooden houses in which they live and work apparently have no meaningful connection to the forests in which trees grow and die. Only people whose relation to the land was already alienated could hold up wilderness as a model for human life in nature, for the romantic ideology of wilderness leaves precisely nowhere for human beings actually to make their living from the land.

This, then, is the central paradox: wilderness embodies a dualistic vision in which the human is entirely outside the natural. If we allow ourselves to believe that nature, to be true, must also be wild, then our very presence in nature represents its fall. The place where we are is the place where nature is not. If this is so – if by definition wilderness leaves no place for human beings, save perhaps as contemplative sojourners enjoying their leisurely reverie in God's natural cathedral – then also by definition it can offer no solution to the environmental and other problems that confront us. To the extent that we celebrate wilderness as the measure with which we judge civilization, we reproduce the dualism that sets humanity and nature at opposite poles. We thereby leave ourselves little hope of discovering what an ethical, sustainable, *honorable* human place in nature might actually look like.

Worse: to the extent that we live in an urban-industrial civilization but at the same time pretend to ourselves that our *real* home is in the wilderness, to just that extent we give ourselves permission to evade responsibility for the lives we actually lead. We inhabit civilization while holding some part of ourselves – what we imagine to be the most precious part – aloof from its entanglements. We work our nine-to-five jobs in its institutions, we eat its food, we drive its cars (not least to reach the wilderness), we benefit from the intricate and all too invisible net-works with which it shelters us, all the while pretending that these things are not an essential part of who we are. By imagining that our true home is in the wilderness, we forgive ourselves the homes we actually inhabit. In its flight from history, in its siren song of escape, in its reproduction of the dangerous dualism that sets human beings outside of nature – in all of these ways, wilderness poses a serious threat to responsible environmentalism at the end of the twentieth century.

By now I hope it is clear that my criticism in this essay is not directed at wild nature per se, or even at efforts to set aside large tracts of wild land, but rather at the specific habits of thinking that flow from this complex cultural construction called wilderness. It is not the things we label as wilderness that are the problem – for nonhuman nature and large tracts of the natural world *do* deserve protection – but rather what we ourselves mean when we use the label. Lest one doubt how pervasive these habits of thought actually are in contemporary environmentalism, let me list some of the places where wilderness serves as the ideological underpinning for environmental concerns that might otherwise seem quite remote from it. Defenders of biological diversity, for instance, although sometimes appealing to more utilitarian concerns, often point to "untouched" eco-systems as the best and richest repositories of the undiscovered species we must certainly try to protect. Although at first blush an apparently more "scientific" concept than wilderness, biological diversity in fact invokes many of the same sacred values, which is why organizations like the Nature Conservancy have been so quick to employ it as an alternative to the seemingly fuzzier and more problematic concept of wilderness. There is a paradox here, of course. To the extent that biological diversity (indeed, even wilderness itself) is likely to survive in the future only by the most vigilant and self-conscious management of the ecosystems that sustain it, the ideology of wilderness is potentially in direct conflict with the very thing it encourages us to protect.

The most striking instances of this have revolved around "endangered species," which serve as vulnerable symbols of biological diversity while at the same time standing as surrogates for wilderness itself. The terms of the Endangered Species Act in the United States have often meant that those hoping to defend pristine wilderness have had to rely on a single endangered species like the spotted owl to gain legal standing for their case – thereby making the full power of the sacred land inhere in a single numinous organism whose habitat then becomes the object of intense debate about appropriate management and use. The ease with which anti-environmental forces like the wise-use movement have attacked such single-species preservation efforts suggests the vulnerability of strategies like these.

Perhaps partly because our own conflicts over such places and organisms have become so messy, the convergence of wilderness values with concerns about biological diversity and endangered species has helped produce a deep fascination for remote ecosystems, where it is easier to imagine that nature might somehow be "left alone" to flourish by its own pristine devices. The classic example is the tropical rain forest, which since the 1970s has become the most powerful modern icon of unfallen, sacred land – a veritable Garden of Eden – for many Americans and Europeans. And yet protecting the rain forest in the eyes of First World environmentalists all too often means protecting it from the people who live there. Those who seek to preserve such "wilderness" from the activities of native peoples run the risk of reproducing the same tragedy – being forceably removed from an ancient home – that befell American Indians. Third World countries face massive environmental problems and deep social conflicts, but these are not likely to be solved by a cultural myth that encourages us to "preserve" peopleless landscapes that have not existed in such places for millennia. At its worst, as environmentalists are beginning to realize, exporting American notions of wilderness in this way can become an unthinking and self-defeating form of cultural imperialism.

Perhaps the most suggestive example of the way that wilderness thinking can underpin other environmental concerns has emerged in the recent debate about "global change." In 1989 the journalist Bill McKibben published a book entitled *The End of Nature*, in which he argued that the prospect of global climate change as a result of unintentional human manipulation of the atmosphere means that nature as we once knew it no longer exists.[17] Whereas earlier generations inhabited a natural world that remained more or less unaffected by their actions, our own generation is uniquely different. We and our children will henceforth live in a biosphere completely altered by our own activity, a planet in which the human and the natural can no longer be distinguished, because the one has overwhelmed the other. In McKibben's view, nature has died, and we are responsible for killing it. "The planet," he declares, "is utterly different now."[18]

But such a perspective is possible only if we accept the wilderness premise that nature, to be natural, must also be pristine – remote from humanity and untouched by our common past. In fact, everything we know about environmental history suggests that people have been manipulating the natural world on various scales for as long as we have a record of their passing. Moreover, we have unassailable evidence that many of the environmental changes we now face also occurred quite apart from human intervention at one time or another in the earth's past. The point is not that our current problems are trivial, or that our devastating effects on the earth's ecosystems should be accepted as inevitable or "natural." It is rather that we seem unlikely to make much progress in solving these problems if we hold up to ourselves as the mirror of nature a wilderness we ourselves cannot inhabit.

To do so is merely to take to a logical extreme the paradox that was built into wilderness from the beginning: if nature dies because we enter it, then the only way to save nature is to kill ourselves. The absurdity of this proposition flows from the underlying dualism it expresses. Not only does it ascribe greater power to humanity that we in fact possess – physical and biological nature will surely survive in some form or another long after we ourselves have gone the way of all flesh – but in the end it offers us little more than a self-defeating counsel of despair. The tautology gives us no way out: if wild nature is the only thing worth saving, and if our mere presence destroys it, then the sole solution to our own unnaturalness, the only way to protect sacred wilderness from profane humanity, would seem to be suicide. It is not a proposition that seems likely to produce very positive or practical results.

And yet radical environmentalists and deep ecologists all too frequently come close to accepting this premise as a first principle. When they express, for instance, the popular notion that our environmental problems began with the invention of agriculture, they push the human fall from natural grace so far back into the past that all of civilized history becomes a tale of ecological declension. Earth First! founder Dave Foreman captures the familiar parable succinctly when he writes,

> Before agriculture was midwifed in the Middle East, humans were in the wilderness. We had no concept of "wilderness" because everything was wilderness and *we were a part of it*. But with irrigation ditches, crop surpluses, and permanent villages, we became *apart from* the natural world. . . . Between the wilderness that created us and the civilization created by us grew an ever-widening rift.[19]

In this view the farm becomes the first and most important battlefield in the long war against wild nature, and all else follows in its wake. From such a starting place, it is hard not to reach the conclusion that the only way human beings can hope to live naturally on earth is to follow the hunter-gatherers back into a wilderness Eden and abandon virtually everything that civilization has given us. It may indeed turn out that civilization will end in ecological collapse or nuclear disaster, whereupon one might expect to find any human survivors returning to a way of life closer to that celebrated by Foreman and his followers. For most of us, though, such a debacle would be cause for regret, a sign that humanity had failed to fulfill its own promise and failed to honor its own highest values – including those of the deep ecologists.

In offering wilderness as the ultimate hunter-gatherer alternative to civilization, Foreman reproduces an extreme but still easily recognizable version of the myth of frontier primitivism. When he writes of his fellow Earth Firsters that "we believe we must return to being animal, to glorying in our sweat, hormones, tears, and blood" and that "we struggle against the modern compulsion to become dull, passionless androids," he is following in the footsteps of Owen Wister.[20] Although his arguments give primacy to defending biodiversity and the autonomy of wild nature, his prose becomes most passionate when he speaks of preserving "the wilderness experience." His own ideal "Big Outside" bears an uncanny resemblance to that of the frontier myth: wide open spaces and virgin land with no trails, no signs, no facilities, no maps, no guides, no rescues, no modern equipment. Tellingly, it is a land where hardy travelers can support themselves by hunting with "primitive weapons (bow and arrow, atlatl, knife, sharp rock)."[21] Foreman claims that "the primary value of wilderness is not as a proving ground for young Huck Finns and Annie Oakleys," but his heart is with Huck and Annie all the same. He admits that "preserving a quality wilderness experience for the human visitor, letting her or him flex Paleolithic muscles or seek visions, remains a tremendously important secondary purpose."[22] Just so does Teddy Roosevelt's rough rider live on in the greener garb of a new age.

However much one may be attracted to such a vision, it entails problematic consequences. For one, it makes wilderness the locus for an epic struggle between malign civilization and benign nature, compared with which all other social, political, and moral concerns seem trivial. Foreman writes, "The preservation of wildness and native diversity is *the* most important issue. Issues directly affecting only humans pale in comparison."[23] Presumably so do any environmental problems whose victims are mainly people, for such problems usually surface in landscapes that have already "fallen" and are no longer wild. This would seem to exclude from the radical environmentalist agenda problems of occupational health and safety in industrial settings, problems of toxic waste exposure on "unnatural" urban and agricultural sites, problems of poor children poisoned by lead exposure in the inner city, problems of famine and poverty and human suffering in the "overpopulated" places of the earth – problems, in short, of environmental justice. If we set too high a stock on wilderness, too many other corners of the earth become less than natural and too many other people become less than human, thereby giving us permission not to care much about their suffering or their fate.

It is no accident that these supposedly inconsequential environmental problems affect mainly poor people, for the long affiliation between wilderness and wealth means that the only poor people who count when wilderness is *the* issue are hunter-gatherers, who presumably do not consider themselves to be poor in the first place. The dualism at the heart of wilderness encourages its advocates to conceive of its protection as a crude conflict between the "human" and the "nonhuman" – or, more often, between those who value the nonhuman and those who do not. This in turn tempts one to ignore crucial differences *among* humans and the complex cultural and historical reasons why different peoples may feel very differently about the meaning of wilderness.

Why, for instance, is the "wilderness experience" so often conceived as a form of recreation best enjoyed by those whose class privileges give them the time and resources to leave their jobs behind and "get away from it all"? Why does the protection of wilderness so often seem to pit urban recreationists against rural people who actually earn their living from the land (excepting those who sell goods and services to the tourists themselves)? Why in the debates about pristine natural areas are "primitive" peoples idealized, even sentimentalized, until the moment they do something unprimitive, modern, and unnatural, and thereby fall from environmental grace? What are the consequences of a wilderness ideology that devalues productive labor and the very concrete knowledge that comes from working the land with one's own hands? All of these questions imply conflicts among different groups of people, conflicts that are obscured behind the deceptive clarity of "human" vs. "nonhuman." If in answering these knotty questions we resort to so simplistic an opposition, we are almost certain to ignore the very subtleties and complexities we need to understand.

But the most troubling cultural baggage that accompanies the celebration of wilderness has less to do with remote rain forests and peoples than with the ways we think about ourselves – we American environmentalists who quite rightly worry about the future of the earth and the threats we pose to the natural world. Idealizing a distant wilderness too often means not idealizing the environment in which we actually live, the landscape that for better or worse we call home. Most of our most serious environmental problems start right here, at home, and if we are to solve those problems, we need an environmental ethic that will tell us as much about *using* nature as about *not* using it. The wilderness dualism tends to cast any use as *ab*-use, and thereby denies us a middle ground in which responsible use and non-use might attain some kind of balanced, sustainable relationship. My own belief is that only by exploring this middle ground will we learn ways of imagining a better world for all of us: humans and nonhumans, rich people and poor, women and men, First Worlders *and* Third Worlders, white folks and people of color, consumers and producers – a world better for humanity in all of its diversity and for all the rest of nature too. The middle ground is where we actually live. It is where we – all of us, in our different places and ways – make our homes.

That is why, when I think of the times I myself have come closest to experiencing what I might call the sacred in nature, I often find myself remembering wild places much closer to home. I think, for instance, of a small pond near my house where water bubbles up from limestone springs to feed a series of pools that rarely freeze in winter and so play home to waterfowl that stay here for the protective warmth even on the coldest of winter days, gliding silently through streaming mists as the snow falls from gray February skies. I think of a November evening long ago when I found myself on a Wisconsin hilltop in rain and dense fog, only to have the setting sun break through the clouds to cast an otherworldly golden light on the misty farms and woodlands below, a scene so unexpected and joyous that I lingered past dusk so as not to miss any part of the gift that had come my way. And I think perhaps most especially of the blown-out, bankrupt farm in the sand country of central Wisconsin where Aldo Leopold and his family tried one of the first American experiments in ecological restoration, turning ravaged and infertile soil into carefully tended ground where the human and the nonhuman could exist side by side in relative harmony. What I celebrate about such places is not *just* their wildness, though that certainly is among their most important qualities; what I celebrate even more is that they remind us of the wildness in our own backyards, of the nature that is all around us if only we have eyes to see it.

Indeed, my principal objection to wilderness is that it may teach us to be dismissive or even contemptuous of such humble places and experiences. Without our quite realizing it, wilderness tends to privilege some parts of nature at the expense of others. Most of us, I suspect, still follow the conventions of the romantic sublime in finding the mountaintop more glorious than the plains, the ancient forest nobler than the grasslands, the mighty canyon more inspiring than the humble marsh. Even John Muir, in arguing against those who sought to dam his beloved Hetch Hetchy valley in the Sierra Nevada, argued for alternative dam sites in the gentler valleys of the foothills – a preference that had nothing to do with nature and everything with the cultural traditions of the sublime. Just as problematically, our frontier traditions have encouraged Americans to define "true" wilderness as requiring very large tracts of roadless land – what Dave Foreman calls "The Big Outside." Leaving aside the legitimate empirical question in conservation biology of how large a tract of land must be before a given species can reproduce on it, the emphasis on big wilderness reflects a romantic frontier belief that one hasn't really gotten away from civilization unless one can go for days at a time without encountering another human being. By teaching us to fetishize sublime places and wide open country, these peculiarly American ways of thinking about wilderness encourage us to adopt too high a standard for what counts as "natural." If it isn't hundreds of square miles big, if it doesn't give us God's-eye views or grand vistas, if it doesn't permit us the illusion that we are alone on the planet, then it really isn't natural. It's too small, too plain, or too crowded to be *authentically* wild.

In critiquing wilderness as I have done in this essay, I'm forced to confront my own deep ambivalence about its meaning for modern environmentalism. On the one hand, one of my own most important environmental ethics is that people should always be conscious that they are part of the natural world, inextricably tied to the ecological systems that sustain their lives. Any way of looking at nature that encourages us to believe we are separate from nature – as wilderness tends to do – is likely to reinforce environmentally irresponsible behavior. On the other hand, I also think it no less crucial for us to recognize and honor nonhuman nature as a world we did not create, a world with its own independent, nonhuman reasons for being as it is. The autonomy of nonhuman nature seems to me an indispensable corrective to human arrogance. Any way of looking at nature that helps us remember – as wilderness also tends to do – that the interests of people are not necessarily identical to those of every other creature or of the earth itself is likely to foster *responsible* behavior. To the extent that wilderness has served as an important vehicle for articulating deep moral values regarding our obligations and responsibilities to the nonhuman world, I would not want to jettison the contributions it has made to our culture's ways of thinking about nature.

If the core problem of wilderness is that it distances us too much from the very things it teaches us to value, then the question we must ask is what it can tell us about *home*, the place where we actually live. How can we take the positive values we associate with wilderness and bring them closer to home? I think the answer to this question will come by broadening our sense of the otherness that wilderness seeks to define and protect. In reminding us of the world we did not make, wilderness can teach profound feelings of humility and respect as we confront our fellow beings and the earth itself. Feelings like these argue for the importance of self-awareness and self-criticism as we exercise our own ability to transform the world around us, helping us set responsible limits to human mastery – which without such limits too easily becomes human hubris. Wilderness is the place where, symbolically at least, we try to withhold our power to dominate.

Wallace Stegner once wrote of

the special human mark, the special record of human passage, that distin-
guishes man from all other species. It is rare enough among men, impossible to any other form of life. *It is simply the deliberate and chosen refusal to
make any marks at all*. . . . We are the most dangerous species of life on the
planet, and every other species, even the earth itself, has cause to fear our
power to exterminate. But we are also the only species which, when it
chooses to do so, will go to great effort to save what it might destroy.[24]

The myth of wilderness, which Stegner knowingly reproduces in these
remarks, is that we can somehow leave nature untouched by our passage.
By now it should be clear that this for the most part is an illusion. But
Stegner's deeper message then becomes all the more compelling. If living
in history means that we cannot help leaving marks on a fallen world, then
the dilemma we face is to decide what kinds of marks we wish to leave. It is
just here that our cultural traditions of wilderness remain so important. In
the broadest sense, wilderness teaches us to ask whether the Other must
always bend to our will, and, if not, under what circumstances it should be
allowed to flourish without our intervention. This is surely a question
worth asking about everything we do, and not just about the natural world.

When we visit a wilderness area, we find ourselves surrounded by plants
and animals and physical landscapes whose otherness compels our attention. In forcing us to acknowledge that they are not of our making, that they
have little or no need of our continued existence, they recall for us a creation
far greater than our own. In the wilderness, we need no reminder that a tree
has its own reasons for being, quite apart from us. The same is less true in
the gardens we plant and tend ourselves: there it is far easier to forget the
otherness of the tree. Indeed, one could almost measure wilderness by the
extent to which our recognition of its otherness requires a conscious, willed
act on our part. The romantic legacy means that wilderness is more a state
of mind than a fact of nature, and the state of mind that today most defines
wilderness is *wonder*. The striking power of the wild is that wonder in the
face of it requires no act of will, but forces itself upon us – as an expression of
the nonhuman world experienced through the lens of our cultural history –
as proof that ours is not the only presence in the universe.

Wilderness gets us into trouble only if we imagine that this experience
of wonder and otherness is limited to the remote corners of the planet, or
that it somehow depends on pristine landscapes we ourselves do not
inhabit. Nothing could be more misleading. The tree in the garden is in
reality no less other, no less worthy of our wonder and respect, than the
tree in an ancient forest that has never known an ax or a saw – even
though the tree in the forest reflects a more intricate web of ecological
relationships. The tree in the garden could easily have sprung from the
same seed as the tree in the forest, and we can claim only its location and
perhaps its form as our own. Both trees stand apart from us; both share

our common world. The special power of the tree in the wilderness is to remind us of this fact. It can teach us to recognize the wildness we did not see in the tree we planted in our own backyard. By seeing the otherness in that which is most unfamiliar, we can learn to see it too in that which at first seemed merely ordinary. If wilderness can do this – if it can help us perceive and respect a nature we had forgotten to recognize as natural – then it will become part of the solution to our environmental dilemmas rather than part of the problem.

This will only happen, however, if we abandon the dualism that sees the tree in the garden as artificial – completely fallen and unnatural – and the tree in the wilderness as natural – completely pristine and wild. Both trees in some ultimate sense are wild; both in a practical sense now depend on our management and care. We are responsible for both, even though we can claim credit for neither. Our challenge is to stop thinking of such things according to a set of bipolar moral scales in which the human and the nonhuman, the unnatural and the natural, the fallen and the unfallen, serve as our conceptual map for understanding and valuing the world. Instead, we need to embrace the full continuum of a natural landscape that is also cultural, in which the city, the suburb, the pastoral, and the wild each has its proper place, which we permit ourselves to celebrate without needlessly denigrating the others. We need to honor the Other within and the Other next door as much as we do the exotic Other that lives far away – a lesson that applies as much to people as it does to (other) natural things. In particular, we need to discover a common middle ground in which all of these things, from the city to the wilderness, can somehow be encompassed in the word "home." Home, after all, is the place where finally we make our living. It is the place for which we take responsibility, the place we try to sustain so we can pass on what is best in it (and in ourselves) to our children.

The task of making a home in nature is what Wendell Berry has called "the forever unfinished lifework of our species." "The only thing we have to preserve nature with," he writes, "is culture; the only thing we have to preserve wildness with is domesticity."[25] Calling a place home inevitably means that we will *use* the nature we find in it, for there can be no escape from manipulating and working and even killing some parts of nature to make our home. But if we acknowledge the autonomy and otherness of the things and creatures around us – an autonomy our culture has taught us to label with the word "wild" – then we will at least think carefully about the uses to which we put them, and even ask if we should use them at all. Just so can we still join Thoreau in declaring that "in Wildness is the preservation of the World," for *wild*ness (as opposed to wilderness) can be found anywhere: in the seemingly tame fields and woodlots of Massachusetts, in the cracks of a Manhattan sidewalk, even in the cells of our own bodies.

As Gary Snyder has wisely said, "A person with a clear heart and open mind can experience the wilderness anywhere on earth. It is a quality of one's own consciousness. The planet is a wild place and always will be."[26] To think ourselves capable of causing "the end of nature" is an act of great hubris, for it means forgetting the wildness that dwells everywhere within and around us.

Learning to honor the wild – learning to remember and acknowledge the autonomy of the other – means striving for critical self-consciousness in all of our actions. It means that deep reflection and respect must accompany each act of use, and means too that we must always consider the possibility of non- use. It means looking at the part of nature we intend to turn toward our own ends and asking whether we can use it again and again and again – sustainably – without its being diminished in the process. It means never imagining that we can flee into a mythical wilderness to escape history and the obligation to take responsibility for our own actions that history inescapably entails. Most of all, it means practicing remembrance and gratitude, for thanksgiving is the simplest and most basic of ways for us to recollect the nature, the culture, and the history that have come together to make the world as we know it. If wildness can stop being (just) out there and start being (also) in here, if it can start being as humane as it is natural, then perhaps we can get on with the unending task of struggling to live rightly in the world – not just in the garden, not just in the wilderness, but in the home that encompasses them both.

Notes

1   Henry David Thoreau, "Walking," *The Works of Thoreau*, ed. Henry S. Canby (Boston, Massachusetts: Houghton Mifflin, 1937), p. 672.

2   *Oxford English Dictionary*, s.v. "wilderness"; see also Roderick Nash, *Wilderness and the American Mind*, 3rd ed. (New Haven, Connecticut: Yale Univ. Press, 1982), pp. 1–22; and Max Oelschlaeger, *The Idea of Wilderness: From Prehistory to the Age of Ecology* (New Haven, Connecticut: Yale Univ. Press, 1991).

3   Exodus 32:1–35, KJV.

4   Exodus 14:3, KJV.

5   Mark 1:12–13, KJV; see also Matthew 4:1–11; Luke 4:1–13.

6   John Milton, "Paradise Lost," *John Milton: Complete Poems and Major Prose*, ed. Merritt Y. Hughes (New York: Odyssey Press, 1957), pp. 280–1, lines 131–42.

7   John Muir, *My First Summer in the Sierra* (1911), reprinted in *John Muir: The Eight Wilderness Discovery Books* (London, England: Diadem; Seattle, Washington: Mountaineers, 1992), p. 211.

8   John Muir, *The Yosemite* (1912), reprinted in *John Muir: Eight Wilderness Discovery Books*, p. 715.

9   William Wordsworth, "The Prelude," bk. 6, in Thomas Hutchinson, ed., *The Poetical Works of Wordsworth* (London, England: Oxford Univ. Press, 1936), p. 536.

10   Henry David Thoreau, *The Maine Woods* (1864), in *Henry David Thoreau* (New York: Library of America, 1985), pp. 640–41.
11   Exodus 16:10, KJV.
12   John Muir, *My First Summer in the Sierra*, p. 238.
13   Frederick Jackson Turner, *The Frontier in American History* (New York: Henry Holt, 1920), pp. 37–38.
14   Owen Wister, *The Virginian: A Horseman of the Plains* (New York: Macmillan, 1902), pp. viii–ix.
15   Theodore Roosevelt, *Ranch Life and the Hunting Trail* (1888; New York: Century, 1899), p. 100.
16   Wister, *Virginian*, p. x.
17   Bill McKibben, *The End of Nature* (New York: Random House, 1989).
18   McKibben, *The End of Nature*, p. 49.
19   Dave Foreman, *Confessions of an Eco-Warrior* (New York: Harmony Books, 1991), p. 69 (italics in original)....
20   Foreman, *Confessions of an Eco-Warrior*, p. 34.
21   Foreman, *Confessions of an Eco-Warrior*, p. 65. See also Dave Foreman and Howie Wolke, *The Big Outside: A Descriptive Inventory of the Big Wilderness Areas of the U.S.* (Tucson, Arizona: Ned Ludd Books, 1989).
22   Foreman, *Confessions of an Eco-Warrior*, p. 63.
23   Foreman, *Confessions of an Eco-Warrior*, p. 27.
24   Wallace Stegner, ed., *This Is Dinosaur: Echo Park Country and Its Magic Rivers* (New York: Knopf, 1955), p. 17 (italics in original).
25   Wendell Berry, *Home Economics* (San Francisco, California: North Point, 1987), pp. 138, 143.
26   Gary Snyder, quoted in *New York Times*, "Week in Review," 18 September 1994, p. 6.

Documents

John Muir on Saving Hetch Hetchy

Source: Century Magazine, Jan. 1909: 464–9.

One of the most visionary proponents of wilderness preservation was John Muir, founder of the Sierra Club, whose dedication to wilderness as a kind of American sacred space was unparalleled at the turn of the last century. Here, Muir extols the virtues of Yosemite National Park's Hetch Hetchy valley, which was about to be flooded to create a dam in order to provide a water source for San Francisco. (The fight over damming Hetch Hetchy was in part a product of the historical forces we examined in chapters 5 and 7. San Francisco needed a new water supply to protect against the kinds of calamitous fires that destroyed much of the city after the 1906 earthquake. The most feasible source of water was in the national park at Yosemite.) Muir's battle to save Hetch Hetchy ended in defeat in 1914, when conservationists, led by Gifford Pinchot, succeeded in having the valley dammed. The incident was a signal split within the conservation movement. Muir's passionate defense of pristine wilderness against Pinchot's utilitarianism presaged later battles over dams, wilderness, and the economic needs of America's increasingly urban population.

Note that Muir portrays the Hetch Hetchy valley as a kind of parallel to the better-known (and very popular) valley of the Yosemite. What other kinds of rhetoric does Muir use to mobilize his readers to protect the Hetch Hetchy valley? How would Muir's references to Indian names for valley features appeal to an American audience? How does Muir's language appeal both to American desires for recreation and to popular sensibilities about religion and nature? For Muir, as for many people today, wilderness preservation had pronounced religious meaning. How do Muir's religious views on the subject of nature compare to the religions of Indian people like the Koyukon? Is he an animist, believing that individual natural features are endowed with spirit? Or are his views more conventional, in which the wilderness is a kind of natural church where one finds divine inspiration?

*   *   *

The fame of the Merced Yosemite has spread far and wide, while Hetch-Hetchy, the Tuolumne Yosemite, has until recently remained comparatively unknown, notwithstanding it is a wonderfully exact counterpart of the famous valley. As the Merced flows in tranquil beauty through Yosemite, so does the Tuolumne through Hetch-Hetchy. The floor of Yosemite is about 4000 feet above the sea, and that of Hetch-Hetchy about 3700, while in both the walls are of gray granite, very high, and rise precipitously out of flowery gardens and groves. Furthermore, the two wonderful valleys occupy the same relative positions on the flank of the Sierra, were formed by the same forces in the same kind of granite, and have similar waterfalls, sculpture, and vegetation. Hetch-Hetchy lies in a northwesterly direction from Yosemite at a distance of about eighteen miles, and is now easily accessible by a trail and wagon road from the Big Oak Flat road at Sequoia.

The most strikingly picturesque rock in the valley is a majestic pyramid over 2000 feet in height which is called by the Indians Kolana. It is the outermost of a group like the Cathedral Rocks of Yosemite and occupies the same relative position on the south wall. Facing Kolana on the north side of the valley, there is a massive sheer rock like the

Yosemite El Capitan about 1900 feet high, and over its brow flows a stream that makes the most beautiful fall I have ever seen. The Indian name for it is Tueeulala. From the brow of the cliff it is free in the air for a thousand feet, then strikes on an earthquake talus and is broken up into a ragged network of cascades. It is in full bloom in June, and usually vanishes toward the end of summer. The Yosemite Bridal Veil is the only fall I know with which it may fairly be compared; but it excels even that wonderful fall in airy, swaying grace of motion and soothing repose. Looking across the valley in the spring, when the snow is melting fast, Tueeulala is seen in all her glory burning in white sunfire in every fiber. Approaching the brink of the rock, her waters flow swiftly, and in their first arching leap into the air a little hurried eagerness appears; but this eagerness is speedily hushed in sublime repose, and their tranquil progress to the base of the cliff is like that of downy feathers in a still room. The various fabrics into which her waters are woven are brought to view with marvelous distinctness by the instreaming sunshine. They sift and float from form to form down the face of that grand gray Capitan rock in so leisurely and unconfused a manner that one may examine their texture and patterns as one would a piece of embroidery held in the hand. Near the bottom, the width of the fall is increased from about twenty-five feet to a hundred feet, and is composed of yet finer tissue, fold over fold – air, water, and sunbeams woven into irised robes that spirits might wear.

A little to the eastward, on the same side of the valley, thunders the great Wapama or Hetch-Hetchy Fall. It is about 1700 feet high, and is so near Tueeulala that both are in full view from the same point. Its location is similar to that of the Yosemite Fall but its volume of water is much greater, and at times of high water may be heard at a distance of five or six miles or more. These twin falls are on branches of the same stream, but they could hardly be more unlike. Tueeulala, in sunshine, chanting soft and low like a summer breeze in the pines; Wapama, in gorge-shadows, roaring and booming like an avalanche. Tueeulala whispers that the Almighty dwells in peace; Wapama is the thunder of His chariot-wheels in power.

... In June and July summer is in prime, and the tide of happy, throbbing life is at its highest. August is the peaceful season of ripe nuts and berries – raspberries, blackberries, thimbleberries, gooseberries, shadberries, currants, puckery choke-cherries, pine-nuts, etc., offering royal feasts to Indians, squirrels, and birds of every feather. Then comes mellow, golden Indian summer, with its gorgeous colors and falling leaves, calm, thoughtful days, when everything, even the huge rocks, seems to be hushed and expectant, awaiting the coming of winter and rest.

Excepting only Yosemite, Hetch-Hetchy is the most attractive and wonderful valley within the bounds of the great Yosemite National Park and the best of all the camp-grounds. People are now flocking to it in ever-increasing numbers for health and recreation of body and mind. Though the walls are less sublime in height than those of Yosemite, its groves, gardens, and broad, spacious meadows are more beautiful and picturesque. It is many years since sheep and cattle were pastured in it, and the vegetation now shows scarce a trace of their ravages. Last year in October I visited the valley with Mr. William Keith, the artist. He wandered about from view to view, enchanted, made thirty-eight sketches, and enthusiastically declared that in varied picturesque beauty Hetch-Hetchy greatly surpassed Yosemite. It is one of God's best gifts, and ought to be faithfully guarded.

Peter Oscar Little Chief requests permission to hunt in Glacier Park

Source: Dept. of the Interior, Glacier Park, Game Protection Files (Part 4), RG 79 Records of the National Park Service, General Records, Central Files, 1907–1939, Box 23, Folder "Game Protection"

Peter Oscar Little Chief was a Blackfeet Indian from Montana. The Blackfeet ceded the western edge of their reservation to the federal government in the 1890s, but they retained the right to hunt, fish, and gather wood on it. They continued to use these lands, particularly for hunting and wood gathering, for decades afterwards. But federal authorities banned them from such activities when they merged the Blackfeet "ceded strip" with the new Glacier National Park in 1910. Peter Oscar Little Chief led a movement to demand the return of hunting rights in the ceded strip in the 1920s and 1930s. Here, he writes to the Secretary of the Interior, requesting permission to hunt in the park.

What are economic conditions like for Little Chief? Blackfeet had been hunting, gathering wood and wild foods, and utilizing the mountains of Glacier National Park for sacred purposes for centuries prior to the creation of the park. Does Little Chief consider it a pristine "wilderness"? If Little Chief could have some other relationship with this landscape than the law allows, what would it be? Would the park still be wilderness? Do you think Little Chief supports opening all of the park to hunting for all people? Or are Blackfeet claims to this landscape his only concern? And what is the response of federal authorities to this request?

November 20, 1915

Honorable F. K. Lane
Secy. of Interior
Washington, D.C.

Hon. Sir:

I kindly ask you to send me a permit to kill one deer and one elk in the Park. There are so many of them any where in the mountains. Some time you can see them from thirty to fifty head but I think that there are more mountain sheep than deers and elk in this Park. If you have no objection to give two head of mountain sheep I shall be very thankful for your kindness towards the Indians because you are the main man to see you and get permit from you no one else but you. The beef very high here and rare besides I have not tasted any meat for number of months ago and I would like to have meat once or more. I am poor man and have big family to support and besides don't make enough money to buy any farming implements and clothing for my family in the year to speak of. . . .

Yours Very Truly

Peter Oscar Little Chief

Dept. of the Interior
Washington
November 27, 1915

Peter Oscar Little Chief
Browning, Montana

Sir:

Acknowledging receipt of your letter of November 20th, requesting permission to kill game in the Glacier National Park . . . I have to state that under existing law the killing of game within the metes and bounds of the Glacier National Park is prohibited. . . .

Respectfully,

E. J. Ayers
Acting Assistant Secretary

National Parks Act, 1916

Wilderness Act, 1964

Finally, we examine two vital pieces of wilderness protection law. The first is the act that created the National Park Service in 1916 (passed partly to appease angry preservationists, who felt that the damming of Hetch Hetchy might have been prevented had the national parks been administered by a separate agency). The second is the Wilderness Act of 1964, which allowed for designation of wilderness areas on federal land, thereby ensuring their protection from many forms of economic development.

Compare these two laws with each other. How do they reflect the kinds of wilderness thought that Cronon describes? Is there room in these laws to accommodate *both* the sincere convictions of environmental thinkers like Muir *and* Indian claimants to the land like Peter Oscar Little Chief? National parks are among the most beloved of American landscapes. How do we reconcile local and Indian opposition to them with their importance to the nation at large? Is the definition of wilderness in the Wilderness Act coherent and feasible? Is there a paradox in the idea of *managing* a wilderness?

* * *

The National Parks Act (1916)

Be it enacted by the Senate and House of Representatives of the United States of America in Congress assembled, That there is hereby created in the Department of the Interior a service to be called the National Park Service. . . . The service thus established shall promote and regulate the use of the Federal areas known as national parks, monuments, and reservations hereinafter specified by such means and measures as conform to the fundamental purpose of the said parks, monuments, and reservations, which purpose is to conserve the scenery and the natural and historic objects and the wild life therein and to provide for the enjoyment of the same in such manner and by such means as will leave them unimpaired for the enjoyment of future generations. . . .

SEC. 3. That the Secretary of the Interior shall make and publish such rules and regulations as he may deem necessary or proper for the use and management of the parks, monuments, and reservations under the jurisdiction of the National Park Service, and any violations of any of the rules and regulations authorized by this Act shall be punished as provided for in section fifty of the Act entitled "An Act to codify and amend the penal laws of the United States," approved March fourth, nineteen hundred and nine, as amended by section six of the Act of June twenty-fifth, nineteen hundred and ten (Thirty-sixth United States Statutes at Large, page eight hundred and fifty-seven). He may also, upon terms and conditions to be fixed by him, sell or dispose of timber in those cases where in his judgment the cutting of such timber is required in order to control the attacks of insects or diseases or otherwise conserve the scenery or the natural or historic objects in any such park, monument, or reservation. He may also provide in his discretion for the destruction of such animals and of such plant life as may be detrimental to the use of any of said parks, monuments, or reservations. He may also grant privileges, leases, and permits for the use of land for the accommodation of visitors in the various parks, monuments, or other reservations herein provided for, but for periods not exceeding twenty years; and no natural curiosities, wonders, or objects of interest shall be leased, rented, or granted to anyone on such terms as to interfere with free access to them by the public: *Provided, however,* That the Secretary of the Interior may, under such rules and regulations and on such terms as he may prescribe, grant the privilege to graze live stock within any national park, monument, or reservation herein referred to when in his judgment such use is not detrimental to the primary purpose for which such park, monument, or reservation was created, except that this provision shall not apply to the Yellowstone National Park. . . .

The Wilderness Act (1964)

SEC. 2. (a) In order to assure that an increasing population, accompanied by expanding settlement and growing mechanization, does not occupy and modify all areas within the United States and its possessions, leaving no lands designated for preservation and protection in their natural condition, it is hereby declared to be the policy of the Congress to secure for the American people of present and future generations the benefits of an enduring resource of wilderness. For this purpose there is hereby established a National Wilderness Preservation System to be composed of federally owned areas designated by Congress as "wilderness areas", and these shall be administered for the use and enjoyment of the American people in such manner as will leave them unimpaired for future use and enjoyment as wilderness, and so as to provide for the protection of these areas, the preservation of their wilderness character, and for the gathering and dissemination of information regarding their use and enjoyment as wilderness; and no Federal lands shall be designated as "wilderness areas" except as provided for in this Act or by a subsequent Act.

(b) The inclusion of an area in the National Wilderness Preservation System notwithstanding, the area shall continue to be managed by the Department and agency having jurisdiction thereover immediately before its inclusion in the National Wilderness Preservation System unless otherwise provided by Act of Congress. No appropriation shall be available for the payment of expenses or salaries for the administration of the National Wilderness Preservation System as a separate unit nor shall any appropriations be available for additional personnel stated as being required solely for the purpose of managing or administering areas solely because they are included within the National Wilderness Preservation System.

Definition of Wilderness

(c) A wilderness, in contrast with those areas where man and his own works dominate the landscape, is hereby recognized as an area where the earth and its community of life are untrammeled by man, where man himself is a visitor who does not remain. An area of wilderness is further defined to mean in this Act an area of undeveloped Federal land retaining its primeval character and influence, without permanent improvements or human habitation, which is protected and managed so as to preserve its natural conditions and which (1) generally appears to have been affected primarily by the forces of nature, with the imprint of man's work substantially unnoticeable; (2) has outstanding opportunities for solitude or a primitive and unconfined type of recreation; (3) has at least five thousand acres of land or is of sufficient size as to make practicable its preservation and use in an unimpaired condition; and (4) may also contain ecological, geological, or other features of scientific, educational, scenic, or historical value.

9
Something in the Wind: Radiation, Pesticides, and Air Pollution

In this chapter we begin to explore the environmental movement. Environmentalism is distinctive from conservationism in some important ways, which we will examine when we get to the documents for this chapter. First we're going to read an article that suggests their similarity. Robert Gottlieb argues that although conservationists have gone down in history as being concerned with outdoor nature, they were just as concerned about protecting nature much closer to home, and in making sure that working people from the cities benefited from clean working environments and accessibility to wilderness. He describes the careers of two conservationists: Alice Hamilton, an early advocate of workplace safety and health, and Bob Marshall, a campaigner for working-class access to national forests and wilderness. He compares their stories with that of Rachel Carson, whose efforts to alert the public to the dangers of chemical pesticides led to the banning of DDT, and who was perhaps the foremost inspiration for environmentalists in the 1960s and 1970s. Gottlieb suggests that in warning about the threats of pollution to working people, and the needs of the broader public in relation to nature, these thinkers were more similar than different. Thus, there are common interests between conservation and environmentalism.

As true as this is, note also that only Carson succeeded in galvanizing a mass movement to advance her cause. What was it about the 1950s that allowed Carson's warnings to reach a broader audience than did Hamilton or Marshall? Between the early twentieth century, when Hamilton and Marshall were active, and the post-World War II era, something had changed.

Reconstructing Environmentalism: Complex Movements, Diverse Roots

Robert Gottlieb

Where We Live, Work, and Play

Given the diverse nature of contemporary environmentalism, it is striking how narrowly the movement has been historically described. In nearly all the standard environmental histories, the roots of environmentalism are presented as differing perspectives over how best to manage or preserve "Nature"; that is, "Nature" outside of the cities and the experiences of people's everyday lives. The primary players in numerous historical texts – the Muirs and the Pinchots – represent those perspectives to the exclusion of other figures not seen as engaged in *environmental* struggles because their concerns were urban and industrial. There has been no place in this history for Alice Hamilton who helped identify the new industrial poisons and spoke of reforming the "dangerous trades;" for empowerment advocates like Florence Kelley who sought to reform the conditions of the urban and industrial environment in order to improve the quality of life of workers, children, women, and the poor; or for urban critics like Lewis Mumford who spoke of the excesses of the industrial city and envisioned environmental harmony linking city and countryside at the regional scale.

In part because of these historical omissions, scholars offer sharply divergent views about the origin, evolution and nature of contemporary environmentalism. Most common explanations place the beginning of the current environmental movement on or around Earth Day 1970. The new movement, they emphasize, came to anchor new forms of environmental policy and management based most directly on the clean-up and control of pollution rather than simply the management or protection of the natural environment. This explanation thus provides a convenient way to distinguish between an earlier *conservationist* epoch where battles took place over national parks, forest lands, resource development, and recreational resources, and today's *environmental* era where pollution and environmental hazards dominate contemporary policy agendas.

The problem with this explanation of such an historical divide in environmentalism is who is left out and what it fails to explain. Pollution issues are not just a recent concern; people have recognized and struggled about these problems for more than a century in significant and varied ways. A history which separates resource development and its regulation from the urban and industrial environment disguises a crucial link which connects both pollution and the loss of wilderness. If we see environmentalism as rooted primarily or exclusively in the struggle to reserve or manage extra-urban "Nature," we find it difficult to link the changes in material life after World War II – the rise of petrochemicals, the dawning of the nuclear age, the tendencies towards over-production and mass consumption – with the rise of new social movements focused on issues of quality of life. And by defining contemporary environmentalism primarily in reference to its mainstream, institutional forms, such historians cannot account for the spontaneity and diversity of an environmentalism rooted in communities and constituencies seeking to address issues . . . of where and how people live, work, and play.

Situating Bob Marshall

To understand this complex movement with diverse roots, it might be best to begin with Wilderness Society founder Bob Marshall, who remains a paradoxical figure within environmentalism. A champion of the poor and powerless, deeply committed to wilderness, and equally forceful about the need to make nature a direct part of people's lives, Marshall is an especially enigmatic figure for those who have defined environmentalism in narrower terms. Yet this intense, always curious radical forester proposed a common thread for a movement split between managers and protectors of the natural environment and those defining their environmentalism on the basis of daily life experiences.

The son of the senior partner in the prestigious, Washington D. C. law firm of Guggenheimer, Untermeyer, and Marshall, Robert Marshall grew up steeped in liberal values, including defense of civil liberties, respect for minority rights, and the fight against discrimination. Encouraged by his father who maintained a strong interest in forest conservation, Marshall decided to launch a forestry-related career. He worked in various capacities for the Forest Service, where he began to view the forests as a necessary retreat "from the encompassing clutch of a mechanistic civilization," a place where people would be able to "enjoy the most worthwhile and perhaps the only worthwhile part of life." Marshall quickly became a strong critic of development pressures on forest lands from private logging companies which had led to a decline in productivity, increase in soil erosion, and "ruination of the forest beauty."[1]

Marshall's compassion for people and powerful desire to be in touch with wilderness eventually led him to adopt two distinctive, yet, for him, compatible positions about wilderness "protection." On the one hand, Marshall feared a loss of the wild, undeveloped forest lands in their spectacular western settings and in the less "monumental" forest areas of the East, such as the Adirondacks. . . . Marshall urged a new organization be formed "of spirited people who will fight for the freedom of the wilderness," and be militant and uncompromising in their stance.[2]

At the same time, Marshall argued that wilderness belonged to all the people, not simply to an elite who wanted such areas available for their own use. Already by 1925, Marshall was writing that "people can not live generation after generation in the city without serious retrogression – physical, moral and mental – and the time will come when the most destitute of the city population will be able to get a vacation in the forest."[3] Marshall was particularly critical of the policies of the National Park Service with their expensive facilities and concessions. . . . This was a particularly appealing position to the Forest Service during the New Deal era, which convinced Marshall to head a new outdoors and recreation office. Through this office, the Forest Service hoped to contrast itself as a "blue collar" alternative to the Park Service.

Despite his agency role, Marshall remained a critic of the Forest Service's pro-development position as well as the Park Service's recreation-oriented policies which ended up destroying wilderness. The criticism of the Forest Service, spelled out in his best known work, *The People's Forests*, was tied to Marshall's overall critique of *private* forestry and its role in injuring the work force, the community, and the land itself. In this book, Marshall advocated public ownership of forest lands in order that "social welfare" be "substituted for private gain as the major objective for management." To Marshall, that meant a new labor and rural economic development strategy and careful land use planning, more research and science, and safeguarding recreational values from "commercial exploitation."[4] . . .

This search for a green retreat, or a "green utopia," became a continuing passion for Marshall, both in his governmental activities and advocacy work. After his return to the Forest Service in 1937, following a stint with the Bureau of Indian Affairs, Marshall laid out this combined social and environmentalist vision. It included subsidizing transportation to the public forests and operating camps at nominal cost for low income people, changing Forest Service practices that discriminated against blacks, Jews, and other minorities, and acquiring more recreational forest land near urban centers. At the same time, he sought to designate wilderness as places "in which there shall be no roads or other provision for the motorized transportation, no commercial timber cutting, and no occupancy under special use permit for hotels, stores, resorts, summer homes, organization camps, hunting and fishing lodges or similar uses. . . ."[5]

Marshall also sought to integrate some of these ideas into the approach of the Wilderness Society, an organization he helped found and finance in its first years of operation. In 1937, Marshall enlisted his close friend Catherine Bauer, a leader in the regional planning movement, to explore the issues of wilderness, public access, and social policy. In a long letter to Marshall, Bauer noted that wilderness appreciation was seen as "snobbish" but that a great many people, even the majority, could enjoy the wilderness, given a chance to experience it. Bauer suggested that "factory workers, who experience our machine civilization in its rawest and most extreme form" could most benefit from wilderness and by doing so could broaden wilderness's political base.[6]

Though Bauer's suggestions reflected Marshall's own approach, they caused concern and consternation among other key figures in the Wilderness Society, especially its executive director, Robert Sterling Yard. Yard worried that the New Deal forester might interest too many "radicals" like Bauer in wanting to influence wilderness policy. Yard and others were also concerned about the redbaiting of Marshall during the late 1930s. These attacks, led by members of the House Un-American Activities Committee, sought to attack Marshall through his non-wilderness activities and financial contributions. Wilderness Society leaders like Yard feared that Marshall's activities might reflect on the organization, and remained skeptical of his advocacy of a democratic wilderness policy. In response to the "democratic wilderness" concept, key Wilderness Society figure Olaus Murie would later write that "wilderness is for those who appreciate" and that if "the multitudes" were brought into the backcountry without really understanding its "subtle values," "there would be an insistent and effective demand for more and more facilities, and we would find ourselves losing our wilderness and having these areas reduced to the commonplace."[7]

Murie's pivotal essay was written a few months after Bob Marshall unexpectedly died in his sleep during an overnight train ride from Washington to New York. In his will, Marshall divided his $1.5 million estate into three trusts: one for social advocacy including support for promoting "an economic system in the United States based upon the theory of production for use and not-for-profit;" a second to promote civil liberties; and a third, for "preservation of wilderness conditions in outdoor America, including, but not limited to, the preservation of areas embracing primitive conditions of transportation, vegetation, and fauna." This last trust came to be controlled by Wilderness Society officials whose approaches were more narrowly conceived (in terms of membership and constituency) and politically limiting (in terms of resource policy) than Marshall's own inclinations. Over time, Bob Marshall's life and ideas began to undergo reinterpretation. His love for wilderness, it was eventually claimed, had really been an exclusive concern. With his death, Bob Marshall, the "people's forester" whose life's mission had sought to link social justice and protected wilderness, would become an uncertain historical figure representing environmentalism's divide between movements, constituencies, and ideas.

Exploring the Dangerous Trades

At the other edge of this historical environmental divide stand the urban and industrial reformers, including advocates such as Alice Hamilton who sought to situate the concern about environmental hazards in the context of urban and industrial life. A compassionate advocate yet cautious and careful researcher, Alice Hamilton can be considered this country's first major urban/industrial environmentalist. Born in 1869 in New York City and raised in Fort Wayne, Indiana, Hamilton decided to study medicine, one of the few disciplines available to this first generation of women able to enter the universities and embark on a professional career. . . .

Even prior to entering medical school at the University of Michigan, Hamilton thought of combining her interest in medicine and science with humanitarian service and social reform. She found the ideal outlet when she moved into the Hull House settlement in Chicago while accepting a position as professor of pathology at the Woman's Medical School of Northwestern University. . . . There [at Hull House], she organized a well-baby clinic, looked into the cocaine traffic endemic in the neighborhood, took part in efforts to improve the quality of health care for the poor, and investigated a serious typhoid epidemic, among other activities. The typhoid epidemic was particularly instructive since Hamilton's investigation eventually helped reveal that a sewage outflow (an episode covered up by the Board of Health) bore direct relationship to the outbreak of the disease in specific neighborhoods. . . .

Hull House also became a staging ground for Hamilton's growing interest in the little understood and poorly treated area of industrial disease. At the settlement house, Hamilton heard countless stories about "industrial poisoning:" carbon monoxide in the steel mills, pneumonia and rheumatism in the stockyards, "phossy jaw" from white phosphorous used in match factories. Though industrial medicine had become an accepted discipline in Europe, its detractors in the U.S. suggested, as Hamilton wryly noted, that "here was a subject tainted with Socialism or with feminine sentimentality for the poor."[8] For

Hamilton, however, the exploration of industrial poisons joined her passion for reform with her desire to pursue a real world-based science.

In 1908, Hamilton's interest in the subject of industrial poisons was further stimulated by her appointment to the Illinois Commission on Occupational Diseases for whom she later became chief medical investigator. It was in this capacity that Hamilton began her famous investigation of the lead industries. Hamilton sought to identify which industries used lead and the kinds of health problems associated with them. In pursuing her research among the lead companies, Hamilton frequently encountered the belief (a kind of ideological rationale for lack of action), that worker unwillingness to "wash hands or scrub nails" represented the primary cause for occupational lead poisoning and that its occurrence was therefore "inevitable." Hamilton also quickly came to realize that lead hazards and health impacts were underreported by workers who concealed their illness out of fear of losing their jobs.[9]

Faced with lack of documentation and information, few resources, company resistance, and workers' fears, Hamilton's investigations, first with the Illinois Survey and subsequently with the Bureau of Labor within the Commerce Department, demonstrated an extraordinary resourcefulness in the pursuit of her "shoe-leather epidemiology." Her search for data required long hours and uneven information; a duty, she felt, "to the producer, not to the product." Hamilton recognized that her compassion as a woman for the victims of the dangerous trades gave her certain advantages in soliciting information. "It seemed natural and right that a woman should put the care of the producing workman ahead of the value of the thing he was producing," Hamilton remarked; "In a man it would have been (seen as) sentimentality or radicalism."[10]

During the next several decades, Hamilton became the premier investigator of occupational hazards in the U.S.. Her research (and advocacy) ranged over a number of industries and toxic substances. Her insights and investigative techniques broke new ground in the areas of worker and community health and anticipated the later interest in the occupational and environmental problems associated with such substances as heavy metals, solvents, and petroleum-based products. Forty years prior to the major environmental debates about the uses of science and technology and the nature of risk, Hamilton was already warning that workers were being used as "laboratory material" by industrial chemists who were introducing new products such as petrochemicals and petroleum distillates "about whose effect on human beings we know very little."[11] ...

Hamilton was also convinced that "control" techniques, such as respirators or other protective devices, were far from adequate, anticipating similar debates within OSHA (the Occupational Safety and

Health Administration) during the 1970s and 1980s. She focused on the impacts from low exposures from substances like lead, anticipating the "no acceptable threshold" argument about certain toxic substances. During debates over the decision by the automotive industry to introduce tetraethyl lead in gasoline during the 1920s, Hamilton became a key critic of the claim that the small amounts of lead involved were not significant.... The question of when environmental or public health factors needed to be considered was critical for Hamilton. "It makes me hope," Hamilton said of the tetraethyl lead controversy, "that the day is not far off when we shall take the next step and investigate a new danger in industry before it is put into use, before any fatal harm has been done to workmen... and the question will be treated as one belonging to the public health from the very outset, not after its importance has been demonstrated on the bodies of workmen."[12]

As her research began to receive attention, Hamilton's standing grew in an area that had largely failed to elicit interest in academic, industry, or government circles. In 1919, she was appointed assistant professor of industrial medicine at Harvard University following Harvard's decision to initiate a degree program in industrial hygiene. The appointment attracted attention since she was the first woman professor in any field at Harvard and the university did not admit women to its medical school. But Hamilton was chosen partly because there weren't any men interested in the position and the medical field and academic world in general still viewed occupational and environmental issues with little interest.

By the 1920s, with the publication of her classic text *Industrial Poisons in the United States*, her increasing prominence in issues of occupational and environmental health, and her participation in organizations like the Workers' Health Bureau, Alice Hamilton had become the country's most effective voice for exploring the environmental consequences of industrial activity. Her interest touched on issues of class, race, and gender in the workplace and the long-term hazards of the production system. A powerful environmental advocate in an era when the term had yet to be invented, Alice Hamilton must be seen as a core figure in the reconstruction of the urban and industrial roots of environmentalism.

Rachel Carson's Legacy

While Alice Hamilton provided a crucial link between work and environment, Rachel Carson, far more celebrated in the annals of environmentalism, anticipated, through her cautionary exploration of the world of synthetic pesticides,[13] a new language of environmental concern, linking urban and industrial issues with fears about the degradation of the natural environment. The publication of *Silent Spring* in 1962 and the ensuing controversy that made it an epochal event in the history of environmentalism can also be seen as helping launch a new era of environmental protest in which the idea of Nature under stress also began to be seen as a question of the quality of life.

Born in the small Western Pennsylvania town of Springdale on the Allegheny River, Rachel Carson as a young woman developed two related passions: nature writing and science research. While teaching biology courses in the evening, Carson took a job with the Bureau of U.S. Fisheries in the late 1930s, and began writing about undersea life. Though her first book, *Under the Sea Wind*, failed initially to generate interest, she continued her desire to write about the oceans and other science-based environmental topics. During the war, as editor of the Bureau of Fisheries publications, she became familiar with new research about the ocean environment which became the genesis of her first successful published book, *The Sea Around Us*.

The Sea Around Us combined Carson's knowledge of oceanography and marine biology, her concern for the harm that had been done to the sea and its life, and a readable style that made her work immediately accessible. The book was an extraordinary success, on the best seller list for eighty-six weeks, more than two million copies sold, and translated into thirty-two languages. Carson was not as surprised as some about the book's public reception and its indication of a popular interest in science. In accepting the National Book Award for *The Sea Around Us*, Carson defined this interest in science as reflecting daily life concerns. "Many people have commented on the fact that a work of science should have a large popular sale," she commented. "But this notion, that 'science' is something that belongs in a separate compartment of its own, apart from everyday life, is one that I should like to challenge. We live in a scientific age; yet we assume that knowledge is the prerogative of only a small number of human beings, isolated and priestlike in their laboratories. This is not true. The materials of science are the materials of life itself. Science is part of the reality of living; it is the what, the how, and the why in everything in our experience. It is impossible to understand man without understanding his environment and the forces that have molded him physically and mentally."[14]

Carson's environmental pursuit of "the what, the how, and the why" in daily experience also made her a logical candidate to investigate the most striking petrochemical success story of the postwar era. By the late 1950s, when she began her work on *Silent Spring*, pesticides had already become a fixture in both agricultural production and other commercial uses, having already fully supplanted all other pest control methods. Their use was of such magnitude that significant episodes of harm to wildlife and immediate health impacts on farmworkers began to be recorded throughout the country, although scientific and technical publications either ignored or dismissed those concerns.

For Carson, pesticides assumed significance as a defining environmental hazard of the post World War II industrial order. In an interview prior to the publication of *Silent Spring*, Carson told the *Washington Post* that while pesticide impacts were not directly equivalent to nuclear fallout, which she characterized as the major environmental hazard of the period, the two were still "interrelated, combining to render our environment progressively less fit to live in."[15] In a period when the question of pollution was only just beginning to receive significant public attention, Carson's research suggested that public health and the environment, human and natural environments, were inseparable. Her insistence that "expertise" had to be democratically grounded, that pesticide impacts were a public not a technical issue decided in expert arenas often subject to industry influence, anticipated later debates about the absence of the public's role in determining risk and in making choices about hazardous technologies. For Carson, natural and human environments were under siege from a science and a technology that had "armed itself with the most modern and terrible weapons." ... Through such writing, Carson sought to not only present information but convince her audience about a new kind of danger, to create in effect a new environmental consciousness.[16]

While sharply criticized by the chemical industry and other pro-industry commentators ... Carson's thesis about reducing pesticide use was even deemed controversial among certain members of conservationist groups. In letters to the *Sierra Club Bulletin*, for example, several Club members employed by the ag-chem industry complained that a favorable review of *Silent Spring* in the publication did not bode well "for the future of the Sierra Club as a leading influential force in furthering objectives of conservation."[18] Privately, Club executive director David Brower complained that some of the group's board members, including those tied to the chemical industry, remained skeptical of *Silent Spring*.[19]

The period following the release of the book was a difficult time for the shy and reserved nature writer who was also going through a debilitating bout with the cancer that caused her death eighteen months after *Silent Spring*'s publication. During this period, Carson continued to counter her critics by elaborating the key elements of her argument: that science and specialized technical knowledge had been divorced from any larger policy framework or public input; that "science" could be purchased and thus corrupted; that the rise of pesticides was indicative of "an era dominated by industry, in which the right to make money, at whatever cost to others, is seldom challenged;" and that the pesticide problem revealed how hazardous technologies could pollute both natural and human environments.[20]

Carson in fact had hoped to refine her core concept of interrelated eco-logical systems in a book about ecology that she was never able to complete, though her thesis would ultimately be developed by others, both analysts and activists. Thus, while an earlier critic of the chemical industry, Alice Hamilton, laid the groundwork for discussing environmental themes in an urban-industrial age, Rachel Carson, with her evocative cry against the silencing of the "robins, catbirds, doves, jays, wrens, and scores of other bird voices," brought to the fore questions about the urban and industrial order that an evolving environmentalism would soon need to face.

Interest Group or Social Movement?

Bob Marshall, Alice Hamilton, Rachel Carson: each serve as signposts for a broader, more inclusive interpretation of the roots of environmentalism. This interpretation situates environmentalism as a complex of social movements that first appeared in response to the rapid urbanization, industrialization, and closing of the frontier that launched the Progressive Era in the 1890s. Pressures on human and natural environments can then be seen as connected, integral to the urban and industrial order. The social and technological changes brought about by the Depression and World War II further stimulated environmentalist views. And if we see Earth Day 1970 not simply as the beginning of a new movement but as the culmin-ation of an era of protest and as prefiguring the different approaches within contemporary environmentalism, we can more fully explain the common-alities and differences of today's complex environmental claims....

Who ... will be able to speak for environmentalism in the 1990s and beyond? Will it be the mainstream groups with their big budgets, large staff, and interest group recognition? Can alternative groups, many of whom reject the term "environmentalist," lay claim to a tradition yet to be considered environmental? Can mainstream and alternative groups find a common language, a shared history, a common conceptual and organizational home?

The figures of Bob Marshall, Alice Hamilton, and Rachel Carson provide a clue. These compassionate, methodical, bitterly criticized figures, accused of being romantics and sentimentalists, biased research-ers and pseudo-scientists, opened up new ways of understanding what it meant to be concerned about human and natural environments. They were figures who transcended the limited discourse of their era, forcing their contemporaries to realize that much more was at stake than one damaged forest or one industrial poison or one dying bird. Their lan-guage was transformative, their environmentalism expressed in both daily life and ecological dimensions.

... How should environmentalism be defined ... ? Should we keep to the narrow definitions that have provided environmental legitimacy for some groups and ideas to the exclusion of others? To learn the lessons of Bob Marshall, Alice Hamilton, and Rachel Carson and how they are linked in their concern for the world we live in helps begin that process of redefining and reconstituting environmentalism in ... less narrow terms. ... It involves a redefinition that leads towards an environmentalism that is democratic and inclusive, an environmentalism of equity and social justice, an environmentalism of linked natural and human environments, an environmentalism of transformation. The complex and continuing history of this movement points the way towards these new possibilities of change.

Notes

1   Marshall's comments are from "Wilderness as Minority Right," an August 27, 1928 article for the *Service Bulletin* of the Forest Service, cited in *A Wilderness Original: The Life of Bob Marshall*, James M. Glover, The Mountaineers, Seattle, 1986, 96.

2   The "region which contains no permanent inhabitants" quote is from "The Problem of the Wilderness," Robert Marshall, *Scientific Monthly*, Vol. XXX, February 1930, 148; The "vast lonely expanse" quote is from *Arctic Village*, Robert Marshall, H. Smith & R. Haas, N. Y., 1933, 198; See also "Bob Marshall and the Alaska Arctic Wilderness," George Marshall, *The Living Wilderness*, Autumn 1970, Vol 34, No. 111, 29–32.

3   The "people can not live" quote is from "Recreational Limitations to Silviculture in the Adirondacks," Robert Marshall, *Journal of Forestry*, Vol. 23, No. 2, February 1925, 176. ...

4   Cited in *The Nation*, December 20, 1933, 696; The quotes from *The People's Forests* (Harrison Smith and Robert Haas, N. Y., 1933) can be found on 123, 211.

5   The quote, "there shall be no roads," is from a draft of a text for the Forest Service that Marshall prepared and is reproduced as "Protection at Last for Wilderness," in *The Living Wilderness*, July 1940, Vol. 5, No. 5, 3.

6   The Bauer/Marshall correspondence is described in *A Wilderness Original*, 218–219.

7   Murie sought to directly associate Marshall with this elite posture in his essay, "Wilderness Is For Those Who Appreciate," *The Living Wilderness*, July 1940, 5; On the redbaiting of Bob Marshall, see "Muddled Millions: Capitalist Angels of Left-Wing Propaganda," Benjamin Stolberg, *The Saturday Evening Post*, February 15, 1941, 9; "High Federal Aides Are Linked to Reds at House Hearing," *New York Times*, August 18, 1938; "WPA Union Called Communist Plan," *New York Times*, April 18, 1939.

8   The "here was a subject" quote is from *Exploring the Dangerous Trades: The Autobiography of Alice Hamilton, M. D.*, Little Brown, Boston, 1943, 115.

9   The "wash hands or scrub nails" quote is from *Exploring the Dangerous Trades*, 122. The concept of industrial lead poisoning "inevitability" is discussed in *The White Lead Industry in the United States, With an Appendix on the Lead-Oxide Industry*, Alice Hamilton, *Bulletin of the Bureau of Labor*, No. 95, Washington D.C., 1912, 190.

10 "It seemed natural and right" is a quote from *Exploring the Dangerous Trades*, 269; the duty "to the producer" quote is from *Industrial Poisons in the United States*, Alice Hamilton, The MacMillan Company, N.Y., 1925, 541.

11 The "laboratory material" quote is from *Exploring the Dangerous Trades*, 294; see also "The New Public Health," Alice Hamilton and Gertrude Seymour, *The Survey*, Vol. XXXVIII, No. 3, April 21, 1917, 59–62; "The Scope of the Problem of Industrial Hygiene," Alice Hamilton, *Public Health Reports*, October 20, 1922, Vol. 37, No. 42, 2604–2608.

12 "What Price Safety? Tetra-ethyl Lead Reveals a Flaw in our Defenses?" Alice Hamilton, *The Survey Midmonthly*, June 15, 1925, Vol. LIV, No. 6, 333.

13 *Silent Spring*, Rachel Carson, Fawcett Crest Edition, N.Y., January 1964.

14 Carson's National Book Award Acceptance Speech is reprinted in *The House of Life: Rachel Carson at Work*, Paul Brooks, Houghton Miflin, Boston, 1972, 127–129.

15 Cited in "Using a Plague to Fight a Plague," Loren Eiseley, *Saturday Review*, September 29, 1962, Vol. XLV, No. 39, 18.

16 *Silent Spring*, Rachel Carson, 262. . . .

17 The "thanks to a woman" quote is from "The Myth of the Pesticide Menace," Edwin Diamond, *Saturday Evening Post*, September 28, 1963, 16–18; The "priestess of nature" quote is from "A Noisy Reaction to Silent Spring," Clarence Cottam, *Sierra Club Bulletin*, January 1963, Vol. 48 No. 1, 4.

18 See Letters in the *Sierra Club Bulletin*, March 1963, 18 and the April–May 1963 issue as well.

19 David Brower, *For Earth's Sake: The Life and Times of David Brower* (Salt Lake Peregrine Smith Books, 1990), 215. . . .

20 Carson's statement is cited in "Silent Spring – III," *The New Yorker*, June 30, 1962, 67.

Documents

"Fallout: The Silent Killer"

Saturday Evening Post, August 29, 1959

The documents in this chapter will help us understand how the global conflict of the 1940s set the stage for new ways of thinking about nature, which was a necessary precondition for the environmental movement. Remember, environmentalism is related to the conservation movement, but ultimately quite different from it. The distinctions are many, but a key one was that while conservationists tended to see science and management as the key to protecting nature and integrating it with the needs of the populace, environmentalists were more suspicious of human abilities to manage nature, and generally more concerned with protecting it from human pollution. They tended to view science as a double-edged sword, capable of doing great good, but often destructive.

There was no greater stimulus to new thinking about nature and its fragility than World War II. The enormous government planning effort that the war required, its unprecedented demands for rapid industrial output, its vast appetite for human lives, and its culmination in the nuclear devastation of two Japanese cities left Americans with a profound sense of their own destructive powers and the fragility of the earth as a whole. Whereas environmental thinkers before the war often worried about preserving American nature, post-World War II thinkers were more concerned about the threat to the global environment. And, as we have observed above, they were less likely to think of human actions in nature as an unqualified good.

One of the reasons for the new environmental skepticism was to be found in the war's greatest technological feat, the harnessing of atomic power for purposes of mass destruction, and its long-term consequences as embodied in nuclear fallout. Fear of nuclear radiation was perhaps the most pervasive legacy of World War II. Beginning with studies of the effects of radiation on Japanese civilians at Hiroshima and Nagasaki, Americans became conscious of a new affliction on earth: radiation poisoning, which often resulted in cellular mutations leading to cancer and leukemia. With the Soviet Union's first successful nuclear test in 1949, the United States entered into a nuclear arms race which would last until the end of the Cold War four decades later. The threat of nuclear devastation hung over the 1950s like a cloud.

Periodic US explosions of nuclear weapons in the deserts of Nevada and in the Pacific Ocean, and Soviet testing in the steppes of Central Asia, led to widespread concern about peacetime nuclear fallout, in particular, strontium 90. This is a radioactive isotope which is blown high into the atmosphere with each explosion before settling to earth thousands of miles away. It turned up in milk (after cows ate it in grass and feed). Because the body chemistry recognizes strontium 90 as calcium, it is taken up into the bones and the teeth, and in the 1950s there was much discussion about the possibility of bone cancers and other maladies among the generation's children as a result of strontium 90 exposure from drinking contaminated milk, or simply breathing tiny amounts of fallout in the air.

These concerns were compounded by the national security context of bomb testing itself. Because government strategists perceived nuclear weapons as the key component of national defense, there was an enormous, often misinformed, and sometimes disingenuous campaign to reassure Americans about the safety of nuclear testing. Because nuclear explosions catapulted radioactive dust into the upper atmosphere, from where it descended around the world, concern about the effect of fallout was global.

In our first document for this section, *The Saturday Evening Post*, a popular weekly magazine, explores the dangers of fallout in a 1959 article. Note the anxiety that surrounds the long-term effects of strontium 90 on the nation's children, and the accompanying fears that government officials are not telling all they know about this issue. What does this article suggest about the impact of nuclear testing on the public's faith in government authorities? On the public's faith in scientists in general? And how did the insidiousness of the strontium 90 threat differ from previous environmental dangers? How is it similar to, or different from, the fear of cholera in nineteenth-century cities?

*   *   *

. . . The pervasive by-product of weapons testing now blankets the entire planet. It contaminates the air, the sea and the soil. It lies twice as thick over the Northern Hemisphere as the Southern, and is more heavily concentrated in the United States than anywhere else on the earth's surface. And every living creature, man included, has in its body a few particles of radioactive strontium 90, some of which will remain for life.

Moreover, the fallout will get worse before it gets better, even if bomb tests are never resumed. The spring of 1959, contrary to some of the forecasts, was radioactively the "hottest" yet, due in large part to the Russian tests of last fall. Scientists estimate that the burden of accumulated bomb debris now floating in the stratosphere, seven to ten miles up, is so great that "drip-out" to the ground will actually increase for seven or eight years before it begins to taper off.

Upon these basic facts of fallout the experts are in fair agreement. But there is sharp and disturbing disagreement among them, and among Government officials, members of Congress and plain ordinary citizens, as to what the fallout figures mean in terms of hazard to the present and future populations of the world.

How concerned should we be, then, about the amounts of radioactivity in the air we breathe, the water we drink, the food we eat, the milk we give our babies and growing children? Is fallout partly responsible for the reported rise in leukemia? Is it also inducing other forms of cancer? Will it shorten our lives through subtle, nonspecific effects, as laboratory-applied radiation has shortened the lives of mice?

And what about the genetic effects? Are we now, without knowing it, sowing bad seed that will cause an increased number of physical and mental defectives to be born to future generations? And finally, are the biological risks, no matter how small or large, worth taking as the cost of developing bigger, cheaper or more "discriminating" nuclear weapons?

Such questions do not lend themselves to quick, precise answers. No scientific issue in many years has so exasperatingly eluded all efforts to lay hands upon the truth. But the public, paying out its tax billions for the bomb tests and the study of their troublesome debris, deserves more understandable answers than it has received.

Moreover, the public's understanding is not improved by semantic efforts to put a benign face on the atom with such "happy" terms as Project Sunshine, the AEC's original name for the fallout-measuring program. One scientist suggested this may have been chosen to counter-act the gloomy impact of an earlier Project Gabriel. In any event, fallout has no more positive connection with sunshine and health than does the bomb itself.

The citizen is more bewildered by reading on one day a warning headline: ATOM TEST RATE CALLED PERILOUS, and on the following morning a reassuring one: STUDY MINIMIZES FALLOUT DANGER. Both appeared in the same newspaper, the trustworthy *New York Times*, and both articles were accurate accounts of testimony at hearings on fallout from nuclear-weapons tests, held last May by the radiation subcommit-tee of the Joint Congressional Committee on Atomic Energy.

The subject's frustrating uncertainties were expressed more specific-ally in testimony of Dr. Charles L. Dunham, director of the Atomic Energy Commission's Division of Biology and Medicine. He was dis-cussing the question of strontium 90, which is deposited, like calcium, in the bones, especially the growing bones of children. "It is possible," Doctor Dunham said, "that the average body burden of strontium ninety in young children over much of the United States could rise to ten units as a result of fallout from weapons testing to date. . . . Bearing these dose estimates in mind, one can on the basis of one current theory estimate a maximum number of fifty to one hundred additional cases of bone cancer per year in the next seventy years, and for leukemia as much as double that number." Then he added, "Of course, there may be no additional cases at all, as the United Nations Scientific Committee was so careful to point out." . . .

The cloudy state of fallout information has long been a topic of critical comment in Congress and in the press, and the blame has usually been placed on the Atomic Energy Commission. Even the commission's own General Advisory Committee recently noted that while the AEC had "released all significant fallout data to other agencies and to the public . . . promptly and completely," the release had "not always been in a form readily understood by the public."

"As a result," the Advisory Committee continued, "the public has been confused about the status of fallout and its implications. There is real need for clear, simple exposition of the facts of fallout in media widely available to the public. We feel that the commission should assume this responsibility. It should be clearly explained to the public that weapons tests have been an essential part of our effort to prevent the occurrence of nuclear war."

That clearer information is needed no one will deny. But there is doubt that a completely unbiased picture should be expected from an agency which, in origin and spirit, is so closely allied to the Defense Department. Wedded to atomic weapons as the main safeguard of peace, it is apt to weigh radioactive hazards by a different scale of values than do those who see the atomic-arms contests as a senseless gallop toward human extinction.

This brings us to the core of the controversy that has kept the public in such a state of confusion. For its picture of fallout the public has had to rely upon the interpretation of fragmentary data by authorities with different viewpoints and policies. They can make the picture dark or light, depending on how they mix emphasis and adjectives with facts that are, at best, incomplete. They can even omit a detail here and there, by accident or for the sake of over-all effect.

What it all boils down to is a question of human risk versus military risk. The United States is faced with the necessity of weighing a definite but as yet unmeasurable hazard against an uncertain benefit. The hazard is that continued nuclear testing – and perhaps even the testing we have already done – will create more physical and mental defectives within the world's future population, and possibly even some cancer or life-shortening in the present generations. The uncertain benefit is that testing will discourage Russia from attacking us. . . .

Actually, radioactivity has been with us from the beginning of life on this planet, a force generated by cosmic rays from outer space and by rocks in the earth's crust. But we were unaware of its existence or its power for good and evil until that remarkable period of 1895–98 when in quick succession Wilhelm Konrad Roentgen produced X rays, Henri Becquerel discovered the natural radioactivity of uranium salts, and Marie and Pierre Curie isolated and identified radium. Almost immediately the early workers with these rays found they would irritate and burn the skin. Later they discovered that the damage could produce cancer; a number of pioneer radiologists lost fingers and lives. In the 1920's radium-dial painters in several plants began to die of bone cancer resulting from tipping their brushes with their lips and swallowing minute amounts of radium.

. . . Distant fallout did occur with the very first atomic explosion, the historic test blast at Alamogordo, New Mexico, on July 16, 1945, but the only people who complained about it were officials of the Eastman

Kodak Company, where a batch of new X-ray film got mysteriously fogged. The trouble was eventually traced to strawboard packaging, made in Vincennes, Indiana, in a process which used Wabash River water apparently contaminated by fallout from the blast.

Alerted by this experience, Eastman set up Geiger counters to monitor not only its wrapping department but the water used in manufacturing and developing. For the next several years no more film was ruined by fallout, in spite of the gradual step-up of the United States testing program – the first Bikini shots in 1946, the Eniwetok series in 1948.

Then in January of 1951 the big Nevada program got under way. Within a few days of the opening shot the instruments at the Eastman plant in Rochester, New York, buzzed a warning. What had set them off was a fresh snowfall, apparently seasoned with atomic dust from Yucca Flat, 2500 miles away.

Thanks to the warning and to adequate filtration of water and air, no film was damaged; but a call went immediately to the Atomic Energy Commission's Health and Safety Laboratory in New York City. The snow covered much of the Eastern United States. . . .

It was now apparent from the analysis of the 1951 "snow-out" that atomic debris not only fell in the immediate vicinity of "ground zero" but could drift thousands of miles across the country and be brought down by precipitation. The New York laboratory, which had been devoting much of its work to safety problems at atomic plants, therefore began to put more emphasis on sampling. By the fall of 1951 it was collecting rainfall and natural background data from more than 200 localities.

During the Nevada series Merril Eisenbud, manager of the AEC's New York Operations Office and today one of the most informed men in the field of atomic radioactivity, was on hand to monitor a shallow underground shot.

"From what we observed in that test," he told me, "we got a strong notion of what might happen if an H-bomb exploded close to the surface, and we were really concerned about the radioactivity aspects, although our predictions didn't agree. Several of us thought the local fallout from the large bombs would be hazardous, and others figured the explosive force would be so great it would blast everything high into the stratosphere and right on out into space."

As later events proved, the superbombs blast the debris into the stratosphere all right, but not on out into space. After a stratospheric "residence time," first estimated at about ten years but now though to be more like four or five, the ashes fall back to earth.

By 1954 the AEC was aware that worldwide fallout measurements would be essential to a full understanding of atomic bomb effects. Since much of the debris from the Pacific tests would drop into the ocean, various schemes were devised for catching it.

"We irradiated iron filings at the Brookhaven National Laboratory," Mr. Eisenbud related, "and dropped them on oil slicks in the Atlantic to see if we could count fallout that way. All we got was seasick. Then on March first, nineteen fifty-four, we were called off that assignment because the shot that exposed the Japanese fishing boat *Lucky Dragon* had given us a lot of new information. It was a very important accident."

It was, indeed. In fact, the fallout behavior of that monster bomb, rated at the equivalent of 15,000,000 tons of TNT, caught the experts way off base. Boldly named Bravo, the test brought more embarrassment than applause. It wiped out an island and tore a great hole in the ocean floor, about as planned. But its radioactive cloud, which meteorologists predicted would drift west from ground zero, soared unexpectedly high into the atmosphere, met a west wind and was blown east. The "hot" ashes fell not only on the luckless fishermen of the *Lucky Dragon* . . . but also on 239 natives of the Marshall Islands, on twenty-eight Americans at weather stations on the island of Rongerik, and on nine scientists in a control blockhouse twenty miles from the firing point. The fishermen were seriously injured – one died – and many of the Marshallese experienced radiation burns, loss of hair and prolonged anemia. The scientists were protected by the blockhouse walls, but still took fairly high doses. . . . It was bad enough that the bomb, twice as powerful as predicted, had dumped its ashes to the east instead of the west. What was more alarming was the size and intensity of the local fallout zone, although a year passed before the United States Atomic Energy Commission released these disturbing details. On February 15, 1955, it announced that "there was sufficient radioactivity in a downwind belt about 140 miles in length and of varying width up to twenty miles to have seriously threatened the lives of nearly all persons in the area who did not take protective measures" and that "about 7000 square miles of territory downwind from the point of burst was so contaminated that survival *might* have depended upon prompt evacuation of the area or upon taking shelter and other protective measures." Actually the people on the Marshall Islands and the United States test personnel were evacuated promptly. . . .

But the most important consequence of the Bravo shot, from the standpoint of better understanding of fallout, was the impetus it gave to the study of worldwide spread of the bomb debris. Cloud-tracking observations and reports from surface ships and ground stations had revealed that the ashes from this multimillion-ton detonation had completely encircled the earth. This finding gave rise to several key questions. How high did the debris go? If it entered the stratosphere, which starts at about 40,000 feet, how much of it got there? How was it distributed and how long would it stay? Would it remain in this lofty reservoir long enough, as some experts predicted, to lose much of its harmful radioactivity? . . .

From Rachel Carson, *Silent Spring*

Reprinted from *Silent Spring* (Boston: Houghton Mifflin, 1962)

Ultimately, fears about nuclear radiation would diminish after 1963, when the USA and the Soviet Union signed an agreement to ban above-ground nuclear testing (although to this day other powers continue to test weapons above ground on occasion). Still, the threat of instant incineration in a nuclear blast became an enduring feature of the Cold War years, serving as a constant reminder to the public that human beings had the potential to destroy the earth, and thereby heightening a new environmental consciousness.

In many ways, concern about fallout precipitated anxieties about other technological wonders. World War II had seen new applications of chemicals to improve human health and control over insect pests. One of the most promising of these was dichloro-diphenyl-trichloro-ethane, or DDT, an insecticide which was applied to American soldiers in Italy as part of a delousing campaign to avert a typhus epidemic. The effort was credited with saving tens of thousands of soldiers. After World War II, until the early 1970s, DDT was used to spray people, crops, swamps, and virtually any other possible zone of infestation by insect pests.

In the 1950s, Rachel Carson, a biologist, bird-watcher, and popular nature writer (her book *The Sea Around Us* had been translated into 35 languages), became concerned over multiple reports of diminishing bird populations. Research led her to connect these reports and a host of other potential dangers to the impact of insecticides, especially DDT. She published her findings in 1962, in *Silent Spring*, the book that would make her world famous as an environmental reformer. If modern environmentalism can be said to have begun with one book, *Silent Spring* is it. The book kicked off a popular campaign to ban DDT, which was finally accomplished in 1974. In this excerpt from Carson's classic, note how her assessment of DDT's impact on human beings and the larger environment draws on popular conceptions of radioactive fallout. Would it have been possible to write the way Carson did, and for a mass audience, if the public had not been familiar with the threat of radioactive fallout?

*   *   *

For the first time in the history of the world, every human being is now subjected to contact with dangerous chemicals, from the moment of conception until death. In the less than two decades of their use, the synthetic pesticides have been so thoroughly distributed throughout the animate and inanimate world that they occur virtually everywhere. They have been recovered from most of the major river systems and even from streams of groundwater flowing unseen through the earth. Residues of these chemicals linger in soil to which they may have been applied a dozen years before. They have entered and lodged in the bodies of fish, birds, reptiles, and domestic and wild animals so universally that scientists carrying on animal experiments find it almost impossible to locate subjects free from such contamination. They have been found in fish in remote mountain lakes, in earthworms burrowing in soil, in the eggs of birds – and in man himself. For these chemicals are now stored in the bodies of the vast majority of human beings, regardless of age. They occur in the mother's milk, and probably in the tissues of the unborn child.

All this has come about because of the sudden rise and prodigious growth of an industry for the production of man-made or synthetic chemicals with insecticidal properties. This industry is a child of the Second World War. In the course of developing agents of chemical warfare, some of the chemicals created in the laboratory were found to be lethal to insects. The discovery did not come by chance: insects were widely used to test chemicals as agents of death for man.

The result has been a seemingly endless stream of synthetic insecticides. In being man-made – by ingenious laboratory manipulation of the molecules, substituting atoms, altering their arrangement – they differ sharply from the simpler inorganic insecticides of prewar days. These were derived from naturally occurring minerals and plant products. . . .

What sets the new synthetic insecticides apart is their enormous biological potency. They have immense power not merely to poison but to enter into the most vital processes of the body and change them in sinister and often deadly ways. Thus, as we shall see, they destroy the very enzymes whose function is to protect the body from harm, they block the oxidation processes from which the body receives its energy, they prevent the normal functioning of various organs, and they may initiate in certain cells the slow and irreversible change that leads to malignancy.

Yet new and more deadly chemicals are added to the list each year and new uses are devised so that contact with these materials has become practically worldwide. The production of synthetic pesticides in the United States soared from 124,259,000 pounds in 1947 to 637,666,000 pounds in 1960 – more than a fivefold increase. The wholesale value of these products was well over a quarter of a billion dollars. But in the plans and hopes of the industry this enormous production is only a beginning.

A Who's Who of pesticides is therefore of concern to us all. If we are going to live so intimately with these chemicals – eating and drinking them, taking them into the very marrow of our bones – we had better know something about their nature and their power. . . .

DDT (short for dichloro-diphenyl-trichloro-ethane) was first synthesized by a German chemist in 1874, but its properties as an insecticide were not discovered until 1939. Almost immediately DDT was hailed as a means of stamping out insect-borne disease and winning the farmers' war against crop destroyers overnight. The discoverer, Paul Müller of Switzerland, won the Nobel Prize.

DDT is now so universally used that in most minds the product takes on the harmless aspect of the familiar. Perhaps the myth of the harmlessness of DDT rests on the fact that one of its first uses was the wartime dusting of many thousands of soldiers, refugees, and prisoners, to combat lice. It is widely believed that since so many people came into extremely intimate contact with DDT and suffered no immediate ill effects the chemical must certainly be innocent of harm. This understandable misconception arises from the fact that – unlike other chlorinated hydrocarbons – DDT *in powder form* is not readily absorbed through the skin. Dissolved in oil, as it usually is, DDT is definitely toxic. If swallowed, it is absorbed slowly through the digestive tract; it may also be absorbed through the lungs. Once it has entered the body it is stored largely in organs rich in fatty substances (because DDT itself is fat-soluble) such as the adrenals, testes, or thyroid. Relatively large amounts are deposited in the liver, kidneys, and the fat of the large, protective mesenteries that enfold the intestines.

This storage of DDT begins with the smallest conceivable intake of the chemical (which is present as residues on most food stuffs) and continues until quite high levels are reached. The fatty storage depots act as biological magnifiers, so that an intake of as little as $\frac{1}{10}$ of 1 part per million in the diet results in storage of about 10 to 15 parts per million, an increase of one hundredfold or more. These terms of reference, so commonplace to the chemist or the pharmacologist, are unfamiliar to most of us. One part in a million sounds like a very small amount – and so it is. But such substances are so potent that a minute quantity can bring about vast changes in the body. In animal experiments, 3 parts per million has been found to inhibit an essential enzyme in heart muscle; only 5 parts per million has brought about necrosis or disintegration of liver cells; only 2.5 parts per million of the closely related chemicals dieldrin and chlordane did the same.

This is really not surprising. In the normal chemistry of the human body there is just such a disparity between cause and effect. For example, a quantity of iodine as small as two ten-thousandths of a gram spells the difference between health and disease. Because these small amounts of pesticides are cumulatively stored and only slowly excreted, the threat of chronic poisoning and degenerative changes of the liver and other organs is very real.

Scientists do not agree upon how much DDT can be stored in the human body. Dr. Arnold Lehman, who is the chief pharmacologist of the Food and Drug Administration, says there is neither a floor below which DDT is not absorbed nor a ceiling beyond which absorption and storage ceases. On the other hand, Dr. Wayland Hayes of the United States Public Health Service contends that in every individual a point of equilibrium is reached, and that DDT in excess of this amount is excreted. For practical purposes it is not particularly important which of these men is right. Storage in human beings has been well investigated, and we know that the average person is storing potentially harmful amounts. According to various studies, individuals with no known exposure (except the inevitable dietary one) store an average of 5.3 parts per million to 7.4 parts per million; agricultural workers 17.1 parts per million; and workers in insecticide plants as high as 648 parts per million! So the range of proven storage is quite wide and, what is even more to the point, the minimum figures are above the level at which damage to the liver and other organs or tissues may begin.

One of the most sinister features of DDT and related chemicals is the way they are passed on from one organism to another through all the links of the food chains. For example, fields of alfalfa are dusted with DDT; meal is later prepared from the alfalfa and fed to hens; the hens lay eggs which contain DDT. Or the hay, containing residues of 7 to 8 parts per million, may be fed to cows. The DDT will turn up in the milk in the amount of about 3 parts per million, but in butter made from this milk the concentration may run to 65 parts per million. Through such a process of transfer, what started out as a very small amount of DDT may end as a heavy concentration. Farmers nowadays find it difficult to obtain uncontaminated fodder for their milk cows, though the Food and Drug Administration forbids the presence of insecticide residues in milk shipped in interstate commerce.

The poison may also be passed on from mother to offspring. Insecticide residues have been recovered from human milk in samples tested by Food and Drug Administration scientists. This means that the breast-fed human infant is receiving small but regular additions to the load of toxic chemicals building up in his body. It is by no means his first exposure, however: there is good reason to believe this begins while he is still in the womb. In experimental animals the chlorinated hydrocarbon insecticides freely cross the barrier of the placenta, the traditional protective shield between the embryo and harmful substances in the mother's body. While the quantities so received by human infants would normally be small, they are not unimportant because children are more susceptible to poisoning than adults. This situation also means that today the average individual almost certainly starts life with the first deposit of the growing load of chemicals his body will be required to carry thenceforth.

All these facts – storage at even low levels, subsequent accumulation, and occurrence of liver damage at levels that may easily occur in normal diets, caused Food and Drug Administration scientists to declare as early as 1950 that it is "extremely likely the potential hazard of DDT has been underestimated." There has been no such parallel situation in medical history. No one yet knows what the ultimate consequences may be.

The Air Pollution Control Act (1955), and the Clean Air Act, with amendments (2001)

At the same time that concern was growing over fallout and pesticides, lawmakers were responding to public demands for action to redress new threats of urban air pollution. The explosion in car ownership after World War II helped increase exhaust emissions at a rapid rate, resulting in smog problems for many cities. California passed some of the earliest clean air legislation in 1947, and with the federal Air Pollution Control Act of 1955, (since renamed the "Clean Air Act," and amended many times), the nation began a long-term effort to control auto and factory emissions and guarantee healthy air. The Clean Air Act has thus been a staple of environmental legislation for almost fifty years. (If you want a sense of how effective it has been, flip ahead to the graph on p. 344.)

Compare the Air Pollution Control Act of 1955 with the beginnings of the federal Clean Air Act as it appeared, after numerous amendments, in 2001. How has the preamble of the act changed its focus? Why is the Surgeon General the central presence in the earlier legislation? In what ways do the changes in the later act's focus speak better to your own concerns about smog than the earlier act?

An Act

To provide research and technical assistance relating to air pollution control.

Be it enacted by the Senate and House of Representatives of the United States of America in Congress assembled, That in recognition of the dangers to the public health and welfare, injury to agricultural crops and live-stock, damage to and deterioration of property, and hazards to air and ground transportation, from air pollution, it is hereby declared to be the policy of Congress to preserve and protect the primary responsibilities and rights of the States and local governments in controlling air pollu-tion, to support and aid technical research to devise and develop methods of abating such pollution, and to provide Federal technical services and financial aid to State and local government air pollution control agencies and other public or private agencies and institutions in the formulation and execution of their air pollution abatement research programs. To this end, the Secretary of Health, Education, and Welfare and the Surgeon General of the Public Health Service (under the super-vision and direction of the Secretary of Health, Education, and Welfare) shall have the authority relating to air pollution control vested in them respectively by this Act.

SEC. 2. (a) The Surgeon General is authorized, after careful investi-gation and in cooperation with other Federal agencies, with State and local government air pollution control agencies, with other public and private agencies and institutions, and with the industries involved, to prepare or recommend research programs for devising and developing methods for eliminating or reducing air pollution. For the purpose of this subsection the Surgeon General is authorized to make joint investi-gations with any such agencies or institutions.

(b) The Surgeon General may (1) encourage cooperative activities by State and local governments for the prevention and abatement of air pollution: (2) collect and disseminate information relating to air pollu-tion and the prevention and abatement thereof; (3) conduct in the Public Health Service, and support and aid the conduct by State and local government air pollution control agencies, and other public and private agencies and institutions of, technical research to devise and develop methods of preventing and abating air pollution; and (4) make available to State and local government air pollution control agencies, other public and private agencies and institutions, and industries, the results of surveys, studies, investigations, research, and experiments relating to air pollution and the prevention and abatement thereof.

SEC.3. The Surgeon General may, upon request of any State or local government air pollution control agency, conduct investigations and research and make surveys concerning any specific problem of air pollu-tion confronting such State or local government air pollution control agency with a view to recommending a solution of such problem.

SEC.4. The Surgeon General shall prepare and publish from time to time reports of such surveys, studies, investigations, research, and ex-periments made under the authority of this Act as he may consider desirable, together with appropriate recommendations with regard to the control of air pollution.

SEC.5. (a) There is hereby authorized to be appropriated to the Department of Health. Education, and Welfare for each of the five fiscal years during the period beginning July 1, 1955, and ending June 30, 1960, not to exceed $5,000,000 to enable it to carry out its functions under this Act and, in furtherance of the policy declared in the first section of this Act, to (1) make grants-in-aid to State and local government air pollution control agencies, and other public and private agencies and institutions, and to individuals, for research, training, and demonstration projects, and (2) enter into contracts with public and private agencies and institutions and individuals for research, training, and demonstration projects. . . .

Clean Air Act as amended (2001)
42 U.S.C. § 7401 et seq.

TITLE I AIR POLLUTION PREVENTION AND CONTROL

SHORT TITLE

42 USC 7401 Note
Sec. 317

This act may be cited as the "Clean Air Act."

PART A Air Quality and Emission Limitations

FINDINGS AND PURPOSES

42 USC 7401
Sec. 101

(a) The Congress finds –

  (1) that the predominant part of the Nation's population is located in its rapidly expanding metropolitan and other urban areas, which generally cross the boundary lines of local jurisdictions and often extend into two or more States;

  (2) that the growth in the amount and complexity of air pollution brought about by urbanization, industrial development, and the increasing use of motor vehicles, has resulted in mounting dangers to the public health and welfare, including injury to

agricultural crops and livestock, damage to and the deterioration of property, and hazards to air and ground transportation;

(3) that air pollution prevention (that is, the reduction or elimination, through any measures, of the amount of pollutants produced or created at the source) and air pollution control at its source is the primary responsibility of States and local governments; and

(4) that Federal financial assistance and leadership is essential for the development of cooperative Federal, State, regional, and local programs to prevent and control air pollution.

(b) The purposes of this title are –

(1) to protect and enhance the quality of the Nation's air resources so as to promote the public health and welfare and the productive capacity of its population;

(2) to initiate and accelerate a national research and development program to achieve the prevention and control of air pollution;

(3) to provide technical and financial assistance to State and local governments in connection with the development and execution of their air pollution prevention and control programs; and

(4) to encourage and assist the development and operation of regional air pollution prevention and control programs.

(c) Pollution Prevention. – A primary goal of this Act is to encourage or otherwise promote reasonable Federal, State, and local governmental actions, consistent with the provisions of this Act, for pollution prevention.

10

Environmental Protection and the Environmental Movement

By the late 1960s, American politicians were beginning to address pervasive concerns about global destruction and insidious environmental threats like radiation, pesticides, and air pollution. Again, the environmental movement that emerged in the late 1960s and early 1970s was different in crucial ways from the conservation movement. Whereas conservationists sought greater control over natural resources in order to use them better, environmentalists more often sought greater restraint in the use of nature, and even a revolution in thinking about it. Conservationists emphasized *production* of natural resources like water, timber, and game through better management of them; environmentalists emphasized *consumption* of nature, and were less convinced that manipulating nature through dams or forest management could ensure the vitality of natural systems.

It is one of the great ironies of environmental history, and a sign of the enormous public support for environmental legislation, that a president with little personal interest in environmentalism would preside over some of its greatest victories. Richard Nixon, a former Republican senator and vice-president with few if any environmental achievements to his credit, was elected President at the height of the Vietnam War, in 1968. As we see in this excerpt from the book *Nixon and the Environment* by J. Brooks Flippen, Nixon was most determined that his Democratic rivals not gain the upper hand by endorsing popular environmental legislation. Like most presidents, Nixon included among his primary goals the shoring up of a broad voter base against possible opponents in the next election. As he saw it, his two most likely future rivals for the presidency were Edmund Muskie, the Democratic Senator from Maine, and Henry "Scoop" Jackson, Democratic Senator from the state of Washington. Both these men were so eager to be seen as pre-eminent environmentalists that they competed with each other to write the strongest environmental legislation possible. Nixon's strategy for outflanking them was to endorse stronger legislation than either of them had envisioned. The result was the stunning passage of the National Environmental Policy Act of 1969.

The reading that follows is in two sections. The first part takes us to the first Earth Day, in April 1970. We explore the rising tide of public environmental concern that brought it about, and the dilemmas this movement posed for the new Nixon administration. The second part of this material takes us back to the year before Earth Day, 1969, and shows how the groundswell of support for environmental protection led to new government policy. Nixon and his rivals competed for the environmental movement's approval, with the result that the National Environmental Policy Act of 1969 (NEPA) became much more aggressive than any of its originators, Democrat or Republican, had intended. The act created the Council on Environmental Quality, but it also included a provision which none of its sponsors noticed: a requirement that any new government project must submit an Environmental Impact Statement (EIS) to assess the project's likely environmental effects. In years to come, this would become the primary tool of environmentalists for slowing or stopping government projects that were environmentally controversial. In your mind, who deserves the credit (or blame) for NEPA's passage: Nixon, his Democratic rivals, or the public? If no politician envisioned the far-reaching impact of the EIS provision, can any of them be credited or blamed for it?

Richard Nixon and the Triumph of Environmentalism

J. Brooks Flippen

"A Wholesale Change in Values"

It was one of the largest demonstrations in American history – an odd gathering of businessmen, housewives, college students, children, workers, and radical antiestablishment militants. Indeed, the amazing turnout represented every strata of American society. In New York, over 100,000 people participated in festivities in Union Square. In Washington, thousands gathered on the mall. In cities from Philadelphia to Los Angeles, a citizenry often divided over issues such as the Vietnam War, racial desegregation, and the economy united in an event part celebration and part earnest protest.

In recent years Earth Day earns only scant notice from an apathetic and preoccupied American public. The first Earth Day on April 22, 1970, however, was different – a significant event in American history and one worthy of the tremendous attention it received. Drawing an estimated twenty million participants and involving over ten thousand schools and two thousands colleges and universities, the first Earth Day and its surprising success represented in many respects the emergence of a powerful new environmentalism. Since the days of President Theodore Roosevelt many Americans had recognized the need to use resources judiciously. They had appreciated that America's natural bounty had limits, and long since had adopted the basic wise-use doctrine of conservation. The many participants of the first Earth Day, however, had broader concerns. They realized that the unrestrained urbanization and industrialization characteristic of the nation's post–World War II economic boom mandated more than the simple need to use natural resources wisely. It demanded broader protection for overall environmental quality, protection for the intrinsic condition of the nation's air, water, and land. Expanding upon the tradition of Progressive-era preservationists, these new environmentalists viewed the earth as an ecosystem with humanity only a part, a part that nevertheless threatened the whole.

The magnitude of the first Earth Day – the apparent breadth of public concern – surprised many observers, for the problems on which the demonstration focused had multiplied rather suddenly, paralleling the nation's rapid postwar economic growth. In the decade and a half after the conclusion of hostilities, the United States emerged as the "affluent society," in the words of Harvard economist John Kenneth Galbraith.[1] By 1960, the nation's population had increased by thirty-five million, with the population growth approaching that of India. The census that year reported a population of 180 million, almost a 20 percent increase over the previous decade. The gross national product was 500 million dollars, more than double the 200 million dollar GNP in 1945. The median family income approached fifty-seven hundred dollars, an increase of almost 50 percent adjusted for inflation.

This growth had a tremendous impact on the way Americans regarded their environment. Rising standards of living allowed more recreational time as well as greater discretionary income. Americans had more time for qualitative experiences along with material necessities, and thus they possessed the means for a greater appreciation of environmental amenities. A host of new appliances appeared on the market – automatic washing machines and dryers, dishwashers, waste disposal units, power lawn mowers, and many others – all significantly reducing the time necessary for normal domestic chores. At the same time the average work week declined from forty-four to almost forty hours. The result was a boom in the recreation business. The making and servicing of pleasure boats, camping equipment, sporting goods, and hunting and fishing gear became multimillion-dollar businesses. Americans purchased almost four million pleasure boats in the 1950s alone. In short, they now had the opportunity to enjoy the outdoors as never before.

The growth in automobile ownership made a retreat to more natural surroundings much easier. From 1945 to 1960 the number of cars increased by 133 percent. Middle-class America now meant two cars, each successive model longer and wider, with more gadgets and bigger fins. The government did its share to facilitate easy access to nature, passing the massive Highway Act of 1956, which provided for thirty-three billion dollars to construct over forty-one thousand miles of new inter-state roads. Vacations in the country were no longer the exclusive domain of the super-wealthy. Although few Americans yet saw the recreation business itself as a threat, most Americans now realized that the environ-ment offered more than simply the extraction of natural resources.

America's phenomenal growth following the Second World War did more than stir a new-found appreciation of nature. It also noticeably began to affect overall environmental quality, to erode the very intrinsic value of nature that Americans were just learning to appreciate. The expansion of the population and economy contributed to massive sub-urbanization. In time, this growth brought more than simply a comfort-able lifestyle; it also brought unforeseen environmental consequences.

Suburbs were not new to America. Satellite communities had grown around American urban centers since the days of horsecars and trolleys. The new migration after the Second World War, however, dwarfed these earlier movements. Mass produced and prefabricated, and best repre-sented by the Levittown community on Long Island, suburbs offered affordable homes away from the problems of inner cities. After fifteen years of depression and war, America had a severe housing shortage. Together with the spread of the automobile, the new suburbs offered a solution. During the 1950s, suburbs grew six times faster than estab-lished cities, with a total of eighteen million new suburbanites. By 1960, one-quarter of Americans lived in such suburban homes. Americans now spoke of a "megalopolis" to describe the miles of sprawling single-family homes that surrounded established urban centers.

The new suburbanite, however, faced a cruel paradox in his or her existence. Economic growth had made suburban life possible, but it also threatened the amenities that he or she had sought in the first place. Landowners, real estate developers, financial institutions, and utility companies all fostered more intensive use of land. Local governments joined in with the hope of securing more tax revenue from higher land values. Two-lane roads became four-lane roads and shopping centers replaced open fields. By 1960, over two thousand shopping centers had sprung up in previously undeveloped land. Billboards, part of the growth of the advertising industry during the same period, soon blighted what natural beauty remained. Suburbia had become in many ways just like the urban areas from which it grew.

The nation's growth contributed to the deterioration of environmental quality in other ways. In many areas construction of waste-treatment centers did not keep pace with the greater population density. This meant that many communities simply dumped raw sewage into nearby rivers and lakes, magnifying the problem of water pollution. The dumping of such sewage led to eutrophication, the overfertilization of water plants. The resulting algal growth blocked the sun from deeper plants, whose subsequent death and decay eliminated the remaining oxygen in the water. This ensured the death of any aquatic wildlife, including fish. In time, the water was devoid of all life, its ecosystem destroyed.

More people and more suburbs often meant more waste, more trash. Municipal waste – residential, commercial, and institutional refuse – constituted millions of tons a year, the elimination of which composed a municipal expense that only education and roads surpassed. During the 1950s, Americans, with their appetite for automobiles, junked almost as many cars per year as they manufactured. Most communities disposed of their waste in city dumps, incinerators, or landfills. Open dumps contributed to disease, contaminating the surrounding water tables, while municipal incinerators often lacked even the most rudimentary pollution-control equipment. Although they were the best alternative, sanitary landfills were the most expensive, and rarely did municipalities allocate adequate funds.

The greatest threat to the quality of the nation's air, however, was not municipal waste, but the growth of the automobile so crucial to the development of suburban life. The internal combustion engine produced unhealthy levels of hydrocarbons, carbon monoxide, and nitrogen oxide vehicular-exhaust emissions. In certain urban areas on hot days the result was a gray, choking haze, air pollution that decreased visibility and irritated eyes. Residents in the rapidly growing community of Los Angeles soon coined a term for this nasty vapor – *smog*, an amalgam of smoke and fog – a term Americans throughout the country soon recognized and adopted.

The automobile was not the only culprit. The electric-power industry, together with other heavy industry, also contributed. America needed her heavy industry to construct suburbia, and it, in turn, needed its electricity; both saw a significant increase in the 1950s. Most of these industries burned fossil fuels, and in doing so contributed to the problem. The burning of oil, gas, and coal released particulate matter and sulfur oxide into the air. This produced an acrid yellow gas, especially from those plants burning high-sulfur coal. Many large industrial cities had reeked with this foul stench since the dawn of the Industrial Revolution, but in the postwar years the problem only compounded, much to the chagrin of the nearby populace.

This manifold threat to the nation's environmental quality – the complex problems facing America's air, water, and land in the postwar world – ensured a popular protest for adequate reform. It was not until the 1960s, however, that the problems worsened to the point that any significant national movement emerged, a movement that ultimately culminated in the first Earth Day in 1970. In 1962, a former researcher for U.S. Fish and Wildlife Service, Rachel Carson, published *Silent Spring*, a text that bemoaned the environmental impact of indiscriminate insecticide use, but had ramifications far beyond the agricultural community. Carson shocked many Americans with her warning that the impetuous pace of human development threatened the natural world. Quickly a best-seller, *Silent Spring* arguably opened the eyes of the American public to the problems that accompanied the prosperity of the postwar world. The Carson book found a receptive audience in the 1960s, an era rapidly evolving as one of the most rebellious, tumultuous decades in American history. Growing numbers of Americans, most notably many among the nation's youth, countered traditional assumptions by rallying against the evils they perceived in American life. The repression of African-Americans and women, the apparent pointlessness of the war in Vietnam, the greed of large corporations, and the drudgery of the average middle-class existence – all increasingly galvanized the young into a potent cultural force that welcomed the basic tenets of the new environmentalism. For many, America needed fundamental change, with protection for environmental quality only one among many examples.

As the 1960s progressed, the problem of environmental deterioration was increasingly before the public, from new collegiate-level courses in "environmental science" to a wave of best-selling books in the wake of *Silent Spring*. The National Advertising Council released a poignant commercial that depicted an American Indian looking out over a littered landscape, a tear rolling down his cheek. Environmental degradation, whether a messy oil spill on pristine beaches or mountains of rusted automobiles taller than nearby buildings, made great copy for television; it was sure to win viewers, a fact not lost upon network executives. Not surprisingly, polls soon registered growing public concern. In 1965, over a quarter of respondents surveyed indicated that they thought air pollution was a serious problem in their own community. For water quality, the figure was over one-third. By 1967, half of the respondents indicated a serious problem in both areas, and by the following year the figure had risen to two-thirds. Respondents did not list environmental deterioration as the most important problem facing the nation, but their growing concern was obvious.

The result was tremendous growth in environmental organizations, both in terms of the number of organizations and the membership within each. Prior to 1960 an average of only three new conservation groups per year appeared on the American scene. Throughout the remainder of the 1960s, the average was eighteen. . . .

. . . [M]ost of the traditional organizations . . . found that their membership rose. The Wilderness Society, for example, doubled its membership over the decade, while the Sierra Club and the National Audubon Society more than doubled theirs. . . . In short, the environmental movement, largely united and obviously growing, appeared to be by the end of the decade a political force hard to ignore.

The potential of this grass-roots environmentalism was evident from the start, its successes slowly building as the movement grew. In the 1950s, preservationists succeeded in blocking construction of two dams that promised to destroy the natural ecosystem of the surrounding lands. A proposal to flood the Dinosaur National Monument with a dam at Echo Park near the Utah-Colorado border galvanized a resistance that surprised the dam's proponents. Similarly, a proposal to build a dam at Hell's Canyon on the Snake River in Idaho sparked an unexpected degree of outrage. Fifty years before, Sierra Club founder John Muir had led a committed band of preservationists in an unsuccessful attempt to block the damming of the beautiful Hetch Hetchy Valley in Yosemite National Park. The success of his philosophical descendants, if nothing else, indicated that a new day for environmental advocates was approaching.

By the 1960s, environmentalists found a friend in President Lyndon Johnson. With a new faith in government activism, the Great Society witnessed the first significant legislation to address the problem of pollution. New laws to create air and water quality standards were revolutionary for their day, if not stringent enough to meet the growing problem. Laws to protect unspoiled wilderness from development, to create a permanent fund for the purchase of parkland, to limit solid waste, and to create a wildlife-refuge system were critical steps in the evolution of federal environmental policy. Most notably, Johnson's Interior Department secretary, Stewart Udall, emerged as a forceful champion of the natural world, in many respects challenging the dominant utilitarian biases of his predecessors. Environmentalists had, according to the Sierra

Club, "no stauncher friend."[2] Perhaps even more apparent to the public was Johnson's wife, Lady Bird. Although many first ladies had adopted a pet cause, Lady Bird's was unique – the preservation of the country's natural beauty. Chairing a presidential commission and hosting a White House conference on the subject, Lady Bird helped pass legislation to limit roadside blight. Her real significance, however, lay in the example she set. The American people should, she insisted, care about their environment.

Congress, of course, played a major role. In most respects, bipartisan support existed for each legislative initiative. Still, taking the lead was Maine Democratic senator Edmund Muskie. Environmental quality was not yet a major political force, but the former governor of Maine already had a long record of activism that proved his interest was genuine. Born and raised in the town of Rumford, Maine, a town so polluted that the stench from its timber industry permeated the daily lives of its citizens, Governor Muskie had made the pollution of his state's rivers a cause célèbre. Elected to the Senate in 1958 and appointed four years later as chair of the Subcommittee on Air and Water Pollution of the Senate Public Works Committee, he was in a position to place his imprint on virtually every pollution bill before Congress. Together with his colleagues in the executive branch, he helped lay the foundation for an environmental policy that the nation needed.

It was, however, still only a foundation. The problems continued to grow throughout the decade, fueling the development of the environmental movement and leading ultimately to the first Earth Day, an unmistakable signal that environmentalism had arrived. Despite a decade of growing concern and accomplishment, for many Americans the thousands gathered in Washington, New York, and other cities on that April day in 1970 served as a wake-up call, an alarm signaling both the pressing nature of the problem and the urgency for additional action. The sheer size of the turnout ensured significant media coverage, but the demonstrators themselves devised tactics to seize headlines. At the University of Minnesota, members of the "Students for Environmental Defense" conducted a mock funeral service for the internal combustion engine, lowering an engine into a coffin buried in downtown Minneapolis. A New Jersey housewife spent weeks sewing red banners with black skulls and crossbones, banners that she then placed on dredging equipment which she believed sullied nearby beaches. Self-styled Yippies at Indiana University were more aggressive, plugging municipal sewage pipes with concrete, while their more orderly colleagues tossed birth-control pills at the crowds. Protesters intended such actions to garner attention – and their efforts proved successful. All three major television networks devoted considerable coverage to the event, while the public broadcasting stations devoted all of their daytime programs to the protection of environmental quality.

The first Earth Day was a fitting culmination to a popular movement, a demonstration that ecology had achieved political capital as never before – and, not surprising given the incredible turnout, politicians listened. Both houses of Congress adjourned for the day, allowing their members to participate in the various activities, invariably extolling their own interest in the matter. . . .

Inside the White House, the approach of the first Earth Day posed a dilemma for President Richard Nixon. The first-term Republican, like many politicians in Washington, recognized the opportunity the occasion posed to sway a wide segment of voters. Environmentalism, it appeared, was particularly strong in critical electoral college states, including Florida, California, New York, and much of New England. Indeed, with polls indicating that the environment was a key issue among the nation's youth, Earth Day offered a chance to score points with an important demographic group, a voting block not traditionally allied with Nixon. The idea of an Earth Day had grown from the original plan for a large "teach-in," a public gathering popular at many large universities at the time. In such events, more common as protests against the Vietnam War, students boycotted classes to attend meetings, where activists led panel discussions, symposia, and lectures. Coordinating the logistics for a "national teach-in on the environment" – Earth Day, as they named it – was a Harvard University graduate student, Denis Hayes, an ambitious and intelligent twenty-five year old who recruited a number of volunteers from Stanford, his undergraduate alma mater. Earth Day, in short, appeared as youth oriented as the nation's burgeoning environmentalism itself, and thus for a conservative administration constituted a rare opportunity. As the ultimate commander-in-chief of America's forces in Vietnam, Nixon was more often than not the object of such a collegiate "teach-in," not a willing participant. He could not, in short, easily ignore it.

Ever the astute politician, Nixon had recognized the potential power of the new environmentalism sweeping the country even before Hayes and the others began molding their "teach-in" into the truly momentous event it became. In addition, his political opposition stood poised to take advantage of the situation if the administration somehow appeared indifferent. Predictably, Muskie prepared an offensive, planning to venture to Harvard and the University of Pennsylvania for speeches demanding additional environmental protection. . . . Muskie was well known nationally, and Nixon ardently believed him to be his most likely opponent in the coming 1972 presidential elections. . . . Muskie had not joined Wisconsin Democratic senator Gaylord Nelson as one of Earth Day's top proponents, top aide Leon Billings recalled, but he recognized

it "as an opportunity to provide political strength to his lonely cru-
sade."[3] Other presidential-caliber Democrats planned to make the
most of the occasion as well. Minnesota senator Hubert Humphrey
scheduled a major speech at an Indiana high school, while Washington
senator Henry Jackson planned the same at the University of Washington. Senator McGovern scheduled his address for Purdue University,
while Massachusetts senator Edward Kennedy chose Yale University.
The Democrats knew the power of this political bloc, Nixon assumed,
and to ignore it completely might prove foolish.

On the other hand, however, Hayes and the other organizers, while
denying their event as a partisan affair, had not exactly welcomed the
administration's overtures in their preparations. They had publicly
trashed the administration's environmental efforts to date as a "billow
of smog," and had turned down an invitation to meet with John D.
Ehrlichman, Assistant to the President for Domestic Affairs and one of
Nixon's closest advisors. Such an impertinent snub to an incumbent
presidential administration did not seem to bother them. "We didn't
think we had anything to chat about," a spokesman for the organizers
sarcastically explained.[4] Such comments reinforced the belief in the
White House that environmentalists were "social activists on the left
side of the political spectrum" harboring a natural antagonism difficult
to bridge. Still remaining were serious questions about whether Nixon
could reach America's youth in any event, especially if the reaction of the
Earth Day organizers was any indication. So many other factors – the
war, the administration's position on civil rights – played into the equation. Any efforts might simply prove futile, a waste of time.

Worse was the possibility of alienating traditional conservative allies.
Many industries anticipated facing the full wrath of environmentalists'
anger on this, their designated day. . . . They did not want to appear to
counter publicly such a popular movement as the new environmentalism, but neither did they plan to support a president who actively and
ardently pushed the environmental agenda. Nixon realized that various
industry representatives and a number of conservatives had already
voiced in private, if not in public, their displeasure over the administration's environmental accomplishments to date. To appear at the
forefront on Earth Day might risk pushing them into direct opposition.

As Earth Day neared, the debate raged within the White House. The
first to recommend a strong administration response in favor of Earth Day
was aide Christopher DeMuth, who recommended to Ehrlichman and
Deputy Assistant to the President for Domestic Affairs John Whitaker, his
immediate supervisor, that Nixon deliver a "substantial presidential address." Ehrlichman had just appointed Whitaker as the White House's
top environmental advisor, and Whitaker, in turn, had realized the intelli-

gence of DeMuth. A recent graduate of Harvard and the same age as Hayes and the other Earth Day organizers, DeMuth argued that a forceful presidential response before the day itself would ensure the "supremacy of the moderate students," not the radical fringe....[5]

Whitaker quickly agreed with DeMuth. A former advance man and scheduler with the Nixon campaign, the forty-three-year-old Whitaker was born in beautiful Vancouver, British Columbia, and held a doctorate in geology from Johns Hopkins University and a long-standing interest in environmental protection. As a boy, he had been shocked by the unsightly grit and grime of the large eastern seaboard cities. His subsequent career in geology had led him to many of the world's most beautiful locales, and by the time of Earth Day Whitaker had found in his assistant DeMuth an instant ally. Ehrlichman, however, was another question. A year older than Whitaker, he also had a background in the environment; he had served for fifteen years as an attorney with a specialization in land-use law. He too recognized the importance of cleaning up the environment and the political potency of the new environmentalism, but as a closer aide to Nixon and with responsibilities beyond simply natural resources, Ehrlichman had reservations about such a strong endorsement as the one Whitaker and DeMuth proposed.

Ehrlichman worried that preparations for Earth Day were not sufficiently bipartisan. Not only had Hayes personally scorned the White House, but the original idea for a day devoted to the environment had come ... from Democratic senator Nelson. Nelson had not agreed with his protégé's ill treatment of Nixon's assistants and had helped recruit California Republican congressman Paul McCloskey as a formal cochair. With a Democrat and Republican officially at the helm, Nelson hoped his colleagues from both sides of the aisle would recognize the importance of the day and look past partisan antics. This did not convince Ehrlichman, who warned Nixon that the entire affair had the potential to turn "anti-Administration."[6] ... Rather than directly endorsing Earth Day, Ehrlichman concluded, Nixon should organize federal workers' participation, but personally remain aloof.

Nixon made no immediate decision, allowing the debate within the administration to spread. Secretary of Interior Walter Hickel, together with his chief advisor, Undersecretary Russell Train, argued that Nixon should declare Earth Day a national holiday and issue an executive order directing government employees to aid their local efforts. "This action would be beneficial not only to our fight for the environment," Hickel wrote, "but also to our continued efforts to involve young people in national concerns."[7] ...

Nixon recognized that preparations were necessary in any event, and thus he could not delay his decision. Weighing the options, Nixon decided on a middle course, a low-risk plan along the lines of what Ehrlichman recommended. The White House would ensure the active participation of its key staff, who would speak throughout the country lauding the president's concern for environmental quality. Nixon, however, would remain quiet, neither issuing an executive order nor even making an official statement beforehand. If it appeared that events were proceeding smoothly – that is, with little violence or criticism of the White House – then Nixon might issue a quick statement to the press, hopefully in time for the evening news. A certain amount of criticism was inevitable, Nixon assumed. He had promised a major environmental address in the future and had his staff actively preparing a program of legislative initiatives. It was an agenda, Nixon hoped, that would establish his environmental credentials regardless of his response to Earth Day, a complete program sufficient in its own right to win the environmental vote. If he tried to steal some of the spotlight on Earth Day, an event for which he had contributed nothing, some would criticize him for grandstanding.

Whitaker and DeMuth had their marching orders. They sent a memorandum to the departments of Interior, Agriculture, Labor, Transportation, and Health, Education and Welfare requesting each to develop a plan of action for the coming day. DeMuth, in turn, would coordinate publicity. The administration, Whitaker wrote DeMuth, should "hit Carson, Cavett and the think-type programs." It should include "young fellas" in its agenda, not simply higher administration figures. DeMuth notified Patrick Buchanan, a young aide and speech writer, that if any administration figure were asked about Earth Day, he should respond positively, noting that Nixon planned future environmental initiatives. To ensure that no administration figure encountered a hostile reception for which he was unprepared, Whitaker instructed DeMuth to "categorize our potential speakers as 'establishment' or 'teach-in' types."[8]

Preparations proceeded according to plan, although not without worries. The Vietnam War continued to rage, with protests on the rise. In the months before Earth Day, Nixon had increased the withdrawal of American troops as part of his "Vietnamization" of the war, but a string of ugly incidents, including the infamous My Lai massacre by American troops, undercut any positive effects domestically. In San Diego, student radicals burned a bank; at Kansas State, others burned down the ROTC building; at Yale, still others set afire books in the Law School library; at the University of California-Berkeley, they fought police for six hours in an antiwar protest. In the eyes of many administration officials, courting the nation's youth appeared to be an increasingly perilous proposition. ... The thought of scores of young people on yet another protest

– whether in support of environmental protection, or whatever – terrified many industry representatives, who began to prepare for the worst-case scenario. Owners of the Forest Industries building in Washington began to board up their first-floor windows, but settled for setting up fir trees in front of the glass. Most officials in the White House had by this point accepted the argument of Whitaker and others that some form of participation was wise, but Vice President Spiro Agnew remained a vocal opponent of any action whatsoever. . . .[9]

These were serious worries for the White House's environmental staff. For Nixon, however, they warranted little of his time. As meticulous and organized as ever, and with his decision made, Nixon turned his attention elsewhere. Indeed, Nixon faced a critical decision, one that for him surely dwarfed his administration's response to Earth Day. The National Security Council had informed him of the damage done by communist supply lines through Cambodia, and Nixon wrestled over the possibility of invading that ostensibly neutral country. With much of America apparently radicalized by the continued fighting, a decision to intervene might pour fuel on the fire. Earth Day would certainly command attention, but Nixon had his mind on other matters.

Nixon had not announced his decision by the time Earth Day arrived, and for this one day nothing competed for the public's attention. Hundreds of administration staffers fanned out as planned, their scripts in hand. His own speech scheduled for Harvard, Train recalled that the staff was "very engaged around the country."[10] . . . Only a handful of incidents nationally resulted in arrests – an amazing fact given the magnitude of the turnout. . . . Overall, Hayes and the other organizers were ecstatic, describing the event as the largest, cleanest, and most peaceful demonstration in American history.

With neither the major riot so many feared nor a significant Vietnam story, the media had more time to assess and critique the event, and the focus quickly turned to the administration. Ignoring the administration's efforts, the headline declared neglect by the White House – the very criticism Nixon had hoped to avoid. His actions – or, more correctly, lack of action – ensured condemnation. . . .

"There was little doubt," Whitaker later wrote, "that the Nixon administration took its licks on Earth Day." CBS's much-admired newsman Walter Cronkite characterized the crowds as "predominantly anti-Nixon." Newsman Daniel Schorr added that while the event offered a rare chance for reconciliation between the nation's youth and its presidential administration, "they went their polarized ways." White House correspondent Dan Rather was more pointed, describing Nixon's reaction as "benign neglect." In many instances, the speakers themselves added jabs at the White House. Addressing a crowd in New York City's

Bryant Park, noted author Kurt Vonnegut, Jr., remarked, "If we don't get our President's attention, this planet may soon die . . . I'm sorry he's a lawyer; I wish to God that he was a biologist." . . . [11]

The week of Earth Day, White House staffers participated in a symbolic cleanup of the polluted Potomac River, with the media properly alerted. The administration, the staged event seemed to declare, did care, after all. The White House had scheduled the event prior to Earth Day, and had in fact touted it for some time to all who would listen. After the criticism of the day, however, the cleanup appeared to be a lame attempt to shield the administration from further rebuke, far from any genuine expression of concern.

It made no difference. On the night of April 30 – only eight days after Earth Day – Nixon went on national television to announce his decision to send troops into Cambodia. It was not an "invasion," Nixon assured his audience. The troops would leave once they had disrupted the enemy's supply lines into neighboring Vietnam. "We will withdraw," he promised. The following morning, speaking to supporters, Nixon made an offhand remark describing student protesters as "bums," a slur the press readily quoted. A reaction to these developments was inevitable, but no one expected the uproar that followed. Viewing the Cambodian excursion as an escalation of the conflict, not a way to a quicker victory, campuses throughout the nation exploded. Students at 450 colleges and universities immediately went on strike. In California, the situation was so bad that Governor Ronald Reagan ordered the entire statewide university system closed. On May 4 the blaze turned to conflagration as National Guard troops at Kent State University in Ohio opened fire on student protesters, killing four.[12]

The entire episode shook Nixon and shocked the country. The United States appeared on the verge of revolution, and, as tempers flared, leaders called for calm. Nixon, unable to sleep early one morning, ventured out unannounced to protesters at the Lincoln Memorial, trying in vain to reach an accord. He cared for the same things they did, he explained, turning to his environmental agenda as evidence of a common denominator. California had the most beautiful beaches in the world, Nixon stated, pointedly adding that he had ordered the San Clemente beach opened as part of "our whole 'quality of life' environmental program."[13]

Nixon's attempt to divert the handful of war protesters with his care for the environment had as little effect as Earth Day in diverting attention from the Cambodian attack. Despite the pressing nature of the problem and the apparent wide-spread American interest, the reality was that public concern for the environment faded when other urgent problems commanded attention. In the words of [the] Sierra Club's

[Philip] Berry: "That stupid war eclipsed the movement."[14] America's new-found interest in preserving environmental quality was a significant development in the nation's social and political evolution, a real break from the assumptions and opinions of the past. With the problem of environmental deterioration a genuine threat to the nation's future, the first Earth Day was, indeed, a momentous event. Ironically, it just did not appear so two weeks later, a fact that no doubt registered with Nixon. . . .

In the end, the story of the first Earth Day tells a great deal about the Nixon administration and the emergence of the modern environmental movement. In a sense it demonstrates both the strengths and weaknesses of the new environmentalism, as well as the manner in which Nixon approached it. Nixon, the consummate political animal, gave no indication of sharing the concerns and hopes of the thousands who gathered on that April day in 1970 but rather gauged his response according to political expediency. Politics inevitably surrounded the day, just as the new environmentalism changed the political dynamics of the era. For many on the White House staff, the matter of environmental protection was more than just politics, but it was, nevertheless, the desire for partisan advantage that consumed the commander-in-chief. The story of the first Earth Day provides ample evidence of Nixon's desire to win the environmental vote, the strength of the Democrats as they resisted his efforts, and the rapidity with which critics condemned the White House. It illustrates, paradoxically, the important nature of the cause as well as the fleeting nature of public vigilance. If nothing else, it demonstrates the critical place of the Nixon administration in American environmental history.

"Ecology Has Finally Achieved Currency" 1969

. . . [The year before,] [a]s the end of [1969] approached, all indications pointed to the passage of [Democratic Senator Henry Jackson's] bill to create a Council on Environmental Quality. It was not just the proposed CEQ, however, that gave Jackson so much confidence. The bill, now known as the National Environmental Policy Act (NEPA), promised to pass both houses strengthened beyond what even Jackson had anticipated, beyond the version passed in the Senate in the summer. Proclaiming it the nation's policy to protect environmental quality, the bill now popular in Congress no longer required the government to issue a "finding" of environmental impact before the approval of any large federal project. It now mandated a "detailed statement," an exhaustive study that had to include possible alternatives to the proposed project.

The bill obligated the government to circulate the statement among the public before approval by the proposed CEQ. If passed, it would stand as one of the nation's most important environmental laws, a cornerstone of the nation's policy for years to come . . .

The "bandwagon" of environmentalism sweeping Congress, Jackson assumed, assured that the conference committee then meeting to iron out the differences between the House and Senate versions would return a bill favorable to environmentalists. In fact, he assumed, he had already overcome the single biggest threat to the bill, a threat not from opponents of stringent provisions, but, ironically, from his colleague in the struggle to protect the environment, Muskie. Muskie's Water Quality Improvement Act, then still under debate, called for a different version of an executive environmental council, not a three-person CEQ, but a five-member Office of Environmental Quality. It was no small dispute, for if Muskie's bill and council prevailed, future environmental issues would fall not under Jackson's Interior Committee, but Muskie's Public Works Committee. In this respect, the struggle was one for environmental prestige. . . . "Scoop [Jackson] wanted a piece of the action," recalled Muskie aide Billings, with Muskie "not too happy about Jackson cutting into his issue." The solution was a compromise that allowed both bills to proceed. To achieve this end, both senators agreed that Jackson's bill would specify his CEQ as the major body for policy considerations, while Muskie's bill would specify his OEQ as the major body for enforcement and support staff. At Muskie's insistence, the agreement provided for a stronger environmental impact-statement requirement in Jackson's bill and otherwise supported the strongest provisions possible.[15]

With leading Democrats on the same page and with the public receptive, Whitaker was blunt with Ehrlichman. The opposition had "run over" the administration. Witnessing a competition so keen that even Muskie and Jackson were struggling among themselves for advantage, Train agreed. Immediate action was still necessary to "take the initiative away from the Democrats" and "identify the Republican Party with concern for environmental quality."[16] It was by November a familiar refrain, but, at last, one that this time carried some weight; Whitaker's task force had finally completed its preliminary agenda for a comprehensive environmental program and it was ready for Nixon's review. For the first time, the administration stood on the brink of a true offensive. Nixon, who up to this point had only concerned himself with environmental policy in a cursory manner, took the sixty-five-page volume with him on Thanksgiving weekend to Key Biscayne. It commanded his full attention, a positive sign for environmentalists if nothing else.

The White House planned Nixon's environmental address for early February, and throughout the waning days of 1969 Whitaker, Ehrlichman, and their staffs worked on final preparations and revisions. Duly impressed by the task force's report, and, as always, aware of political opportunities, Nixon had one additional chance to divert attention from Jackson, Muskie, and the Democratic juggernaut. Just after Thanksgiving, Congress passed new, stronger wildlife legislation. The bill expanded the nation's endangered-species lists to include mollusks and crustaceans, and more importantly prohibited the importation of species considered in danger of extinction on a worldwide basis. With over 275 species of mammals and 300 species of birds threatened around the globe, wildlife advocates had lobbied for the bill for years. It was a solid piece of legislation with little apparent economic cost, and the White House had no doubts that Nixon should sign it. Apart from Hickel, however, the administration had taken little role in the bill's passage, and Whitaker worried that the media would praise its "large Democratic sponsorship." The wise course was not to stage an elaborate signing ceremony as Hickel recommended, but a private one. This allowed the White House to control coverage by mailing environmental groups pictures of the signing ceremony. With less traditional coverage and fewer Democrats present, more credit flowed to the administration.[17]

On December 5, 1969, Nixon signed the Endangered Species Conservation Act of 1969, his first chance to sign into law significant environmental legislation.[18] It was not, however, his last. Twelve days later the conference committee working on NEPA submitted its report, which included almost all the stringent provisions upon which Jackson and Muskie had agreed. Under pressure from the House conferees, the report added the qualifying phrase "to the fullest extent possible" to its impact statement requirement, and it mandated each agency to "consult" with CEQ, not receive its approval. In all other respects, however, the report was as forceful a statement of environmental policy as supporters had hoped.

The committee report sailed through both houses of Congress, reaching Nixon's desk just after Christmas. Once again, Nixon faced a decision on a bill largely authored and supported by his political opposition. Surprisingly, no one in the White House recognized the significance of the impact-statement requirement, the only true coercive portion of the bill and the one in which environmentalists placed so much faith.[19] No executive agency recommended against approval, despite potential conflicts with the new CEQ. In the years to come, Nixon would come to regret this oversight, but at the end of his first year in office, the bill appeared only a minor nuisance. Another environmental council – and, if Muskie's water pollution bill were later to pass, the possibility of a third – promised duplication and overlap. Nevertheless, the nation needed a coherent environmental policy and Nixon still held the right to appoint the new council's members. He might simply deactivate or ignore one of the bodies if jurisdictional issues hampered efforts. In any event, as Whitaker noted and Ehrlichman agreed, to veto the bill was to court political disaster, for the environmental "bandwagon" ensured a congressional override. A veto would cast Nixon as anti-environment just as the administration was finally prepared to unveil its long-awaited program. An opportunity still existed, Whitaker and Ehrlichman agreed. Just as with the endangered-species bill, Nixon could co-opt the legislation as his own. If he were to stage properly the signing ceremony, choose his words wisely, and follow with credible appointments, NEPA could work in the administration's favor.[20] Coupled with his coming environmental message to Congress, it would finally win the political initiative that the White House had so long sought....

Notes

1 John Kenneth Galbraith, *The Affluent Society* (Boston: Houghton Mifflin, 1958)....
2 *Sierra Club Bulletin* 53, no. 1 (January 1968): 7....
3 Interview, Author with Leon Billings, June 26, 1998.
4 Quoted in Steve Cotton, "What Happened," *Audubon* 72, no. 4 (July 1970): 113.
5 Memo, Christopher DeMuth to John Ehrlichman and John Whitaker, Dec. 4, 1969, Folder "485-OA#2977, Environment," Box 63, Egil Krogh Files, White House Special Files (hereafter cited as WHSF), Richard Nixon White House Papers, Richard Nixon Presidential Materials Project (hereafter cited as RNPMP), National Archives II, College Park, Maryland; John Whitaker, *Striking a Balance: Environment and Natural Resources Policy in the Nixon–Ford Years* (Washington, D.C.: American Enterprise Institute, 1976), 29.
6 Memo, John Ehrlichman to Richard Nixon, Dec. 5, 1969, Folder "EX NR Natural Resources, 1 of 3, 1969–1970," Box 1, Natural Resources Files, White House Central Files (hereafter cited as WHCF), RNPMP.
7 Interview, Author with Walter Hickel, Mar. 27, 1998; Memo, Walter Hickel to Richard Nixon, Dec. 16, 1969, Folder "485-OA#2977, Environment," Box 63, Egil Krogh Files, WHCF, RNPMP; Memo, John Whitaker to Russell Train, Dec. 11, 1969, Folder "June–December, 1969, 6 of 6, December, 1969," Box 1, John Whitaker Files, WHCF.
8 Memo, John Whitaker to Secs. Hardin, Hickel, Finch, et. al., Jan. 8, 1970, Folder "White House, Environment, 1970," Box 9, Edward David Files, WHCF, RNPMP; Memo, John Whitaker to Christopher DeMuth, Jan. 16, 1970, Folder "January–April, 1970, 1 of 4, January, 1970," Box 2, John Whitaker Files, WHCF, RNPMP; Memo, Christopher DeMuth to Patrick

Buchanan, Jan. 29, 1970, Folder "Environmental Briefing, January–February, 1970," Box 13, Patrick Buchanan Files, WHCF, RNPMP; Memo, John Whitaker to Christopher DeMuth, Feb. 2, 1970, Folder "January–April, 1970, 2 of 4, February, 1970," Box 2, John Whitaker, WHCF, RNPMP.

9 Walter Hickel, *Who owns America?* (Englewood Cliffs, N.J.: Prentice-Hall, 1971), 239; Stephen E. Ambrose, *Nixon: The Triumph of a Politician, 1962–1972* (New York: Simon and Schuster, 1989), 334, 338; Cotton, "What Happened," 114.

10 Interview, Author with Russell Train, July 8, 1998.

11 Cronkite, Schorr, and Rather quoted in Whitaker, *Striking A Balance*, 7; Vonnegut and Hayes quoted in Cotton, "What Happened," 113–14.

12 *Public Papers of the Presidents, Richard Nixon, 1970* (Washington, D.C.: U.S. Government Printing Office, 1971), 405–10; Nixon quoted in Ambrose, *Nixon, Triumph*, 345, 348.

13 Ambrose, *Nixon, Triumph*, 355–56.

14 Interview, Author with Philip Berry, June 19, 1998.

15 Interview, Author with Leon Billings, June 26, 1998.

16 Memo, John Whitaker to John Ehrlichman, Nov. 18, 1969, Folder "440-OA 2975, Conservation," Box 63, Egil Krogh Files, WHSF, RNPMP; Memo, Russell Train to John Ehrlichman, Nov. 3, 1969, Folder "485-OA 2977, Environment," Box 63, Egil Krogh Files, WHSF, RNPMP.

17 Memo, John Whitaker to Ken Cole, undated, Folder "Endangered Species Act," Box 60, Charles Colson Files, WHSF, RNPMP; Memo, Dwight Chapin to Richard Nixon, Dec. 2, 1969, Folder "EX NR Fish-Wildlife, 1 of 7, 1969–1970," Box 3, Natural Resources File, WHCF, RNPMP; Memo, Russell Train to John Whitaker, Aug. 26, 1969, Folder "EX NR Fish-Wildlife, 1 of 7, 1969–1970," Box 3, Natural Resources Files, WHCF, RNPMP; Victor B. Scheffer, *The Shaping of Environmentalism in America* (Seattle: University of Washington Press, 1991), 158–59.

18 Presidential Statement on Signing of Wildlife Bill, Dec. 5, 1969, Folder "Endangered Species Act," Box 60, Charles Colson Files, WHSF, RNPMP; *New York Times*, Dec. 6, 1969, 1.

19 Interview, Author with John Whitaker, July 23, 1996....

20 Memo, John Whitaker to John Ehrlichman, Dec. 24, 1969, Folder "EX FG 251, EQC; FG 251, CCE, Terminated July 1, 1970, 2 of 2," Box 1, Cabinet Committee on the Environment Files, WHCF, RNPMP; Memo, John Whitaker to Lee DuBridge, Dec. 17, 1969, Folder "June–December, 1969, 6 of 6, December, 1969," Box 1, John Whitaker Files, WHCF, RNPMP; Memo, Wilfred Rommel to Richard Nixon, Dec. 30, 1969, Folder "Ex FG 251, EQC; FG 251, CCE, Terminated July 1, 1970, 2 of 2," Box 1, Cabinet Committee on the Environment Files, WHCF, RNPMP; Kent Portney, *Controversial Issues in Environmental Policy* (Newbury Park, Calif.: Sage, 1992), 41; Richard N. L. Andrews, *Environmental Policy and Administrative Change: Implementation of the National Environmental Policy Act* (Lexington, Mass.: Lexington Books, 1976), 13.

Documents

National Environmental Policy Act (1969)

The first document is an excerpt from the National Environmental Policy Act. You may want to read it over just to see what such a highly-charged, movement-oriented piece of law looks like. In what ways does it provide clues to its own political origins? Do you find any indication, in its wording or in its provisions, of the widespread concerns about air pollution, litter, or other environmental degradation?

*   *   *

An Act

Be it enacted by the Senate and House of Representatives of the United States of America in Congress assembled, That this Act may be cited as the "National Environmental Policy Act of 1969".

PURPOSE

SEC. 2. The purposes of this Act are: To declare a national policy which will encourage productive and enjoyable harmony between man and his environment: to promote efforts which will prevent or eliminate damage to the environment and biosphere and stimulate the health and welfare of man; to enrich the understanding of the ecological systems and natural resources important to the Nation; and to establish a Council on Environmental Quality.

TITLE I

DECLARATION OF NATIONAL ENVIRONMENTAL POLICY

SEC. 101. (a) The Congress, recognizing the profound impact of man's activity on the interrelations of all components of the natural environment, particularly the profound influences of population growth, high-density urbanization, industrial expansion, resource exploitation, and new and expanding technological advances and recognizing further the critical importance of restoring and maintaining environmental quality to the overall welfare and development of man, declares that it is the continuing policy of the Federal Government, in cooperation with State and local governments, and other concerned public and private organizations, to use all practicable means and measures, including financial and technical assistance, in a manner calculated to foster and promote the general welfare, to create and maintain conditions under which man and nature can exist in productive harmony, and fulfill the social, economic, and other requirements of present and future generations of Americans.

(b) In order to carry out the policy set forth in this Act, it is the continuing responsibility of the Federal Government to use all practicable means, consistent with other essential considerations of national policy, to improve and coordinate Federal plans, functions, programs, and resources to the end that the Nation may –

(1) fulfill the responsibilities of each generation as trustee of the environment for succeeding generations;

(2) assure for all Americans safe, healthful, productive, and esthetically and culturally pleasing surroundings;

(3) attain the widest range of beneficial uses of the environment without degradation, risk to health or safety, or other undesirable and unintended consequences;

(4) preserve important historic, cultural, and natural aspects of our national heritage, and maintain, wherever possible, an environment which supports diversity and variety of individual choice;

(5) achieve a balance between population and resource use which will permit high standards of living and a wide sharing of life's amenities; and

(6) enhance the quality of renewable resources and approach the maximum attainable recycling of depletable resources.

(c) The Congress recognizes that each person should enjoy a healthful environment and that each person has a responsibility to contribute to the preservation and enhancement of the environment.

SEC. 102. The Congress authorizes and directs that, to the fullest extent possible: (1) the policies, regulations, and public laws of the United States shall be interpreted and administered in accordance with the policies set forth in this Act, and (2) all agencies of the Federal Government shall –

(A) utilize a systematic, interdisciplinary approach which will insure the integrated use of the natural and social sciences and the environmental design arts in planning and in decisionmaking which may have an impact on man's environment;

(B) identify and develop methods and procedures, in consultation with the Council on Environmental Quality established by title II of this Act, which will insure that presently unquantified environmental amenities and values may be given appropriate consideration in decisionmaking along with economic and technical considerations;

(C) include in every recommendation or report on proposals for legislation and other major Federal actions significantly affecting the quality of the human environment, a detailed statement by the responsible official on –

(i) the environmental impact of the proposed action,

(ii) any adverse environmental effects which cannot be avoided should the proposal be implemented,

(iii) alternatives to the proposed action,

(iv) the relationship between local short-term uses of man's environment and the maintenance and enhancement of long-term productivity, and

(v) any irreversible and irretrievable commitments of resources which would be involved in the proposed action should it be implemented.

Prior to making any detailed statement, the responsible Federal official shall consult with and obtain the comments of any Federal agency which has jurisdiction by law or special expertise with respect to any environmental impact involved. Copies of such statement and the comments and views of the appropriate Federal, State, and local agencies, which are authorized to develop and enforce environmental standards, shall be made available to the President, the Council on Environmental Quality and to the public as provided by section 552 of title 5. United States Code, and shall accompany the proposal through the existing agency review processes;

(D) study, develop, and describe appropriate alternatives to recommended courses of action in any proposal which involves unresolved conflicts concerning alternative uses of available resources;

(E) recognize the worldwide and long-range character of environmental problems and, where consistent with the foreign policy of the United States, lend appropriate support to initiatives, resolutions, and programs designed to maximize international cooperation in anticipating and preventing a decline in the quality of mankind's world environment;

(F) make available to States, counties, municipalities, institutions, and individuals, advice and information useful in restoring, maintaining, and enhancing the quality of the environment;

(G) initiate and utilize ecological information in the planning and development of resource-oriented projects; and

(H) assist the Council on Environmental Quality established by title II of this Act.

SEC. 103. All agencies of the Federal Government shall review their present statutory authority, administrative regulations, and current policies and procedures for the purpose of determining whether there are any deficiencies or inconsistencies therein which prohibit full compliance with the purposes and provisions of this Act and shall propose to the President not later than July 1, 1971, such measures as may be necessary to bring their authority and policies into conformity with the intent, purposes, and procedures set forth in this Act.

SEC. 104. Nothing in Section 102 or 103 shall in any way affect the specific statutory obligations of any Federal agency (1) to comply with criteria or standards of environmental quality, (2) to coordinate or consult with any other Federal or State agency, or (3) to act, or refrain from acting contingent upon the recommendations or certification of any other Federal or State agency.

SEC. 105. The policies and goals set forth in this Act are supplementary to those set forth in existing authorizations of Federal agencies.

The Endangered Species Act (1973)

Political competition to capture the support of the environmental movement led Richard Nixon to endorse more environmental legislation in the same period. Among the measures he endorsed were the creation of the Environmental Protection Agency in 1970, the first Endangered Species Conservation Act (in 1969), and a more rigorous version of the same law in the Endangered Species Act of 1973. This last piece of legislation would become one of the most celebrated and contested of environmental achievements.

What specific concerns appear to have motivated public support for this legislation? How is it different in tone from earlier legislation like the National Parks Act of 1916?

* * *

AN ACT

To provide for the conservation of endangered and threatened species of fish, wildlife, and plants, and for other purposes.

Be it enacted by the Senate and House of Representatives of the United States of America in Congress assembled. That this Act may be cited as the "Endangered Species Act of 1973". . . .

FINDINGS, PURPOSES, AND POLICY

SEC. 2. (a) FINDINGS. – The Congress finds and declares that –

(1) various species of fish, wildlife, and plants in the United States have been rendered extinct as a consequene of economic growth and development untempered by adequate concern and conservation;

(2) other species of fish, wildlife, and plants have been so depleted in numbers that they are in danger of or threatened with extinction;

(3) these species of fish, wildlife, and plants are of esthetic, ecological, educational, historical, recreational, and scientific value to the Nation and its people;

(4) the United States has pledged itself as a sovereign state in the international community to conserve to the extent practicable the various species of fish or wildlife and plants facing extinction, pursuant to –

  (A) migratory bird treaties with Canada and Mexico;

  (B) the Migratory and Endangered Bird Treaty with Japan;

  (C) the Convention on Nature Protection and Wildlife Preservation in the Western Hemisphere;

  (D) the International Convention for the Northwest Atlantic Fisheries;

  (E) the International Convention for the High Seas Fisheries of the North Pacific Ocean;

  (F) the Convention on International Trade in Endangered Species of Wild Fauna and Flora; and

  (G) other international agreements.

(5) encouraging the States and other interested parties, through Federal financial assistance and a system of incentives, to develop and maintain conservation programs which meet national and international standards is a key to meeting the Nation's international commitments and to better safeguarding, for the benefit of all citizens, the Nation's heritage in fish and wildlife.

  (b) PURPOSES. – The purposes of this Act are to provide a means whereby the ecosystems upon which endangered species and threatened species depend may be conserved, to provide a program for the conservation of such endangered species and threatened species, and to take such steps as may be appropriate to achieve the purposes of the treaties and conventions set forth in subsection (a) of this section.

  (c) POLICY. – It is further declared to be the policy of Congress that all Federal departments and agencies shall seek to conserve endangered species and threatened species and shall utilize their authorities in furtherance of the purposes of this Act.

From Paul Ehrlich, *The Population Bomb*

Reprinted from Paul Ehrlich, *The Population Bomb* (New York: Sierra Club Publishers, 1969)

Finally, we should take note of the sense of impending doom which preoccupied environmentalists in the 1970s, and which in many ways has continued to characterize the movement and energize its reformist zeal. Among its most fearsome prophecies were those that predicted global destruction through overpopulation. The most eloquent and arguably sensational prophet of population catastrophe in the twentieth century was Paul Ehrlich, a population biologist whose book *The Population Bomb* was published by the Sierra Club in 1969. The movement for controlling global population was already several decades old by this time. (In fact, Ehrlich appropriated the title of his book from a series of pamphlets published in the 1950s by Hugh Moore, a multimillionaire whose fortune derived from the manufacture of Dixie Cups.) Ehrlich's book resonated particularly well with the gathering sense of global crisis brought on by the continuing Cold War and the fear of nuclear devastation. Predicting widespread environmental harm from global population growth by 1980, Ehrlich urged Americans to restrain their population growth, and to begin facilitating birth control around the world. His proposals were (and are) controversial. In particular, he urged more developed nations to select which less-developed nations they should help through "triage," a concept borrowed from military medicine. Those nations which refused to take measures to lower their birth rates should be cut off from US foreign aid.

There are many ways of criticizing Ehrlich's arguments (and we shall return to these in the last chapter). Read this document for the sense of overwhelming crisis it conveys. Does he feel that all people should restrain their growth? Or is he more concerned about some peoples than others? Is there a racial dimension to his perceptions of overpopulation?

*   *   *

The battle to feed all of humanity is over. In the 1970's the world will undergo famines – hundreds of millions of people are going to starve to death in spite of any crash programs embarked upon now. At this late date nothing can prevent a substantial increase in the world death rate, although many lives could be saved through dramatic programs to "stretch" the carrying capacity of the earth by increasing food production. But these programs will only provide a stay of execution unless they are accompanied by determined and successful efforts at population control. Population control is the conscious regulation of the numbers of human beings to meet the needs, not just of individual families, but of society as a whole.

Nothing could be more misleading to our children than our present affluent society. They will inherit a totally different world, a world in which the standards, politics, and economics of the 1960's are dead. As the most powerful nation in the world today, *and its largest consumer,* the United States cannot stand isolated. We are today involved in the events leading to famine; tomorrow we may be destroyed by its consequences.

Our position requires that we take immediate action at home and promote effective action world-wide. We must have population control at home, hopefully through a system of incentives and penalties, but by compulsion if voluntary methods fail. We must use our political power to push other countries into programs which combine agricultural development and population control. And while this is being done we must take action to reverse the deterioration of our environment before population pressure permanently ruins our planet. The birth rate must be brought into balance with the death rate or mankind will breed itself into oblivion. We can no longer afford merely to treat the symptoms of the cancer of population growth; the cancer itself must be cut out. Population control is the only answer.

Man can undo himself with no other force than his own brutality. It is a new brutality, coming swiftly at a time when, as Loren Eiseley says, "the need is for a gentler race. But the hand that hefted the axe against the ice, the tiger, and the bear now fondles the machine gun as lovingly."

The roots of the new brutality, it will become clear from *The Population Bomb,* are in the lack of population control. There is, we must hope and predict, a chance to exert control in time. We would like to predict that organizations which, like the Sierra Club, have been much too calm about the ultimate threat to mankind, will awaken themselves and others, and awaken them with an urgency that will be necessary to fulfillment of the prediction that mankind will survive.

It was only twelve years ago that we even suggested, in any Sierra Club publication, that uncontrolled population was a menace. We went far enough to write: "People are recognizing that we cannot forever continue to multiply and subdue the earth without losing our standard of life and the natural beauty that must be part of it.... These are the years of decision – the decision of men to stay the flood of man."

I have understood the population explosion intellectually for a long time. I came to understand it emotionally one stinking hot night in Delhi a couple of years ago. My wife and daughter and I were returning to our hotel in an ancient taxi. The seats were hopping with fleas. The only functional gear was third. As we crawled through the city, we entered a crowded slum area. The temperature was well over 100, and the air was a haze of dust and smoke. The streets seemed alive with people. People eating, people washing, people sleeping. People visiting, arguing, and screaming. People thrusting their hands through the taxi window, begging. People defecating and urinating. People clinging to buses. People herding animals. People, people, people, people. As we moved slowly through the mob, hand horn squawking, the dust, noise, heat, and cooking fires gave the scene a hellish aspect. Would we ever get to our hotel? All three of us were, frankly, frightened. It seemed that anything could happen – but, of course, nothing did. Old India hands will laugh at our reaction. We were just some overprivileged tourists, unaccustomed to the sights and sounds of India. Perhaps, but since that night I've known the *feel* of overpopulation.

11
Environmental Racism and Environmental Justice

The modern environmental movement was born in the 1960s, and almost upon its birth it came under fire for not being inclusive enough, and for defending the recreational landscapes of white, middle- and upper-class people at the expense of America's minority-dominated inner cities and the rural and urban workplaces of blue-collar people. In recent years, this critique of environmentalism has inspired calls for environmental justice, demands for a more inclusive environmental movement, and allegations that zones of environmental destruction correlate suspiciously with the living spaces of poor and non-white Americans.

Ellen Stroud suggests that environmental racism might be more difficult to extirpate than it seems. In her study of environmental pollution in Portland, Oregon, she finds that city officials sacrificed some areas to industrial development partly because of popular (and incorrect) perceptions that those areas were overwhelmingly home to minority residents. As polluting industries in those neighborhoods increased, minority neighborhoods also expanded, partly because people of color had few other places where they could buy homes. The end result was that minority people flocked to one of the most toxic areas in the city, in part because of its cheap home prices. Will it be possible to avoid environmental racism without also creating a less racially divided society? Given the interlocking nature of the factors at work here, racism that leads city authorities to zone minority neighborhoods for industry, and racism that prevents minority residents from moving out, what are the best approaches to ameliorating environmental racism?

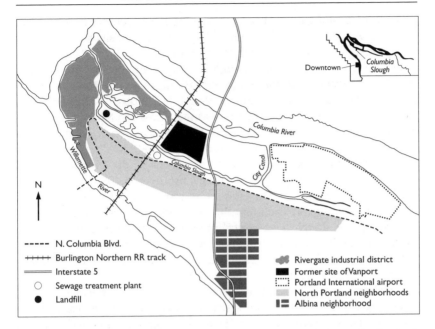

Map 11.1. The Columbia Slough and the North Portland Peninsula, Portland, Oregon. This map illustrates important locations on the North Portland Peninsula and along the lower Columbia Slough. Map by Maria Buhigas.

Troubled Waters in Ecotopia: Environmental Racism in Portland, Oregon

Ellen Stroud

Though the Columbia Slough in North Portland is easy to locate on a map – it is the narrow, eighteen-mile waterway just south of the Columbia River, along Portland's northern boundary – it is difficult to reach (see map 11.1).[1] The maze of industrial buildings, the tangle of highways, and the tall barbed wire fences make it hard to get a close look. But if you park next to the truck depot at the dead-end of Fourteenth Place, you can climb up the grassy, trash-strewn dike to see the still, murky water of the slough, Portland's most polluted waterway. You can see the high fence and barbed wire above the dike on the other side of the slough, which is about one hundred feet wide here. You can see the dike separating the upper slough and the lower slough, which were divided in the 1920s as a flood control measure. A pump station, surrounded by barbed wire, sits atop this dike, pumping water from east to west. It is a mini-dam.

On the near bank of the slough, across from the big metal pipes carrying the water from the pumping station, a sign declares the slough a hazard: "Warning: The Columbia Slough Is Polluted." The warning is printed in six languages – English, Spanish, Russian, Khmer, Vietnamese, and Laotian – and pictures drive the message home: don't swim in the water, don't drink the water, and don't eat the fish. The slough water is toxic and poses a severe risk to members of the North Portland communities who, despite the warnings, fish here for food.

Millions of gallons of Portland's raw sewage are dumped into this slow-moving waterway each month, and more than two hundred industries along the slough have contributed to its contamination. De-icing fluid from the Portland International Airport, pesticides from farms and golf courses, and leaching toxins from a municipal landfill all drain into the slough. Toxic sludge lines the slough's floor.

Local residents, environmentalists, city officials, and business leaders have long engaged in hotly contested debates about how to deal with the mess at the Columbia Slough. Headlines demonstrate that concern about the slough is nothing new. The Portland *Oregonian* reported a "Protest Against Columbia Slough Filth" in August of 1935. Thirty-five years later, in 1970, the *Oregon Journal* was telling "The Columbia Slough Story: 'Open Sewer' Poses Stinking Hazard." In 1993, headlines in the Portland *Oregonian* proclaimed, "Health Officials Report Finding PCBs in Fish," and "Slough Work Overdue." ... Conditions had reached crisis level.

But the slough was not always this filthy. Long-time North Portland resident John Bonebrake recalls the slough in the 1910s, before the dikes, the dams, the industry, and the sewage. "I remember it in my mind as a nice, little wavey slough," says Bonebrake, who was born in 1910. He tells of cottonwood trees lining the waterway, of a dozen or so smaller sloughs and marshes connecting it to the Columbia River. He tells of hunting owls and arrowheads and of fishing and swimming only a short walk from his childhood home. These days, Bonebrake says, "It's nothing but a stagnant, stale, smelly stream." ... He charges that the city cut corners with sewage treatment and made too many concessions to polluters, favoring higher profits over a clean waterway.[2]

Environmental and community activists in Portland agree that the slough has been sacrificed to industry. Northwest Environmental Advocates, a Portland environmental group, charges that the city allowed the slough to become and remain polluted because the communities affected by the slough are primarily communities of color. According to Richard

Brown, a community activist who works with Portland's Black United Front, many of the people who have fished for years for subsistence along the slough are African Americans and recent immigrants. Although the warning signs at the slough may now be discouraging people from eating the fish that they catch there, many of these same people live near the slough, and are therefore at continued risk of exposure to the toxins located there.

The charge of environmental racism is persuasive. The slough is the most polluted waterway in Portland, and possibly in the state. And the neighborhoods along the slough have some of the highest percentages of African-American and recent immigrant residents of any neighborhoods in the state, a correlation which is consistent with national patterns. In recent years, community and environmental activists have documented the fact that non-white people in the United States are significantly more likely than white Americans to live near toxic hazards, and the campaign against "environmental racism" and for "environmental justice" has gained momentum. . . .

The connection between toxic pollution and poor and non-white communities has been widely accepted, not only by activists, but by government agencies as well. In 1992, the EPA published a study that found that "racial minority and low-income populations experience higher than average exposures to selected air pollutants, hazardous waste facilities, contaminated fish and agricultural pesticides." . . . [3] However, the history of this correlation between severe pollution and minority communities is extremely complex. There is not a single racist culprit, nor any one policy or type of policy which can be blamed. When I use the term "environmental racism" to describe what I have found at the Columbia Slough, I do not intend to imply specific, conscious racist action. Rather, I use the term to designate the geographic and social results of the many interwoven policies and ideas which have created such a striking correlation. Some of these policies and ideas have involved conscious racism; many have not. However, their combined result is discriminatory.

. . . The history of this discriminatory landscape . . . is the result of many overlapping historical processes. The politics and geography of industrial location, wartime changes in Portland's population and economy, the limited goals and achievements of Oregon's environmental movement, and changing perceptions of the North Portland neighborhoods all contributed to the creation of the area's social and environmental landscapes. Since World War II, the land near the Columbia Slough has appeared on the cognitive map of many Portlanders as a throw-away place, an area best suited to industry and waste. That perception, which has a multiplicity of origins, is as much a cause as an effect of the environmental disaster at the slough. Portlanders in power thought the North Portland Peninsula was a disaster, and so it was.

Pollution was rampant at the Columbia Slough before the settlement of a significant minority population on the North Portland Peninsula. Moreover, the concerns of the slough's residential neighbors have long been subordinate to business interests in the area. However, when the area became identified with minority residents during World War II, the assault on the local environment intensified. For industrial developers, city planners and later, environmental activists, the association of the peninsula with African-American residents contributed to a perception of the area as degraded, and therefore as an appropriate place for further degradation.

In this article, I trace the history of the environmental degradation of the Columbia Slough since World War II, with particular attention to the lower slough and to the neighborhoods that run along it on the North Portland Peninsula. I argue that by the mid-1970s, at which time the environmental movement had gained considerable influence elsewhere in Portland, and the minority population of the North Portland Peninsula was again on the rise, environmental activists, local politicians and many business owners considered the slough to be beyond hope as anything but a sewer channel. Portland environmentalists' willingness to sacrifice the slough in order to secure gains elsewhere, and civic leaders' vision of North Portland as a "natural" industrial site, a vision reinforced by ideas about who did and who should live in the area, profoundly shaped the peninsula. The result was a landscape of inequity.

The Changing Peninsula

Until the 1940s, the great majority of the people who lived on the North Portland Peninsula near the slough were working-class people of European ancestry. The jobs that accompanied the industry-friendly development of the peninsula, development which was encouraged by the area's proximity to the conjunction of the Willamette and Columbia Rivers, helped to maintain the respectable working-class reputation that the area had earned as early as the turn of the century. Like other waterfront areas in the early twentieth century, the North Portland Peninsula attracted industry because of the transportation and sewage disposal options that the waters offered.

The first businesses along the Columbia Slough included slaughterhouses, stockyards, a meat packing plant, a dairy farm, a shingle company, and a lumber mill. Sewage from these businesses flowed directly into the slow-moving slough. In an attempt to increase the slough's current and flush the sewage more quickly downstream to the Willamette River, the city built a canal between the Columbia River and the slough in 1920, although the plan was never much of a success because the canal was repeatedly plugged by silt. In 1932, the City of Portland began operating a garbage dump on the marshy north bank of the slough, a site attractive because of the area's topography and its proximity to navigable water. Pollution was plaguing the waterway, as it was many waterways in industrializing cities. However, when wartime changes in demographics and industry transformed the image of the North Portland Peninsula, the slough came under a new, intensified industrial assault. Problems at the slough were no longer typical, but exceptional.

The outbreak of World War II pushed Portland's already strained housing situation to a crisis. War industry workers flooding into Portland found few places to live. In response to the influx of workers, the city formed the Housing Authority of Portland in 1941, but the authority was slow in finding a solution for the problem. The first members of the authority were a real estate agent, a banker, a landlord, and a trade union leader, each of whom was decidedly in favor of finding free market solutions to the housing crisis. Not surprisingly, they did not vigorously pursue public housing construction on the scale necessary to abate the crisis.

In July of 1942, after months of deliberation, the Housing Authority finally authorized the construction of almost 5,000 new housing units, 93 percent of them located on the North Portland Peninsula. The North Portland area made sense for a number of reasons; open space was available for building, and the people in the housing developments would be close to war-time jobs in the factories along the Willamette and the Columbia. In addition, the character of peninsula neighborhoods was a factor. The *St. John's Review*, a North Portland newspaper, reported in March of 1942 that the projects were being planned "only in those districts where property values will not be hurt by the construction." Elite neighborhoods were not candidates for public housing.[4]

This modest start, however, came nowhere near satisfying the anticipated need for 32,000 new units in the Portland area. War industry owners, whose ability to step up production was limited by the availability of housing for workers, were frustrated with the slow pace of Portland's new Housing Authority. One of these owners took the housing business into his own hands. Henry J. Kaiser realized that the lack of housing in Portland was threatening his ability to recruit the army of workers that his war-time production schedule at his Oregon Shipbuilding Corporation factories demanded. Kaiser went straight to the federal government. . . .

In August of 1942, the Federal Public Housing Authority approved Kaiser's plan to build cheap wooden apartment buildings on 650 acres of lowlands near the Columbia Slough, just outside Portland city limits. Before the construction of Kaiserville, which was later renamed Vanport City, this area between the slough and the Columbia River had been marsh, pasture, and farmland. It was bounded on all four sides by dikes between fifteen and twenty-five feet high, which had kept the waters of both the slough and the river from flooding the farmland. . . .

Kaiser shipyard workers began moving into Vanport apartments in December of 1942, just four months after construction had begun. . . . By early November of [1943] the population had reached 39,000, making it Oregon's second largest city. The population remained near 40,000 until shipyard production waned at war's end. . . . The post-war population finally stabilized at around 18,500. It remained at that level until the city was wiped out by flood in 1948. Despite its short life, Vanport had a dramatic effect on the image of the peninsula.

Although the Housing Authority of Portland eventually administered sixteen different wartime housing projects, Vanport housed more people than those other projects combined. Indeed, Vanport was not only Oregon's largest wartime housing complex; it was the largest in the nation. However, while the new city helped to alleviate Portland's war-time housing crisis, it did not solve Portland's housing problem. Neither Vanport nor the rest of the city's housing projects, with the exception of about five hundred units at the Columbia Villa and Dekum Court developments, were intended as permanent housing. . . . Despite the housing crisis and the North Portland Peninsula's potential role in alleviating that crisis, industrial development remained the primary goal for the area. Indeed, the fact that public housing had been located on the peninsula seemed to accelerate rather than retard the push for industrial development. Politicians and planners argued that the kinds of people that public housing attracted demonstrated that public housing was not in the peninsula's best interest.

During the war, the North Portland Peninsula acquired a reputation as an area of industry, housing projects, and black residents. The first two characterizations were accurate, but the third was not. Nevertheless, the identification of North Portland with African Americans contributed to the perception of the area as blighted, suitable only for industry and for those who could not afford to live elsewhere. Many white city residents, politicians and businessmen were beginning to see North Portland as a throw-away zone.

Although North Portland was not a predominantly black area in the 1940s, the promise of jobs at Henry Kaiser's shipyards had attracted large numbers of African Americans to the Portland area for the first time, and many of them, along with many white migrants, found housing on the peninsula. In 1940, only 1,800 black people lived in Oregon. By 1944, that number had grown to about 15,000, with over one third living in Vanport. Though many white families moved out of Vanport at the war's end, most black families remained, in part because racist real estate practices and restrictions kept them from moving to many places in Portland.

Having African Americans as neighbors was a new experience for most Portlanders, and although African Americans never accounted for more than 28 percent of the population of Vanport, or more than 18 percent during the war years, the community quickly acquired a reputation as a "negro project." This was the first identification of the slough area with a minority population.

Initially, Vanport had been hailed as a "miracle" of city planning and public housing, with good cause. Community life was strong, the schools were integrated, and childcare was provided for the families of shipyard workers. The apartments were small but well-designed, and all vital services were provided within the walls of the city. In comparison with large federal wartime housing projects elsewhere in the country, living conditions and community life at Vanport were quite good, and racial conflicts were few. Nevertheless, almost immediately after it was built, residents, Portland leaders and federal officials began to criticize the development. The buildings were flimsy, heating was insufficient, and noise from the nearby factories was disturbing. In addition, officials fretted about the undefined but often cited "negro problem."[5]

The Housing Authority of Portland was very worried about the "negro problem." As early as 1943, Housing Authority commissioners were regularly spending portions of their meetings anxiously discussing the "negro situation." They were concerned, among other issues, about Vanport events that they described as "mixed dances (negro & white)."[6] . . .

In the years immediately following the war, as white families moved away and the black proportion of the population increased, Vanport's reputation as a black area intensified. Many Portland residents saw the housing development, unfairly and incorrectly, as a crime-ridden, black-dominated neighborhood. Indeed, as late as 1970, researchers reported in a demographic study done for the Center for Urban Education in Portland that "most" of Vanport's residents had been black, an assertion that was based on reputation, but not on fact. Because of its reputation as a "problem" area, few Portland residents who had not been living there were sorry to see it disappear in the flood of 1948. Indeed, by that time, many city officials and businessmen had spent years pushing to tear down the housing at Vanport and create an industrial park in its place.

As early as February of 1945, the Housing Authority of Portland was making plans for the destruction of Vanport. At a meeting that month, the commissioners agreed to vigorously pursue a plan "for post-war industrial development of Vanport City." . . . [7]

As luck would have it, a flood did the job for the Housing Authority. May of 1948 brought heavy rains and particularly warm weather, both of which contributed to unusually high water levels in Oregon's rivers. On Memorial Day, the waters of the Columbia River, behind Vanport's northern dike, and Smith Lake, behind the western dike, were fifteen feet above the city floor. The waters in the Columbia Slough, to Vanport's south, were quickly rising, too. . . . Shortly after 4:00 P.M., floodwaters crashed through the railroad dike to the west, and a ten-foot wall of water careened through Vanport, sweeping buildings off their flimsy foundations, sending them reeling through town as residents rushed to escape. More than two thousand people were initially declared missing in the flood; fifteen people were confirmed as dead and another eighteen missing. The next day, the Denver Avenue dike to the east of Vanport gave way. . . .

The Columbia River had reclaimed its flood plain. Vanport was not rebuilt, and its eighteen thousand residents had to find housing elsewhere. White residents scattered throughout the city. Most black residents moved to Albina, a run-down part of town south of the North Portland Peninsula, just across the Willamette River from Portland's Central Business District. Historically, Albina had been a stop-over district for recent immigrants of European descent, and it held the most densely built housing in the city. The neighborhood was one of the few areas in Portland from which black people were not excluded by racist white homeowners and real estate agents, who employed tactics ranging from restrictive housing covenants to outright violence in order to exclude African Americans from most neighborhoods in the city. By the 1930s, Albina had become the center of Portland's small black community, and when the flood destroyed Vanport, the development's black residents had little choice but to seek housing in that already overcrowded district. It was not until a fair housing law was passed in Oregon in 1959 that such residential segregation would be declared illegal. . . .

Although black residents had left the North Portland Peninsula and would not move back there in large numbers until the 1960s, the area's reputation as a black neighborhood would continue to encourage the placement of industry there. The disappearance of this major housing project on the peninsula, coupled with the endurance of a reputation of blight, helped to clear the way for intensive industrial development nearby at a time when environmentalists were beginning to secure gains elsewhere in the city. The swampy and flood-prone Vanport site itself, however, never became an industrial site; instead, a park and a golf course occupy the land today.

In addition to changes in the social landscape, the flood brought dramatic changes to the physical environment. The canal that the city built in the 1920s between the slough and the Columbia River to create a stronger current in the slough had always been difficult to maintain. When the Vanport flood sealed the entrances to the canal once again, the city council and the Port of Portland decided not to bother unblocking it. With the canal sealed, the slough was entirely cut off from Columbia River water, as it remains today. However, the fact that the current disappeared for good in the late 1940s did not cause a change in the amount of sewage and industrial waste dumped into the slough. It only slowed the sewage's trip down stream.

In the early 1950s, conditions of the slough became so bad that millworkers refused to handle logs that had traveled through the water. Meat-packing plant waste, hog ranch waste, and lumber and shingle mill waste would cling to the logs as they floated down the slough to the mills. Related concerns drove many of the industries which relied on navigation of the slough to relocate in the early 1950s, and by 1965, all commercial traffic on the slough had stopped. Industrial developers choosing sites near the slough after this point saw proximity to the waterway as a benefit not for transportation purposes, but rather for the disposal of wastes.

Until the 1950s, Portland's sewers dumped the city's waste, untreated, into the Willamette River and the Columbia Slough. In an attempt to clean up the local waterways, the City of Portland finally began building a sewage treatment plant in the late 1940s, which began operating in 1951. Unfortunately, this by no means solved the peninsula's sewage woes. The plant, which provided for the treatment of much of Portland's sewage before discharging it into the Columbia River, contributed significantly to the improvement of the water quality of the slough and the rivers. However, the city placed the plant itself on the banks of the slough. The peninsula was still collecting the city's sludge.

Also, despite the new plant, not all sewage was treated before it reached the waterways. Although many of the industries which had been dumping their sewage into the slough began to send their sewage to the treatment plant, a number of businesses which were not connected to city sewers continued to send their waste into the slough. In addition, although the city sewers had been rerouted to the treatment plant, the plant was not always able to handle all the sewage sent there. When storm water mixed with the sewage, it exceeded the treatment plant's capacity. At these times, the sewers would overflow and the mixture of sewage and stormwater would spill over weirs, or gates, in the sewer pipes and fall into the Willamette and the slough. Such an occurrence, frequent in rainy Portland, is called a "combined sewer overflow" or "CSO." Although this arrangement was far superior to dumping all raw sewage directly into the water, CSOs were still a serious problem facing the slough.[8] . . .

Meanwhile, with the help of Portland real estate developers and city officials, many new industries were finding homes along the slough. . . .

In the 1950s, Portland city planners began to turn to strategies of "urban renewal" in order to plan for the city's future development and to fix what were seen as existing development problems. . . .

A significant component of Portland's urban renewal plan included decisions about where to allow industry within the city. Industry was considered a major cause of blight in residential neighborhoods, and therefore a blight removal and prevention plan had to pay close attention to the placement of industry. In analyzing areas to determine where industrial expansion was appropriate, the Planning Commission took many factors into account, including prior industrial development, traffic capacity, and the availability of land.

Other factors which the commission considered were indicated in a handwritten outline for a Planning Commission report on expanding the city's industrial sector. The report, the purpose of which was to provide recommendations for maintaining and improving industrial districts within the city and to recommend new sites, listed "housing condition and population characteristics" as factors to consider in industrial zoning and development decisions. The population characteristics the outline specifically called attention to were "stability," "income," and "non-white" status. The implication was that low-income minority neighborhoods were the most appropriate for industry. Other neighborhoods would be protected from industrial blight. This practice of placing industry in areas that were considered to be already blighted by industry and by demographics would continue throughout the 1970s and 1980s.[9]

The impression left by Vanport that the peninsula was a "minority" area encouraged the siting of industry there. Among the businesses that opened along the slough in the post-war years were numerous metal production plants and chemical plants, a wood-treatment facility, and a construction materials plant, which contributed to the accumulation of lead, Pentachlorophenol (PCP), polychlorinated biphenyls (PCBs), cyanide, chromium, hydrochloric acid, dioxins and other pollutants in the slough. Ironically, by the time that African Americans returned to the North Portland Peninsula in substantial (though not majority) numbers, they were finding affordable housing in neighborhoods that had been devalued, and rendered toxic, in part by the idea that there were black residents living there.

Ecotopia and the Slough

In the 1970s, Oregon began to acquire a reputation as "ecotopia," a place where the environmentalists were in charge and people lived in balance with nature. This is a reputation that has in large part endured until today. Oregon is associated with environmentalist governor Tom McCall, the bottle bill, the dramatic cleanup of the Willamette River, and a novel system of state-wide environmentally-sensitive land use planning.... The Columbia Slough, however, is not simply a forgotten waterway that missed the environmental fervor. Rather, it is a sacrificed waterway. The Willamette River cleanup was paid for, in part, by the filth of waterways like the slough and neighborhoods like those of the North Portland Peninsula.

Historian Carl Abbott writes that by the 1980s, Portland had gained "a reputation for strong-minded and environmentally sensitive metropolitan planning." Tom McCall, Oregon's governor from 1967 to 1974, was in large part responsible for this reputation.[10] During his first term as governor, McCall oversaw the creation of the Oregon Department of Environmental Quality and the concerted effort to clean up the Willamette River, which had been so polluted that fish suffocated in its waters. He also pushed through the five "B" bills, which "required removal of billboards, reasserted public ownership of ocean beaches, set minimum deposits on beverage bottles and cans, allocated money for bicycle paths from highway revenues, and tied bonding for pollution abatement to the growth of total assessed values."[11]

Perhaps the most dramatic environmental accomplishment of McCall's administration, however, was the establishment [of] the Land Conservation and Development Commission in 1973, the job of which was to oversee local compliance with newly established state-wide land use planning goals. Among the goals, which were revised in 1974, were the preservation of farm land, the energy-efficient use of land, and the definition of urban growth boundaries to set limits on urban sprawl.[12]

The urban growth boundaries, in particular, changed the face of land use planning in Oregon. In the 1950s and 1960s, Oregon had been experiencing rapid suburban growth. Single family homes on large plots were eating away at the state's open space and at the land on which Oregon's farming and resource industries depended. The urban growth boundaries contained that sprawl by encouraging the intensive development of urban areas and by setting limits on development outside of the boundaries. Metropolitan growth began to be seen as an environmental disaster, and Oregonians wanted to protect against the peril of "Californication."[13]

... Much like the urban renewal plans of the 1950s, this urban growth plan of the 1970s protected the environments of middle and upper-class neighborhoods, while promising the more intensive development of those areas which had already been degraded. The neighborhoods of the North Portland Peninsula fell into this latter category. ...

Although planners paid much attention to the regional economic and environmental aspects of metropolitan planning, they did not give much consideration to the different experiences that different groups would have under the new, environmentally sensitive plans. Not all neighborhoods and not all people would find themselves in cleaner, more environmentally sound surroundings. The case of the Columbia Slough and the neighborhoods of the North Portland Peninsula provide an example of how land use regulations affected different groups of people in different ways. At the slough, it is clear that land use regulations worked against the working-class and minority peoples who lived there. At a time when much of the state was being cleaned up, the Columbia Slough stagnated. ... This had become an industrial area, one of the few places in the state that was allowed to remain filthy, so that industry could thrive while the rest of the state was provided with a cleaner, healthier environment.

Plans for Tom McCall's Willamette River Greenway project set aside park and recreation areas and open space along the Willamette River and its tributaries. However, although the plan included substantial portions of many of the small waterways contributing to the Willamette, the slough was not among the beneficiaries of the project. The Columbia Slough was just outside of the Greenway boundaries, and was instead zoned for industry. This meant that the area near the slough would shoulder a much larger and more concentrated share of local industry and industrial pollution.

North Portland residents protested what they saw happening to their neighborhoods. In 1971, an article in the *Oregonian* quoted Oregon Marine Board director Robert Rittenhouse describing the Columbia Slough as "the rottenest stream in the Northwest." The same article explained that the Port of Portland saw the slough as "playing a key role" in the long-range industrial planning of the area, and hinted at the reason that the waterway was not being included in cleanup plans: "The slough is close to thousands of North Portlanders, many retired and with low incomes – people with little political power." The article went on to describe how many of the neighborhood people favored using the slough, not as a drainage or sewage canal, and not for navigation, but for recreation and for food. "Fish caught there in the past have supplemented the diet of some people with skimpy grocery budgets," the article reported.[14]

However, in the early 1970s, the Port of Portland was not focusing on the slough as a neighborhood resource. Rather, it was concentrating on the possibilities for expanding industrial development in the slough area. . . . Cleaning the slough, though still discussed, began to be portrayed as a lofty but impractical goal.

Port of Portland General Manager George M. Baldwin proposed putting flood gates at the slough's mouth at the Willamette River. This would have closed the slough to navigation but offered more flood protection to the Rivergate Industrial District (see map 11.1), development of which had begun in 1965, and which the Port hoped would become home to hundreds of industries. . . .

When area industry owners responded that the slough should remain open for navigation and was a vital waterway for industry, Port officials argued that the slough's conditions were so bad that neither navigation nor recreational use were practical ideas. . . . With the water already so fouled, the Port argued, the most sensible use of the slough was as a drainage ditch.

Other business owners argued that all that was needed to clean the slough was a good flush, which the Columbia River could provide if the city canal were reopened. Assistant Port Manager Adam Heineman disagreed, arguing that cleaning the slough by flushing it with Columbia River water would be impractical. "There's so much filth and pollution already in the slough it would take years for it to clean itself out naturally," he said. This debate continues today, with most environmentalists joining the anti-flushing faction. . . . [15]

The Oregon State Game Commission, in assessing the ecological impact of the Port's plan for the Columbia Slough area, wrote in approval that "concentrating, rather than scattering, industry and residential areas minimizes damage to wildlife by preserving natural habitat and open spaces. . . . " Clearly, the North Portland area was being sacrificed so that the "best habitat," in other parts of the city and state, could be preserved. [16]

Residents of the peninsula were not pleased with the proposals, and they resented the process by which those proposals had been reached. As early as 1971, area residents were upset that the public had had no part in the planning of a large industrial district on the peninsula. . . .

In response to public demands for participation in the decision making process, the Army Corps of Engineers held a public workshop in June of 1973 to try to form a citizens' advisory committee to provide input on decisions made about flood control in the area, but at the meeting, residents felt intimidated by the presence of members of so many government agencies. Members of the Army Corps of Engineers were joined at the meeting by representatives of the Port of Portland, the

Columbia Region Association of Governments, the Multnomah County
Planning Division, the Oregon State Marine Board, the Oregon State
Water Resources Board, the City of Portland Parks Bureau, the U.S.
General Accounting Office, the Bonneville Power Administration, and
the Oregon State Highway Division. In addition, representatives from
many area industries, including Union Pacific Railroad Company, Moar
Lumber Company, and Upland Industries Corporation were there. The
primary purpose of the meeting was supposed to be the solicitation of
citizen involvement. However, fewer than half of the almost seventy
people who filled out attendance cards after the meeting identified
themselves as area homeowners, residents or members of neighborhood
organizations.

The residents had barely been notified of the meeting, as Clifford
Nelson observed:

> I think the main reason [that more people aren't here at the meeting] is
> that where you advertise the average citizen never looks at; for example, I
> just found the article by happenstance and came over here. I found it down
> in the corner of the market reports. It seems to me that you should send
> the meeting notices to "Occupant." This would be better than putting it in
> the Daily Journal of Commerce. How many citizens read that news-
> paper?[17]

Nor did residents feel welcome. Mary Runyon complained at the meeting, "The residents have been pushed around by various agencies and
the fact that there are so many agencies represented here tonight gives us
the feeling we are being overpowered." Clifford Nelson agreed with her.
"Many of the people who are doing so much talking do not live down
here. Why is there so much talk if they do not live down here?" he asked.
He was told by Joe Heidel of the Army Corps of Engineers that living in
the area was no prerequisite to being interested in the slough.[18]

The meeting was a confusing affair. The Corps of Engineers wanted to
limit the topic of discussion to their area of jurisdiction, flood control,
and the related issues of recreation, water quality improvement, and fish
and wildlife habitat. However, area residents wanted to broaden the
discussion. Their interests included public health, industrial zoning,
proximity of housing to industry, and rights of property owners, among
other issues. There was no clear sense of what the meeting was intended
to accomplish, and many people were left irritated and confused....

At the end of the workshop, participants were asked to submit their
names, addresses and areas of interest to the Corps of Engineers representatives, who would then coordinate committees to work on various
topics. City documents show no indication of specific follow-up

meetings, although the North Portland Citizen's Committee, a coalition of eight North Portland neighborhood associations, members of which had been at the Army Corps meeting, became more active in issues relating to the slough shortly after this workshop.

In October of 1974, the North Portland Citizen's Committee held a conference titled "North Peninsula Environment '74: Lakes, Lands & Livability." Sharon Roso, who compiled the conference report, had participated in the Army Corps workshop the previous year. This conference was designed specifically with the needs of the community residents in mind. The purpose of the conference, according to Roso, was "to find out agency plans for and needs of that area, and for local people and agency people to ask specific questions regarding lakes, land and livability...." Among the agencies the committee invited to participate in the conference were the Corps of Engineers, the Port of Portland, the Portland Landfill, the Department of Environmental Quality (DEQ), the Multnomah County Planning Bureau, the Portland Planning Bureau and the Columbia Region Association of Governments. The conference culminated with North Portland residents mapping their priorities for their environment, which they then presented to the various agencies.[19]

...Water quality was something the residents did not want to see compromised in any way.

The citizens were also highly concerned about air quality.... The citizens' requests made it clear that they felt as though their neighborhood was being used as a dumping ground. "Treat the North Portland Peninsula as a natural resource rather than as an area for dumping industry unwanted in cleaner areas, or a site for maximum development, or maximum profit," they requested of the Port. The area residents were also concerned with noise pollution and increased traffic through their area.[20]

Among the specific requests outlined in the conference report were requests that the city engineer plan to eliminate the St. John's Landfill within the decade, and that the city and county planning bureaus avoid zoning the areas around the Columbia Slough for heavy industry. In addition, the area residents asked that the Department of Environmental Quality set and enforce strict air-quality standards....

Almost all of the community's requests were ignored. The slough area was zoned for heavy industry, and the St. John's Landfill was kept open until it could hold no more garbage in 1991. The DEQ continued to issue permits to polluting industries, including industries which dumped factory waste directly into the slough. And the North Portland Peninsula remained a dumping ground for industry that no one wanted anywhere else....

City of Portland records describing citizen participation in neighborhood meetings in the 1970s offer no indication of the class or ethnicity of the area residents who attempted to influence planning decisions for North Portland. However, the fact that the 1973 meeting was not widely publicized suggests that those citizens who found out about the meeting and made arrangements to attend were among the best-connected and most politically active members of the North Portland Peninsula community. The fact that even this group felt bullied by government agencies and ignored by the planning bureaucracy suggests the extent to which this predominantly working-class area was excluded from the decision-making processes affecting their community.

Also during the 1970s, the minority population of the peninsula was on the rise, as more African Americans and recent immigrants began to find housing in the neighborhoods near the slough. In 1950, when only 4 percent of Portland residents were classified as non-white in the federal census, the census tracts along the slough reported similar numbers. By 1970, in most of the census tracts along the lower Columbia Slough, the percentage of non-white residents was at least twice as high as the city-wide average. In 1990, the census reported that the minority proportion of the population on the peninsula had continued to increase. That year, 7.6 percent of the residents of the Portland metropolitan area were classified as black, and 15 percent were classified as non-white.... By this time, fully one quarter of Portland's African-American residents lived in the immediate vicinity of the slough, and the proportion living in the old Albina district had significantly declined.

The decline in the number of African-American residents in the Albina district was due in part to urban renewal projects undertaken there during the 1950s and 1960s. Many Albina residents were displaced by the construction of the Portland Coliseum in the 1950s and by the construction of Interstate Five in the 1960s.... [M]any African Americans continued to face opposition when they sought housing in many Portland neighborhoods. Census statistics show that most African-American Portland residents found housing near the Albina district even after large blocks of housing were razed to make way for the sports arena and the highway. Historian Carl Abbott has pointed out that the center of Portland's African-American population has shifted to the north in recent decades, toward the Columbia Slough.[21]

Indeed, houses closer to the slough were in better condition than many in the old Albina district, and census information suggests that a move from the Albina area to the neighborhoods of the North Portland Peninsula was a move up. In 1970, in the census tracts which had been the center of the old Albina district and which were still each over 40 percent black in 1970 (one tract was over 77 percent black), the median family income in 1969 was less than $5,300. That same year, the median family income for the Portland Metropolitan Area as a whole was $10,463. In the census tracts along the slough, where the black population was increasing, family incomes were closer to the city-wide median. In one of the tracts along the lower slough, the median family income was $7,549; in each of the other tracts, the median was over $8,000. The 1990 census showed a similar pattern. . . . Likewise, 1990 home values were significantly higher closer to the slough, though still well below the city-wide median.

In Portland, African Americans moving out of the old ghetto district in search of better homes have found those better homes in one of the most toxic areas of the city. As one drives north through the old Albina district and onto the North Portland Peninsula, the improvement in housing conditions is obvious. The homes are in better condition, there is more space between houses, and there are more and bigger lawns. The sewage and industrial filth that pollute the neighborhoods are not so visible at first glance. As in Gary, Indiana, better housing for many African Americans has meant worse water and worse air.

The pollution and industrial development which have kept property values lower on the peninsula, which were in turn encouraged by assumptions about the types of people who did and should live in these neighborhoods, meant that relatively inexpensive housing was available here for African Americans looking for better housing, and for working-class white Portlanders, and for recent immigrants from Vietnam, Cambodia, Laos, Eastern Europe, Mexico and Central America. . . . As part of its recent campaign to educate people against eating fish caught in the Columbia Slough, the Portland Bureau of Environmental Services commissioned a survey which suggests that the majority of people who eat fish caught in the slough are recent immigrants.

It is not sufficient to say that low-income white and non-white Portlanders live near the slough because housing there is inexpensive due to its proximity to industry. A long history of development and zoning decisions coupled with discriminatory housing practices and inequitable environmental policies have created the North Portland landscape of the 1990s, in which the most toxic neighborhoods in the city also have the highest proportion of minority residents. City planners, politicians, developers, real estate agents, home owners, landlords, and environmentalists have all contributed to the creation of the Portland landscape in which inexpensive housing is most accessible to working-class whites, African Americans, and recent immigrants in the most toxic part of the city.

Postscript

. . . In the quarter century since the residents of the North Portland Peninsula voiced their frustration at plans for their neighborhoods, the city and the Port have held dozens of meetings about pollution at the slough and development on the peninsula. Also during that time, Rivergate Industrial District has become home to more than sixty manufacturing, distribution and warehousing businesses. The Port has added more than seventy million cubic yards of fill to the industrial park to build it up and reduce the chance of flooding. Whether the slough should be completely closed for better flood control or reopened for navigation remains a subject of controversy. Only in the past several years has cleaning the slough re-entered the debate at an official level. As late as the early 1990s, when public officials discussed a clean-up of the slough, it was often peripheral to discussion of development concerns.

Since 1972, the city and the Port have conducted more than forty studies of the slough, and they have debated at least eight different plans for altering its conditions. . . . However, despite the fact that the city has spent more than twenty years and $14 million studying this toxic waterway and talking with the area residents about the problems in their neighborhood, the slough remains an environmental disaster.

As the City of Portland has begun to recognize the environmental crisis of the Columbia Slough, it has begun to recognize that African Americans and recent immigrant groups have been bearing a disproportionate share of the burden of that crisis. In 1993, the activist lawyers of Portland's legal environmental group Northwest Environmental Advocates threatened to sue the city for violating the Federal Clean Water Act, and the city took notice. Since then, there has been progress.

In September of 1993, in response to the lawsuit threatened by Northwest Environmental Advocates in July of that year, the Portland City Council voted to spend $125 million to eliminate all combined sewer overflows on the slough, which environmentalists and many city officials viewed as only the first step in an extensive and expensive clean-up project. Heavy rains in 1996 and 1997 and the accompanying sewer overflows prompted repeated warnings about dangerous water and fish in the slough, and it wasn't until early 1998 that almost $32 million in construction contracts were awarded to begin work on "the Big Pipe," a 3.5 mile long conduit intended to collect sewage and rainwater that would otherwise flow directly into the slough during storms.

But the sewers are only a part of the problem. Every time it rains, the raw sewage that flows into the slough is joined by polluted groundwater, industrial wastes, chemicals from the Portland Airport, and toxins leaching from the St. John's Landfill. Another study in the seemingly endless series of studies, this one released in 1997, argues that the slough is too polluted to ever properly clean up. Meanwhile, the city continues to issue warnings about swimming and fishing in the slough, and people continue to fish there, and to swim.

Ultimately, however, in focusing on water quality in the slough, city officials are focusing on a single piece of a larger problem. The intensive industrial development that plagues the peninsula continues, with no change of pace or development strategy in sight, and the people who live on the peninsula are still being exposed to a disproportionate share of the pollution these industries produce. Until the environmental crisis of the peninsula as a whole is addressed, and until the environment there is recognized as an integral part of Oregon's larger landscape, the situation is not likely to improve. . . .

Notes

1 A slough (pronounced "sloo") is a swampy waterway or marsh with very little current, if any.

2 John Bonebrake, telephone interview by author, 5 May 1994, Portland, written record in possession of the author.

3 Marianne Lavelle and Marcia Coyle, "Unequal Protection: The Racial Divide in Environmental Law," *National Law Journal* 15 (21 September 1992), S1.

4 "Report on a Proposed General Policy from a Program of Temporary Defense Housing for Portland," Portland: Housing Authority of Portland, 1942. Parr Archives, Series 0605-02, Location: 06-06-60, Folder 6/58; *St. John's Review*, 20 March 1942, 1.

5 Manley Maben, *Vanport* (Portland: Oregon Historical Society Press, 1987), 25–28, 31; Carl Abbott, *Portland: Planning, Politics, and Growth in a Twentieth-Century City* (Lincoln: University of Nebraska Press, 1983), E. Kimbark MacColl, *Growth of a City: Power and Politics in Portland, Oregon, 1915–50* (Portland, Or.: Georgian Press, 1970), 578

6 Housing Authority of Portland Minutes, July 1943, Parr Archives, Series 0605-02, Location: 06-06-58, Folder 4/7; Housing Authority of Portland Minutes, 20 April 1944, Parr Archives, Series 0605-02, Location: 06-06-58, Folder 4/16; Housing Authority of Portland Minutes, 16 September 1943, Parr Archives, Series 0605-02, Location: 06-06-58, Folder 4/9; Maben, *Vanport*, 89–90.

7 Housing Authority of Portland Minutes, 15 February 1945, Parr Archives, Series 0605-02, Location: 06-06-58, Folder 4/26.

8 Joe Fitzgibbon, "Now-Ailing Slough Has Rich History," *Portland Oregonian*, 16 September 1993, 5; *Toxic Waters*. CSOs still plague the slough. During the rainy season, 70 percent of the lower slough's flow comes from CSOs.

9 Planning Commission, handwritten outline of report [1960s]. Parr Archives, Series 7706-15, Location: 10-10-14, Folder 3/2. The Planning Commission was following a standard national convention by making investment and development decisions based on the perceived stability of neighborhoods. See Kenneth T. Jackson, *Crabgrass Frontier: The Suburbanization of the United*

States (New York: Oxford University Press, 1985), Chapter 11, for a discussion of Federal Housing Administration redlining practices.

10   Abbott, *Portland*, 248–49.

11   Ibid., 250–51; Brendt Walth, *Fire At Eden's Gate: Tom McCall and the Oregon Story* (Portland: Oregon Historical Society Press, 1994), 327.

12   Abbott, *Portland*, 251–52.

13   Ibid., 248, 250.

14   Jim Kadera, "Polluted Columbia Slough Faces Clean-up Problems," *Portland Oregonian*, 1 August 1971, 11.

15   Ibid. "Columbia Slough Flood Control Plan Receives Approval of County Board," *Portland Oregonian*, 1 May 1970, 29.

16   Quoted in "The Columbia Slough: Its History and Current Status," City of Portland Report, June 1972, Parr Archives, Series 7706-06, Location: 10-09-33/1, Folder 1/2.

17   "Rivergate-North Portland Survey Study Workshop Notes," 3; "Rivergate-North Portland Survey Study Workshop Attendance", 6, Columbia School, Portland, 14 June 1973, Parr Archives, Series 7706-06, Location: 10-09-33/1, Folder 1/3.

18   "Rivergate-North Portland Survey Study Workshop Notes," 3, 5, Columbia School, Portland, 14 June 1973, Parr Archives, Series 7706-06, Location: 10-09-33/1, Folder 1/3.

19   Sharon Roso, compiler, "North Peninsula Environment '74: Lakes, Lands & Livability – A North Portland Conference," (Portland: North Portland Citizen's Committee, 1974), 1, Parr Archives, Series 5000-1000-01. Location 09-07-22, Folder 2/35: 1.

20   Ibid., 2, 3.

21   Abbott, *Portland*, 26; Stuart McElderry, "The Problem of the Color Line: Civil Rights and Racial Ideology in Portland Oregon, 1944–1965" (Ph.D. diss., University of Oregon, 1998), 235, 315, 325.

Documents

Lois Gibbs on toxic waste and environmental justice

Reprinted from *Toxic Struggles: The Theory and Practice of Environmental Justice*, ed. Richard Holrichter (Philadelphia: New Society Publishers, 1993)

The movement for environmental justice in many ways grew out of the populist rebellion against toxic wastes hidden or deposited in residential areas without the knowledge of homeowners. The most famous instance of this kind occurred in the early 1970s, in Love Canal, in New York state. Residents of Love Canal discovered that their neighborhood's peculiarly high rate of childhood deafness and other maladies, as well as foul-smelling sludge that leaked into basements and exploding rocks on the playground of the neighborhood school, were connected to the area's secret history as a dumping ground for waste products of Hooker Chemical Company. Lois Gibbs was a local housewife who led the campaign to compensate the largely working-class residents of the Love Canal community. Here she speaks about her own experience as a working-class woman at Love Canal and her view of the environmental struggle to which she has dedicated her life ever since.

How is this different from the environmental movement that Robert Gottlieb discussed in chapter 9? Compare and contrast the role of Lois Gibbs with that of Alice Hamilton and Rachel Carson. What would Lois Gibbs think of William Cronon's arguments about wilderness and the need to take greater responsibility for nature close to home?

* * *

When my mother asked me what I wanted to do when I grew up, I said I wanted to have six children and be a homemaker. I moved into Love Canal, and I bought the American Dream: a house, two children, a husband, and HBO. And then something happened to me, and that was Love Canal. I got involved because my son Michael had epilepsy, and my daughter Melissa developed a rare blood disease and almost died because of something someone else did. I never thought of myself as an activist or an organizer. I was a housewife, a mother, but all of a sudden it was my family, my children, and my neighbors. I believed in democracy, but then I discovered that it was government and industry that abused my rights. But my experience is not unique.

Every day across the country people distressed about the health and well-being of their families demand justice. Families who have diligently paid their taxes, farmers who have struggled for generations to keep their family farms, poor families desperately trying to break the pattern of poverty and give their children a fighting chance: they have typically suffered the greatest inequities. They are the families who make up the backbone of our country, to whom politicians play for votes, and those for whom corporations design and direct their advertising.

These are the people who make up the grass-roots movement for environmental justice. This movement, in hundreds of local and regional organizations, is typically led by women, working-class people, and people of color. Many, particularly the women, have never been involved in any political issue before and have been galvanized primarily by their concern for their children's safety. Women in Texas, for example, organized against the pollution they believed was causing brain cancer in their children. A mother of a child born severely retarded became a leader in a movement against a battery recycler in Throop, Pennsylvannia, that contaminated her neighborhood with lead. A mother of two autistic children in Lemonster, Massachusetts, discovered that there were over one hundred autistic children in her community, a statistic she believes is the result of policies at a nearby Foster-Grant sunglasses plant. The heartbreak and struggles can be heard in every state in this country.

Although these leaders became involved because of a single issue or problem, they quickly recognized the interconnections with other injustices they face daily. They realize that the root of their problem is the lack of organized political power, deteriorating neighborhood conditions, poverty, and race. Increasingly, they are beginning to recognize the international dimensions of the problem and make common cause with others around the world, such as during the United Nations Conference on Environment and Development (UNCED) in Rio de Janeiro in June, 1992. Community leaders understand, for example, that the dump or incinerator in their community is only a symptom of a larger problem: the lack of political power to resist the companies and public officials who put it there. As they battle with various bureaucracies to resolve the crisis that brought them together, they begin to identify links among issues and build an even broader coalition for change.

As a result, these leaders now build bridges with civil-rights and labor organizations, housing groups, and those fighting for adequate health care for all. As these groups join together, they develop the skills, information sources, and means of communicating the dangers they face to a wider public. These new alliances and cooperative work can achieve real democracy.

Those in power, however, fearful of these new alliances and the potential for resistance, have begun to drive wedges between the diverse groups. They are concerned about citizens rethinking how and what is produced and for whom. Such rethinking may lead to more democratic ways of decision making about ecological matters.

Community leaders are making connections with other environmental organizations and developing partnerships with local nonenvironmental groups. Civil-rights leaders, economic development groups, healthcare advocates, and women's groups are increasingly addressing more basic forms of oppression and unequal power. Alliances at the local and state level result in national coalitions. The First National People of Color Environmental Leadership Summit, held in Washington, D.C., in October, 1991, was a prime example of diverse groups with many issues devising a plan to force social change.

A major goal of the grass-roots movement for environmental justice is to rebuild the United States, community by community. Many people no longer accept the either-or rhetoric of jobs vs. the environment, health care vs. housing, or education vs. economic development. They know that there are numerous choices. This movement, working from the bottom up, builds powerful community organizations that enact strong local laws, launch ballot initiatives, and run their own candidates for office at all governmental levels.

From United Church of Christ, *Toxic Wastes and Race in the United States*

In the years since Lois Gibbs first asked what was causing the strange ailments in her town, numerous communities of color have had similar experiences to that of the mostly white, blue-collar residents of Love Canal. Charges of widespread environmental racism in American society were enhanced by the report of the United Church of Christ in 1987, which substantiated what many minority critics of environmentalism have been saying for a long time: environmental pollution is directed towards communities of color.

As you read this excerpt from their report, consider: is environmental racism a new phenomenon, or is it just another face of racism? How does this report about pollution in communities of color compare to the environmental history of Georgia's rice plantations and Indian experience generally?

*   *   *

The findings of the analytical study suggest the existence of clear patterns which show that communities with greater minority percentages of the population are more likely to be the sites of commercial hazardous waste facilities. The possibility that these patterns resulted by chance is virtually impossible, strongly suggesting that some underlying factor or factors, which are related to race, played a role in the location of commercial hazardous waste facilities. Therefore, the Commission for Racial Justice concludes that, indeed, race has been a factor in the location of commercial hazardous waste facilities in the United States.

The findings of the descriptive study suggest an inordinate concentration of uncontrolled toxic waste sites in Black and Hispanic communities, particularly in urban areas. This situation reveals that the issue of race is an important factor in describing the problem of uncontrolled toxic waste sites. We, therefore, conclude that the cleanup of uncontrolled toxic waste sites in Black and Hispanic communities in the United States should be given the highest possible priority.

The magnitude of the problem of hazardous wastes in racial and ethnic communities demands that an aggressive action plan be implemented, combining the best efforts of environmental agencies, corporations, environmental organizations, legislators, churches, civil rights and community-based organizations. The Commission for Racial Justice is therefore recommending a series of actions that have the potential for making the broadest social and political impact with respect to existing and potential hazardous waste problems in racial and ethnic communities.

Immediate attention should be focused on areas where the existence of operating hazardous waste facilities and uncontrolled sites may pose a serious threat to public health and overall community development. Seven metropolitan areas have been identified for particular attention due to the high number of Blacks, Hispanics and other racial and ethnic persons residing in them. They are: (1) Memphis, Tennessee; (2) St. Louis, Missouri; (3) Houston, Texas; (4) Cleveland, Ohio; (5) Chicago, Illinois; (6) Atlanta, Georgia; and (7) Los Angeles, California. Many of the recommendations of this report will focus on programs and actions to address hazardous waste problems in these and similar metropolitan areas.

The Letter that Shook a Movement

Sierra, May/June 1993, p. 54

Partly as a result of the report by the United Church of Christ, the Southwest Organizing Project, an Albuquerque-based community organization, and Louisiana's Gulf Coast Tenant Leadership Development Project sent letters to the ten major American environmental reform organizations, including the Sierra Club, Friends of the Earth, and the Environmental Defense Fund, protesting years of neglect on environmental issues relevant to poor and minority peoples. One of these letters is reproduced here. What did SWOP mean by "Third World" communities in the United States?

The environmental justice movement, a loose coalition of hundreds of grassroots groups led by people of color, was born out of a challenge to the country's largest environmental organizations. Below are excerpts from a letter sent by the Southwest Organizing Project on March 15, 1990, to what's known as the "Group of Ten": the Sierra Club, Sierra Club Legal Defense Fund, Friends of the Earth, The Wilderness Society, National Audubon Society, Natural Resources Defense Council, Environmental Defense Fund, National Wildlife Federation, Izaak Walton League, and National Parks and Conservation Association.

*   *   *

We are writing this letter in the belief that through dialogue and mutual strategizing we can create a global environmental movement that protects us all. . . .

For centuries, people of color in our region have been subjected to racist and genocidal practices, including the theft of lands and water, the murder of innocent people, and the degradation of our environment. Mining companies extract minerals, leaving economically depressed communities and poisoned soil and water. The U.S. military takes lands for weapons production, testing, and storage, contaminating surrounding communities and placing minority workers in the most highly radioactive and toxic work sites. Industrial and municipal dumps are intentionally placed in communities of color, disrupting our cultural lifestyle and threatening our communities' futures. Workers in the fields are dying and babies are born disfigured as a result of pesticide spraying.

Although environmental organizations calling themselves the "Group of Ten" often claim to represent our interests, in observing your activities it has become clear to us that your organizations play an equal role in the disruption of our communities. *There is a clear lack of accountability by the Group of Ten environmental organizations towards Third World communities in the Southwest, in the United States as a whole, and internationally.*

Your organizations continue to support and promote policies that emphasize the cleanup and preservation of the environment on the backs of working people in general and people of color in particular. In the name of eliminating environmental hazards at any cost, across the country industrial and other economic activities which employ us are being shut down, curtailed, or prevented while our survival needs and cultures are ignored. We suffer from the end results of these actions, but are never full participants in the decision-making which leads to them. . . .

We . . . call upon you to cease operation in communities of color within 60 days, until you have hired leaders from those communities to the extent that they make up between 35 and 40 percent of your entire staff. We are asking that Third World leaders be hired at all levels of your operations. . . . Also provide a list of communities of color to whom you furnish services, or Third World communities in which you have organizing drives or campaigns, and contacts in those communities. . . .

It is our sincere hope that we can have a frank and open dialogue with your organization and other national environmental organizations. It is our opinion that people of color in the United States and throughout the world are clearly an endangered species. Issues of environmental destruction are issues of our immediate and long-term survival. We hope that we can soon work with your organization in helping to assure the safety and well-being of all peoples.

12
Backlash against the Environmental Movement

Because the events examined in this chapter are relatively recent, we await a comprehensive historical evaluation of them. For this reason, this chapter and the next do not have the kind of scholarly discussion that has opened every other chapter in this book. Rather, we shall look exclusively at documents from the era, in an attempt to generate insights into the leading issues of the period, and hopefully to inspire questions that could lead to good research in these areas, also.

The many successes of the environmental movement perhaps made inevitable some kind of backlash against it. Critics of environmentalism were vaulted to power with the election of Ronald Reagan in 1980. Reagan appointed prominent anti-environmentalists to key positions in his administration. The most notable of these was James Watt, a lawyer at one of the most vehemently anti-environmental law firms in the country. Watt became Secretary of the Interior Department, which is responsible for stewarding America's natural resources, including wilderness areas and the national parks.

For environmentalists, the Reagan administration marked the end of their movement's golden age. As we shall see below, Reagan's opposition to environmentalism had some paradoxical outcomes which were not without benefit to the movement. But the last decade of the twentieth century saw the efflorescence of Reaganite anti-environmentalism to a *bona fide* political movement of its own. The increasingly conservative turn of the United States Congress under the Clinton administration, culminating in Republican, anti-environmental majorities in 1994, threatened to make environmentalism a dissident movement without the kind of sway it held in the 1960s and 1970s, when politicians of both parties eagerly supported it.

Documents

Carl Pope, "The Politics of Plunder"

Reprinted from *Reagan as President: Contemporary views of the Man, his Politics, and his Policies*, ed. with commentary by Paul Boyer (Chicago: Ivan R. Dee, 1990)

In our first document, Carl Pope, currently president of the Sierra Club, reflects on the paradoxical impact of the Reagan administration on the environmental movement. Reagan remained extraordinarily popular throughout his administration, and he was re-elected to a second term in 1984. But his environmental policies, through which he sought to roll back many of the achievements of the movement in the previous two decades, were rarely successful. Oddly, Reagan's antagonism seems to have galvanized support for environmentalism. Is environmentalism now such a part of American culture that it has reshaped politics beyond the need for an easily identifiable "movement"? Was the Reagan administration bad for the environmental movement? Or was it an ally in disguise?

*   *   *

At half past four on election day, 1980, Sierra Club volunteers and staff gather around a borrowed television set at the Club's San Francisco headquarters to watch the returns.

For the first time the Club has conducted a major voter-education drive. It's been a discouraging effort. Republican presidential candidate Ronald Reagan has barnstormed the country, attacking the Carter administration and even its Republican predecessors for turning environmental agencies over to "extremists." He has made some outlandish statements, ranging from a promise to invite the steel and oil industries to rewrite the EPA's regulations to a charge that 80 percent of the nation's air pollution problems are caused by chemicals released by trees. Despite growing controversy over Reagan's reactionary environmental stands, polls indicate that he is likely to defeat the incumbent, Jimmy Carter.

Groans fill the room as soon as the television is turned on. Even though the polls will remain open for several hours in the far West, the networks are already proclaiming Reagan the winner.

Spirits slump further as the Senate and House results pour in. In state after state, senators who have fought for the environment are being upset by their opponents. . . . Frank Church of Idaho, one of the Senate's leading proponents of wilderness, is narrowly defeated by Steve Symms, a virulent advocate of public-land exploitation. By seven o'clock only a scattering of sorrowful Sierra Clubbers remain at the election-night party.

The next morning it is clear that very few pro-environment candidates have managed to claw their way to the top of the Reagan avalanche. Representative Morris Udall, chair of the House Interior Committee, is reelected, as are most of the other key environmental players in the House. Of the environmental leaders in the Senate facing strong 1980 challenges, only Alan Cranston of California wins a decisive victory. Senator Gary Hart of Colorado wins, but barely.

Reagan's coattails are so long that the Republicans finally wrest control of the Senate from the Democrats. The new chair of the Senate Energy Committee, with jurisdiction over the nation's public-land and energy resources, is Symms' ideological soulmate and fellow Idahoan, James McClure. The new head of the Senate Agriculture Committee is archconservative and wilderness foe Jesse Helms of North Carolina.

"The end of the environmental movement" is proclaimed by NBC News (along with the demise of feminism and civil rights). Mainstream Republicans who served on the staffs of environmental agencies under presidents Nixon and Ford, some of whom worked for Reagan when he was governor of California in the late 1960s and early '70s, are passed over for jobs. By Inauguration Day environmental policy is firmly in the hands of the "sagebrush rebels" – abrasive, conservative ideologues from the West. The rebels' antigovernment bias is strongly supported by Office of Management and Budget (OMB) Director David Stockman, a former Republican congressman from Michigan who only months earlier told Congress that toxic waste dumps are not a proper federal concern.

The Reagan Era has begun.

Today environmentalists are breathing slightly easier, and counting the few days left in Reagan's reign. The Sierra Club has moved to larger headquarters, a necessary response to a membership that soared from 180,000 during the Carter years to 480,000 in September of 1988. Ironically, Ronald Reagan has motivated far more people to join the Club and other environmental organizations than all of his predecessors combined.

Reagan, in effect, has reinvented the national environmental movement. He has done so with appointments and policy initiatives that have offended and alarmed the American people – efforts consistent with the President's general hostility toward activist government and his unlimited faith in private economic institutions. But it is one thing to promise to get the government off the taxpayers' backs. It is an altogether different proposition – and an unacceptable one to most Americans – to relieve polluting industries of the burden of complying with environmental laws. It's one thing to extol the virtues of free markets; it's another to extend that principle *ad absurdum*, offering to sell national parks to geothermal companies or amusement-park operators.

For nearly eight years the American people have been confronted with a difficult choice. In the White House a charismatic political leader has made taxpayers an appealing promise of limited government. A majority of voters have felt that Reagan and his economic programs fit well with their values of personal freedom and achievement. At the same time, in the EPA, in the Department of the Interior, in the OMB, and elsewhere in the federal bureaucracy, Reagan's zealous and often hard-edged political appointees have openly displayed their contempt for the environmental values and programs that have long since become an accepted part of American life.

The public's reaction has been to support Reagan as a person, but to make sure that his anti-environmental ethic is not translated into concrete policy. Citizens demanded and got the ouster of Interior Secretary James Watt, EPA Administrator Anne Burford, and EPA Assistant Administrator Rita Lavelle – the first generation of Reagan's hard-line appointees. They joined environmental groups and told pollsters that their commitment to those issues was stronger than ever before. In 1984 they elected a Congress that stopped virtually all of Reagan's anti-environmental initiatives.

Faced with this formidable resistance, the Reagan administration gradually abandoned the environmental front. By the middle of Reagan's second term his administration's new initiatives were far closer to the mainstream than to the privatized, deregulated world the President's pre-inauguration team had laid out. The administration came in adamantly opposed to federal cleanup of abandoned hazardous waste dumps, for instance, yet eventually agreed to a strong Superfund bill that would provide for just that.

Now, at the end of Reagan's second term, it's clear that the past eight years have not turned out to be as disastrous as the environmentalists who watched the 1980 election returns feared; nor have U.S. businesses reaped the rich harvest they anticipated in the early months of 1981. The most disappointed of all must be the ideologues, the Watts, Burfords, and Stockmans. They had their best shot ever at the American environmental ethos. Yet they strengthened, rather than weakened, the public's determination to protect the environment – and that is one of the more surprising legacies of Ronald Reagan. . . .

There can be no question that Reagan's appointees tried on numerous fronts to weaken America's commitment to the environment.

– They talked loosely of selling some units of the National Park System, and for eight years regularly proposed eliminating federal funding for park acquisition.

– A dentist from South Carolina, James Edwards, began dismantling conservation and renewable-energy programs soon after he was named Secretary of Energy.

– Through Reagan's Task Force on Regulatory Reform, headed by Vice President George Bush, the OMB's Stockman targeted scores of environmental regulations that were later weakened, delayed, or eliminated.

– Administration officials offered mineral leases at bargain-basement prices on millions of acres of public land. They recommended putting the entire outer continental shelf (OCS) on the auction block, under lease procedures that ranged from honest giveaways to outright corruption. In its first ten OCS lease sales, the administration managed to transfer titles to prime oil tracts for $7 billion less than would have been realized using the leasing methods of previous administrations.

– Reagan appointees rebuffed repeated pleas from Canada for a reduction of the acid rain that is destroying its forests, its economy, and life in its lakes. Instead of solutions, some Reaganites talked of "more studies" while Stockman made scornful references to "billion-dollar fish."

– Appointees at the EPA crippled the Superfund toxic-waste-cleanup program, and the program's key administrator, Rita Lavelle, went to jail.

– Morale at the EPA, the National Park Service, the Fish and Wildlife Service, and the Bureau of Land Management collapsed in the face of inadequate budgets, the administration's repeated refusals to enforce the laws, and its political interference in regulatory decisions....

[But] hundreds of thousands of Americans stood up to Reagan, Bush, Watt, and Burford and preserved and strengthened the country's environmental ethic. Good laws were passed and harmful ones blocked; lawsuits argued and won on their merits; scoundrels evicted from office. More people signed the Sierra Club's petition to remove Watt from Interior than had ever simultaneously petitioned Congress on any other issue. Thousands of dedicated civil servants in public agencies resisted the efforts of political appointees to disrupt the execution and enforcement of the nation's environmental statutes. The media covered environmental issues with more intensity than ever before. State and local governments assumed much of the burden that the Reaganites refused to shoulder.

Thanks in large part to environmentalist campaigns, more acreage was added to the National Wilderness Preservation System in the lower 48 states under Reagan than under any other president. Twenty-nine new wildlife refuges were established, encompassing a total of 500,000 acres;

200 new plants and animals were added to the nation's list of endangered species. The Clean Water Act, the Resources Conservation and Recovery Act, and the Comprehensive Environmental Response, Compensation, and Liability Act (the Superfund) have all been reauthorized and greatly strengthened. Lead is finally being phased out of gasoline after two generations of use. An international agreement to reduce the production of chlorofluorocarbons (CFCs), chemicals that destroy the protective stratospheric ozone layer, has been ratified. Oil leasing along the California coast has been stalled, and the Arctic National Wildlife Refuge is still closed to oil drilling.

Just this summer, the Senate renewed the Endangered Species Act by the largest margin ever – 92 to 2. A majority of the House of Representatives, including 64 Republicans, went on record as favoring a massive strengthening and renewal of the Clean Air Act. The Senate declined to confirm Robert Bork and Bernard Siegan, viewed by environmentalists as Reagan's two worst judicial nominees.

In the end, even the delegates to the Republican National Convention in August demonstrated surprising disagreement with Reagan's environmental policies. In a survey conducted for the Sierra Club and other conservation groups, the delegates showed strong support for federal leadership in protecting the country's natural resources.

But . . . we should not forget that on mountaintops and beaches, in small woodlands and majestic rainforests, in cities and playgrounds, in the oceans and the atmosphere itself, reminders of the Reagan Era will linger for decades. . . .

Eight precious years have been lost. The patterns set by Reagan's policies could have irreversible consequences in ten, or twenty, or thirty years – very brief times to change the direction of cumbersome national and international economies and polities. . . .

We now need a global environmental Reconstruction. We need to ask of ourselves and our leaders more self-discipline than ever before, in part to compensate for the callousness of the last eight years. We need greater fidelity to facts, in part because our most recent leaders tried to wish them away. We need above all to remember that time matters, that events have consequences, and that the world is a wondrous and intermingled web that, when torn in one place, may unravel a thousand miles or a hundred years away.

S. Fred Singer, "The Costs of Environmental Overregulation"

Reprinted from *Human Events*, August 7, 1993

Consistently, political opponents of the environmental movement emphasized a stark choice for voters: clean environment or good jobs. The assumption that any society can have only one of these is the core argument of today's anti-environmentalists. Our last two documents of this section examine this claim. S. Fred Singer, a prominent critic of the environmental movement, argues that "over-regulation" of the environment strangles business.

*   *   *

Few will dispute the need for some kind of regulation in a complex society such as ours. However, as the level of regulation in the United States has grown exponentially – measured either in number of laws or in pages of the Federal Register (62,928 pages in 1992) – we may be approaching the critical level where in fact the economy is being strangled, where enterprise is restrained, where entrepreneurship is stifled. Indeed, the level of regulatory costs is now in excess of $600 billion per year.

Environmental regulation accounts for a significant portion of today's regulatory cost burdens. Prof. Murray Weidenbaum of the Center for the Study of American Business estimates that one-quarter of the regulatory costs are connected with the environment, and that this is the fastest-growing segment.

As the Clinton Administration and Congress consider clean water, wetlands and other environmental legislation in the next few months, we need to ask the following questions:

Do we need more stringent environmental controls for better human health and ecological values?
Are the additional benefits worth the additional cost?
How clean is clean?

The answers to these questions are not easy to come by and require a lot of scientific data and understanding.

Initially, environmental regulation did prove to be cost-effective. Removing the first large increment of pollutants from water and air probably produced more benefits than it cost. In the last 20 years there have indeed been tremendous improvements in the quality of the air, and of streams and lakes.

But removing the last few per cent of pollution is enormously expensive and often not even within the reach of technology.

Science tells us that there is little if any additional return from the complete elimination of "hazards" such as pesticides, asbestos, dioxin, radon and various air pollutants. Most gains come from eliminating the initial 90% – which is generally simple and cheap – rather than from eliminating the last 1% – which is frightfully difficult, in many cases virtually impossible, and in almost all instances extremely costly. The goal of zero risk is not only unrealistic, but unattainable and infinitely costly.

The enormous expense of further curbing effluents from power plants, factories and cars and now, in Los Angeles, from dry-cleaning shops, the corner garage, and the bakery down the street as well – must be passed along to the consumer through higher prices. Otherwise these establishments have to fold.

As sales fall due to higher prices and some firms cannot maintain their viability, workers lose their jobs. Small business, in particular, cannot afford the specialists to fill out the innumerable forms needed for emission permits, or to take the precise measurements required, or to employ the myriad of environmental consultants, lawyers, and just plain paper pushers.

Furthermore, the way in which environmental controls are enforced contributes significantly to their burden.

Courts and juries are holding companies with deep pockets guilty of "criminal" offenses for environmental accidents, like the Exxon Valdez. The assigning of liability post-facto, often hitting not the actual polluter but those who can afford to pay, is dampening new investment.

Although this disincentive is impossible to quantify, the fear of exposure to enormous costs must be having a crimping effect on economic growth.

Investors are increasingly wary of putting their money in the United States because any serious environmental mishap with which they could be remotely connected might subject them to huge liabilities.

One cannot stress enough the importance of sound science in setting environmental regulations. There are many examples too of misguided regulations based on pseudo-science or worse, and applied without regard for geographic differences or other commonsense factors.

The 1990 Clean Air Act gives us many good examples.

One title of the law deals with air toxics, the emission of substances that could conceivably cause cancer. The problem is that the cancer risk is calculated for a susceptible person who is maximally exposed to the atmosphere for 70 years, and that the risks are computed based on dubious scientific data.

Furthermore, the analysis neglects the obvious: The fact that the person will be indoors for much of his life exposed to an indoor air quality that is likely to be much more hazardous. Even so, cancer risk, normally about 25%, would be reduced to only 24.99999%, but at a cost of many billions of dollars that could have been used to save many more lives by reducing more down-to-Earth risks.

Yet another title deals with the acid rain problem, the acidification of rain by sulfur dioxide from coal-burning power plants. It calls for emissions reduction nationally of 10 million tons per year, a nice round number for which there is no scientific justification whatsoever, except that it would cut the remaining emissions in half.

Over the last 20 years, the emissions have already been reduced by 25% to 30% without much noticeable impact on acidity.

Furthermore, the science has changed completely since the early '80s when there appeared to be some cause for concern about the health of lakes and forests. By the end of the decade these fears had disappeared.

A major scientific study, conducted under government auspices, had demonstrated that most small lakes affected are naturally acidic and that forests are not harmed. This new scientific evidence was never disputed; it was simply ignored.

Those who wanted to pass the extremely expensive control legislation that would add some $5 to $10 billion to the cost of electricity simply declared the scientific studies to be "not policy-relevant."

One final example: the precipitous phase-out of production of chloro-fluorocarbons (CFCs). The policy decisions here were driven by hype and fear, by false stories of blind sheep and rabbits in Patagonia, and by exaggerating the fear of skin cancer.

Press releases about ozone depletion always refer to it as "worse than expected." The question was never raised whether the theory underlying the expectations was wrong, whether the observations were wrong, or whether both were wrong; yet these are the only logical choices.

What can be done about excessive regulation, not supported by scientific evidence, yet imposing tremendous costs on the economy, destroying jobs, and discouraging entrepreneurs and small business enterprises?

Somehow to use President Clinton's words the public must be made to "feel the pain." In other words, there is hope, provided the public can be educated about the cause-and-effect relationship between overregulation and the loss of jobs and lower standards of living.

One way to do this is by having people pay directly for what is judged to promote environmental quality. Within the next few years, motorists will face not only higher gasoline taxes but also greatly increased costs in monitoring car emissions and in recharging or replacing air-conditioning systems.

Perhaps these and other similar instances of direct, out-of-pocket costs will lead to a kind of consumer revolution, which in turn can lead to an overhaul and rationalization of our whole system of environmental regulation.

The purpose of environmental regulation is to improve human health and protect ecological values. But once past the initial level, further clean-up gains little in the way of health benefits.

Households could take the estimated $1,500 per year that they pay for environmental regulations and spend it better on food and shelter and proper medical care. It is well-recognized that "wealthier makes healthier." And cleaner, too.

Mark Douglas Whitaker, " 'Jobs vs. Environment' Myth"

Institute for Southern Studies news release (18 November 2000)

The Institute for Southern Studies counters arguments like Singer's with a study which, they claim, indicates that states with the most stringent environmental regulations also have the highest per capita income. Is there a simple choice to be made between clean environments and good jobs? Or is the issue more complicated?

*   *   *

STATES RANKED ON ECONOMIC & ENVIRONMENTAL HEALTH

States with the best environmental records also offer the best job opportunities and climate for long-term economic development. That's the conclusion of a study released today by the Institute for Southern Studies, a non-profit research center in Durham, North Carolina.

"In the 2000 elections, political leaders were still debating about whether protecting the environment will cost jobs," says Chris Kromm, a co-author of the report and Director of the Institute [chris@southernstudies.org]. "What this study finds is that the trade-off myth is untrue. At the state policy level, efforts to promote a healthy environment and a sound economy go hand-in-hand."

The study, entitled Gold and Green 2000, uses two separate lists of indicators to evaluate each state's economic performance, and the stresses on the natural environment. The 20 economic indicators include annual pay, job opportunities, business start-ups, and workplace injury rates; the 20 environmental measures range from toxic emissions and pesticide use, to energy consumption and urban sprawl. [For complete results, please visit http://www.southernstudies.org] Keith Ernst, J.D., Research Director at the Institute [keith@southernstudies.org], and Jaffer Battica, a research associate, were the other co-authors.

The report ranks states on each indicator, and the sum of ranks produces a state's final score. Comparing the two lists reveals remarkable correlations:

*** Seven states rank in the top 15 for both economic and environmental health. Vermont, Rhode Island and Minnesota rank in the top six on both lists. Other "top performers" with high marks on both scales are Colorado, Maryland, Maine, and Wisconsin.
*** Conversely, 10 states – mostly in the South – are among the worst 15 on both lists. For example, Louisiana ranks 48th on economic performance and 50th on the environment. Others in the cellar are: Alabama, Texas, Tennessee, Mississippi, Indiana, Arkansas, West Virginia, Kentucky, and South Carolina.

Gold and Green 2000 is an updated version of a similar study authored by the Institute in 1994. The original study had similar findings, and the authors observe that comparisons of the 1994 and 2000 reports offer a useful yardstick for gauging which states are improving – or falling behind – on their environmental and economic records. For example:

*** While there was some jockeying among "bottom performers" – those ranking in the lower 15 on both environmental and economic scales – since the 1994 edition of the study, only two states managed to escape from the bottom of the barrel in 2000: Ohio and Oklahoma.
*** Since 1994, the list of environmental and economic "top performers" – those with high environmental and economic scores – has seen more turn-over, with Rhode Island and Maine adding themselves to the honor role. While New Hampshire and Massachusetts continue to post strong economic numbers, greater environmental threats removed them from the top of the list.

Similarly, the strong environmental records of Hawaii and Oregon could not offset these states' sub-par economic performance.

"Now we have two similar studies that point to the same conclusion: states can have a strong economy and protect the environment," co-author Ernst says. "And states that sacrifice their natural resources for quick-fix development aren't improving their long-term economic prospects."

The study comes at a time when bitter battles have broken out over the supposed conflict between jobs and the environment. For example, in June of this year, national African-American and Latino labor leaders released a widely-reported study – commissioned by the coal industry-backed Center for Energy and Economic Development – opposing the

Kyoto global climate treaty due to a perceived threat to "Black and Hispanic jobs." Across the country, local conflicts have pitted environmentalists against logging businesses, chemical companies, and other industries, who in turn raise the specter of job losses due to environmental standards.

But Gold and Green 2000 joins a growing chorus of experts who argue that, while businesses may invoke the "jobs versus the environment" trade-off to resist regulation, the myth is unfounded. For one, environmental regulation comes at a small cost.

"Even in the most highly regulated industries, the cost tops out at two to three percent of total operating costs," says Dr. James Barrett, environmental economist at the Economic Policy Institute. "Clearly, when industry says its going to shut down or move, it's not the environmental laws that are causing this."

Barrett also observes that steps can easily be taken to prevent economic dislocation. When environmental standards do impact industry – most frequently, companies that are already in decline – the answer is not to prolong the life of polluting or unsustainable businesses, but to ensure a "just transition" of workers to new jobs.

"Many people are talking about 'just transition' today, but there's been little effort to devise policies that work," Barrett says. As a model, he points to the Trade Adjustment Assistance Act, enacted in the 1960s and designed to assist workers laid off due to trade agreements. The Act has been little-used by workers, mostly because it provides no income support to supplement the training it offers to employees seeking new jobs – an oversight that could be easily fixed.

"This study shows that sustainable development is a matter of political will," says Kromm of the Institute. "States that protect their natural resources also cherish their human resources. And states seeking quick-fix, unsustainable development end up sacrificing both workers and the environment."

13
Legacies

As in the previous chapter, there are no historical essays in this one. Rather, we will focus on a few examples of ongoing environmental concerns which suggest how much we are still "in" environmental history. If there is one thing environmental history teaches, it is that we cannot live apart from nature. Any decision about living or, for that matter, dying shapes the environment around us in some way. What follows is a set of brief examinations about how we continue to shape the world's nature, sometimes in surprising and, yes, hopeful ways.

What the future holds is not for any historian to say. But if the course of American environmental history is any indication, it will be more complicated than we expect. And it will reveal as much about who Americans are as about the nature they encounter.

Documents

Ben J. Wattenberg, "The Population Explosion is Over"

New York Times Sunday Magazine, 23 November 1997

Our first document returns us to the fears of population explosion which Paul Ehrlich introduced us to in chapter 10. For generations, environmental thinkers have anguished over the fate of the earth given the seemingly inexorable increase in human populations. Ben Wattenberg, a journalist, suggests that such concerns are increasingly out of place in the world today. The larger problem, according to Wattenberg, is what appears to be a sustained decline in the birth rates of world populations in the late 1990s. Although populations are still growing, the growth has slowed. This has led some analysts to warn of a new danger on the horizon: diminishing populations which would pose a fiscal and political crisis, especially in developed countries. How do Wattenberg's warnings compare with Paul Ehrlich's fears about the population bomb?

* * *

For 30 years, one notion has shaped much of modern social thought: that the human species is reproducing itself uncontrollably, and ominously. In his best-selling book of 1968, "The Population Bomb," Paul Ehrlich warned that "the cancer of population growth must be cut out" or "we will breed ourselves into oblivion." He appeared on the Johnny Carson show 25 times to sell this idea. Lester Brown's "29th Day" compared people to geometrically multiplying waterlilies; on the 30th day, the world would end. A study by the Club of Rome (which it later renounced) described how rapacious humans would soon "run out of resources."

Several generations of schoolchildren have been taught these lessons; the State Department endorses them. A 1992 documentary on Ted Turner's CNN described the impending global chaos "as the planet's population grows exponentially," and just a few days ago, Turner and his wife, Jane Fonda, were honored at a gala for Zero Population Growth, which preaches the mantra of out-of-control overpopulation. The issue of global warming, linked to soaring population growth deep into the next century, is front-page news.

Thirty years of persistent alarm. But now, mounting evidence, from rich nations and poor, strongly suggests that the population explosion is fizzling. Earlier this month, for the first time ever, the United Nations Population Division convened expert demographers to consider aspects of low and tumbling fertility rates. That discussion is a step toward a near-Copernican shift in the way our species looks at itself. Never before have birthrates fallen so far, so fast, so low, for so long all around the world. The potential implications – environmental, economic, geopolitical and personal – are both unclear and clearly monumental, for good and for ill.

The Plot Thins

The free fall in fertility can best be seen in "World Population Prospects: The 1996 Revision," an eye-opening reference book published by the

United Nations, from which most data used here are drawn. From 1950 to 1955, the global "total fertility rate" (roughly speaking, the average number of children born per woman per lifetime) was five. That was explosively above the so-called replacement rate of 2.1 children, the level needed to keep a population from falling over time, absent immigration. This scary growth continued for about 15 years until, by 1975 to 1980, fertility had fallen to four children per woman. Fifteen years after that, the rate had fallen to just below three. Today the total fertility rate is estimated at 2.8, and sinking.

Five children per woman. Then four. Then three. Then less than three. In estimating the population for the year 2050, demographers were caught with their projections up. Suddenly, worldwide, 650 million people were "missing." Many more will be missing soon. They will never be born.

But what about women in those teeming less-developed countries (L.D.C.'s) – those swarming places where the population bomb was allegedly ticking most loudly? Even there, the fuse is sputtering. The L.D.C. fertility rate in 1965 to 1970 was six children per woman. Now it's three, and falling more quickly than ever before in demographic history.

Those are broad numbers. Consider some specific nations. Italy, a Catholic country, has a fertility rate of 1.2 children per woman, the world's lowest rate – and the lowest national rate ever recorded (absent famines, plagues, wars or economic catastrophes). India's fertility rate is lower than American rates in the 1950's. The rate in Bangladesh has fallen from 6.2 to 3.4 – in just 10 years.

European birthrates of the 1980's, already at record-breaking lows, fell another 20 percent in the 90's, to about 1.4 children per woman. The demographer Antonio Golini says such rates are "unsustainable." Samuel Preston, director of the University of Pennsylvania's Population Studies Center, recently calculated what will happen if European fertility changes and moves back toward a rate of 2.1. Even then, by the year 2060, when its population levels off, Europe will have lost 24 percent of its people. Japanese and Russian rates are also at about 1.4 children.

In Muslim Tunisia, over three decades the rate has fallen from 7.2 to 2.9. Rates are higher, but way down, in Iran and Syria. Fertility rates are plunging in many (though not all) sub-Saharan African nations, including Kenya, once regarded as the premier demographic horror show. Mexico has moved 80 percent of the way toward replacement level.

In the United States, birthrates have been below replacement for 25 straight years. There was an uptick in the late 1980's, but rates have fallen for five of the last six years. The National Center for Health Statistics reports solidly lower levels for early 1997, which will "continue the generally downward trend observed since early 1991" and will soon be reflected in U.S. Census Bureau projections.

This sounds strange. After all, we have gone through a half-century of the greatest population growth in history, and such growth has not quite ended. What's happening is that two powerful trends – the population explosion and the baby bust – are now at war. They can coexist, but only for a while. The recent evidence makes it clear which of these trends will prevail: the baby bust.

The population explosion is a long-distance runner. From 1750 to 1950, global population increased from 1 billion to 2.5 billion. From 1950 to 2000, it will increase to 6 billion. Remarkable. But the baby bust is also a marathon player. In America in 1790, women bore an average of 7.7 children. Benjamin Franklin saw children "swarming across the countryside like locusts." But for two centuries, except for a bump during the baby boom, American fertility has fallen steadily. Since 1972, the fertility rate has averaged 1.9. (Among the lowest rates are those experienced by Jewish women and black women with college degrees.)

An explosion *and* a bust? It sounds contradictory. But the number of potential mothers today was set two and three decades ago, when they were born, and when birthrates were much higher. And the rates in most less-developed countries, though falling rapidly, are still above replacement. Life expectancy has been climbing. These factors create "population momentum," which automatically yields more people – for a while.

Soon, however, reflecting the recent sharp reduction in fertility, the number of potential mothers will be much lower than previously anticipated. Fertility will most likely drop below replacement level in many less-developed countries. It already has in 19 of them, including Cuba, China, Thailand and, probably soon, Brazil. The momentum then turns the other way. (A bust, like an explosion, moves in geometric progression.)

What next? There are arguments, as well there should be, when dealing with the future. The U.N.'s "medium variant" projection shows a global population of 9.4 billion people in 2050. Because of its "medium" designation, this Mama Bear projection is cited most often. But its central assumption is questionable: that all nations will move to a fertility rate of about 2.1 children per woman by 2050. Based on current data, this scenario seems implausible. Indeed, the experts met at the U.N. to change some assumptions in the medium-variant projections – downward. . . .

Where Did Everybody Go?

What is causing this birth dearth? Paul Demeny, the editor of Population and Development Review, points to the famous "demographic transition" theory, which he describes as the move "from high fertility and high mortality to low fertility and low mortality, with lots of complicated and contradictory things going on in the middle."

One of the main factors pushing this transition is urbanization – reflecting the shift from wanting more children to help on the farm to wanting fewer mouths to feed in the city. Among the many other factors are more education for women, legal abortion, higher incomes, unemployment yielding *lower* incomes, greater acceptance of homosexuality, new aspirations for women, better contraception (including "morning-after pills," endorsed by new Food and Drug Administration guidelines), later marriage, difficulty conceiving at older ages, more divorce and vastly lower infant-mortality rates. When parents know their children will survive, fertility rates plummet.

These trends toward modernization are continuing, along with some new ones. For example, the black American fertility rate is down to about the national average; black teen-age birthrates have declined by 20 percent since 1991. (On the other hand, advances in infertility treatment and a small increase in births among women in their later 30's slightly mitigate the trend toward lower fertility.)

Demographic transition theory explains, or at least describes, the downward arc of high fertility rates. But there is no theory (yet) that explains why, when or how long-term below-replacement fertility rates would ever go back up.

Therefore What?

Speculation is in season. When people have fewer babies and live longer, the median age of society climbs. In 1990, about 6 percent of the world's population was over age 65. By 2050, that figure will be in the 15-to-19 percent range – prompting a "grayby boom." By having relatively few children, people today are eroding the population base that should pay for their pensions in their old age. In 1955 there were nine American workers to support each Social Security recipient. Today there are three. By 2030, the number is expected to be two.

Where will the money come from? No one knows. Perhaps from funds not spent to support children who are never born. Perhaps from tax increases or benefit cuts – both tough to sell politically. Perhaps from immigration or higher fertility. Perhaps from the partial privatization of Social Security or from long-term economic growth more robust than expected.

For the environment, the prospect of fewer people than expected should be good news. The specter of a population explosion has been the Archimedean lever of environmental thinking: more people cause more pollution, more people use more resources and more affluent people do more of both. Environmentalists and population activists, long at the forefront of providing family-planning services, can appropriately claim much credit for the brighter outlook. (Not unrebutted, though: others argue that modernism, urbanization, education and wealth driven by market economics have done much of the job.)

But the good news may make it more difficult to sell bad news. For example, the demographic models used in global-warming calculations are based on projections keyed to a population of 11.5 billion people. Inevitably, these numbers will have to be revised sharply downward, and the threat will be reduced. But even if there are not as many billions as were expected, there will be enough billions to make a big mess. The case for exaggeration has been diminished; the case for environmental realism remains powerful. . . .

Eventually, demography blends into psychology. There is likely to be a lot more personal sadness ahead. There will be missing children and missing grandchildren. In an article in The Public Interest titled "World Population Implosion," the demographer Nicholas Eberstadt, of Harvard and the American Enterprise Institute, looks ahead and writes that "for many people, 'family' would be understood as a unit that does not include any biological contemporaries or peers" and that we may live in "a world in which the only biological relatives for many people – perhaps most people – will be their ancestors." Lots of people without brothers or sisters, uncles, aunts or cousins, children or grandchildren – lonelier people.

A lonelier world? It's not lonely enough now? Some observers say that friends and colleagues will become "like family." Do not count on that if you end up in a nursing home. Young DINK's (double income, no kids) may be cute. Old LINK's (low income, no kids) may be tragic. Clergymen say that the saddest funerals are those in which the deceased has no offspring.

"Pronatalist" policies, like the newly enacted $500-per-child tax credit, are important, but the results are uncertain. And even now, we seem to be moving toward a more atomized life. During the most affluent moment in history, so many young people say they can't afford to have two children. People well into their 60's look vainly for grandchildren. Adoption, already excruciatingly difficult, may well become more so. Will the rest of the country look like Manhattan, which as this magazine has reported has the country's largest concentration of people living alone (48 percent) except for a former leper colony in Hawaii?

First the population was growing too fast. Now in many places it has sunk too low too quickly, with more to come. Is there cause for concern?

Certainly, but not for despair. The demographers at the U.N. conference were not talking about a world where people can't control their destiny. Quite the opposite. We are in control, and are changing how we see ourselves and our world.

From *World Population Prospects*

Reprinted from *World Population Prospects: The 1996 Revision* (New York: United Nations, 1998) and *The 2000 Revision* (2001)

Although it is too soon to see if birth rates will slow as much as Ben Wattenberg and others have speculated, the following excerpts from the United Nations *World Population Prospects*, in 1996 and 2000, suggest that the growth curve continues to slow.

* * *

1996

The present publication provides the results of the United Nations *1996 Revision* of global population estimates and projections. At mid-1996, the world population stood at 5.77 billion. Between 1990 and 1995, the world population grew at 1.48 per cent per year and increased by 81 million persons per year on average. The current population growth rate is the lowest recorded since the Second World War. This is significantly below the 1.72 per cent per annum at which population had been growing between 1975 and 1990, and much below the 87 million persons added each year between 1985 and 1990, which stands now as the peak period in the history of world population growth.

2000

Executive summary

The *2000 Revision* is the sixteenth round of global demographic estimates and projections undertaken by the Population Division of the Department of Economic and Social Affairs since 1950. These population estimates and projections provide the standard and consistent set of population figures that are used throughout the United Nations system as the basis for activities requiring population information.

Among the key findings of the *2000 Revision* are:

1   World population reached 6.1 billion in mid-2000 and is currently growing at an annual rate of 1.2 per cent, or 77 million people per year. Six countries account for half of this annual growth: India for 21 per cent; China for 12 per cent; Pakistan for 5 per cent; Nigeria for 4 per cent; Bangladesh for 4 per cent, and Indonesia for 3 per cent. By 2050, world population is expected to be between 7.9 billion (low variant) and 10.9 billion (high variant), with the medium variant producing 9.3 billion. . . .

2   The population of more developed regions, currently 1.2 billion, is anticipated to change little during the next 50 years because fertility levels are expected to remain below replacement level. However, by mid-century the populations of 39 countries are projected to be smaller than today (e.g., Japan and Germany 14 per cent smaller; Italy and Hungary 25 per cent smaller; and the Russian Federation, Georgia and Ukraine between 28 to 40 per cent smaller).

3   The population of the less developed regions is projected to rise steadily from 4.9 billion in 2000 to 8.2 billion in 2050 (medium variant). This projection assumes continuing declines in fertility; in the absence of such declines, the population of less developed regions would reach 11.9 billion instead of the projected 8.2 billion. Particularly rapid growth is expected among the group of 48 countries classified as least developed. Their population is expected to nearly triple between 2000 and 2050, passing from 658 million to 1.8 billion, despite the fact that their fertility is projected to decline markedly in the future.

4   The difference between the projected population in 2050 according to the *2000 Revision* (9.3 billion) and that projected in the *1998 Revision* (8.9 billion) is 413 million people. Higher future fertility levels projected for the 16 developing countries whose fertility has not yet shown signs of a sustained decline are responsible for 59 per cent of that difference. The somewhat higher recent fertility estimated in the *2000 Revision* for several populous countries (e.g., Bangladesh, India and Nigeria) accounts for a further 32 per cent of that difference.

Graph of Economic Growth and Air Emission Trends, 1970–2000

Environmental history can at times become a frightening and even depressing field, for it is full of stories about human destructiveness and the seemingly continual drumbeat of ecological decay. But in fact, we should remember the

Comparison of growth areas and emission trends

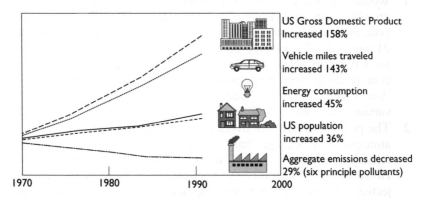

US Gross Domestic Product
Increased 158%

Vehicle miles traveled
increased 143%

Energy consumption
increased 45%

US population
increased 36%

Aggregate emissions decreased
29% (six principle pollutants)

1970   1980   1990   2000

Figure 13.1. Graph of economic growth and air emission trends. Between 1970 and 2000, gross domestic product increased 158 percent, energy consumption increased 45 percent, vehicle miles traveled increased 143 percent, and U.S. population increased 36 percent. At the same time, total emissions of the six principal air pollutants decreased 29 percent.

many environmental victories of the past, the campaigns that brought clean water and banished cholera, and the Clean Air Act and other legislation of the last 50 years which has in fact done a great deal to reduce and contain environmental damage.

Graph of Atmospheric CO_2 Concentration, 1958–1997

The most ominous environmental threat in the minds of many people is that of global warming, brought on by increasing quantities of heat-trapping gases in the atmosphere. Among the most notable of these is carbon dioxide. The rising concentration of carbon dioxide in the atmosphere, much of which is thought to come from human activities such as the combustion of fuel for industry, transportation, and home heating, is one of the most prominent of these. Charles Keeling has monitored CO_2 concentrations in the atmosphere since 1958. The graph shown in figure 13.2 reflects the rising concentration of CO_2 since the 1950s. There is considerable seasonal fluctuation, denoted by the wiggles in the line. This is caused by CO_2 decline in the spring and summer, as plants burst into leaf and begin to transpire more of the gas in the growing season, causing the number of CO_2 parts per million to

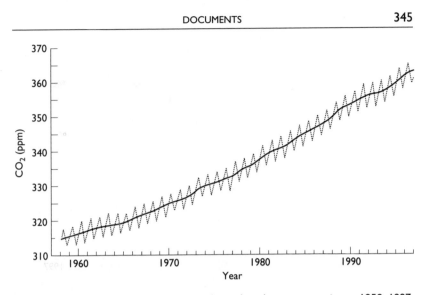

Figure 13.2. Global atmospheric carbon dioxide concentrations, 1958–1997. Source: Mauna Loa Observatory, 40th Anniversary Commemoration and Dedication of the NDSC Building (U.S. Department of Commerce, 1997).

dip measurably. Nonetheless, the long-term trend is clearly one of increased CO_2 content in the atmosphere. For many people, the link between this graph and the rising median temperature of the atmosphere is ominous.

The Triumph of Diplomacy?: Atmospheric CFC Graph, 1977–1996

Yet, even the graph shown in figure 13.3 should not cause us to abandon hope. In the late 1980s, there was similar consternation about the threat of choroflourocarbons, or CFCs, which were a prominent component in refrigeration systems around the earth and which, released into the air by industrial processes, drift upward into the stratosphere, where they destroy ozone molecules at the rate of one per second. Since ozone is vital to protecting the earth from the most harmful of the sun's radiation, there was worldwide anxiety about the thinning ozone layer. Subsequent diplomatic efforts resulted in a worldwide ban on CFCs, and their replacement in refrigeration systems by less harmful chemicals. The graph shows the effect of this, with a flattening out of the CFC concentrations in the atmosphere. Over time, CFCs currently in the air will decay, and ozone will naturally regenerate in its absence.

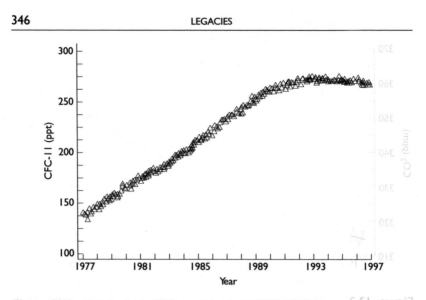

Figure 13.3. Atmospheric CFC concentrations, 1977–1996. Source: U.S. Environmental Protection Agency, "National Air Quality: 2000 – Status and Trends – Six Principal Pollutants," http://www.epa.gov/oar/aqtrndoo/sixpoll.html.

Index